FAMOUS AMERICAN CRIMES AND TRIALS

FAMOUS AMERICAN CRIMES AND TRIALS

Volume 1: 1607–1859

Edited by Frankie Y. Bailey
and Steven Chermak

Praeger Perspectives

Crime, Media, and Popular Culture

PRAEGER

Westport, Connecticut
London

Library of Congress Cataloging-in-Publication Data

Bailey, Frankie Y.

    Famous American crimes and trials / Frankie Y. Bailey and Steven Chermak.

      p. cm.—(Crime, media, and popular culture, ISSN 1549-196X)

    Includes bibliographical references and index.

    Contents: Vol. 1. 1607–1859—v. 2. 1860–1912—v. 3. 1913–1959—v. 4. 1960–1980—v. 5. 1981–2000.

      ISBN 0-275-98333-1 (set : alk. paper)—ISBN 0-275-98334-X (vol. 1 : alk. paper)—ISBN 0-275-98335-8 (vol. 2 : alk. paper)—ISBN 0-275-98336-6 (vol. 3 : alk. paper)—ISBN 0-275-98337-4 (vol. 4 : alk. paper)—ISBN 0-275-98338-2 (vol. 5 : alk. paper)

      1. Criminal justice, Administration of—United States—Case studies. 2. Criminal justice, Administration of—United States—History. I. Chermak, Steven M. II. Title. III. Series.

HV9950.B3 2004

364.973—dc22   2004050548

British Library Cataloguing in Publication Data is available.

Library of Congress Catalog Card Number: 2004050548

ISBN: 0-275-98333-1 (set)

       0-275-98334-X (vol. I)

       0-275-98335-8 (vol. II)

       0-275-98336-6 (vol. III)

       0-275-98337-4 (vol. IV)

       0-275-98338-2 (vol. V)

ISSN: 1549-196X

First published in 2004

Praeger Publishers, 88 Post Road West, Westport, CT 06881
An imprint of Greenwood Publishing Group, Inc.
www.praeger.com

Printed in the United States of America

The paper used in this book complies with the Permanent Paper Standard issued by the National Information Standards Organization (Z39.48-1984).

10 9 8 7 6 5 4 3 2 1

Contents

Set Foreword

Famous American Crimes and Trials covers over four centuries, from the colonial era to the end of the twentieth century, in five volumes. In each volume, we introduce the social and historical contexts in which the cases appearing in the volume occurred. We discuss the evolution of the criminal justice system and the legal issues that were dominant during that time period. We also provide an overview of the popular culture and mass media, examining in brief the nexus between news/entertainment and the criminal justice system. In each introduction, we also identify the common threads weaving through the cases in the volume.

Many of the cases featured in these five volumes provide examples of what Robert Hariman (1990) describes as "popular trials," or "trials that have provided the impetus and the forum for major public debates" (p. 1). As we note elsewhere, cases generally achieve celebrity status because they somehow encapsulate the tensions and the anxieties present in our society; or, at least, this has been the case until the recent past. In the last half-century, the increasing importance of television (and more recently the internet) in delivering the news to the public, and the voracious appetite of the media for news stories to feed the twenty-four-hour news cycle, has meant that stories—particularly crime stories—move quickly into, and sometimes as quickly out of, the public eye. So, as we address in volume 5, we now have a proliferation of crime stories that vie for the status of "famous." It remains to be seen whether these cases will have true "staying power" in the same sense as the cases that are still remembered today after many decades or centuries.

Oddly enough, some cases that were celebrated, though attracting a great deal of public attention when they occurred, have now disappeared from

American collective memory. Perhaps some of these cases for one reason or another only touched a public nerve at the time because they resonated with some passing interest or concern, or fit some media theme. Occasionally, such forgotten cases are rescued from the dustbins by a journalist, a true-crime writer, or a historian and undergo a new wave of public attention. That has happened with several of the cases that appear in these volumes. Perhaps the rediscovery of such cases reflects their relevance to current social issues; or perhaps these cases are interesting to modern readers because they are not only enthralling stories but because they occurred in the past and are now entertaining "period" pieces.

We think that the reader will agree that the cases included in these volumes are among the most important of each era. Since space was limited, many famous cases had to be excluded, but many of these have been covered in other books or media. The cases that are included cover each crime, the setting, and the participants; the actions taken by law enforcement and the criminal legal system; the actions of the media covering the case; the trial (if there was one); the final resolution of the case; the relevant social, political, and legal issues; and, finally, the significance of the case and its impact on legal and popular culture.

REFERENCE

Hariman, R. (1990). *Popular trials: Rhetoric, mass media, and the law.* Tuscaloosa, AL: University of Alabama Press.

Series Foreword

The pervasiveness of media in our lives and the salience of crime and criminal justice issues make it especially important to provide a home for scholars who are engaged in innovative and thoughtful research on important crime and mass media issues.

This series will focus on process issues (such as the social construction of crime and moral panics), presentation issues (such as images of victims, offenders, and criminal justice figures in news and popular culture), and effects (such as the influence of the media on criminal behavior and criminal justice administration).

With regard to this latter issue—effects of media/popular culture—as this foreword was being written the *Los Angeles Times* and other media outlets reported that two young half-brothers (ages 20 and 15) in Riverside, California, had confessed to strangling their mother and disposing of her body in a ravine. The story was attracting particular attention because the brothers told police they had gotten the idea of cutting off her head and hands to prevent identification from a recent episode of the award-winning HBO series, *The Sopranos*. As the *Los Angeles Times* noted, this again brought into the spotlight the debate about the influence of violent media such as *The Sopranos*, about New Jersey mobsters, on susceptible consumers.

In this series, scholars engaged in research on issues that examine the complex nature of our relationship with media. Peter Berger and Thomas Luckman coined the phrase the "social construction of reality" to describe the process by which we acquire knowledge about our environment. They and others have argued that reality is a mediated experience. We acquire what Emile Durkheim described as "social facts" through a several-prolonged process of personal experience, interaction with others, academic education, and, yes, the mass media. With regard to crime and the criminal justice system, many people acquire much of their information from the news and from entertainment media. The issue raised by the report above and other anecdotal stories of "copy cat" crime is how what we consume—read, watch, see, play, hear—affects us.

What we do know is that we experience this mediated reality as individuals. We are all not affected in the same way by our interactions with mass media. Each of us engages in interactions with mass media/popular culture that are shaped by factors such as social environment, interests, needs, and opportunities for exposure. We do not come to the experience of mass media/popular culture as blank slates waiting to be written upon or voids waiting to be filled. It is the pervasiveness of mass media/popular culture and the varied backgrounds (including differences in age, gender, race/ethnicity, religion, etc.) that we bring to our interactions with media that make this a particularly intriguing area of research.

Moreover, it is the role of mass media in creating the much discussed "global village" of the twenty-first century that is also fertile ground for research. We exist not only in our communities, our cities, and states, but in a world that spreads beyond national boundaries. Technology has made us a part of an ongoing global discourse about issues not only of criminal justice but of social justice. Technology takes us to events around the world "as they happen." It was technology that allowed Americans around the world to witness the collapse of the World Trade Center's Twin Towers on September 11, 2001. In the aftermath of this "crime against humanity," we have been witnesses to and participants in an ongoing discussion about the nature of terrorism and the appropriate response to such violence.

Frankie Y. Bailey and Steven Chermak
Series Editors

Acknowledgments

We would like to thank the contributors who worked so hard on the individual chapters. The contributors are a very diverse group, but they all share a passion for the cases they tackled. We appreciate their hard work and their willingness to quickly respond to our suggestions for revision. Many of the contributors have published frequently about a case, but they took the approach we requested in these chapters to offer fresh insights into their work. Other contributors had not written specifically about a case but answered our solicitation because they were curious about it. Our thanks to all of them for producing very insightful and entertaining accounts of the most important cases and trials that have occurred throughout the history of the United States.

The staff at Greenwood Publishing contributed significantly to bringing this project to publication. We are especially grateful to Suzanne Staszak-Silva, Senior Editor at Greenwood, for encouraging us to work on this five-volume set. We considered several different ways to approach the organization of the five volumes, and we appreciate her insights and suggestions for organizing the work by historical era. We were both skeptical about being able to cover so many different cases in such a short amount of time, but her energy was contagious and she was able to convince us of the great potential for such a large project. Mariah Krok was the Developmental Editor for the volumes, and we would like to thank her for being such an effective liaison between the contributors and us. We were able to avoid the many problems that can arise from a project with so many different contributors because of her ability to keep us organized. Thanks to Dan Harmon for tackling the very arduous task of tracking down illustrations and seeking permissions.

The staff at Capital City Press was terrific to work with: special thanks to Bridget Wiedl.

Steve's wife was incredibly supportive and interested in the work of this project. Alisha and I welcomed Mitchell into our family during this project. Thanks to him for deciding to sleep through the night on occasion—this is when most of the work got done.

Frankie Y. Bailey and Steven Chermak

Introduction

Frankie Y. Bailey and Steven Chermak

The United States has often been described as an "experiment in democracy." Perhaps it might be more accurate to say that the United States has been a case study in the collision between democratic ideals and the use and abuse of power in a heterogeneous society. The democratic ideals that are said to define the United States are ever subject to interpretation. The question of exactly what rights are "unalienable," and for whom and how that question should be translated into public policy, is a matter of ongoing controversy and debate. This controversy becomes evident as we examine the issues raised in the cases throughout these five volumes and the responses of the criminal justice system, the media, and various groups in the larger society to the problems posed in these cases.

THE CREATION OF A NEW COUNTRY

American history books attest to the fact that the first permanent settlement in the "New World" was in Jamestown, Virginia, in 1607. We are also told of the first New England settlement, marked by the Pilgrims' first Thanksgiving celebration in Plymouth, Massachusetts, in 1621. Virginia and Massachusetts would provide the setting for many dramatic events in early American history.

In Virginia, the democratic ideals and the Enlightenment beliefs of the "founding fathers" clashed with their more pragmatic self-interests in the perpetuation of the system of slavery. In the courtrooms of Massachusetts during this time, legal confrontations over heresy in Puritan society, rebellion against Great Britain, and, later, abolitionist offensives against slavery, took place. These events, however, are not to downplay the importance of the developments taking place in the other colonies.

In Pennsylvania, for example, one of the two models for the modern American penitentiary system evolved from an experiment in rehabilitation that began at the Walnut Street Jail in Philadelphia; New York City was the setting for an early courtroom confrontation concerning freedom of the press in the Peter Zenger sedition case; and, later, in the 1830s, New York City became the birthplace of the "penny press."

Each of the colonies, later to become states, had a role to play in creating the country that would be the United States. By the nineteenth century, the young nation had survived its adolescent growing pains. However, as the cases in this first volume illustrate, although some issues had been resolved by the nineteenth century, others—particularly those about which the founding fathers had reached unsatisfactory compromises—lingered on. If by the nineteenth century the issues of religious freedom, freedom of the press, and the question of what constituted treason had been to some extent resolved, one burning issue—slavery—still loomed large. Moreover, the increasing pace of urbanization had produced new concerns about urban disorder. A country born of riots and rebellions continued in the nineteenth century to experience social conflicts that sometimes led to violence.

LAW AND JUSTICE IN EARLY AMERICA

By the late eighteenth century, the U.S. Constitution would define the relationship between the states and the federal government, preserving certain rights for the states; would mandate the separation of church and state; would create the three branches of government, placing certain powers in the hands of the president, the Congress, and the Supreme Court; but at the same time would create a system of checks and balances. Before the Revolutionary War, and before the Constitution settled these matters that were crucial to the creation of a country, the colonial governments had dealt on their own with the social, political, and legal issues presented in the cases that reached their courtrooms.

The colonies along the Atlantic reflected the unique characteristics of their founders. If the early settlers of Massachusetts could be defined by their preoccupation with religion, those of Virginia could as easily be defined by their preoccupation with their "tobacco boom" and its cultivation as a cash crop for the British market. What the colonies that eventually joined as the United States of America shared was that, in all of them, immigrants from

Britain were either the original settlers or would later displace the Dutch, the French, or the Spanish. By the time the Constitution was enacted, the United States was a country in which British laws, values, and attitudes provided the foundation for the American system of justice. Even though the British immigrants did eventually throw off the controlling hand of the "mother country," they did not completely discard British common law and judicial precedent. Nor did they completely reject the religion or the culture that had bred them. Although others—other European immigrants, slaves from Africa, Native Americans, Asians, and Mexicans—interacted with these British immigrants and played important roles in the colonies and later the country, it was the British immigrants who would claim the right to determine the destiny of the new country and, in doing so, define the meaning of justice.

The conflicts that plagued the British settlers were generally rooted in the beliefs and values that they had brought with them when they crossed the ocean. In Puritan Massachusetts in the seventeenth century, one such conflict concerned the matter of religious orthodoxy. In chapter 1 of this volume, Kathy Warnes examines the case of Mary Dyer, a Quaker woman who became a martyr for her religion. As Warnes explains, the Dyer case should be understood within the context of the tensions within Puritan society that had earlier led to the prosecution of Antinomian Anne Hutchinson (with whom Mary Dyer had been associated) and of such others who were deemed heretics. Though we are often told that the Puritans came to the New World seeking religious freedom, the Puritan elders responded with extreme unease to challenges to religious orthodoxy and authority. It has been argued that their engagement in repressive justice, including corporal punishment, banishment, and the execution of a few heretics such as Mary Dyer, must be understood within the larger context of the threats perceived by the Puritans to their survival. In chapter 2, Tammy Denesha examines the 1692 Salem witch trials and the hysteria that gave birth to the accusations. She discusses the various theories offered over the centuries to explain what happened and why. She notes the central roles that females (girls and women) played in these courtroom dramas as both the accusers and the accused in the trials.

As Norton (2002) observes, in this regard the Salem witchcraft trials were unusual, because young girls were not generally the principal accusers, and the role played by a female servant was also unusual. In fact, as in England, women were not granted full status in the colonies, or in the states in the post-Revolutionary era. Married women were subordinate to their husbands concerning such matters as ownership of property and custody of children. They did not possess the right to vote or to pursue professions such as law and medicine. However, they were protected from prosecution for some offenses by the concept of *feme covert*, which displaced responsibility for a woman's offense to her husband. This concept did not, however, apply to the crime of murder, particularly *petit treason*, or the murder of a husband.

As Salita S. Bryant discusses in chapter 6, a pregnant woman might also "plea her belly," that is, she might ask for commutation of her death sentence because she was with child. As Bryant discusses, this became an issue in the 1778 case of Bathsheba Spooner. Spooner, the daughter of a despised loyalist to the British cause, was put on trial for conspiring with her young lover and two British soldiers to kill her husband. When convicted of the crime, she attempted to plea her belly. However, lacking modern medical techniques to determine pregnancy, two examining committees of midwives were divided among themselves about whether Spooner was with child. The authorities allowed the execution to go forward—only to discover that Bathsheba Spooner was indeed pregnant.

The Spooner case is one of those that have proved durable not only because of the melodramatic nature of the events—an affair, a murder conspiracy, and the execution of a pregnant woman—but because it serves as a historical reference in a continuing debate about the execution of women. The "chivalry factor" has always played a role when Americans debated putting convicted women to death. Of course, this was only true with some women. Lower-class women and women of color were, it has been argued, rarely the beneficiaries of such chivalry. As we see with the Spooner case, even for middle-class white women, politics and the dread of *malice domestic* could outweigh concerns about subjecting a woman to the ultimate punishment.

As for men in early America, the roles they assumed were determined mostly by their ability to claim and exercise power. As Kathy Warnes discusses in chapter 3, on occasion such claims to power could take the form of a pirate such as Blackbeard, who demonstrated a masterful ability to promote his own ferociousness. Bred by a tradition of international privateering that was common among the British, French, and Spanish, Blackbeard the Pirate and his motley crew plied the waters of the Atlantic. But pirates such as Blackbeard could exist only for a time, before they were killed or captured by colonial warships.

In the aftermath of the Revolutionary War, greater threats seemed to come from within the young country itself. As Brandon K. Webster and Jennifer H. Childress discuss in chapter 7, during the Whiskey Rebellion, the federal government in the east faced rebellion on the western frontier by settlers who resented the tax on whiskey, which threatened their livelihood. In the first use of federal forces against Americans, soldiers were sent to arrest the rebellious and bring them to trial. The resolution of this episode was less costly in lives than it might have been. This rebellion came somewhat later than Bacon's Rebellion in 1676 against Virginia elites. It also followed the Revolutionary era, during which the Founding Fathers themselves, and other good patriots, had taken up arms against the British government, declaring "no taxation without representation." During the Revolutionary era, the Boston Massacre in March 1770, in which colonists attacked and were fired upon by British soldiers, led to a courtroom trial in which the well-known defense attorneys for the British soldiers addressed the vigilante actions of the colonists who had been killed. This is the subject of chapter 5 by Marcella Bush Trevino.

AFTER THE REVOLUTION: DEFINING FREEDOM IN THE NEW COUNTRY

In the aftermath of the Revolution, the patriots attempted to define the limits of freedom. Clearly, freedom did not include the liberty to engage in treason against the United States. As Joanne Barker discusses in chapter 8, the actions of Aaron Burr, who seemed to be mounting a secession movement in the western United States that involved collusion with the Spanish government, brought this question to center stage. In deciding the Burr case, the Supreme Court took on the task of defining treason. Burr was acquitted, but he retained the notoriety of a man who had engaged in a duel in which Alexander Hamilton, a political enemy, was killed, and who might not have been completely trustworthy. However, he was not, the Court had decreed, guilty of treason, and with this decree the Court made it more difficult, in effect, to allege treasonous actions by domestic political rivals.

But determining the limits of freedom was even more pressing for those at the bottom of the social ladder. As historians assert, in the colonies prior to the Revolution, freedom was best described as a matter of degree. In colonial Virginia, for example, landowners controlled the labor of white indentured servants from Europe, and of the Africans, who were first treated as indentured servants but by mid-seventeenth century began to be legally assigned to slave status. The laws of Virginia—and of colonies in the South and the North—reflected these degrees of freedom. The simmering conflicts in the colonies reflected the concerns of those in power that those without it might rise up and attempt to overthrow them. In the case of indentured servants, laws punished certain crimes—such as running away—by prolonging the period of indenture. Even so, most indentured servants did eventually work off their contracts (by paying back the cost of passage assumed by their employers). When such young men (women were less of a concern) gained their freedom, the task for those in power was to ensure that these men did not threaten the class hierarchy. Modern historians have argued that one way this was done was by creating racial distinctions that superseded class. Such distinctions were also deemed necessary to maintain the slave system that was in place in the colonies by the late seventeenth century. In the South, the slave code controlled a black population that in some places outnumbered that of whites. The slave system rested on assumptions about black inferiority that allowed white masters to treat black slaves as property rather than persons. This perception would later be incorporated into the Constitution and supported by Supreme Court decisions such as that in *Dred Scott*, in which the Court declared that a black man had no rights that a white man must recognize. The institution of slavery required the creation and enforcement of a dual system of justice—one for free whites and one for slaves (Morgan, 1975; Sellin, 1976; Finkelman, 1993; Bailey and Green, 1999).

Those blacks who were not slaves fell somewhere in between the two systems. They enjoyed some of the benefits of freedom, but even in the North bore some of the restrictions placed on slaves. In the North, they could and did agitate along with white abolitionists to eliminate slavery. By the nineteenth century, the resistance of these abolitionists to the Fugitive Slave Act, the federal law that required the cooperation of Northern law enforcement officers in the recovery and return of escaped slaves, resulted in dramatic events such as the Shadrach courtroom rescue, which Kathryn Mudgett recounts in chapter 13.

The conflicts about slavery and the international slave trade were at the heart of an earlier case involving the slaves who rebelled aboard the slave ship *Amistad*. In chapter 10, Kathy Warnes explores the legal issues that faced the courts in New Jersey, Connecticut, and finally the Supreme Court as various parties laid claim to the *Amistad* and its cargo. The question was whether the Africans who had seized their freedom were slaves under international law or free men who had defended themselves against kidnappers.

THE EVOLUTION OF THE MEDIA

The evolution of the early American media has been described as the movement from the religious to the secular. Newspapers are not an important factor in the cases of seventeenth-century New England. The first, preliminary effort at an American newspaper was Benjamin Harris's *Publick Occurrences* in Boston in 1690. However, because of trouble with the Massachusetts licensing act and Harris's conflict with the local authorities, his career as a newspaper publisher came to an end after the first issue. Fourteen years later, in 1704, John Campbell's *Boston News-Letter* became the first American newspaper with continuing publication.

Because the first American newspaper appeared later in the history of the colony, the contemporary accounts we have of the trial of Mary Dyer and of the witchcraft trials in Salem take the form of pamphlets, papers, and books published by those who were involved in or witnessed the events. As in Europe, ballads and broadsheets, as well as gallows sermons and the confessions of those facing execution, were important in the recording and recounting of criminal cases. At the local level, where no newspapers existed, word of mouth played an important role in the dissemination of information (Norton, 2002).

The eighteenth century begins the movement away from control of crime news by ministers involved in the execution process as confessors to, by the nineteenth century, the involvement of lawyers, novelists, and eventually journalists in the framing of such news (Cohen, 1993). In chapter 4, Emily Gillespie examines the John Peter Zenger case, in which the government charged a newspaper printer with sedition. The case occurred during a time when newspapers were openly partisan organs that expressed the opinions of political parties. The outcome of the Zenger case has been described as having landmark importance in the struggle for freedom of the press. But even more critical to a viable press was its ability to reach the masses.

During the Revolutionary era, American patriots such as Samuel Adams used their publications as propaganda tools in the struggle against British rule. Adams himself was editor of the "radical" newspaper the *Independent Advertiser*. He was also a regular contributor to the *Boston Gazette and Country Journal*. Two of Adams's associates, Benjamin Edes and John Gills, were the publishers of the *Boston Gazette*, which by 1764 "was the nerve center of the Boston Radicals" (Emery and Emery, 1984, p. 69). Another journalist of this era, Thomas Paine, achieved fame with his pamphlet *Common Sense*, which was "copied by many of the colonial newspapers of 1776" (Emery and Emery, 1984, p. 80). Paine's pamphlet became a rallying cry for the revolutionary movement.

In similar fashion, nineteenth-century abolitionists who were agitating against slavery used their newspapers as vehicles for expressing their own revolutionary sentiments. In 1831, William Lloyd Garrison launched the *Liberator*. That newspaper came four years after *Freedom's Journal*, the first black-published newspaper in the United States. In 1847, Frederick Douglass, the escaped slave and abolitionist leader, began publishing the *North Star*. These abolitionist newspapers were routinely banned in the southern states, where selling or distributing them was a criminal offense.

However, by the nineteenth century, technology was in place for the mass production and distribution of newspapers. In 1830s New York, the penny press was born, offering an alternative to those working-class readers who could not afford the subscription price of the newspapers available. The first such newspaper was Benjamin H. Day's *New York Sun* in 1833. James Gordon Bennett's *New York Herald* followed it soon after, in 1835. In 1841, Horace Greeley began publication of the famous *New York Tribune*, a newspaper that marked "the maturing of the press for the masses" (Emery and Emery, 1984, p. 147). What the publishers of the penny press and its descendants achieved was to move away from focusing on partisan politics and the concerns of the elite to other events, including crime news, that concerned the mass reading public.

The cases in this volume offer an intriguing look at early America, the evolving justice system, and the expanding mechanisms for reporting crime. It should be noted here that the modern police department (based on the London model) came into being to deal with urban disorder at roughly the same time when the penny press appeared as a medium through which urban dwellers could read about crime. Early newspaper reporters developed relationships with the police, and a regular feature in these papers was a police column or crime beat. As Andrea L. Kordzek and Carolyn Levy discuss in chapter 9, the Helen Jewett murder case provided the perfect opportunity for the new "pennies" to carve a role for themselves as crime news reporters. The Jewett case was a New York City case. Like the Mary Rogers murder case of the 1840s, the Jewett case raised issues of gender relations and morality in an urban setting. When Helen Jewett, a high-class brothel prostitute, was killed and set on fire in her room and a young clerk put on trial for her murder, the penny press editors had an opportunity to engage not only in sensational reporting but also investigative journalism as they sought the truth about Helen Jewett.

During this era, other cases provided opportunities for sensational reporting. Three such cases are recounted in this volume. In the Bickford murder case (chapter 11), the defense was unusual. An abusive man (himself married and a father) had engaged in a scandalous affair with a married woman (who had left her husband for various liaisons). He claimed that he had murdered her while sleepwalking. The sensational aspects of this case were rivaled by another New England case. In chapter 12, Karen Elizabeth Chaney examines the elite social context of the Parkman case. Rediscovered by the public in recent years, this is the story of a Harvard medical professor who murders and dissects a former friend and colleague to whom he owes money. Chaney examines the impact of this case and its coverage on the upper-class community in which it took place. A third case that received heavy newspaper coverage in antebellum America raised issues that are still relevant to the insanity defense. In chapter 14, John McClymer looks at the Daniel Sickles murder trial, the first case in which the defendant argued that he had been suffering from temporary insanity at the time of the murder. In Sickles' case, he claimed he had been rendered so by discovering his wife's adulterous affair with another man. In a public street, he shot the man with whom she had betrayed him.

In the final chapter of volume 1, Russell L. Hanson examines another famous case from 1859—John Brown's raid on Harpers Ferry and the trial that followed. At the time, the question posed by Brown's contemporaries was whether Brown was a madman or a martyr. Whatever he was, his contemporaries sensed that his raid on the federal arsenal in Virginia had propelled the country a step closer to war. Davidson and Lytle (1992) write, "Most historians would agree that the Harpers Ferry raid was to the Civil War what the Boston Massacre had been to the American Revolution: an incendiary event. In an atmosphere of aroused passions, profound suspicions, and irreconcilable differences, Brown and his men put a match to the fuse. Once their deed had been done and blood shed, there seemed to be no drawing back for either North or South. The shouts of angry men overwhelmed the voices of compromise" (pp. 123–124).

Even after John Brown lay "moulderin' in his grave," it was difficult—as the rhetoric flew between North and South—to turn back from the course that had been set decades earlier when the decision was made to retain the institution of slavery in the United States Constitution. As Abraham Lincoln assumed the presidency, the southern states began to secede from the Union. Through the cases in volume 1, we travel from colonial Massachusetts to a country on the verge of civil war.

REFERENCES

Bailey, F. Y., and Green, A. P. (1999). *Law never here: A social history of African-American responses to crime and justice.* Westport, CT: Praeger.

Cohen, D. A. (1993). *Pillars of salt, monuments of grace: New England crime literature and the origins if American popular culture, 1674–1860.* New York: Oxford University Press.

Davidson, J. W., and Lytle, M. H. (1992). The madness of John Brown: The uses of psychohistory. In *After the fact: The art of historical detection* (pp. 122–147). Vol. 1. New York: McGraw-Hill.

Emery, E., and Emery, M. (1984). *The press and America: An interpretive history of the mass media* (5th ed.). Englewood Cliffs, NJ: Prentice-Hall.

Erikson, K. (1966). *Wayward Puritans.* New York: Wiley.

Finkelman, P. (1993). The crime of color. *Tulane Law Review, 67*(6), 2063–2112.

Gilje, P. A. (1996). *Rioting in America*. Bloomington: Indiana University Press.

Hariman, R. (Ed.). (1990). *Popular trials: Rhetoric, mass media, and the law*. Tuscaloosa: The University of Alabama Press.

Morgan, E. S. (1975). *American slavery, American freedom: The ordeal of colonial Virginia*. New York: W. W. Norton.

Norton, M. B. (2002). *In the devil's snare: The Salem witchcraft crisis of 1692*. New York: Knopf.

Sellin, J. T. (1976). *Slavery and the penal system*. New York: Elsevier.

1

Quaker Mary Dyer: Twice under the Hangman's Noose

Kathy Warnes

My life not availeth me in comparison to the liberty of truth.
—Mary Dyer Memorial, Founders' Park, Portsmouth, Rhode Island
(Rogers, 1896, p. 2)

As far as the Puritans of Boston were concerned, Mary Dyer richly deserved to be the first woman executed in America for practicing her Quaker religious beliefs. On June 1, 1660, as her body dangled from the huge old elm on Boston Common that the Puritans used for a hanging tree, one of them self-righteously pointed out, "This is what happens to heretics" (Rogers, 1896, p. 2).

The Puritans had founded the Massachusetts Bay Colony in the early seventeenth century to translate their ideal of a religious "city on a hill" to a practical example for the Puritans back in England. They desired to purify the Church of England from what they considered "popish" and sinful practices, and they felt that if they provided a godly example, the Church of England would reform itself. They were not prepared to tolerate any doctrine or group that challenged their partnership between church and state or their ideas about salvation. The Puritans feared and despised dissenters

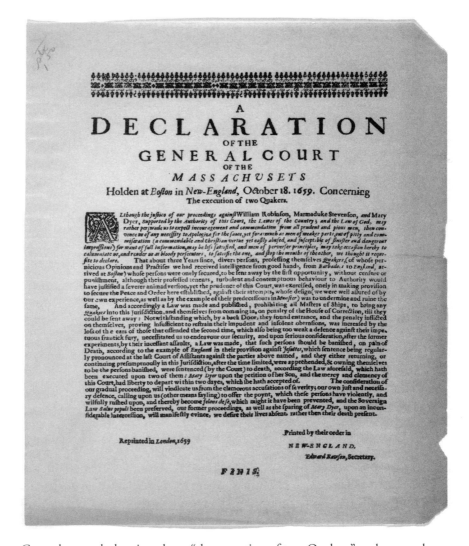

General court declaration about "the execution of two Quakers" and mercy shown to Mary Dyer, October 18, 1659. (Courtesy of Library of Congress)

and banished them from their settlements. In the case of the Quakers, the Puritan authorities took their intolerance and fear a step further and legally executed at least five Quakers in Boston in the late seventeenth century. They persecuted and banished countless others.

The Puritan leaders of the Massachusetts Bay Colony considered Quakers and others who dared to differ with them heretics and blasphemers. The

Mary Dyer being led to execution. (The Granger Collection, New York)

Records of the Governor summed up their attitude: "The doctrine of this sect of people . . . tends to overthrow the whole gospell & the very vitalls of Christianitie" (Notable Women Ancestors).

The Puritan hierarchy thought that women contributed nothing to religion and should be subordinate to and guided by men. They viewed outspoken, courageous women like Anne Marbury Hutchinson and Mary Dyer with alarm and took immediate steps to silence them. Even Puritan men, such as Roger Williams, who didn't conform to Puritan doctrines were banished from the Massachusetts Bay Colony. Williams, a minister from Salem, Massachusetts, objected to the way that the early white settlers took land from the Native Americans, and he spoke out against the religious intolerance of the Puritans. By 1636, the General Court of Massachusetts Bay Colony had banished him, stating in their decree of banishment that he had expressed dangerous ideas and objections against the authority of the magistrates and that he had six weeks to leave Massachusetts. Although the Puritan authorities agreed to allow Williams to remain until spring, he continued to speak out against them, and they resolved to send him back to England.

Before the magistrates could deport him to England, Roger Williams fled into the wilderness in the middle of a severe winter. Narragansett Indian chiefs Canonicus and Miantonomi welcomed him into their villages and deeded him land to establish a new colony. Williams called his new colony Rhode Island and his new settlement Providence. He acknowledged the contributions of the Narrangansetts when he said, "were it not for Canonicus . . . Rhode Island would not be" ("Trials without Justice," chap. 3, par. 4).

Williams founded his settlement on principles of total democracy, and other groups, such as Baptists and Quakers, who had been banished from the Massachusetts Bay Colony, found refuge in Rhode Island. Soon, Rhode Island and the more authoritarian Massachusetts clashed over issues of citizenship, law, and religious freedom. Mary Dyer and Anne Hutchinson were at the forefront of this epic struggle.

THE DYERS AND ANNE HUTCHINSON: THE BIRTH OF TROUBLE

Mary Barrett Dyer was born about 1610 in London, England. After her husband, William Dyer, served an apprenticeship, he and Mary were married in St. Martin-in-the-Fields, London, on October 27, 1633. William was a milliner in the New Exchange, a member of the Fishmongers' Company, and a Puritan. In 1634 or early 1635, when Mary was still in her early twenties, the Dyers immigrated to Massachusetts, where they were admitted to the Boston First Church on December 13, 1635. They were among the best citizens, being above reproach and above average in education and culture. William became a freeman of the Massachusetts Bay Colony on March 3, 1635, and he held many positions of public importance. He was elected clerk in 1638, and on December 14, 1635, and January 16, 1637 or 1638, William was granted land at Rumney Marsh in Chelsea, Massachusetts.

George Bishop, the Quaker chronicler who wrote about Mary after her death, described her as "a Comely Grave Woman, and of a goodly Person and one of a good Report, having a Husband of an Estate, fearing the Lord, and a Mother of Children" (New England Historical and Genealogical Register, 1940, p. 300).

Governor John Winthrop of Massachusetts, less flattering, described Mary as "the wife of one William Dyer, a milliner in the New Exchange, a very proper and fair woman, and both of them notoriously infected with Mrs. Hutchinson's errors, and very censorious and troublesome, she being of a very proud spirit, and much addicted to revelations" (Winthrop, 1644, p. 44).

William and Mary Dyer openly supported Anne Hutchinson, who preached doctrines of individual contact with God without benefit of church or minister and assured, instead of predestined and earned, salvation. Immediately, she encountered the prejudice and intolerance of Massachusetts Bay Colony's stern male leaders. Though her husband was one of Boston's leading citizens, Anne's charisma and learning (as well as her midwife skills) threatened the Puritan leaders, as did her teaching. She believed that faith through the covenant of God's grace, not deeds or the covenant of works, saved people. She summarized her doctrines:

As I do understand it, laws, commands, rules and edicts are for those who have not the light which makes plain the pathway. He who has God's grace in his heart cannot go astray. ("Trials without Justice")

Mary Dyer and Anne Hutchinson became friends, and when Mary's third child was about to be born, she turned to Anne and her midwifery skills. The Dyers already had two children. William, who was baptized on October 24, 1634, in London, England, lived only three days and was buried on October 27, 1634. Samuel was baptized on October 20, 1635, in Boston, Massachusetts. (Around the year 1660, Samuel married Anne Hutchinson, the granddaughter of Anne Marbury Hutchinson.) Eventually, the Dyers would have six more children: the stillborn daughter born October 17, 1637, in Boston; William, born about 1640 in Newport, Rhode Island; Mahershallahasbaz, born about 1643 in Newport; Henry, born about 1647 in Newport; Mary, born before 1650 in Newport; and Charles, born about 1650 in Newport.

When Mary Dyer went into premature labor on October 17, 1637, she called Anne to her side, along with Jane Hawkins, another midwife. Governor Winthrop of Massachusetts noted in his *History of New England* that Jane Hawkins was later banished from Boston for "practicing medicine," and lived in the woods. While living in Portsmouth, Rhode Island, she practiced midwifery, and she assisted in the delivery of the "monster" child of Mary Dyer (Winthrop, 1853, p. 45).

After hours of agonizing labor, Mary gave birth to a stillborn daughter who was badly deformed. William and Anne agreed that the birth had to be kept secret—if the Boston magistrates found out about the deformed baby, they would accuse Mary and Anne of sin and demonic possession. English law did not permit a midwife to deliver or bury a child secretly, so Anne immediately consulted Reverend John Cotton about whether or not to publicly record the stillbirth. With surprising compassion, Reverend Cotton dismissed the ancient folk wisdom that said that the death of an infant was divine punishment for the sins of the parents, and he told her to ignore the law and bury the child in secret. Jane Hawkins and Anne buried the stillborn child, and the birth and burial remained a secret for five months.

In the meantime, Anne continued her preaching as well as her midwifery. Anne attracted men as well as women to the meetings that she held in her Boston home, and every week, more and more people crowded into her home to hear her preach. In November 1637, the Boston Puritans disenfranchised and disarmed dozens of Anne's followers, including William Dyer. In March 1638, the alarmed and scandalized Puritan authorities charged Anne with heresy.

Governor Winthrop was Anne's chief accuser, and the verdict was obvious even before the trial. The governor's attitude toward women resounded when he said to her, "We do not mean to discourse with those of your sex" ("Trials without Justice").

At the end of the trial, Governor Winthrop read the verdict: "Mrs. Hutchinson, the sentence of the court you hear is that you are banished from out of our jurisdiction as being a women not fit for our society, and are to be imprisoned till the court shall send you away" ("Trials without Justice").

When Anne countered, "I desire to know wherefore I am banished," Governor Winthrop answered curtly, "Say no more. The court knows wherefore and is satisfied" (Plimpton, 1994, p. 63). Governor Winthrop and the Puritan authorities decreed that Anne Hutchinson and her entire family be banished from Massachusetts, and they left to live near Providence in the Rhode Island settlement that Roger Williams had established (Plimpton, p. 63).

On March 22, 1638, when Hutchinson was excommunicated from the Boston church and walked out the door, Mary Dyer walked with her. Several women gathered outside the church, whispering and pointing. One of them asked, "Who is that woman accompanying Anne Hutchinson?"

Another woman answered, "She is the mother of a monster!" (Plimpton, 1994, p. 63).

The women in the community had gossiped so extensively about Mary Dyer's deformed baby that Governor Winthrop heard the rumors and questioned Reverend Cotton. The reverend confessed that he had helped bury a deformed child five months previously. Governor Winthrop ordered the child exhumed, and he and other clergymen examined it. According to Winthrop's (Governor Winthrop of Massachusetts wrote a classic journal that is in Colonial historiography) *Journal*, Mary Dyer, for being "notoriously infected with Mrs. Hutchinson's errors," had been divinely punished for this sinful heresy by delivering a stillborn "monster." He included graphic descriptions of the child in his journal and in letters that he sent to England and Massachusetts Bay Colony, New England. Governor Winthrop used the child to demonize Dyer and Hutchinson as "unnatural" women. In pamphlets bursting with lurid details, he declared that "Mary Dyere had borne a monster child with talons instead of toes" (Winthrop, 1853, p. 47). Reverend Cotton Mather also discussed the story of Mary Dyer's monster child in his *Magnalia Christi Americana*.

MEETING THE "INNER LIGHT" OF THE QUAKERS

After the scandal of their deformed child, William and Mary Dyer and their children were excommunicated and followed the Hutchinson family to safety and freedom in Rhode Island. William became one of the founders of Portsmouth, and on March 7, 1638, he and seventeen other men signed the compact of Portsmouth. The other men respected him enough to elect him clerk. The Dyers ultimately settled in Newport, Rhode Island, and by March 19, 1640, William had acquired 87 acres of land. He served as secretary for the towns of Portsmouth and Newport from 1640–1647, as general recorder in 1647, and as attorney general from 1650–1652. At different times he held other offices including commissioner, deputy general solicitor, and secretary of the council.

For fourteen years, the Dyers lived peacefully in Rhode Island. Then, in 1652, William and Mary traveled to England with Roger Williams and John Clarke to persuade the English government to revoke the powers it had granted William Coddington.

William Coddington had also supported the controversial religious beliefs of Anne Hutchinson, and the Puritan authorities forced him to leave Massachusetts for the island of Aquidneck in Narragansett Bay, where he established a community at Pocasset, later Portsmouth, Rhode Island, in northern Aquidneck. Anne had also settled in Portsmouth after her banishment from Massachusetts, but William and she quarreled, and Coddington moved his settlement to Newport in 1639. In 1640, Portsmouth and Newport united, with Coddington as governor. In 1651, he obtained a patent from Parliament establishing Aquidneck as a separate colony. Roger Williams, William Dyer, and John Clarke traveled to England to try to persuade Parliament to revoke the patent. Mary accompanied her husband. The events of that trip transformed Mary Dyer's religious thinking and propelled her on a fatal collision course with the Puritan authorities in Boston.

During her five-year stay in England (William returned to Rhode Island in 1653), Mary Dyer met George Fox, the founder of the Society of Friends, or Quakers, whose doctrine of the "Inner Light" was similar to Anne Hutchinson's ideas. An essential part of the Quaker message concerned the "Inner Light of Christ," or the idea that Christ taught people himself and that they did not need intermediaries like priests, ministers, books, or churches to have a relationship with Christ. Quakers believed people could attain a direct knowledge of the spirit of Christ. They believed that by "waiting on the Lord," they could learn the will of God through direct communication. George Fox believed that the state should not control the Church of England, and in 1643, he began to preach sermons throughout England, arguing that people did not need consecrated buildings and ordained ministers to gain salvation. Women were allowed to speak in Quaker worship services and to preach. By 1656, English Quakers had stopped attending Anglican services and refused to pay tithes. George Fox, as the instigator and leader of this unorthodox activity, clashed with the authorities, and they arrested him for his subversive teachings. The Quakers were persecuted in England because of their unconventional beliefs and forms of worship. Over 13,000 Quakers were arrested during the reign of Charles II, and 338 died in prison or from violent attacks during their religious meetings. Some of the Quakers migrated to New England, where their views clashed with those of Puritans (Besse, 2000, p. 76).

Quaker beliefs both openly and implicitly challenged the authority of the priest or minister or church, and they were accused of anarchy, heresy, and blasphemy, as well. It is ironic that a group such as the Quakers, who believed that they were living under God's guidance and claimed Christ as their lord and teacher, would be charged with blasphemy. Perhaps the blasphemy charge originated from the Quaker conviction that all people could possess the Inner Light: the Light of Christ. Some who charged the Friends with blasphemy interpreted the inner light as a Quaker claim to divine powers, assuming a Godlike nature for themselves. The most common charges against Quakers were transgressions like "disorderly behavior," "breach of the peace," and "contempt of court." In Britain, Quakers were imprisoned and several were whipped; but none were executed, as they were in America.

FROM CONVERSION TO CONTROVERSY

Mary Dyer became a Quaker during her stay in England, and her conversion significantly affected the rest of her life. By 1657, when Mary returned from England to Boston, Puritans had already passed anti-Quaker laws. Puritan ministers led the persecution of Quakers. The Reverend John Norton, a pastor of the Boston First Church, where the Dyers had been members, agitated for the passage of a law of banishment under penalty of death upon return. In 1659, he wrote the vindication of the Massachusetts authorities for putting Quakers to death. Reverend John Wilson, another pastor of the Church, wrote, "I would carry fire in one hand and fagots in the other to burn all the Quakers in the world. . . . Hang them or else"—he drew his finger across his throat in a cutting motion (Rogers, 1896, p. 15).

By 1658, anti-Quaker sentiment had reached a fever pitch in Massachusetts. The anti-Quaker laws were harsh. Quakers could be branded with an *H* for "heretic" and their tongues cored with hot irons. Punishments for their first offenses were tailored as warnings against further offenses. A first offender could be whipped, jailed, and banished. If caught again, the Quaker would have his head put into a stock and an ear nailed to a board and cut off. A third offense required the other ear to be lopped off. The punishment for a fourth offense was immediate death. John Endicott, who had succeeded John Winthrop as governor of the Massachusetts Bay Colony in 1649, sought and won the death penalty as the ultimate punishment for Quakers who had been banished but returned to the Colony. He feared that if he allowed the Quakers to express their beliefs in Massachusetts Bay Colony, the church–state partnership might collapse.

There was nothing in the Massachusetts Bay Colony charter that permitted the imprisonment of anyone on the grounds of his or her religious beliefs, so Governor Endicott invented legal tactics to remove the Quakers. The Massachusetts General Court met in mid-October 1656 and 1657 and passed several laws against "the cursed sect of heretics . . . commonly called Quakers." These laws permitted banishing, whipping, and such corporal punishment as cutting off ears and boring holes into tongues. On October 14, 1656, the Court ordered that any shipmasters bringing Quakers or any other "Blasphemous heretics" should pay a fine of 100 pounds, and "they must be brought back from where they came or go to prison" (Rogers, 1896, p. 15).

The Massachusetts General Court then spelled out what it would do to any Quaker who evaded the law and successfully returned to the Colony. The Court decreed that such a person must go to the House of Correction and be severely whipped, kept constantly at work, and not allowed to speak to anyone. They set up a system of fines: fifty-four pounds for having any Quaker books or writing "concerning their devilish opinions, forty pounds for a second offence, and the House of Correction for a third offence . . . until there be a convenient passage for them to be sent out of this land." These laws were read on the street corners of Boston against the backdrop of beating drums (Rogers, 1896, p. 15).

Unaware of the new laws and the imprisonment of fellow Quakers, Christopher Holder, John Copeland, Mary Dyer, and Anne Burden arrived in Boston and disembarked. The Puritan authorities immediately arrested them and put them in prison. The women protested, but they were kept in darkened cells with boarded-up windows and not allowed to talk to anyone. The Puritans confiscated Mary's Quaker papers and books and burned them. Mary finally slipped a letter to her husband through a crack to friendly hands outside the jail, but it took a long time to reach him in Newport, Rhode Island.

Two and a half months later, Governor Endicott had an unexpected visitor. William Dyer barged into his home, insisting that the governor free his wife Mary immediately. Governor Endicott knew that the Boston Church had disenfranchised William, but the Boston authorities respected him for his prominent position in Rhode Island. He felt that Massachusetts would have to free Mary because of William's prestige, but only on the condition that William be put under a bond and swear on his honor that if his wife were allowed to return home, he was "not to lodge her in any town of the colony nor to permit any to have speech with her on the journey." Mary could not return to Massachusetts under any circumstances. William Dyer agreed to these conditions and, reluctantly, so did Mary (Rogers, 1896, p. 16).

Returning home to Rhode Island in 1657, Mary became a prominent Quaker minister, traveling through the settlement and preaching the Quaker doctrine of the Inner Light. Her beliefs rejected oaths of any kind, taught that gifts and prophecy did not depend on gender, and contended that women and men were equal in church worship and organization. In 1658, she was expelled from the Puritan New Haven settlement for preaching Quaker doctrine.

Conditions for Quakers in Massachusetts continued to worsen. In a stormy session on October 19, 1658, the Massachusetts General Court passed, by a single vote, a law banishing Quakers under pain of death. In June 1659, Quakers William Robinson, a merchant of London, and Marmaduke Stephenson of Holderness, then in Rhode Island, were, in the Quaker phrase, "moved by the Lord" to enter Massachusetts. Patience Scott, Anne Hutchinson's eleven-year-old niece from Providence, and a man named Nicholas Davis from Plymouth Colony, accompanied them. The authorities promptly threw them in jail to wait for the next meeting of the Court of Assistants in September. Mary Dyer heard of their imprisonment and visited them in the summer of 1659. The Boston authorities threw Mary in prison as well (Rogers, 1896, p.18).

In a letter dated August 30, 1659, William Dyer chastised the Massachusetts Bay Colony for imprisoning his wife without evidence or legal right. He compared the General Court's members to the "Popish inquisitors" of the thirteenth century, pointing out that they also had acted as "judge and accuser both." He identified the most important ideological issue in the case when he expressed outrage that the Puritans, who had fled persecution in England, should, in their turn, persecute Quakers. "Surely you or some of you, if ever you had the courage to looke a bishop in the face, cannot but remember that the (first, second) or third word from them was, You are a Puritane are you not, & is it not so (here) in N(ew) England, the magistracy having . . . assumed a coercive power of conscience, the first or next word?" (Burgess, 2000, p. 45).

Among the others who protested Mary Dyer's sentence were her son William; Governor John Winthrop Jr. of Connecticut; and Governor Thomas Temple of Nova Scotia. On September 12, 1659, the Massachusetts General Court released the Quakers from prison and banished them from the Colony, vowing to execute them if they returned. Nicholas Davis and Mary Dyer did not return, but William Robinson and Marmaduke Stephenson felt that it was their duty to remain and continue their ministry, determined to confront and defy the anti-Quaker laws and try to change them.

Within a month, the Massachusetts authorities again arrested William Robinson and Marmaduke Stephenson and once again clapped Christopher Holder in jail. The threat of further torture hung over them like the shadow of a noose. Mary Dyer, Hope Clifton, and Mary Scott, Christopher's future wife and Anne Hutchinson's niece, walked through the forest from Providence to Boston to plead for the release of the prisoners. On October 8, 1659, as Mary spoke to Holder through the prison bars, the authorities arrested her as well and put her in prison with her fellow Quakers.

The motives and actions of the Quakers—Christopher Holder, William Robinson, Marmaduke Stephenson, and Mary Dyer—resembled the tactics of Dr. Martin Luther King Jr.'s nonviolent resistance in the civil rights movement of the 1960s. The Quakers deliberately challenged Massachusetts Governor Endicott's right to enforce the death penalty. They returned to the battlefield as soon as they were released from prison, ready to die if necessary, yet never retaliating with violence. They fought the Boston Puritans with passive resistance, religious appeals, and the unshakable conviction of the righteousness of their cause. The issues between Quakers and Puritans were clear. The Quakers defied the unjust Puritan laws and dared martyrdom. How far would the Puritan authorities fight the challenge to the might and right of their authority?

Not everyone felt sympathy with the Quaker cause, even centuries after their struggles. Early-twentieth-century historian Hubert H. Bancroft, in his history *The Great Republic*, appeared to side with the Puritans in his narrative of Quaker zeal and the Puritan-Quaker clash of the late seventeenth century. He stated that "the treatment which the Quakers experienced in Massachusetts was much more severe than that of the Anabaptists, but certainly much more justly provoked" (Morris, 1902, p. 35). Regarding the Massachusetts controversy, he remarked:

The penal enactments resorted to by the other settlements than Rhode Island served only to inflame the impatience of the Quaker zealots to carry their ministry into places that seemed to them to stand so greatly in need of it; and the persons who had been disappointed in their first attempt returned almost immediately to Massachusetts, and, dispersing themselves through the colony, began to proclaim their mystical notions, and succeeded in communicating them to some of the inhabitants of Salem . . . the apostles of Quakerism raised their voices in vilification of everything that was most highly approved and revered in the doctrine and practice of the provincial churches. Seized, imprisoned, and flogged, they were again dismissed with severer threats from the colony, and again they returned by the first vessels they could procure. The government and a great majority of the colonists were incensed at their stubborn pertinacity, and shocked at the impression which they had already produced on some minds, and which threatened to corrupt and subvert a system of piety whose establishment, fruition, and perpetuation supplied their fondest recollections, their noblest enjoyment, and most energetic desire.

EXECUTED TWICE

The accounts of Mary Dyer's death are more sympathetic to the Quaker cause. On October 19, 1659, Mary, William Robinson, and Marmaduke Stephenson were brought before Governor Endicott and his assistants. The Puritan officials demanded to know why the prisoners again had come into their jurisdiction after they had been banned from Massachusetts on the pain of death. The Quakers stated that they came in obedience to God. The next day, October 20, 1659, the Quaker prisoners were again brought before the magistrates. Governor Endicott called the prisonkeeper to pull off the hats of the Quakers. Addressing William Robinson and Marmaduke Stephenson, he pronounced a sentence of death on them. Then the guards brought Mary Dyer to the bar of the court, and the governor pronounced sentence upon her: "Mary Dyer, you shall go from hence to the place from whence you came, and from thence to the place of execution, and there be hanged till ye be dead" (Plimpton, 1994, p. 67).

Governor John Winthrop Jr. of Connecticut appealed to the Massachusetts authorities not to condemn the Quakers to death. Colonel Thomas Temple also pleaded with the Massachusetts magistrates to banish the prisoners and spare their lives. He promised that he would take them, give them a house to live in, corn to eat, and land to plant so that they would be able to provide for themselves within a year. He pledged that if they returned to Massachusetts, he would take them away at his own expense. But Governor

Endicott, Reverend John Wilson from the Boston Church, and other Puritan authorities were determined that the Quakers must die.

The Massachusetts authorities set October 27, 1659, as the date for the triple execution and began to prepare for it. People came to the prison windows to talk to the condemned Quakers. The authorities put the male prisoners in irons and detailed a special force of soldiers "to watch with great care the towne, especially the prison." Captain James Oliver was ordered to recruit 100 soldiers "proportionally out of each company in Boston, completely armed with pike and musketeers with powder and bullet," to escort the prisoners to the place of execution. Later, the order was modified so that thirty-six of the soldiers would remain in and around town and the rest went to the place of execution (Rogers, 1896, p. 22).

The execution day arrived, and Captain Oliver and his military guard waited to escort the prisoners. The marshal and the jailer brought the two Quaker men from the jail and Mary Dyer from the House of Correction. At the prison, William Robinson, Marmaduke Stephenson, and Mary Dyer bade joyful farewells to their friends, thanking God that He had found them worthy of suffering in his name and praying that He would keep them faithful to the end. The condemned Quakers walked forward hand in hand, Mary between the two men. The Marshal asked her whether she were not ashamed to walk hand in hand between two men much younger than she. Mary answered, "It is an hour of the greatest joy I can enjoy in this world. No eye can see, no ear can hear, no tongue can speak, no heart can understand, the sweet incomes and refreshings of the spirit of the Lord which now I enjoy" (Rogers, 1896, p. 23).

The crowd of people pressed around the prisoners. The guards made a steel ring around them, and when the prisoners tried to speak again, the authorities ordered the drums to be beaten to drown them out. The prisoners were marched to the great Boston Common elm that served as the gallows. In *Criminal Trials* (1841), Chandler wrote, "These executions are supposed to have taken place on Boston Common, probably where the Hollis Street Church now stands. The halters were adjusted round the neck of the prisoner, he was forced to climb a ladder leading to the limb to which the other half of the halter was attached. Then the ladder was pulled away. The execution was rude though effective" (1841, p. 44).

The prisoners arrived at the elm tree, and Reverend John Wilson of Mary Dyer's Boston Church tauntingly asked them, "Shall such Jacks as you come in before authority with your Hats on?"

William Robinson replied, "Mind you, mind you, it is for not putting off the Hat we are put to Death" (Rogers, 1896, p. 34).

The prisoners said tender farewells to each other. William Robinson, who was the first to climb the ladder, said, "I suffer for Christ in whom I lived, and for whom I die." Marmaduke Stephenson mounted the ladder next. He said to the people, "Be it known unto all this day, that we suffer not as evil-doers but for conscience sake" (Rogers, 1896, p. 34).

Mary came next. Expecting to die momentarily, she waited at the foot of the elm tree with a rope around her neck. She watched the executioners snatch the ladder from under the feet of her friends and their lifeless bodies swinging in front of her. The hangman bound her arms and legs and tied her skirts around her feet. Her face was covered with a handkerchief that Reverend Wilson, who had been her pastor when she lived in Boston, had loaned the hangman. She stood on the ladder with the rope around her neck, in calm serenity, expecting to die. Then, the hangman loosened the halter from her neck. He untied her and told her to come down the ladder. She did not speak and she did not move. People around her so persistently tried to pull her down that she had to ask them to wait a while so she could ask the Lord what to do. The people pulled her and the ladder down together, and the marshal took her down in his arms. The marshal led Dyer back to prison.

The Massachusetts Puritans had known all along that Mary would not be executed, but they had sent her to the gallows with her friends to test her fortitude and shake her constancy. Mary's son William had presented a petition to the Massachusetts court. The Court's decision was as follows:

Whereas Mary Dyer is condemned by the Generall Court to be Executed for hir offences, on the petition of William Dier, hir sonne, It is ordered that the said Mary Dyer shall have liberty for forty-eight hours after this day to depart out of this jurisdiction, after which time, being found therein, she is forth with to be executed, and in the meanetime that she be kept a close prionser till hir sonne or some other be ready to carry hir away win the aforesaid tyne; and it is further ordered, that she shall be carried to the place of execution, and there to stand upon the gallowes, with a rope about her necke till the rest be executed, and then to returne to the prison and remajne as aforesaid. (Rogers, 1896, p. 37)

When Dyer returned to prison and understood the nature of her reprieve, she rejected it. The next morning she wrote to the Massachusetts General Court, refusing to accept the reprieve from her persecutors. She said to the Puritan authorities, "My life is not accepted, neither availeth me, in comparison with the lives and liberty of Truth and Servants of the living God, for which in the Bowels of Love and Meakness I sought you; yet nevertheless with wicked Hands have you put two of them to Death" (Rogers, 1896, p. 37).

The courage and faith of Quakers like William Robinson, Marmaduke Stephenson, and Mary Dyer turned the people against the Puritan authorities. The magistrates were confused. They did not know what to do with Mary. The reprieve had been kept secret, and neither William Dyer nor anyone else arrived to take Mary away. The day after her friends' execution, some officials came, took her in their arms, set her on horseback, and conveyed her fifteen miles toward Rhode Island. They left her with a horse and man to be conveyed further. Unwillingly, Mary returned to Rhode Island in the company of four horsemen who followed her fifteen miles south of Boston. There three of the horsemen returned, and the remaining man escorted her to Rhode Island.

People were upset about the way the Massachusetts authorities treated Mary Dyer. They were so vocal that the Puritans went on the defensive. They claimed credit for her reprieve and industriously sought to soften the judgment of the citizens upon the martyrdom of William Robinson and Marmaduke Stephenson by pointing out how considerate they had been to Mary Dyer.

Safe in her own home, Mary sought the company of other Quakers. She rowed herself across Long Island Sound on Shelter Island where a group of Indians had approached her, asking if she would hold Quaker meetings with them. Now Mary was safe, but she was not content. The Quaker persecutions in Massachusetts bothered her. She was especially upset at the Puritan attempt to vindicate the executions of William Robinson and Marmaduke Stephenson. She believed that the mercy that the Puritan authorities extended to her was just a diversion to pacify popular indignation. She told her family that she must return to Boston to "desire the repeal of that wicked law against God's people and offer up her life there." She wanted either to defy the authorities and force them to annul their unjust laws or, by her death, to sway public opinion enough that the law would be repealed. In late April 1660, obeying her conscience and defying the law, Mary once again set off for Boston without telling her husband where she was going. She arrived in Boston on May 21, 1660.

A week later, William Dyer heard that Mary had left Shelter Island for Boston. Quickly he wrote to the magistrates of Boston, and Governor Endicott received the letter and presented it to the General Court. In his letter, Dyer appealed to Governor Endicott for mercy to his wife:

Little did I dream that ever I should have occasion to petition you in a matter of this nature, but so it is that through the devine providence and your benignity my sonn obtayned so much pitty and met yo hands as to enjoy the life of his mother, now my supplication to you affectionately, the life of my deare wife. Tis true I have not seen her above this half year & therefore cannot tell how in the frame of her spiritt she was moved thus againe to runn so great a Hazard to herself, and perplexity to me & mine & all her friends & well wishers; so itt is from Shelter Iland about by Pequid Narrangansett & to the Towne of Providence she secretly & spedyly journyed, & as secretly from thence came to your Jurisdiction, unhappy journy may I say, & woe to that generation say I that gives occasion thus of grief & troble (to thos that desire to be quiett) by helping one another (as I may say) to Hazard their lives for I know not whatt end or to what purpose: if her zeale be so greatt as thus to adventure, ohn Lett your favoure & Pitty surmount itt & save her, not your forwonted compassion bee conquered by her inconsiderate madness, & how greatly will you're renowne be spread if by so conquering you become victorious. (Massachusetts Archives X, p. 266)

The governor did not sympathize with William Dyer. Mary had caused the Massachusetts authorities too much trouble, and she had no right to come back in defiance of their orders. The General Court summoned Mary to appear before the magistrates on May 31, 1660.

"Are you the same Mary Dyer that was here before?" Governor Endicott asked her. "You will own yourself a Quaker will you not?" the governor continued. Mary assured him that she was indeed the same Mary Dyer who had appeared in front of the last General Court. She also assured him that she was a Quaker.

Then the governor said, "Sentence was passed upon you the last General Court; and now likewise—You must return to the prison, and there remain till tomorrow at nine o'clock; then thence you must go to the gallows, and there be hanged till you are dead."

Dyer replied, "This is no more than what thous saidst before."

"But now it is to be executed. Therefore prepare yourself tomorrow at nine o'clock," the governor told her sternly.

Mary said, "I came in obedience to the will of God to the last General Court, desiring you to repeal your unrighteous laws of banishment on pain of death; and that same is my work now, and earnest request, although I told you that if you refused to repeal them, the Lord would send others of his servants to witness against them."

The governor asked her a telling question. "Are you a prophetess?"

She answered, "I speak the words that the Lord speaks in me and now the thing has come to pass."

The governor had heard enough of this blasphemy. Beckoning a prison guard, he shouted, "Away with her! Away with her!" (Rogers, 1896, p. 38)

On the morning of June 1, 1660, a band of soldiers escorted Mary from her prison cell to the gallows a mile away. The magistrates tried to cut off communication between Dyer and her followers and anyone else in the crowd who might feel compassion for her. Despite the efforts of the magistrates, some of Mary's followers inched close enough to her to appeal to her to leave Boston. "Mary Dyer, don't die. Go back to Rhode Island where you might save your life. We beg of you, go back!"[1]

Mary refused on the grounds that she was obeying the will of the Lord and would be faithful to His will until she died.

The soldiers led her, sandwiched between drummers, through the streets. With a constant rat-a-tat-tat in front and behind her, Mary Dyer walked to her death.

On Boston Common, the drums were quieted and Captain John Webb spoke, attempting to justify the actions of the Massachusetts authorities. "She has been here before and had the sentence of banishment upon pain of death and has broken the law in coming again now," he said. "It is therefore *she* who is guilty of her own blood."

Mary disagreed with him. "Nay, I came to keep blood guiltiness from you, desiring you to repeal the unrighteous and unjust laws of banishment upon pain of death made against the innocent servants of the Lord. Therefore, my blood will be required at your hands who willfully do it."

Then she turned toward the crowd. "But, for those who do it in the simplicity of their hearts, I desire the Lord to forgive them. I came to do the will of my Father, and in obedience to this will I stand even to death."

Her old Puritan pastor Reverend John Wilson urged Mary to repent and "be not so deluded and carried away by the deceit of the Devil."

Mary replied, "Nay man, I am not now to repent."

John Norton asked Mary, "Would you have the elders pray for you?"

She answered, "I desire the prayer of all the people of God."

Someone from the crowd shouted, "It may be that she thinks there is none here."

Another voice called, "Did you say you have been in Paradise?"

Mary answered, "Yes, I have been in Paradise several days and now I am about to enter eternal happiness."

Captain John Webb signaled to Edward Wanton, officer of the gallows, and he adjusted the noose. Mary mounted the scaffold herself, a small smile illuminating her face. Pastor Wilson had his large handkerchief ready to put over her head so that no one could see her expression the moment that she entered her paradise, instead just the image of her swaying body.

As Mary Dyer's neck snapped, the crowd stood silently. Then a spring breeze lifted her limp skirt and billowed it out like a flag. One of the bystanders who had applauded her execution spoke a fitting tribute to her. "She hangs there as a flag for others to take example by," observed General Atherton, one of her persecutors (Rogers, 1896, p. 39).

Another written epitaph resonated just as elegantly simple and poignant. "Mary Dyer, wife of William Dyer of Newport in Rhode Island: She was put to death at the Town of Boston with y like cruil hand as the martrys were in Queen Mary's time, and there being upon y 31 day of y 3 mo., 1660" (Friends' Record Book).

MARY DYER'S GIFT TO FREEDOM OF RELIGION IN AMERICA

The next day, the gravediggers buried Mary Dyer in an unmarked grave on Boston Common. The Puritan clergy had provided no mercy for Mary, but her death inspired more protests against the anti-Quaker laws. Not only did the Puritan authorities persecute the Quakers, but they also punished the citizens of Massachusetts who gave them shelter, food, attended their meetings, or simply protested the inhumanities perpetrated against them. Ordinary Puritans and people of other beliefs began to find the courage to express their disagreement with Puritan policy toward the Quakers. They saw nothing in Quaker doctrine that was adverse to Christianity. Rhode Island and other colonies got along with the Quakers, and people felt that the Massachusetts Puritans' persistence in prosecuting Quakers reflected badly on the Puritans' religious beliefs. In spite of the frantic attempts of the Boston magistrates to rid themselves of the Quakers, they failed. Gradually, people began to consider Dyer's death a martyrdom, even in Massachusetts. Her death brought about the easing of anti-Quaker statutes, and only one more Quaker was executed after her.

Public indignation about the treatment of Quakers influenced the Massachusetts General Council. Governor Endicott raved at his fellow magistrates for what he considered their weakness, but his tantrums did no good, for they refused to execute any more Quakers. Instead, the Massachusetts General Council ordered the Quakers to be sent to England for trial and punishment. King Charles II, ruler of England, issued a royal mandate for the release of the Quakers, which ordered the Massachusetts authorities to do the following:

Send the said Persons (Quakers) whether condemned or imprisoned over to this our Kingdom of England, together with their respective Crimes and Offences laid to their charge, to the End such Course may be taken with them here, as shall be agreeable to our Laws and their demerits. And for so doing, these our Letters shall be your sufficient Warrant and Discharge. Given at our Court at Whitehall, the 9 September 1661, in the thirteenth Year of our Reign. (Besse, 2000, p. 225)

Quakers celebrated this questionable clemency, but it did not last for long. The royal order was modified on October 8, 1662, and the Puritan persecutions of the Quakers resumed. John Endicott pursued the Quakers with relentless cruelty until March 1665, when his death ended his holy war against them. Governor Richard Bellingham succeeded Endicott, but he did not persecute the Quakers as zealously. In November 1675, Quaker persecution was revived by the passage of a law prohibiting Quaker meetings; and in May, 1677, the law further provided that constables should make diligent search for meetings and could break open any door where peaceable entrance was denied them. Quaker men and women were seized, dragged to jail, imprisoned, fed only bread and water, fined, and publicly whipped. For nearly twenty years, persecution of the Quakers continued, but with decreasing severity.

Meanwhile, in 1649 in England, the authorities imprisoned George Fox, the founder of the Society of Friends, at Nottingham for interrupting a church service; and in 1651 he was imprisoned at Derby under a new blasphemy law.

As the Quaker movement spread in the 1650s, the pattern of opposition and frequent imprisonment developed. During the 1650s, Friends began building meeting houses and establishing local worship groups. In 1689, the Toleration Act was passed in England, greatly reducing the pressure on all dissenters by making it an offense to disrupt the worship of others. People recognized the Quaker principle of taking no oaths and respected it. Quakers perhaps were regarded as a peculiar people, but no longer were considered a threat to secular or religious authority. In the forty years between 1650 and 1690, Quakers continued to establish and consolidate their faith and spread it throughout the world (Murray-Rust).

By the end of the seventeenth century, the descendants of the Puritans and the larger society had transformed the authoritarian Puritan way of life into accommodation and toleration of colonial society's diversity. Puritan control of Massachusetts had lasted only sixty years. Mary Dyer, acting upon the courage of her convictions and her deep faith, helped transform fanatical Puritanism and fanatical Quakerism into a tolerance that more closely resembled the principles of freedom of speech and religion. Her death helped to bring America closer to practicing its idealism.

In 1959, the Massachusetts General Court erected a bronze statue in the memory of Mary Dyer on the grounds of the State House in Boston. The statue of her friend, Anne Hutchinson, stands in front of the other wing of the State House.

THE ROLE OF THE MEDIA IN REPORTING QUAKER LIFE

The stories of Mary Dyer and her fellow Quaker martyrs were not covered in contemporary colonial newspapers, because the first continuously published newspaper in Boston, the *Boston News-Letter*, did not appear until April 24, 1704. The activities of the Quakers are reported in later colonial newspapers such as the *South Carolina Gazette*, the *Pennsylvania Gazette*, and the *Virginia Gazette*. The *Virginia Gazette* issues of 1737 and 1756 offer some interesting insights into how Quakers were regarded in England and why they immigrated to the colonies. The *Virginia Gazette* even featured a story about the family of William and John Dyer, possible descendants of Mary.[2]

The eyewitness accounts of Mary Dyer's life have survived through the eyes, histories, and broadsides of her persecutors and through the letters of her husband.

NOTES

1. All direct quotes and dialogue in these sections are taken from (Rogers, 1896, p. 38).

2. A page from the 1737 *Virginia Gazette* can be viewed at: http://www.pastportal. com/cwdl_new/VA_Gazet/Images/VG/1737/0084hi.jpg

REFERENCES

Besse, J. (2000). *Sufferings of early Quakers: Yorkshire 1652 to 1690*. Facsimile of the 1753 edition (Vol. 2). Compiled by Michael Grady. London.

Burgess, R. S. (2000). *To try the bloody law: The story of Mary Dyer*. Burnsville, NC: Celo Valley Books.

Chandler, P. W. (1844). *American criminal trials*. Boston: T. H. Carter.

Friends' Record Book, Portsmouth, Rhode Island.

Massachusetts Archives X. Mary Barrett Dyer. *Notable women ancestors*. Retrieved from http://www.rootsweb.com/~nwa.dyer.html

Morris, C. (Ed.). (1902). *The great republic by the master historians* (Vol. 1). New York: R. S. Belcher, Co.

Murray-Rust, D. M. *Quakers in brief*. Retrieved from http://www.cryst.bbk.ac.uk/~ubcg09/dmr/chap2.htm

New England Historical and Genealogical Register. (1940, July, Vol. 94).

Plimpton, R. (1994). *Mary Dyer*. Boston: Branden Publishing.

Rogers, H. (1896). *Mary Dyer of Rhode Island: The Quaker martyr that was hanged on Boston Common, June 1, 1660*. Providence: Preston and Rounds.

Trials without justice. Mary Dyer. Retrieved October 16, 2003, from http://www. lawbuzz.com/justice/mary/mary.htm

Winthrop, J. (1644). *A short story of the life, reign, and ruine of the Antinomians familists & libertines that infected the churches of New-England*. Plymouth, MA.

Winthrop, J. (1853). *The history of New England from 1630 to 1649*. Boston: Little, Brown.

2

Witch Trials, 1692:
Madness in Salem

Tammy A. Denesha

On June 10, 1692, Bridget Bishop made the long walk to Gallows Hill led by Sheriff Jonathan Corwin. She must have been amazed that her case had come this far and no one stopped it. She must have been wondering what she had done that was so bad. Was it that she had outlived two husbands? Was it that she owned a tavern? No, more likely it was because she had not lived up to the strict Puritan standards of the time. She liked a drink now and then, she enjoyed her colorful clothing, and yes, she wasn't afraid to speak her mind. But was any of this sufficient cause for her to be hanged as a witch?

Twelve years earlier, Bridget Bishop had been in a similar circumstance. After the death of her first husband, she was accused of witchcraft. But then she was found innocent. How could this possibly have happened again?

On April 18, 1692, a warrant was issued for her arrest. The warrant charged Bishop with "sundry acts of witchcraft." The next day, Bishop was examined by Judge John Hathorne and Sheriff Corwin. During the examination, Bishop was accused of afflicting two girls, Mercy Lewis and Ann Putnam. When the accusations were made, even Bishop's family turned against her; her third husband did not come to her defense, and her brother-in-law claimed she conversed with the Devil himself.

The trial of George Jacobs of Salem for witchcraft. (Courtesy of Library of Congress)

Found guilty of witchcraft, Bridget Bishop was the first to be hanged for that crime, but over 150 others would also be accused during the witch trials in Salem, Massachusetts. This was not the first time accusations of witchcraft had been made in New England, but it would be the first and last mass trial of accused witches in colonial America. The question for historians was, and continues to be, why the witchcraft hysteria occurred at that time and in that place.

WHAT IS WITCHCRAFT?

To begin to understand what happened in Salem in 1692, it is important to strip away the modern meanings of witchcraft. Today's "witches" come in many forms. The most common reference to witches is to those who practice Wicca, a nature-based religion. While there is no one true Wiccan religion, the basic tenets are the same across variations. Wicca has its roots in the pagan religions of old. Wiccans believe in the male and female divines, and that the male and female forces of the universe complement and complete each other. Wiccans celebrate the earth, and their holy days coincide with the solstices. True Wiccans also believe that what evil you do comes back to you threefold. In Wicca there is no devil; there is no hell.

The "witches" of Salem in 1692 were a far cry from the Wiccans of today. The witches feared by the people of Salem were alleged disciples of the Devil and inflicted pain and suffering on their neighbors. In the imaginations of

Witch Hill, Salem, Massachusetts. (Courtesy of Library of Congress)

Salem residents, witches could be anywhere and anyone. Even the most devout could be accused of siding with the Devil. Barstow (1994), in her book about the European witch-hunts, tells us:

Since long before the sixteenth century, people had believed that some persons had supernatural power, the ability to perform good or harmful magic (or both). A good witch, or cunning woman, as these magic workers were often called, might, for example, heal persons or animals by incantations or potions; she might just as readily kill with a curse or the evil eye. In either case, she possessed a power to be reckoned with. By the sixteenth century, many—especially among the elite—began to hold a new belief, namely, that such supernatural power came from the devil, who bestowed it chiefly on women in return for their absolute obedience to him. (p. 20)

It was from this environment, from Europe where witches were believed to both exist and to be disciples of the Devil, that the Puritans of Massachusetts had come. In Europe the techniques of witch-hunting were already well developed. In fact, as early as 1486, two Dominican priests in Germany, Kramer and Sprenger, had published the "witch hunter's manual," *Malleus Maleficarum* (Barstow, 1994, p. 171). Therefore, when the Puritans in Salem begin to suspect they had witches among them, their perceptions were shaped by the beliefs that they had brought with them when they crossed the Atlantic.

THE AFFLICTIONS

On January 20, 1692, the afflictions began. The first girls to be afflicted were Elizabeth Parris, age nine, daughter of Reverend Samuel Parris; and Abigail Williams, age eleven, niece of the reverend. The girls' symptoms included seizures, screaming, and babbling. Parris did not rush to the conclusion that the girls had been bewitched. In fact, he seems first to have looked for a medical explanation. Puritan physicians were unable to provide one, and in their society, "[m]edical and demonic explanations were not mutually exclusive." The ministers and gentlemen that Parris consulted suspected "the hand of Satan." They advised patience (to allow for the working of providence) and prayer (Harley, 1996, p. 317). Therefore, services were held to pray for guidance and deliverance from the evil that afflicted the girls. But soon more girls begin exhibiting symptoms.

The town elders pressured the girls to tell them who was causing these strange fits or who was hurting them. Finally, the girls broke down and began naming their tormentors. They accused Sarah Good, Sarah Osborne, and Tituba, a slave who lived in the household of Reverend Samuel Parris, of practicing witchcraft. Sarah Good was an elderly woman who committed a grave sin in the eyes of the Puritans—she did not go to church. Sarah Osborne was a homeless beggar. Both denied any connection to witchcraft. Tituba was another story; of the three women first accused, Tituba was the most alien to the society in which she lived.

THE FIRST EXAMINATIONS

Sarah Good, Sarah Osborne, and Tituba were examined by Judge Hathorne and Sheriff Corwin. Good and Osborne maintained their innocence. During the questioning, the girls, now eight of them, would cry, yell, and thrash on the floor. They claimed that even there, in the courtroom, the specters of Good, Osborne, and Tituba were afflicting them. Soon, the accusers would have the proof they needed.

As a girl, Tituba was apparently brought to Barbados to be sold as a slave. She was bought by Reverend Parris and brought to Boston in 1680 along with another slave named John Indian. To save herself from the hangman's noose, Tituba confessed to being a witch. She spent three days confessing to her crimes. She told of animals that came to her and asked her to serve them. She told of mystical creatures sent by the other accused witches to torment her and lead her to witchcraft. She spoke of a tall man who tempted her with gifts and asked her servitude. These requested services included pinching the afflicted children and, in her spectral form, attacking them with knives.

Tituba said that the tall man had brought a book that he asked her to sign. This was the "Devil's book," signed by those that had given themselves over to his powers. She also told of gatherings of witches, know as Sabbaths, where the witches would fly together to a mysterious place and dance under the moon. She claimed that Sarah Good and Sarah Osborne were witches as well and that they had all made pacts with the Devil. Tituba, Sarah Good, and Sarah Osborne were sent to jail in Boston, where Osborne died two months later from natural causes. Instead of ending the witchcraft hysteria, Tituba's confession and arrest only added fuel to the fire. In the minds of the frightened residents of Salem, where there was one witch, there had to be more.

MORE ACCUSED WITCHES

During April 1692, the girls continued to suffer the afflictions, and they continued to name other witches. There was George Burroughs, a former minister of Salem Village Church who had left over a pay dispute and was known to have mistreated his wives. The girls said that Burroughs was the leader of their coven and made them sign the Devil's book.

There was Rebecca Nurse, who was seventy-one years old when she was accused. Nurse was originally found not guilty; but then the girls protested and the judge asked the jury to reconsider their "not guilty" verdict. So the jury continued to deliberate, and when Nurse failed to respond to the jury's questions (most likely due to her age-related hearing loss), the jury reversed its judgment and found her guilty.

There was Elizabeth Proctor, who ran the family tavern and whose grandmother was once suspected of witchcraft. At the time of her conviction, Proctor was pregnant. In accordance with the common law practice of allowing a woman to "plea her belly," her accusers showed mercy and did not hang her right away. Proctor was one of the lucky ones. By the time her baby was born, the hysteria was over. Not so lucky was her husband, John Proctor. Outspoken and known to have a temper, he spoke out publicly against the witch trials and defended his wife's innocence. For his troubles, he was also accused of witchcraft and hanged.

There was Martha Corey, known to be a religious woman, but she, too, was outspoken, and she had an illegitimate mulatto child fathered by an unnamed man. Martha's husband, Giles Corey, was one of the most famous victims of the witchcraft hysteria. Corey was a wealthy landowner and not well liked by his neighbors. Knowing that if he pled guilty he would be subject to forfeiture of his property, and that if he pled innocent he would still most likely be hanged, Corey refused to enter a plea. Judge Hathorne and

Sheriff Corwin were not happy with this turn of events, and they set about making him answer their charge. On September 19, Corey, well over eighty years old at the time, was forced to lie in a field and was covered by a board while heavy stones were laid upon his chest. Each morning, the sheriff would ask Corey how he pleaded, and each morning, Corey responded with two words: "more weight." The weights were so heavy upon Corey's chest that his tongue began to protrude from his mouth and the sheriff pressed it back inside with a stick. After several days, Giles Corey's chest collapsed and he died; the sheriff never did get a plea.

THE TENSE POLITICAL CLIMATE IN SALEM

Even before the witchcraft hysteria, tensions divided the community between Salem Town and Salem Village. The 600 residents of Salem Village were divided into two factions: those who wanted to separate themselves from Salem Town and those who did not. The farming families, from the western part of town, believed that the individualistic nature of the Salem residents in the eastern part of town near the harbor was contrary to the rules of good Puritanism. When Boyer and Nissenbaum (1974) examined the map of Salem, they found that twelve of the fourteen accused came from the eastern section; thirty-two of the thirty-four adults who testified against the accused came from the western section (Davidson and Lytle, 1992, p. 36). Clearly, the political climate in Salem seemed to play a role regarding who was accused and by whom. But as Davidson and Lytle (1992) observe, although what was at work here was clearly more complex than village politics, it is important to consider "Salem Village's uneasy relation to its social parent Salem Town" (p. 36).

Among the farming families in Salem Village were the Putnams. In 1689, the large Putnam family, along with Reverend Samuel Parris, separated from Salem Town and formed their own Puritan congregation. Reverend Parris was not very popular, and, by 1691, the Salem Village committee, in opposition to him, was elected. This action served to widen the divide between the Salem factions and solidify the ill feelings between them.

When Reverend Parris became minister of the new congregation, he received much more than was normally granted a minister. In addition to a reasonable salary, he was also given title to the parsonage and surrounding land. Those who opposed this new congregation stopped attending his services and, more importantly, stopped paying their taxes. Without that tax money, Reverend Parris's salary was in jeopardy.

The reverend had a family to support, and his wife was ill. He expected his niece to care for his sick wife and take care of the household chores.

Playtime was unknown to the children of the Parris household. Their only respite was reading and listening to Tituba's stories. Soon many of the local girls were gathering at the Parris house to hear these tales.

Some later historians of the witch trials alleged (as her reputation darkened) that Tituba stories of voodoo, demons, and witchcraft were the sources of the rituals that the girls engaged in as they played forbidden games. However, some modern historians have suggested that these superstitious rituals—such as seeking the face of a future husband by dropping an egg into water—had British roots. Whatever the combination of Caribbean and Anglo influences, the games they played were potent in their effects on these village girls. They led to the symptoms that their elders attributed to bewitchment. They led to the accusations that these girls, as the star witnesses, made against those who they alleged were their tormentors.

THE WITCH HYSTERIA SPREADS

During the spring of 1692, the girls continued to accuse their friends and neighbors of being witches. The accused were not a homogeneous group, except that, in one way or another, most were outsiders to the core of Salem society. In *Salem Possessed* (1976), Paul Boyle and Stephen Nissenbaum discuss this issue of the accused as outsiders. They note that 82 percent of the accused lived outside the boundary of Salem Village, some from towns bordering the village and others from towns throughout northeastern Massachusetts. The authors discuss that even many of the accused who lived in Salem Village had only recently come to live there and had been found to be disruptive to the Puritan way of life—for example, Bridget Bishop, the scarlet-wearing tavern owner; and Sarah Osborne, who had had an illicit relationship prior to marriage.

In the cases of accused women, family members were also sometimes the targets of accusation—as in the case of Giles Corey, husband of Martha; and John Proctor, husband of Elizabeth, to name a couple. Regarding this gender aspect of the witch trials, crime historian Lawrence Friedman (1993) observes:

Town rivalries and factions worked as irritants beneath the surface, perhaps. There was a gender aspect, too. Not all witches were women, but most of them were. . . . In some subtle and not so subtle ways, the war against witches was also a war against women; or at least against disorderly, troublesome, deviant women. (pp. 46–47)

Interestingly, the girls also named strangers as witches—people the girls most probably never came into contact with before the accusations. One must wonder how the girls knew the names and residences of "witches" they had never before met. One such accusation came from Abigail Williams. In early May, Abigail began talking about a woman named Elizabeth Cary from the neighboring town of Charlestown. Upon hearing that she was being accused of witchcraft, Elizabeth and her husband Nathaniel traveled to Salem to try to resolve what they believed was surely a simple misunderstanding. Upon arrival in Salem, the Carys found a witchcraft examination in progress and decided to observe to get a better understanding of the state of affairs. The Carys wondered what Abigail Williams would do in the presence of Elizabeth. During the ongoing examination, the girls made no move in response to the Carys. Even after inquiring the names of the strangers in the courtroom, the girls still did nothing. It was only during an adjournment of the examination that the girls suddenly, en masse, began crying out Elizabeth Cary's name in accusation.

While the Carys had only presented themselves in the court to clear up a misunderstanding, they were soon embroiled in the hysteria. A warrant was quickly produced for Mrs. Cary, and she was led before the magistrates to be questioned. When the girls and Tituba's husband, John Indian, entered the courtroom, John began to show signs of the afflictions, and the girls soon accused Mrs. Cary of causing his fit. The court then ordered Mrs. Cary to touch John to relieve his spasms. After a brief struggle, his fit ended, and Mrs. Cary's status as a witch was "proven." She was then sent to jail in Boston to await the opening of the witch trials (Starkey, 1969, pp. 139–142).

THE WITCH TRIALS OF 1692

The girls accused so many of witchcraft that a special court was created to hear the witch trials, the Court of Oyer and Terminer (literally "hear and determine").[1] Seven judges were originally appointed to the Court. Only one, Bartholomew Gedney, was from Salem. Of the others, four were from Boston: Samuel Sewall, John Richards, William Sergeant and Wait Winthrop. Nathan Saltonstall was from Haverhill, and the Chief Justice of the Court was William Stoughton, a known witch-hunter from Dorchester.

When the Court convened in early June, it began by not only reviewing the testimony given in the examinations, but by accepting the examination record as a fact already proven. The only new business the Court conducted was taking testimony on occurrences after the examination and overseeing the jury deliberations.

The Court of Oyer and Terminer allowed types of evidence that would be laughed at now, but that were deadly serious then, including "spectral evidence" and the finding of "witch marks" on the body. Davidson and Lytle write:

Spectral evidence involved the visions of specters—likenesses of the witches—the victims reported seeing during their torments. The problem was that spectral evidence could not be corroborated by others; generally only the victim saw the shape of her tormentor. Furthermore, some people argued that the Devil might assume the shape of an innocent person. What better way for him to spread confusion among the faithful? (1992, p. 25)

In the beginning, however, the magistrates accepted this evidence. What were undoubtedly dreams, fantasies, and/or hallucinations were taken as fact. Today we know that these specters tell us more about the accusers' state of minds than about the guilt of the accused.

The girls claimed that it was not the physical person of Sarah Good or Bridget Bishop who was tormenting them and cavorting with the Devil, but their specters or ghosts. The girls claimed to see these specters flying through the air, ruining crops and scaring farm animals. Was spectral evidence truly the driving force behind the witchcraft hysteria, or was there something more concrete? It has been suggested that the opportunity to seize the property of those who confessed or who were found guilty played a role in the prosecution. However, Brown (1993) convincingly disputes the allegation that the opportunity for forfeitures motivated the officials. Under seventeenth-century British law, a person who had committed a felony (at the time, a felony was punishable by death) was also liable to have his personal estate forfeited to the king. However, Massachusetts had, earlier in the century, taken a more lenient position regarding seizures. During the witch trials, even though British law was applied, Brown concludes, "All individuals who suffered forfeiture fell into one of three legal categories; they stood mute, or fled from justice, or had been convicted of witchcraft. With the exception of the forfeitures for flight, in which the sheriff and his officers likely exceeded their authority, the cases adhered to common law rules of forfeiture" (p. 91).

Moreover, Sheriff Corwin "seized only the offenders' goods—their 'movable property' or 'personal chattel'" (Brown, p. 97), rather than their land. However, as they stood on trial for their lives, accused witches were not allowed legal counsel, could not present witnesses on their behalf, and had no avenues for appeal. Defendants were allowed to speak on their own behalf, question their accusers, and present evidence of their innocence. However, without legal counsel, the defendants were woefully unprepared for what awaited them at trial.

The official records of the Court of Oyer and Terminer were lost, so it is impossible to completely know and understand what happened. However, based on the preliminary examinations and accounts written at the time, an understanding of the procedure can be achieved. On June 2, 1692, Bridget Bishop was the first to be tried in the Court. The proceedings commenced with a meeting of the "Grand Enquest," or grand jury. Bishop was probably chosen first to be tried because the evidence against her seemed the most compelling. The evidence against her included the finding in her cellar of small dolls stuck with pins, and the fact that a pig she sold to a neighbor kept returning to her farm. Neighbors accused Bishop of signing the Devil's book and flying through the countryside in the form of a demon.

At this time, witnesses were also summoned to testify against Rebecca Nurse, John Willard, and John Proctor. The Court asked witnesses to examine the bodies of the accused for "witch marks." These were nipple-like marks from which the accused woman's "animal familiar" (a small household animal thought to assist the witch in the devil's bidding) could suck milk. They were even more suspicious if they appeared and disappeared in different places on the body. In all likelihood, the marks found on the accused were natural birthmarks, moles, and blemishes.

During the proceedings, numerous witnesses described the torments suffered by the afflicted girls at the hand of Bridget Bishop, and they also told tales of her previous "evil" deeds. Witnesses claimed Bridget was involved with strange accidents that befell her enemies, the deaths of children who crossed her path, and sickness in neighboring farms' livestock. Witnesses also claimed that Bridget, in her spectral form, appeared in the bedrooms of men at night. Perhaps it is this testimony that sheds light on why Bridget was accused, and the first to be tried. Bridget was known to wear provocative clothing (for the time), she owned a tavern, and the men of Salem and the neighboring towns may have found her too much of a temptation. Bridget's husband even suspected her of witchcraft. He claimed that she was a bad wife, outspoken, and independent.

As part of the gathering of evidence, Bridget's current and previous houses were searched. In the cellar of her previous home, searchers found dolls made of rags with pins stuck in them, similar to voodoo dolls. When confronted with them, Bridget was unable to provide a satisfactory explanation. But since she had not lived in the house for several years, one must wonder whether the dolls had been put there by a different tenant (Norton, 2002, pp. 204–207).

After all the witnesses and evidence had been presented, the jury found Bridget guilty, and the judges sentenced her to hang. However, there was a problem: at the time, witchcraft was not punishable by death. It was not until after the trial and sentencing that the Massachusetts court revived an old law making witchcraft a capital offense. Thus, Bishop's sentence was carried out, and she was the first to hang from the old oak tree at Gallows Hill.

After her trial, there was a delay in the proceedings. At the time, the reason for the delay was hidden from the public, but it is now known that one of the judges, Nathaniel Saltonstall, appalled at the conduct of the court and direction of the prosecutions, resigned from the bench. He believed that spectral evidence was not definitive proof of wrongdoing and that without spectral evidence, there was very little else to condemn Bridget Bishop. However, Nathaniel Saltonstall's resignation did nothing to calm the hysteria.

The remaining judges, attempting to avoid questions at a later date, sought guidance on proper court procedures. The governor of the Massachusetts Bay Colony, Sir William Phips, felt that the matter was out of his area of expertise and knew that writing to the Crown in England for guidance would only delay matters (by this time the jail was overflowing with accused witches). With nowhere else to turn, the judges sought the advise of the Puritan ministry.

On June 15, 1692, a group of twelve ministers from Boston, led by Cotton Mather, issued their guidance to the Court. They urged caution and asked the Court to look with favor upon those alleged witches with no previous history of illegal or immoral activities. As for spectral evidence, the ministers suggested that demons could take the form of innocents and that, therefore, the acts of the specters could not always be attributed to those accused.

By this time, however, the jails were overflowing with those accused of being witches. The prisoners were kept in cells according to their social stations and financial means. Prisoners were required to pay for their shackles and their food. Those who could not pay were kept in the smallest of cells, no bigger than standing coffins.

In August 1692, another group of accused witches were brought to trial. This group included the Reverend George Burroughs, John and Elizabeth Proctor, George Jacobs, John Willard, and Martha Carrier. All six were found guilty, and all but the pregnant Elizabeth were hanged at Gallows Hill on August 19.

John Proctor, Elizabeth's husband, had come to Salem in 1666 when he leased a large farm south of the village. Proctor was a "Renaissance man" and entrepreneur: while he ran his farm, his wife and daughter ran the family tavern. After his father's death, Proctor inherited land in neighboring Ipswich, which he continued to manage. It was through these various ventures that he became well-known and prominent in the Salem area. But the tides turned quickly that summer in 1692 Salem; even Proctor's former friends, neighbors, and business acquaintances could not save him.

John Willard had the misfortune of marrying into the Wilkins family. Margaret Knight, granddaughter of a prominent Salem Village merchant, was the first in her family to marry someone from outside Salem Village. Her family looked with suspicion upon Willard, and during the course of the hysteria, ten members of the Wilkins family accused him of witchcraft. Willard was blamed for the death of seventeen-year-old Daniel Wilkins, who was struck down by an unknown ailment. Soon after, Ann Putnam accused Willard of murdering thirteen residents of Salem Village (Boyer and Nissenbaum, 1976, pp. 195–199).

On September 9, after six months in prison, Martha Corey finally stood trial. Martha, wife of Giles Corey, maintained her innocence and stood bravely before the judges. Martha was a strong, independent woman and very secure in her faith. She was a regular churchgoer and thought her faith would shield her against accusations of witchcraft. However, her faith was not enough. After her conviction of witchcraft, Martha Corey was excommunicated from Salem church.

Also tried and condemned along with Martha Corey were Alice Parker, Mary Bradbury, Dorcas Hoar, Mary Easty, and Ann Pudeator. When faced with her imminent execution, Dorcas Hoar broke down and confessed her crimes. In an effort to save herself, she accused others of witchcraft. Regarding the confessions of the accused, Davidson and Lytle (1992) observe that as a strategy, confessing was indeed the best way to stay alive because "Puritans could be a remarkably forgiving people. They were not interested in punishment for its own sake" (p. 26). However, in the context of the witch trials, those who confessed found themselves in the position of then having "to demonstrate their sincerity by providing details of their misdeeds and names of other participants. The temptation must have been great to confess and, in so doing, to implicate other innocent people" (p. 26).

Mary Bradbury also escaped execution, but by an entirely different method. When a petition signed by over a hundred friends and supporters failed to bring about a stay of execution, bribing the jailer apparently worked. Mary escaped from jail and was cleared after the hysteria ended.

Not all who were accused were found guilty. Sarah Buckley and her daughter, Mary Withridge, were accused of witchcraft. The two women spent over eight months in jail before their eventual acquittal in early 1693. Perhaps it was the testimony of Sarah's former ministers that saved her, or perhaps it was just time for the bloodlust to end.

Six months and nineteen hangings later, the hysteria did begin to die down. The townsfolk had begun to doubt what they were doing. How could

George Burroughs flawlessly recite the Lord's Prayer if he was a witch? Why would Giles Corey choose to be crushed to death rather than confess his crimes? These questions and many others were on the lips of Salem Village residents that fall. And then, the girls went too far.

SALEM: SEEKING FORGIVENESS FOR ERRORS IN JUDGMENT

In October 1692, the afflicted girls accused the wife of the newly arrived governor of Massachusetts Bay Colony of being a witch. Incensed, Governor Phips ordered the Court of Oyer and Terminer dissolved and the prisoners released. Almost as quickly as the hysteria began, it was done. But for many, it was not over. Not all prisoners ordered released were free to go. Many had no money and could not pay for their food and their cells. They were kept locked up until payment was made. Those who were convicted and had forfeited their property never got it back.

After the hysteria, one of the judges, Samuel Sewall, issued a public apology. In the five years following the trials, Sewall had experienced a series of personal and family tragedies. The afflictions of the colony (imperial interference, Indian wars, loss of charter, the witch trials) had also continued. As Lovejoy (1997, p. 359) observes, "From 1660 to the end of the century, then, God's displeasure for New England's declining piety and loss of direction grew increasingly obvious." At least, it did to the people. January 15, 1697 was set aside as a day of fasting. On that day, Sewall and the other colonists begged forgiveness and sought renewal of their covenant with God (Lovejoy, 1997, p. 364). Sewall stood in church while his confession was read. He blamed himself for errors in judgment that led to the deaths of many and the perpetuation of the hysteria. Many of the jurors, too, sought forgiveness. They wrote that they were swayed by Satan and condemned their neighbors to death against their own good judgment.

Not everyone would admit to being misguided. Judge William Stoughton, now governor of Massachusetts Bay Colony, never asked for forgiveness. While Governor Stoughton was the one to authorize the fast day, his only confession was to an honest error and not to any malice. But in 1706, Ann Putnam, one of the first of the afflicted girls, begged forgiveness from the community, apologizing for her actions. With Putnam at his side, the Reverend Joseph Green read her confession to the congregation. In attendance that day was the family of Rebecca Nurse, who was put to death by the accusations of Putnam and her friends. Ann Putnam asked to be humbled before God and declared that Satan had deluded her into accusing her neighbors of witchcraft. She asked for forgiveness in the deaths of Rebecca Nurse and her sisters. Putnam must have felt her own mortality as she humbled herself, seeking forgiveness for her sins. Her request was granted—Reverend Joseph Green and the congregation forgave the repentant Ann Putnam.

MODERN THEORIES OF COLONIAL FEAR AND ANXIETY

While hunting for witches was neither new nor novel, the Salem trials continue to fascinate us. Only twenty "witches" were executed; a small number compared to the thousands put to death in Europe during the Middle Ages. In the years since the witchcraft hysteria of 1692, many theories have been put forth to explain the bizarre and tragic actions of the people of Salem. In one of the earliest twentieth-century accounts of the trial, *The Devil in Massachusetts* (1969), Marion Starkey places responsibility for the hysteria not with the initial group of afflicted girls, but with the older girls who came later. Starkey sees the girls' fear of their religion's constraints, combined with continuous suppression of their natural instinct for fun and pleasure, as the catalyst for the hysteria.

In his sociological study of seventeenth-century Puritan Massachusetts, *Wayward Puritans*, Kai Erikson (1966) asserts that the witch trials of Salem should be viewed in conjunction with the earlier Puritan responses to Antinomians, such as Anne Hutchinson, and Quakers, such as Mary Dyer. Erikson argues that, like persecution of perceived religious heretics, the witch trials reflected the Puritans' sense of threat from without and within. The Puritans, Erikson asserts, experienced a series of perceived "crime waves" to which they responded with repressive justice. The witch trials were the culmination of these episodes in which the fears and anxieties of the Puritans assumed the "shape of the Devil," represented in 1692 by the alleged witches who they put on trial.

In *A Delusion of Satan* (1997), Frances Hill holds culpable the pervasive climate of intolerance and fear, coupled with a few unscrupulous individuals taking advantage of the opportunity to further their own personal agendas and pad their own pocketbooks. Even more recently, Mary Beth Norton, in her book *In the Devil's Snare* (2002), argues that the witch trials in Salem must be understood in the context of the Indian wars that were threatening the New England frontier. She also points out that the witch trials in Salem should be described as witch trials in Essex County, because although the trials occurred in Salem, the accusations affected people living in a much broader area. Many of these people had earlier been forced to retreat from the frontier to the more settled areas of New England as a first, a second, and finally a third Indian war occurred, driving them from their homes.

Norton asserts that it was the Puritans' singular worldview that led to the hysteria. The Puritans believed that they were a people chosen by God to bring their religion to a land of heathens ruled by the Devil. The Puritans saw their God in every aspect of their daily lives. They saw messages from God in shooting stars, plagued crops, storms, epidemics, even in the good fortunes of themselves and others.

The Puritans believed that the spiritual world was all around them—they believed that they were surrounded by both God and the Devil; and since God was omnipotent, the Devil was limited in his actions by what God would allow him to do. Therefore, any tragedy credited to the Devil must also be credited to God, and thus God must be punishing the Puritans. Prior to the witchcraft hysteria, the Salem area was embroiled in wars with the Indians; in this context, the girls' sighting of a "black man" tormenting them can be attributed to their fear of the Indians. The first group of afflicted girls showed symptoms not unknown to the Puritan world. Other groups of girls throughout New England had shown similar signs of affliction in the years leading up to 1692. However, none of these earlier instances spread. They were limited to the original girls who showed the symptoms, and no others joined them. Thus, there was no room for the hysteria to grow.

However, in Salem in 1692, the afflictions spread like a plague. It is possible that this spread was a symptom of posttraumatic stress, possibly a form of mass hysteria caused by the political and social climate. Fear of Indian attacks and grieving the loss of friends and loved ones in the Indian wars provided a portion of the context in which the witchcraft hysteria occurred.

There have been other theories put forth as well. Was the water tainted with a natural hallucinogen? Did the grain ferment and cause a drunken state among the participants? Were the afflicted suffering from a disease never before diagnosed? Or was the Devil truly at work in Salem in 1692?

THE TRIALS AS VIEWED IN AMERICAN CULTURE

Because there were no local newspapers available during the time of the Salem witch trials, Norton (2002) points out that much of the information the residents of Salem, the county of Essex, and New England received came to them by word of mouth—by "gossip." Norton writes:

Behind most events in the crisis lay gossip. With one very short-lived exception, late-seventeenth-century New England had no locally produced newspapers or magazines, and so information spread primarily through talk among neighbors, friends, and relatives. . . . Understanding the dynamics of the witchcraft crisis requires paying attention to the ways in which news was transmitted from person to person, farm to farm, town to town. . . . People must have constantly discussed the most recent fits and complaints of the afflicted, along with other news stemming from examinations and, later, trials. (Norton, p. 6)

In the aftermath of the trials, the earliest works to examine the episode were produced by the Puritans themselves. After a brief moratorium by Governor Phips on witchcraft publications, several works appeared in 1693. These included *Cases of Conscience* by Increase Mather. Historian Chadwick Hansen (1969) describes this work as "remarkably even-tempered for a document written in the fall of 1692, and it is a lucid explanation of the truths concerning spectral evidence which the Boston clergy had propounded from the beginning" (pp. 186–187). However, Mather's son, Cotton Mather, "converted himself from a man who, during the trials, had been one of the most cogent critics of the court's methods to the man who, once the trials were over, became their chief apologist" (Hansen, 1969, p. 171). In his condemnation of the court's methods, Cotton Mather had been in agreement with his father. However, both later refused to condemn the members of the court (p. 171). In *The Wonders of the Invisible World*, published in 1693, although probably circulated in manuscript long before, Cotton Mather not only failed to condemn the witch trials in Salem, he also sought excuses for what had happened. Hansen asserts that because of "this hasty, ill-considered, overwrought, partisan defense of his friends," Mather "was the first to fasten the false image of witch hunter on himself" (p. 172). This image of Mather was one that would be taken up by future chroniclers of the trials.

In 1868, Henry Wadsworth Longfellow published a verse drama titled "Giles Corey of Salem Farm." His drama followed earlier works about the case by Rev. Charles W. Upham, who had published *Lectures on Witchcraft* (1831) and then, almost forty years later, *Salem Witchcraft* (1867). According to Hansen (1969), Upham, who served both as minister and mayor of Salem, was "chiefly responsible" for perpetuating the view of Cotton Mather "as a man who instigated witchcraft trials to satisfy his own lust for fame and power" (Hansen, 1969, p. 172). Upham served as the model for Judge Pyncheon in Nathaniel Hawthorne's *The House of Seven Gables* (p. 172).

During the nineteenth century, the witchcraft trials were discussed in scholarly works such as the centenary edition of George Bancroft's *History of the United States* (1876). In the twentieth century, the trials were the subject of a number of full-length books by historians, including those discussed above regarding modern theories. But perhaps the work best known to general audiences is Arthur Miller's *The Crucible* (1953). Two movies have been based on Miller's play. Oddly, the first production was a French–East

German collaboration in 1956, originally titled *The Witches of Salem*, later *The Crucible*. The famed French actors Simone Signoret and Yves Montand recreated their stage performances in the leading roles. A more recent remake of the movie, *The Crucible* (1996), was actually the first American production of the work, starring Daniel Day-Lewis, Winona Ryder, and Paul Scofield.

As several modern historians and literary scholars have noted, the treatment of the slave Tituba in both the historians of the witch trials and the fictional works has been particularly intriguing. In the contemporary documents of the trial, Tituba was always identified as an Indian. But gradually she underwent a literal darkening process, becoming first half-white, half-Negro (a mulatto), and finally being depicted as black. At the same time, the accounts of her character and of her dabbling in magic also became darker in tone. Modern fictional works such as Ann Petry's novel for young adults, *Tituba of Salem Village* (1964), redeemed the slave woman and gave her a voice. This is especially true in French author Maryse Condè's *I, Tituba, Black Witch of Salem* (2000), which features a foreword by political activist and academic Angela Davis. However, the uses to which the mythical persona of Tituba have been put since seventeenth-century Massachusetts clearly remind of us of the ongoing social discourse about race/ethnicity, gender, class, and marginality in America.

While many believe that what happened in Salem could never happen again, it has and it will. The accusations haven't always been "witchcraft," and the punishments haven't always been death; however, the fear and hysteria remain the same. During World War II, it was fear of the Japanese that led to hundreds of American citizens born of Japanese descent to be interred in camps to protect the "real" Americans. In the 1950s during the McCarthy hearings, it was the fear of and search for communists that led many of those suspected to flee the country and others to lose their friends, families, and the ability to support themselves by confessing to being communists. It was in this atmosphere that playwright Arthur Miller wrote *The Crucible*, his account of the Salem witchcraft trials. Astute readers and viewers could plainly see the parallels between the witchcraft hysteria and the communism hysteria.

The effects of the Salem witch trials were far-reaching, both in distance and in time. But the Salem of today bears little resemblances to the Salem of 1692. The Salem of today is a mecca of tolerance and a testament to the human desire to learn from prior mistakes. Today, people travel from all over the world to visit Salem, Massachusetts. Salem has become a haven for "witches"; both those pretending to be magical witches and those who practice the religion known as Wicca. On any given day in Salem, you can visit the Witch History Museum, the Witch Dungeon Museum, the Witch

Museum, the Witch Village, and other exhibits. You can participate in the trial of Bridget Bishop in the award-winning play *Cry Innocent* at Salem Town Hall. You can shop at the Broom Closet, Witch Tee's, or Crow Haven Corner, a magical shop owned by the "official witch of Salem," Laurie Cabot. In October, you can participate in "Haunted Happenings," a month-long festival that celebrates all things "witch-y" and wild. You can go on the Terror Trail Tour or the Haunted Footsteps and hear more "interesting" versions of the life of Sheriff Corwin and the death of Giles Corey. A town that was once shamed by its connection to the witch trials now embraces the witch culture and seeks to educate and inform, so that history will never repeat itself.

NOTE

1. Friedman (1993) notes: "The phrase was used in some places as an ordinary name for certain criminal courts; but the phrase has sometimes been applied to a court specifically commissioned to hear criminal case arising out of some incident or disorder" (p. 46).

REFERENCES

Barstow, A. L. (1994). *Witchcraze: A new history of the European witch hunts.* New York: Pandora.

Boyer, P. S., and Nissenbaum, S. (1976). *Salem possessed: The social origins of witchcraft.* Cambridge, MA: Harvard University Press.

Brown, D. C. (1993). The forfeitures at Salem, 1692. *The William and Mary Quarterly, 50,* 85–111.

Davidson, J. W., and Lytle, M. H. (1992). The visible and invisible worlds of Salem. In J. W. Davidson and M. H. Lytle (Eds.), *After the fact: The art of historical detection* (Vol. 1, pp. 22–46). New York: McGraw-Hill.

Erikson, K. (1966). *Wayward Puritans: A study in the sociology of deviance.* New York: Wiley.

Friedman, L. (1993). *Crime and punishment in America.* New York: Basic Books.

Hansen, C. (1969). *Witchcraft at Salem.* New York: George Braziller.

Hansen, C. (1974). The metamorphosis of Tituba, or why American intellectuals can't tell an Indian witch from a Negro. *New England Quarterly, 47,* 3–12.

Harley, D. (1996). Explaining Salem: Calvinist psychology and the diagnosis of possession. *The American Historical Review, 101*(2), 307–330.

Hill, F. (1997). *A delusion of Satan: The full story of the Salem witch trials.* New York: DaCapo Press.

Lovejoy, D. S. (1997). Between Hell and Plum Island: Samuel Sewall and the legacy of the witches, 1692–1697. *The New England Quarterly, 70*(3), 355–367.

Norton, M. B. (2002). *In the devil's snare: The Salem witchcraft crisis of 1692.* New York: Knopf.

Rinaldi, A. (1994). *A break with charity: A story about the Salem witch trials.* New York: Gulliver Books.

Salem witch trials, 1692: A chronology of events. Retrieved from http://www.salemweb.com/memorial/index.shtml

Starkey, M. L. (1969). *The Devil in Massachusetts: A modern inquiry into the Salem witch trials.* New York: Anchor Books.

3

Blackbeard the Pirate: Seventeenth-century Public Relations Professional

Kathy Warnes

"I'm a better man than all ye milksops put together!"
—Edward Teach (Lee, 1974, p. 26)

Even outside of North Carolina, where he was killed by a Royal Navy lieutenant, people shudder when they hear the name "Blackbeard the Pirate." Ordinary people reading about him and historians writing about him have portrayed him as evil, vicious, and the worst pirate of all time. Edward Teach would be pleased at this appraisal of his character. It is exactly the image that he worked so hard to create.

Blackbeard the Pirate, or Edward Teach, was an English pirate notorious for his forays against shipping in the West Indies, the Spanish Main, and the coast of North Carolina. His life story is interwoven with legend and fact, much like the history of piracy. His real name was Edward Teach, or Thatch, or various other phonetic spellings such as Thach or Thache. Unusual for mariners in his time, he was intelligent and literate. He was centuries ahead of his time in understanding the importance of image, reputation, and psychological warfare. He was a skillful manager of ships and men, but his human weaknesses like greed and lust for adventure and women brought

Painting by Frederick Judd Waugh titled *Buccaneers* (ca. 1910). (Courtesy of Library of Congress)

about his downfall. His life and career were played out against a backdrop of European and North American power struggles for control of the seas and a new continent.

Little is known of his early life, but it is thought that he was born in Bristol, England. One source, writer Norman C. Pendered, claims that nothing at all was known about Blackbeard's early life, but he does conclude that Blackbeard was born in Bristol, England (1975, p. 6).

The North Carolina Maritime Museum factsheet on Blackbeard the Pirate states that documents suggest that Bristol, Jamaica, or even Philadelphia could possibly have been his birthplace. It is not surprising that he chose to follow the sea, being a native of one of these places. It is commonly believed that Blackbeard was somewhere between thirty-five and forty years old when he died in November 1718, so that would place his birth around 1680 (North Carolina Maritime Museum).

According to Robert E. Lee, author of *Blackbeard the Pirate: A Reappraisal of His Life and Times* (1974), Teach was born into an intelligent, respectable, and well-to-do family, and it's probable that he abandoned his real name and used an alias to protect his family. He could read and write because he corresponded with merchants, and at the time of his death on November 22, 1718, he had letters from the chief justice and secretary of the Province of North Carolina, Tobias Knight, in his pocket. He seemed to be equally at ease with ruffians and governors (1974, p. 4).

Other writers, like A. B. C. Whipple, say that Teach was a bastard, an orphan, or a starving ragamuffin growing up in filth, disease, and the cellar homes of sewage-flooded Bristol (1957, pp. 47–49). Pirates usually obscured their origins so that when they returned to their real lives, they would leave no traces of their pirate lives. If Edward Teach followed this pirate axiom, he followed it expertly.

TRACKING THE GOLDEN AGE OF PIRACY TO TEACH

Teach may have become a pirate because he read pirate adventure stories like *The Buccaneers of America* (1684), by John Esquemeling, which were about the daring deeds of French, Dutch, and English pirates. He and other adventurous boys could have read and dreamed over Richard Hakluyt's *Divers Voyages*, published in 1582, which celebrated both the discovery of America and pirating as part of that discovery. A few centuries later, in 1883, writer Robert Louis Stevenson bequeathed the romance of piracy to new legions of readers when he published his fictional pirate story, *Treasure Island*. J. M. Barrie's play, *Peter Pan*, was first performed in 1904 and gave pirate literature "Captain Hook" and later generations of moviemakers material to continue the pirate legend.

The Edward Teach revealed through historical documents may not have been politically ambitious, but he lived in a politically ambitious country, which may have influenced his turn toward piracy. The English, anxious for England to become master of the seas, encouraged piracy. If England had not used pirates and privateers, North America might have become Spanish. England endowed privateering and piracy with a high level of legitimacy, and this helped usher in the Golden Age of Piracy, roughly from 1680–1730. It is significant that an island nation like England did not have a strong professional navy for a long period of her history. Instead, much of her naval power rested in a merchant fleet that was called into service as privateers. This practice dated back to 1243 when King Henry III licensed three private merchant ships to wage war on France. Merchant syndicates actually outfitted pirate vessels and sent them out for profit, and they were welcomed in the colonies. If the price was good and the merchandise desirable, people did not ask questions.

When the Pope divided the New World between Spain and Portugal in 1494, his action set the stage for decades of war. Other countries wanted a part of the gold that the Spanish took from the Aztecs of South America, and clashes between countries clamoring for treasure were inevitable. Colonial expansion grew, creating more and more shipping to carry gold and other goods. Competing interests of colonial powers made it easy for ambitious sailors to always find a way to legalize acts of piracy.

The part of the New World coast from South America through the Caribbean to Northern Florida was known as the "Spanish Main." From ports along these coasts, Spanish galleons—large treasure ships—sailed for Europe. The European powers began attacking these ships and taking the gold for themselves.

Outfitting ships was expensive, and one low-cost way to raise a fleet was to issue "letters of marque" that entitled owners of private ships to outfit them for war to attack enemy ships. In return for official permission, a ship's owner split any captured booty with the royal treasury. Men who sailed under letters of marque were called *privateers*. In effect, privateers were legal pirates, at least legal to the governments that employed them. Sir Francis Drake, who started his career in 1570, was a hated pirate to Spain; but a hero in England, where Queen Elizabeth knighted him. During one expedition he captured 300,000 pounds of booty for the English treasury, and he also attacked Spanish towns and mule trains carrying gold.

There was a downside to using privateers. Often these independent captains were tempted to attack ships of countries other than those their countries warred against. Also, in times of peace, thousands of men who had been trained to attack ships and seize goods were left jobless. The temptation to turn pirate during hard times proved to be irresistible to many men.

On the other hand, North African pirates had a license to rob English ships, and Madagascar pirates of the eighteenth century represented the French king's interests. The area where the pirates operated was called the Barbary Coast, a name that formerly applied to the coast of North Africa from the western border of Egypt to the Atlantic Ocean. From the 1500s to the 1800s, Islamic states under the sovereignty of the Ottoman Empire occupied this coast. In the early 1500s, these states became centers for pirates.

In 1630, Spain, England, and France signed a treaty that allowed the English and French to colonize some of the lands along the Spanish Main. Many European settlers wound up on the island of Hispaniola—now Haiti and the Dominican Republic. One of the main sources of food on the island was the wild pig originally introduced by the Spanish. The settlers barbecued the pigs on open fires called *buccans* or *boucan*, and from this the settlers eventually got the title *buccaneers*.

Becoming nervous over the many buccaneers on Hispaniola, the Spanish sent hunters to slaughter the pigs. This action backfired because the buccaneers, with their food supply gone, turned to piracy to survive. Many of the buccaneers referred to themselves as the "Brethren of the Coast." They moved to the island of Tortuga off the coast of Hispaniola and made it a pirate stronghold.

Sir Henry Morgan was probably the most famous buccaneer. Born in Wales in 1635, he joined a pirate crew from Tortuga in his teens and swore an oath as a member of the Brethren of the Coast. He and some friends outfitted their own ship, elected Morgan captain, and successfully staged their first raid. Many more followed. Morgan became a vice admiral in the buccaneer fleet and quickly became very rich and famous. Later, Morgan settled down on a plantation he had purchased in Jamaica. King Charles II knighted him and made him deputy governor of Jamaica. In 1688, he died a well-respected man.

Few pirates enjoyed a life like Morgan's. Some were caught, tried, and hanged, their bodies left to rot as a warning to other sailors. Many more died of disease or alcoholism. But for the most part, in the late 1600s, piracy promised an exciting life. The spirit of adventure, love of gold, and hatred of Spain lured pirates. In the seventeenth and eighteenth centuries, the Bahamas became a spot where piracy flourished. Its New Providence Island was especially well-placed for piracy. Some of the better-known pirates during "The Golden Age of Piracy" included Captain William Kidd, Captain Henry Morgan, and, of course, Edward Teach—or Blackbeard.

Religious competition between England and Spain—Protestant versus Catholic—also affected piracy during this Golden Age. After the English Civil War, King William III became monarch of both England and Holland, and, in 1689, William III declared war on France, which produced clashes between English and French shipping in northern New England. Queen Anne's War began in 1701 and continued for nearly twelve years. The war generated more severe conflicts, including border fighting with the Spaniards in the South (of what is now the United States) as well as with the French and their Indian allies in the North. By having England and Holland, both Protestant countries, allied in a war with Catholic France and Spain, piracy and privateering against French and Spanish targets gained further legitimacy as part of a wider religious war (Morgan, 1930, p. 379).

The peace treaties among England, France, and Spain that were signed in 1697 were other factors pushing many patriot privateers into outlaw piracy. Low-grade hostilities never stopped, but another forty years would go by before England declared war against Spain. Without official war, there was a surplus in mariner labor, since the Royal Navy no longer needed to fill its ranks. Sailors' wages dropped in peacetime, and many mariners had become accustomed to the financial gains that could come from plunder. These factors led many to careers in piracy (Rediker, 1987, p. 32).

In addition, some of the democratic ferment that was part of the Roundhead, or Puritan, Party of the English Civil War seems to have translated itself into the pirate world. Nearly 100 years before the American and French Revolutions, the operations on the decks of hundreds of pirate ships were essentially democratic. Pirate crews commonly elected the captain and made most noncombat decisions with a majority vote. Under such a system, captains often had few rights or perks beyond those of common crewmen and could be replaced at any time with a vote (Rediker, 1981, p. 209).

Many pirate crews, including Blackbeard's crew, listed blacks on their rosters. Blackbeard proved to be democratic in his treatment of black sailors. On one hand, he captured slavers' ships and sold the slaves for profit. On the other hand, he included blacks in his crew and treated them and paid them the same as his white crewmembers. A few of his black crewmembers were even hanged later as punishment for serving under him.

Pirates, one of the lowest social classes in Anglo-American society, set up entirely new and radical social orders on board these outlaw ships. They elected their captains, and at the beginning of a voyage they drew up articles that defined the social contract that governed all sailors. They used the command structure of the captain only when in battle. For most other decisions, the majority ruled. They also distributed the loot from their raiding very evenly. The fact that mariners on the bottom rungs of society operated democratically outside of the law and existing social structure and did it successfully speaks well of pirate political acumen.

Piracy as a means of social mobility in the late seventeenth and early eighteenth centuries took some interesting forms. During a time of rigid social structure, some common mariners were able to use both the popular image of piracy and wealth potential to move from the lowest rungs of society to the highest. Henry Morgan advanced from being an outlaw pirate to a knight and then to deputy governor of Jamaica. William Kidd rose from lower-class mariner to pirate, to privateer, to being both wealthy and politically connected at the highest levels in the Tory Party in London. Because pirates operated outside the law, they were also outside the social confines of society, and therefore they could move more easily than most from one social class to another.

For the most part, Blackbeard embodied the positive aspects of being a pirate. Pirates were mostly strict sea robbers and did not plunder, burn, steal, or commit atrocious crimes on land. They acquired geographical and navigational knowledge that they passed on to others. Most pirates intended to become incredibly rich from their exploits, return home with untarnished family names, retire, and live lives of luxury and ease in the best society. Perhaps piracy was a necessary evil in the conquest of the rolling and turbulent oceans.

Even when the European powers signed peace treaties, piracy was not completely banished from the New World's coasts. In 1713, the Treaty of Utrecht brought an end to the War of Spanish Succession. Suddenly, thousands of seamen were released from military service, and few jobs were available. Many went to sea again as pirates. Some of the most famous pirate captains emerged from this period: Captain Kidd, Black Bart Roberts, Calico Jack, and Blackbeard. Blackbeard had the worst reputation, but he was not the cruelest pirate of his era. That title belonged to Captain Edward Low, a psychopathic pirate who enjoyed torturing his captives to force them to reveal hidden valuables.

Navigational acts and the almost constant wars of England combined to create piracy and make it an integral part of early colonial American life. At first, public sentiment favored pirates. Many colonists considered the pirate captains to be public benefactors. Colonial governors in America also issued letters of marque that permitted privateers to plunder merchant ships of enemy countries and keep the spoils. Pirate loot was important in the colonial economy. Some of the money used for the 1693 founding of the College of William and Mary—about 300 pounds—came from pirate loot. Blackbeard spent his early apprentice years as a privateer (Johnson, 1724, p. 69).

LEARNING THE PROFESSION OF PIRACY

In his book *A General History of the Robberies and Murders of the Most Notorious Pirates*, Captain Charles Johnson documented that Blackbeard sailed for some time out of Jamaica on privateer ships during Queen Anne's War and that "he had often distinguished himself for his uncommon boldness and personal courage" (Johnson, 1724, p. 45).

Blackbeard went to the West Indies during the War of the Spanish Succession. Active in privateering, he turned pirate at the war's end in 1713. Although his first recorded act of piracy took place in 1716, he might have started earlier, further blurring the line between privateer and pirate. Eventually, Teach found a berth on a merchantman, deserted in the Caribbean, and made his way to New Providence, where he met and made friends with Captain Benjamin Hornigold. Hornigold enjoyed a reputation as the most fierce and talented privateer, and the Brethren of the Coast esteemed him highly. As a young hand aboard Hornigold's pirate ship, Blackbeard demonstrated a marksman's eye, an affinity for dirty infighting and, according to Captain Johnson, a thirst for blood rivaling any other pirate's of the time. Hornigold made Blackbeard his protégé.

Blackbeard continued to learn piracy, studying the art and craft of weapons with increasing interest. Most pirates' weapons of choice were pistols, knives, cutlasses, boarding axes, and pikes. Their flintlock pistols, fitted with hooks for attaching to the belt or to a broad leather sling across the chest, were of large caliber and accurate only at a comparatively short distance. They could fire only one shot at a time, and there was always the chance of a misfire because of an incorrectly placed flint or damp primary powder. To make sure he or she had continuing firepower, a pirate had to carry several braces of pistols while attacking an enemy. Blackbeard was said to have carried twelve pistols (Whipple, 1957, pp. 47–49).

Edward Teach christened himself Blackbeard for the spectacular beard that he had discovered he could grow with no extra work. Effortlessly, he had grown "a matted, greasy, mass of jet-black hair, which covered nearly all of his face and hung down to his chest." His bushy and bristly eyebrows added to the forbidding countenance he was constructing. Tall, robust, and broad-shouldered with a hard-muscled strength, Blackbeard was an imposing physical presence (Whipple, 1957, p. 46).

Writers do not agree about Blackbeard's dress or drinking deportment. One stated that Blackbeard dressed to enhance his physical assets. He sported a broad hat, a waistcoat, and cravat—frequently all black—and usually wore knee boots. Sometimes he wore a long-skirted coat of brightly colored silk or velvet with huge cuffs turned back to the elbows, gaudy-hued knee breeches, and low shoes with huge buckles. He made himself as daring and horrifying in appearance as in deeds.

Another writer described Blackbeard as dirty, hairy, and smelling like liquor, sweat, and swill. Food, slime, and blood usually streaked his coat and breeches. He pinned rather than patched his clothes. His hands were the size of barrel tops and were caked with old dirt. His ears were shaped like bat wings and mutilated, his eyes bulging and red-veined. His nose was twisted and broken, his lips raw and curling. He was a perfect slob and usually drunk. Another writer described him as "having an amazing capacity for alcohol and was never known to pass out drunk" (Whipple, 1957, p. 9).

Blackbeard learned to dress the part of a pirate, especially when it was time to fight. In battle, he wore a sling across his shoulders, in which he fixed two or three pistols, hanging in holsters. In the broad belt strapped around his waist he carried an assortment of pistols and daggers, and an oversized cutlass. For a finishing touch, he tucked, under the brim of his hat on each side, fuses made of hemp cord about the thickness of a pencil and dipped in a solution of saltpeter and limewater. These burned slowly, about twelve inches an hour, and were the same fuses as those used to touch off the cannons on board ship. When set afire, the curling wisps of smoke added to the frightfulness of his appearance. He strung himself with pistols and cutlasses. He braided his greasy beard and pulled a hat low over his brow. At the instant of boarding an enemy ship, he stuck slow-burning matches in his hair. Sailors were superstitious in the early eighteenth century, and since Blackbeard liked to strike at night, the sight of his well-braided beard, glistening guns, swords, and the fizzing matches lighting his face convinced many a sailor that Satan himself was boarding their ship. They did not need to be convinced to surrender.

Blackbeard was never recorded as killing or maiming his captives or burning his prizes if his victims cooperated. He sent the ships he did not keep on their way after first looting them thoroughly. If everyone did as he ordered, looting was the extent of Blackbeard's damage. The slightest resistance or arguments to his commands prompted him to set an example, though. In his reevaluation of Blackbeard, writer Robert E. Lee said, "If a victim did not voluntarily offer up a diamond ring, Blackbeard chopped it off, finger and all. This nearly always impressed the victim, who could be counted on to impress all to whom he related his experience." These tactics also saved time, but their most important effect was to spread the word that Blackbeard operated on the premise of rewarding those who cooperated and punishing those who did not (Lee, 1974, p. 26).

On one occasion, having had a dram too much to drink, Blackbeard challenged his crew to make a replica of hell aboard ship with him and see how long they could endure it. They all went into the ship's hold, closed the hatches, filled several pots with brimstone and other combustible material, and set them on fire. Soon the men were coughing and gasping for air as the hold filled with suffocating fumes. All of the men but Blackbeard quickly scrambled for fresh air. When Blackbeard finally came topside, he snarled, "Damn ye, ye yellow ——. I'm a better man than all ye milksops put together!" (Pendered, 1975, p. 26).

Blackbeard's reputation traveled through the colonial port cities and the rolling Atlantic waves faster than he did.

COMMANDING *QUEEN ANNE'S REVENGE*

In 1717, Blackbeard commanded a sloop and cruised in company with another vessel under Captain Benjamin Hornigold. In November of that year off the island of St. Vincent, the two pirate sloops closed on a large French merchantman, the *Concorde*, and captured it. Blackbeard took it as his own flagship, refitted it as a forty-gun warship and renamed it the *Queen Anne's Revenge*.

A factsheet about the *Queen Anne's Revenge* from the North Carolina Maritime Museum sheds some light on why Blackbeard rechristened the *Concorde* the *Queen Anne's Revenge* and gives a tantalizing hint about his politics. Documents reveal that a vessel called the *Concorde* was built in England about 1710 and captured by the French from the English during Queen Anne's War in 1711. Following some modifications, it was utilized as a merchantman and eventually sold to Spain. A few years later, it was returned to France and again underwent a transformation. It was refitted as a slave ship, and during its initial voyage from the West African coast in 1717, Blackbeard captured it off the island of St. Vincent. The *Concorde's* armament was reportedly strengthened to as many as forty guns, and it carried as many as 150 pirates. According to French sources, the ship was about 104 feet long and weighed about 300 tons. As well as changing the *Concorde's* name to *Queen Anne's Revenge*, Blackbeard increased its armament and its reputation (North Carolina Maritime Museum).

In 1717, the British-appointed governor of the Bahamas was empowered to grant pardons to privateers-turned-pirates. Benjamin Hornigold and others sailed to the Bahamas and accepted the King's mercy. Blackbeard, however, continued to cruise the West Indies on his new flagship, looking for pirate opportunities.

Blackbeard's signature victory came when the *Queen Anne's Revenge* encountered the British thirty-gun man-of-war HMS *Scarborough*, which the English Crown had sent out to deal with him. Rather than run from the warship with his faster vessel, Blackbeard decided to battle the British man-of-war. He prided himself on never having run away from a battle. The *Queen Anne's Revenge* and HMS *Scarborough* began a running duel that lasted for hours, and the British warship was definitively losing the fight to the skillful pirate crew. The British captain realized that he was losing the battle and began to withdraw. Blackbeard allowed him to withdraw, since he saw no purpose in continuing to attack a warship that would not have the kind of cargo that the pirates wanted. Blackbeard's reputation grew dramatically after this battle. A pirate who could defeat a British man-of-war deserved respect.

Shortly afterward, Blackbeard encountered the pirate sloop *Revenge* from Barbados, commanded by Major Stede Bonnet, the educated "gentleman pirate" who had been a wealthy landowner before turning to piracy. When Blackbeard saw the elegantly dressed Major Bonnet, he laughed uproariously. The two pirates became friendly and agreed to sail together as partners. Soon Blackbeard realized that Bonnet was not much of a seaman, and he sent one of his own lieutenants to take command of *Revenge* while Bonnet went aboard *Queen Anne's Revenge* as a "guest."

Bonnet's crew enthusiastically cooperated with Blackbeard. The two *Revenges* were soon joined by another captured sloop, the *Adventure*, which Blackbeard assigned Israel Hands to command. One-hundred-odd years later, Robert Louis Stevenson used the name *Israel Hands* as one of Long John Silver's fellow pirates in his classic fiction novel *Treasure Island*.

Aboard his own vessel, Blackbeard was a savvy leader who kept his men from voting him down or throwing him overboard by capturing so many rich prizes that they were left too happy to disagree with him. Ashore, he was loud and sometimes arrogant, but open-handed and good-hearted. His fellow pirate captains respected and sometimes feared him.

Legend surrounds Blackbeard's visits ashore. Blackbeard and his crew indelibly marked the history of a community. Rumor had it that dogs, cats, birds, and other creatures credited with premonition fled the area an hour or two before the *Queen Anne's Revenge* sailed into the harbor. The *Revenge* always muscled in under full sail, shoving aside existing channel markers, cutting across the bows of fishermen, and terrifying anyone who might be out rowing.

The crew would quickly let down the anchor chain, furl the sails, and all swarm into boats and head to shore. They did not bother to leave a guard because harbor thieves knew better than to steal anything from Blackbeard's ship. The crew hit the beach whooping and shouting as they ran. They crashed through the doors of the nearest tavern. The tavernkeeper gave the place over to the pirates and fled, often with enough money from Blackbeard to keep him for the rest of his life. Blackbeard ordered drinks all around from the barmaids, and after emptying the pockets of the drunken men, the women left, too. Eventually the pirates used their mugs for free-for-all target practice. A tangled wreckage of chairs, tables, and broken mugs littered the tavern. Drunken men, wheezing and sobbing, lay on the floor with a tide of rum, ale, and brandy washing over their bodies.

Through the years, Blackbeard had built up a tolerance to alcohol, but not to women. Many writers portray him as a ladies' man. Robert E. Lee says, "Few pirates treated women or girls with greater respect than Blackbeard. . . . He would not let a girl serve him a drink, he preferred to serve the drink to the girl" (Lee, 1974, p. 22).

Serving drinks to many women, Blackbeard appreciated them all, until a particular one would become his favorite while he stayed in port. Before he left port, he usually proposed marriage to the current woman of his dreams and brought her aboard the *Queen Anne's Revenge*. The first mate would solemnly read the marriage service and pronounce them man and wife. Then they would go ashore to celebrate. Although likely none of the girls considered themselves legally married to Blackbeard, they gained certain prestige and enhancement of their business dealings with other sailors and pirates when they were known as "Blackbeard's wife." Within a day or two of leaving port, Blackbeard forgot about his new wife. To his crew, Blackbeard's marriages, all fourteen of them, were a running joke.

Blackbeard set up his headquarters outside the town of New Providence—now Nassau—in the Bahamas. He established himself at the foot of a hill east of what is now the center of Nassau. Atop the hill he built himself an impressive watchtower; its remains are still there today. From it, he could see far across the blue-green waters of the Atlantic. Blackbeard would descend the tower and the steep narrow trail to the pathway below. He and some of his favorite crew set up a few tents under a huge tree, and he held court where he traded loot, interviewed volunteers for his next cruise, and planned its itinerary and drank more rum. He rarely stayed long, only a few weeks. Blackbeard was one of the 2,000-odd pirates who gathered at New Providence, but expanded their range to the British colonies. Beginning in 1716, he set sail from the Bahamas and made his way up the eastern shore of North America. Two of his favorite retreats were Bath Town and Ocacock Island (Ocracoke) in North Carolina. Ocacock Inlet served the port of Bath Town, which was the principal port of entry. Numerous bays, coves, and secluded spots in the Pamticoe Sound (Pamlico) and the Pamticoe and Neuse Rivers provided hideouts. The appearance of a sail on the horizon with the skull and crossbones flags whipping in the breeze struck fear into the hearts of law-abiding colonial citizens. Blackbeard often added more flags to enhance the fear factor.

BLOCKADING CHARLESTON, SOUTH CAROLINA

In May 1718, Blackbeard's fleet appeared at Charleston, South Carolina, with a force of 400 pirates and six vessels. They stopped every vessel entering and leaving the harbor for the next week and plundered the cargo and the belongings of the passengers. Blackbeard sent a landing party ashore. The landing party returned to the *Queen Anne's Revenge* with many high-ranking citizens as prisoners, hoping they would be useful. Blackbeard sent one of the hostages and two of his crew to deliver a ransom note in which he stated that he was holding the citizens for medical supplies, and threatening to kill them all if he did not get what he wanted. Several days later, he received his medical trunk and, true to his word, he released all the prisoners without loss of life. Historians speculate that Blackbeard must have been ill to take this drastic action. No one knows how many of his crew were ill, but the numbers must have been great enough for him to risk a confrontation with a city by taking some of its most illustrious citizens hostage. He continued to plunder vessels, and almost ten were looted before Charleston acted on the problem.

At this point in his career, Blackbeard decided to retire from pirating and take advantage of the same pardon that his mentor Benjamin Hornigold had taken advantage of earlier. He devised a plan that would allow him and about forty of his crew to keep the most valuable of their plunder. He would load one ship with his best treasure and leave the rest of the crew behind. On

June 10, 1718, at Topsail Inlet, now known as Beaufort Inlet, North Carolina, *Queen Anne's Revenge* either "accidentally" ran aground on a sandbar or was sunk in a storm and finished off by Blackbeard, depending on which historian is telling the story. Blackbeard called Israel Hands from *Adventure* to help him free the ship.

While Hands was helping *Queen Anne's Revenge*, he also ran aground. Blackbeard then told Bonnet that he should seek the pardon, too, and Major Bonnet agreed, especially after Blackbeard promised that he would return the command of *Revenge* to him. Shortly afterward, Bonnet and some of his crew left on a small boat to accept the pardon at nearby Bath, North Carolina. In October 1718, Bonnet and his crew were captured near present-day Wilmington, North Carolina and taken to Charleston, where they were tried for piracy. All except four were found guilty and hanged that November 8. Bonnet escaped briefly, but was recaptured and hanged on December 10, 1718.

Blackbeard and the crews of the sunken ships escaped to the other two vessels. Quarrels broke out, and Blackbeard put many of the men ashore. Some made their way to Virginia, where they were captured and hanged. Then Blackbeard, with twenty to thirty followers, proceeded to Bath, North Carolina, to accept the previously announced royal grant of mercy. The exact arrangement between Blackbeard and Governor Charles Eden is unknown, though rumor had it that Governor Eden and Tobias Knight, the secretary of North Carolina, were hospitable to pirates and granted certain favors to them in return for pirate loot. In the open Atlantic, Blackbeard and his men came upon a French slaver, captured it, and brought it into Bath, North Carolina. Blackbeard, with the tacit consent of Governor Eden, held his own slave auction and made a small fortune.

Blackbeard and his men collected their pardons from the governor, and Blackbeard soon settled in Bath Town, where he lived from 1716 to 1718. Promising to live an honest, upright life, Blackbeard stayed until his gold ran out, but then he returned to his old trade. During this period, Governor Eden and Blackbeard spent much time together, and it is believed that the governor had access to Blackbeard's loot because the two had become friends. During his second amnesty in Bath, Blackbeard selected his fourteenth bride. She was sixteen-year-old Mary Ormond, the daughter of a Bath County planter. Governor Eden performed the marriage ceremony, and Blackbeard built a home on Plum Point facing Old Town Creek—now Bath Creek— right across the creek from Tobias Knight, secretary of North Carolina and Governor Eden's right-hand man (Johnson, 1724, p. 49).

However, by mid-1718, pirate life had tempted Blackbeard out of retirement, and he was once again pirating, although at times he tried to cover it up. While off Ocracoke Island in September 1718, Blackbeard spotted another pirate: Charles Vane. The two pirate ships saluted each other, and soon the two crews gathered for a few days of typical pirate celebrating.

Earlier, in August 1718, Blackbeard and his men had gone to Philadelphia to negotiate unsuccessfully with Governor William Keith of Pennsylvania for landing rights and reciprocal trade agreements as privateers. On August 11, 1718, Governor Keith issued a warrant for the arrest of Blackbeard and his crew. On October 17, 1718, the governor submitted a bill of ninety pounds to cover the expenses of an expedition of two sloops, commanded by Captains Raymond and Taylor, sent out to the nearby capes to pursue Blackbeard.

In the meantime, Blackbeard once again received an official pardon, this time from King George I, but he was unable to take advantage of it—it arrived at Bath Town about a month after he was killed (Pendered, 1975, p. 86).

LOSING HIS BATTLE AMID CHANGING TIMES

According to tradition, late in the autumn of 1718, Blackbeard formed a secret partnership with North Carolina Governor Charles Eden and his secretary Tobias Knight, who was also the collector for North Carolina. Under this arrangement, Blackbeard brought in several prizes, including a large French merchant ship, which he claimed to have found abandoned at sea. With his newfound wealth, Blackbeard led the life of a libertine, forcing planters to provide him with supplies and levying tolls on vessels plying the Pamlico River. The final straw came when Blackbeard ran into Ocracoke Inlet with a prize. He had collected a huge armory and was planning to set up a semi-permanent headquarters on the long, narrow island that stood between Pamlico Sound and the open sea.

Realizing that their governor would do nothing to solve their plight, the North Carolina planters addressed a list of complaints to the lieutenant governor of Virginia, Colonel Alexander S. Spotswood, who in turn referred the matter to Captains George Gordon and Ellis Brand of the HMS *Pearl* and the HMS *Lyme*, two British frigates stationed in the James River. When Lieutenant Governor Spotswood told the captains about the problem, they informed the governor that their large men-of-war would not be able to maneuver through the inlet and engage Blackbeard in among the shoals of the sound. They would, however, provide the men if the governor could find some shallow-draft sloops. Spotswood took the gamble; he would raise the money privately to provide the sloops.

Lieutenant Governor Spotswood used his own money to lease two sloops, *Ranger* and *Jane*, for the job, and they were fitted out and manned from the frigate. Robert Maynard, first lieutenant of the *Pearl*, was selected to lead the two ships for the hunt while Captain Brand of HMS *Lyme* would lead the ground forces.

Ocracoke Inlet was Blackbeard's favorite anchorage. It is located about thirty miles southwest of Cape Hatteras and fifty miles northeast of Cape Lookout. Blackbeard's base of operations was near the southern tip of Ocracoke Island—one of the sand islands of the Outer Banks—which is eighteen miles long and from one-half to two miles wide. He usually anchored in a narrow channel on the sound side, to the extreme right, after passing through the inlet from the Atlantic. The spot is located south of Springer's Point, near Ocracoke Inlet, and has been known as Teach's Hole since the 1700s. Legend has it that during the long night before his death, Blackbeard, impatient for the dawn, cried out, "O Crow Cock, O Crow Cock," and from that came the name Ocracoke (Greater Hyde County North Carolina Chamber of Commerce).

Another night-before-his-death legend about Blackbeard concerns his treasure. Through the night, as Blackbeard waited for Maynard to make his move, he drank in his cabin. One of his crew asked him, "If ye die on the morrow, does your wife, Mary, know where ye buried the treasure?" Blackbeard laughed and replied, "Damn ye, my friend, nobody but me and the Devil know where it's hid—and the longest liver will get it all" (Pendered, 1975, p. 35).

The two sloops set out for Blackbeard's hideout at Ocracoke Island and arrived late on November 21, 1718. The next morning, November 22, 1718, the battle began. The two leased sloops were unarmed, so they had to fight only with small guns and swords. Blackbeard's sloop, *Adventure*, had nine guns, so he was able to fire at the approaching sloops. At their approach, *Adventure* set sail and fired at the sloops, but with very little wind, there was not much speed in the chase. Oars were needed.

Ranger was essentially knocked out from a lethal broadside shot from *Adventure*, so Maynard moved in alone with *Jane*. *Jane* managed to damage *Adventure* enough to slow her down, and Maynard ordered most of his crew below decks to bluff Blackbeard into thinking the crew had been killed. His bluff worked, and when the two ships drew alongside each other, Blackbeard and several of his crew boarded *Jane*.

At this time, Maynard's armed and waiting crew surfaced from below deck, and a raging hand-to-hand battle ensued. Soon Maynard and Blackbeard were fighting each other in a duel of naval officer versus pirate. After Black-beard wounded Maynard's fingers with a cutlass blow, Maynard moved back and shot him, but this did not stop Blackbeard. Several other *Jane* crewmen fought Blackbeard before his numerous wounds eventually overcame him. It has been stated in lore that Blackbeard was decapitated with a sword-blow to the back of the head during the fighting rather than having his head removed after his death. Maynard himself later commented that Blackbeard fell with at least five gunshot wounds and at least twenty sword wounds.

Found in Blackbeard's vessel after he was slain at Ocracoke Inlet were several memoranda written by his own hand in the ship's log: "Such a dry, run all out:—Our company somewhat sober—A damned confusion amongst us! Rogues a plotting—Great talk of separation so I looked sharp for a prize—Such a day took one, with a great deal on liquor on board, so kept the company hot, damned hot; then all things went well again" (Johnson, 1724, p. 58).

Lieutenant Maynard ordered Blackbeard's head severed from his body and suspended from the bowsprit of the sloop *Jane*. The rest of Blackbeard's corpse was thrown overboard. According to legend, when the headless body hit the cold water, it defiantly swam around the sloop several times before it sank.

Maynard and his crew used Blackbeard's head as irrefutable proof that they had killed the pirate chieftain, enabling them to collect the reward of ninety pounds of sterling offered by the Colony of Virginia. The hideous trophy hung from the bowsprit of Maynard's sloop when he arrived in Bath Town, as well as weeks later when he triumphantly returned to the waters of Virginia's James River (Cooke, 1953, p. 304).

According to Virginia legends and a number of writers' statements, Blackbeard's skull dangled from a high pole in the west side of the mouth of the Hampton River for many years as a warning to seafarers. The place is still known as Blackbeard's Point. In time, officials took down the grim souvenir and fashioned it into the base of a large punch bowl. Writer Thomas Watson states that the bowl "was long used as a drinking vessel at the Raleigh Tavern in Williamsburg" (Greater Hyde County Chamber of Commerce).

In addition to Blackbeard, Captain Johnson names these pirates as killed in the battle: Philip Morton, gunner; Garrett Gibbens, boatswain; Owen Roberts, carpenter; Thomas Miller, quartermaster; John Husk, Joseph Curtice, Joseph Brooks, and Sril and Nathaniel Jackson (Johnson, 1724, p. 24).

The victorious Virginia invasion forces did not depart from North Carolina until late December, 1718, because they needed extra time for wounds to heal and vessels to be repaired for the return voyage to Virginia. They used some of the time to trace rumors of hidden treasure, never found, and in collecting evidence to be used in the forthcoming trial of their prisoners.

Lieutenant Governor Spotswood learned of the North Carolina invasion's success before Lieutenant Maynard and his vessels returned to Virginia waters. In one of his customarily lengthy letters of the Council of Trade and Plantations, dated December 22, 1718, he explained in great detail how he had personally planned and executed the expedition in the utmost secrecy, concluding that he felt he had prevented Blackbeard and his crew from disrupting trade in the Plantations and ruined their master plan, which was "that of the pyrats fortifying an Island at Ocracock Inlett and making that a general rendevouze of such robbers" (Colonial State Papers, pp. 1717–1718).

On March 11, 1719, Spotswood informed his council that five of the prisoners captured on Blackbeard's sloop were Negroes, and that "he desired the opinion of this Board whether there be anything in the circumstances of these Negroes to exempt them from undergoing the same Tryal as other pirates." The council believed that the Negroes ought to be tried in the same manner as the others "and if any diversity appears in their circumstances the same may be considered on their tryal" (McIlwaine, 1925–1945, Vol. 3, p. 496).

Israel Hands, Blackbeard's former first mate, whom Blackbeard had shot through the knee only a short time before, and five former members of Blackbeard's crew were rounded up in Bath Town. These men and the survivors of the battle of Ocracoke, numbering about fifteen men, were tried in Williamsburg on the charge of piracy. Johnson stated, "There were taken to Virginia fifteen persones, thirteen of whom were hanged." Samuel Odell was acquitted, and Israel Hands was later pardoned. Johnson lists the names of those hanged as John Carnes, Joseph Brooks Jr., James Blake, John Gills, Thomas Gates, James White, Richard Stiles, Caesar, Joseph Philips, James Robbens, John Martin, Edward Salter, Stephen Daniel, and Richard Greensail (Johnson, 1724, pp. 54–56).

The defeat and death of Blackbeard underscored the decline of the age of pirates and privateers. Blackbeard must have suspected that the great days of piracy were coming to an end because times were changing. In a telling action, Governor Woodes Rogers, operating out of Nassau, effectively cleaned out the pirate nests in the West Indies. Piracy was becoming less legal and less profitable, and governors were less willing to provide bases for pirates. Pirates could not exist without bases.

Although he had captured over forty ships during his career, and plundered countless others, Blackbeard's death did not immediately end piracy along the Atlantic coastline. In 1721, Virginia established batteries on the James, York, and Rappahannock Rivers and set up lookouts with beacons to watch for approaching pirates. Acts of Parliament, strict enforcement, and the development of international law were among the chief factors eliminating piracy. As England rebuilt and improved its navy, the chances of pirates being caught and punished became greater. The profits from piracy were not in keeping with the risks. Power-driven ships and the telegraph were also factors in ending piracy.

One of the distinctive characteristics of the Golden Age of Piracy was the concentration of pirate activities in the Caribbean and Africa. During this time, these areas were key hubs of merchant shipping that the Royal Navy only marginally controlled. By the 1720s and 1730s, the British Empire had extended its reach and was attempting to bring the pirates under control. These Empire efforts pushed many pirates to other bases of operation in the Indian and Pacific Oceans. A major reason for pushing the pirates out of the Caribbean was that the English colonies there were transitioning from raiding colonies to major sugar producers. As the Caribbean colonies began to produce their own wealth, the pirates ceased to be allies and became a problem.

The same thing can be said of the North American colonies. As cooperation and trade between the thirteen colonies increased and Britain became the common enemy, the colonies found it more and more expedient to present a united front in discouraging pirates from plundering their shores. The pirates themselves sensed the changes in the political winds. From the beginning of the Golden Age of Piracy in the 1680s, some pirates recognized the migration trends and moved to the less-controlled areas of the seas (Ritchie, 1986, p. 26).

Perhaps Blackbeard hastened his downfall by allowing greed to blind him to the changing nature of piracy. In sinking his flagship, he sank his own career. Intersal, a private group licensed by the State of North Carolina, found the wreck of the *Queen Anne's Revenge* on November 21, 1996. On November 22, 1996, the 278th anniversary of Blackbeard's death, the North Carolina Underwater Archaeology Unit confirmed the wreck as the *Queen Anne's Revenge*. The wreck was originally buried under sand with only an anchor fluke visible above the seabed. Preliminary excavation revealed a number of large cannon. The wreck is still being explored (North Carolina Maritime Museum).

BLACKBEARD AND THE MEDIA

Rather than being the most notorious pirate of his age, as characterized by some writers and historians, Blackbeard was one of the best public relations people of all time. Three centuries later, the image of himself he created for the public is still alive in the minds of twenty-first-century people. Word of mouth and reputation spread Blackbeard's notoriety much more quickly than newspapers, since the latter were relatively scarce in the eighteenth century. But true to Blackbeard's persona, both the first newspaper in the colonies and a famous printer wrote about him. John Campbell, bookseller and postmaster of Boston, printed the *Boston News-Letter* on April 24, 1704, on a single page printed on both sides. Appearing weekly, the *Boston News-Letter* usually featured news from London journals, but one of the most sensational stories that the *News-Letter* published when it was the only newspaper in the colonies was an account of Blackbeard's death. Benjamin Franklin also contributed to the pirate's media hype of Blackbeard by publishing a broadside ballad about him. Titled "The Downfall of Piracy," the broadside echoes the *Boston News-Letter* report and provides an example of Benjamin Franklin's earliest writing.[1]

As for Blackbeard, people still search for his treasure, rumored to be buried at many sites along the Atlantic seaboard. The real Blackbeard remains as well hidden and as well advertised as his purported treasures.

NOTE

1. "The Downfall of Piracy" can be found in its entirety at http://www.english.udel.edu/lemay/franklin/1719.html

REFERENCES

Colonial State Papers, Vol. 30. (1717, August; 1718, December). Sect. 800.

Cooke, A. L. (1953). British newspaper accounts of Blackbeard's death. *Virginia Magazine of History and Biography, 61.*

Greater Hyde County North Carolina Chamber of Commerce. Retrieved from http://www.ocracoke~nc.com/blackbeard/tales/tales.htm

Johnson, Capt. C. (1724). *A general history of the robberies and murders of the most notorious pirates.* London.

Lee, R. E. (1974). *Blackbeard the pirate: A reappraisal of his life and times.* North Carolina: John F. Blair.

McIlwaine, H. R. (Ed.). (1925–1945). Executive Journals of the Council of Colonial Virginia. Virginia State Library.

Morgan, W. T. (1930). The British West Indies during King William's War, 1689–97. *The Journal of Modern History, 2*(3).

North Carolina Maritime Museum. Blackbeard the pirate. Retrieved September 13, 2003, from http://www.ah.dcr.state.nc.us/sections/maritime/blackbeard

Pendered, N. C. (1975). *Blackbeard, the fiercest pirate of all.* North Carolina: Times Printing Co.

Rediker, M. (1981). Under the banner of King Death: The social world of Anglo-American pirates, 1716–1726. *William and Mary Quarterly, 38*(2), 203–227.

Rediker, M. (1987). *Between the devil and the deep blue sea*. New York: Cambridge Press.

Ritchie, R. (1986). *Captain Kidd and the war against the pirates*. Cambridge, MA: Harvard University Press.

Whipple, A. B. C. (1957). *Pirates: Rascals of the Spanish Main*. New York: Doubleday & Co.

4

The Sedition Trial
of John Peter Zenger:
The Power
of the Printed Word

Emily Gillespie

In November 1734, New York printer John Peter Zenger was arrested under orders from the governor and his council and accused of engaging in seditious libel: printing words that might threaten or humiliate the government. If charged and convicted, Zenger would be subject to fines and/or imprisonment. The trial that followed has been called "the first chapter in the epic of American liberty" (Katz, 1972, p. 1). The commanding role of the judge, combined with the political nature of the charge, classified the Zenger trial as a political trial. It was also a trial that resolutely tackled both the issues of a free press and that of the people's right—using their power as a jury—to contradict and override a partisan government and judge who were resolute about obtaining a guilty verdict. Most importantly, the prosecution of John Peter Zenger was a trial where honesty battled law, where the line between what was legal and what was right blurred, and where justice was in the eye of the beholder.

The law of libel had been established in England to prevent any individual from publishing information that might reflect poorly upon the government and cause disorder or uprising among the people. Due to its broad definition, libel underwent serious changes with each new government administration. Thus, in colonial America, the level of press freedom might change

Zenger, an American printer and journalist, in the dock defended by Andrew Hamilton at his trial for seditious libel in New York City, 1735. (The Granger Collection, New York)

from governor to governor depending on how easily the current governor felt threatened. Furthermore, according to the law, the truth of the printed information was irrelevant; the publisher of any text, true or false, which could be construed as threatening the government, its officials, or the country's stability, was guilty of seditious libel. The important issue was how provoking the printed material appeared; thus, it was often the case that "the greater the truth, the greater the libel" (Finkelman, 1994, p. 27).

Those tried for seditious libel faced a jury of their peers. However, in seditious libel trials, the jury was only permitted to render a "special" verdict; they were only to decide whether, in fact, the publisher was guilty of printing and distributing the text in question and whether that text discussed members of the government. It was then the responsibility of the judge or judges to determine whether the text was indeed seditious (Finkelman, 1994; Katz, 1972).

The Zenger trial, however, took place during a time when tradition and "what had always been" were starting to come under serious attack, and this limited role of the jury was not well received within the colonies (Belknap, 1994). This was fortunate, for Zenger and his counsel, Andrew Hamilton, counted on the likelihood that most Americans felt this way. Hamilton argued that, despite tradition, juries should be able to render a general verdict and by doing so determine both fact and law. English precedent, however, was not in Hamilton's favor, and therefore the prosecution was justifiably shocked when, after only ten minutes of deliberation, the jury returned a verdict of not guilty.

BACKGROUND: THE KEY PLAYERS AND THE SETTING

The Key Players

Hatred, love, distrust, pity: a well-written character will draw each of these emotions from a reader or moviegoer so that the reader will return again and again to hear a story, almost as if he were meeting an old friend. The characters involved in the trial of John Peter Zenger were not composed to make his case more interesting, yet their dynamic personalities and extraordinary life events could not have been scripted to tell a better story.

As in most stories, those individuals involved in the Zenger case were divided into two conflicting groups. The first of these groups, the Morrisites, were dedicated in their attempt to remove the governor from power, and they were responsible for involving Zenger in his libelous behavior and defending him during his trial. Yet, it is important to remember that these men were not seeking long-term political reform, but an immediate change in political power. The Morrisite Party earned its name from Chief Justice Lewis Morris, who engaged in behavior that challenged Governor William Cosby and was subsequently removed from his position. As a man, Morris was described as proud, influential, aristocratic and ambitious; as a politician, he was wholly discontented with the actions of the governor and the political leaders who surrounded the governor (Buranelli, 1957).

Perhaps the first Morrisite who deserves mention is Zenger himself. Originally from the Palatine area of Germany, John Peter Zenger was born in 1697 and traveled with his parents to America in 1710. Zenger's father perished on the journey and so, upon arriving in the colonies, his mother apprenticed the thirteen-year-old Zenger to William Bradford, New York's public printer. Zenger studied under Bradford for eight years before leaving for Pennsylvania where he married Mary White, who gave him a son before she died. He then left Pennsylvania and traveled to Maryland to start a print shop. After both this endeavor and a later partnership with Bradford failed, Zenger started another print shop where he made his living printing religious works, a number of texts in Dutch, and a few pamphlets that criticized the church or state. Despite his experience at printing, Zenger never learned to properly write in English and thus served only in the capacity of printer; yet, it would be he who was arrested, imprisoned, and tried for seditious libel (Buranelli, 1957; Kaltenborn, 1957).

Also important was Rip van Dam, a Dutchman who traveled to New York to become a merchant and served as senior member of the provincial council. This post enabled him, after the death of the previous governor, to be appointed acting governor of New York, where he devotedly served the people of New York until Cosby's arrival. It was Van Dam's dispute with Cosby, upon his arrival, that initiated the chain of events that would eventually lead to the Zenger trial. However, arguably the most indispensable member of the Morrisite Party was James Alexander.[1] Alexander was a Scotsman; as such, he supported James Stuart (James VIII), son of King James VII of Scotland, and participated in the 1915 Jacobite uprising against King George I. After the revolt failed due to incompetent leadership under the Earl of Mar, Alexander fled to America and became a scholar. Though his position remained anonymous, Alexander also served as editor of the *New York Weekly Journal* and was the first American to edit a paper in a manner promoting freedom of the press and to publish articles without the government's consent.

Alexander also served as defense counsel for both Van Dam and Zenger. It was likely he influenced, if not designed, the famous defense Andrew Hamilton (a Scottish immigrant and all-around scholar who gained fame for his opposition to the Pennsylvania governor and for his design of Independence Hall) used to free Zenger (Buranelli, 1957; Katz, 1972). Alexander's assistance during the construction of Zenger's defense, however, does not discount the importance of Hamilton's role in the Zenger trial. Hamilton accepted the case pro bono and his dominating, dynamic, and confident personality likely played a large role in his successful defense of Zenger (Buranelli, 1957; Finkelman, 1994; Wiggins, 1997). Hamilton was assisted in the defense of Zenger by William Smith, another prominent New York lawyer (Buranelli, 1957).

In direct opposition to the Morrisites, the governor's men supported the current governor and were instrumental in securing a conviction against Zenger. The most obvious of the governor's men was Governor William Cosby himself. From all accounts, Cosby was an appalling man, described by historians as haughty, greedy, and selfish. More importantly, Cosby appeared to have had a long history of corruption and improper behavior. In fact, Cosby had previously been removed from his position as governor of

Minorca for seizing the cargo of a Spanish merchant ship and then, as England and Spain were in a time of peace, altering government records to cover his tracks. It appears that this type of behavior only continued after Cosby reached America, where he used his position of power not to help the people of New York, but to fill his own coffers and replenish his depleted fortune. How did such a man become appointed governor of New York? Records indicate that Cosby was likely only able to remain in positions of authority because he was married to the sister of the Earl of Halifax, a member of the king's privy council, and was a friend of his wife's cousin the Duke of Newcastle, who was the secretary of state for the region that included New York (Buranelli, 1957; Finkelman, 1994; Wiggins, 1997).

Two of the governor's men became involved because the connection was advantageous for their career. The first of these men was from the Delancey family and, as such, harbored significant negative feelings toward the Morrisites and Zenger. Justice James Delancey was young, only thirty-two years of age, and relatively inexperienced when Cosby fired Morris and appointed Delancey chief justice. He would serve in this position throughout the events preceding Zenger's arrest and preside over the printer's trial.

The other man did not harbor this strong resentment; rather, his circumstances forced him to engage in behavior opposing Zenger. Prior to the formation of the *New York Weekly Journal*, William Bradford printed the *New York Gazette*, the only newspaper in New York at that time. Bradford was not by nature a supporter of the governor; however, negative experiences involving the government in Philadelphia inspired him to seek favor from the New York government. Thus, Bradford received £50 per annum and the title of King's Printer for the Province of New York in exchange for his agreement that the articles in the *Gazette* would be screened prior to printing and approved by a government representative. Bradford was, in fact, little more than a marionette, whose strings were pulled by Francis Harison, the governor's man in charge of editorial policy at the *Gazette*. His paper, however, played a key role in the media debate surrounding the Zenger case.

The Setting

A far cry from the teeming city of strangers it is today, New York in the early-to-mid 1700s was a simple, modest town. In fact, with approximately 8,000 free persons and an additional 2,000 slaves, the city granted its citizens very little privacy. This created the perfect environment for very intense relationships among friends and foes to develop and heated interactions between those in these relationships to ensue (Wiggins, 1997). Perhaps this is why for a number of years prior to the Zenger trial, New Yorkers had been dividing into two rival political parties, the Popular Party, also known as the Morrisite Party, and the Government Party. These two political parties, for the most part, followed a second key New York rivalry between the Morris and Delancey families. For years, these two families had struggled for power in trade and government, and in the years immediately preceding the Zenger trial, this familial/political alliance, and the resulting controversy, reached almost unprecedented levels (Buranelli, 1957; Wiggins, 1997).

Yet, in the months proceeding August 1732, the people of New York were content with their state and their government. It did not, however, take long for Cosby's nature to turn welcome to wariness and eventually to open hostility. The state assembly had voted to pay Cosby a stipend for duties he claimed to have performed while still in England. Cosby complained that the amount granted by the assembly was not high enough; at the same time he demanded that Van Dam also pay him, as tradition dictated necessary, half of the salary Van Dam earned while acting as governor until Cosby's arrival to the colonies. Van Dam responded to Cosby's demand by stating that he would be pleased to provide this amount, around £1975.8.10, on one condition: Van Dam requested that Cosby provide him with half of the monies Cosby had received for holding the governorship prior to his arrival in America, which totaled around £6407.18.10. Obviously Cosby realized that, by this equation, he would be forced to pay Van Dam a considerable amount of money and firmly rejected the terms of the suggestion. Van Dam responded by simply refusing to hand over the monies Cosby requested, forcing Cosby to solicit the courts and ask them to order Van Dam to pay.

This was a serious problem as Cosby, who was chancellor of the Court of Chancery in New York, could not rule on his own lawsuit. This problem was further confounded by Cosby's realization that using the Supreme Court of New York would mean placing the decision in the hands of a jury, who would likely rule in favor of their countryman Van Dam.

Cosby solved this problem by declaring that his case would be heard by the three Supreme Court judges who served as a special court of equity called the Exchequer Court. This decision enabled the three judges on the court, all appointed by the governor, to hear Cosby's lawsuit and provide a ruling without ever involving a jury. This action fell within the legal powers of the governor and, in fact, it was not the first time members of the Supreme Court had served as an Exchequer Court (Buranelli, 1957; Katz, 1972; Wiggins, 1997). In principle, equity courts were designed to separate the law from an emotional jury and the technicalities of law and allow judges to make a fair and humane ruling. Instead, the courts provided judges with the opportunity to rule as they wished, unheeded and unchecked by the people. Thus, the majority of the colonists, including Chief Justice Morris, were staunchly against the usage of an Exchequer Court (Finkelman, 1994). Americans felt that this type of proceeding displayed an arbitrary and dangerous form of justice and, thus, it had not been used in New York for a number of years (Buranelli, 1957; Katz, 1972; Wiggins, 1997).

The Exchequer Court heard Cosby's case in the spring of 1733, and at the end of arguments the three-judge panel was unable to come to a unanimous decision. As the lawyers prepared to address the panel, they were ordered by Morris not to argue the case; instead the attorneys were instructed to argue whether or not the court even had a right to hear the case. This surprised Attorney General Richard Bradley, who was prosecuting the case; however, Morris' instructions were not a surprise to Alexander and Smith, who had been forewarned that this would happen (Buranelli, 1957; Finkelman, 1994).

Thus, the counsel for Van Dam argued that the Exchequer Court itself was unequal and unjust. Two of the judges, James Delancey and Frederick Philipse, adamantly opposed this assertion. However, Chief Justice Lewis Morris agreed with the argument put forth by Van Dam's lawyers (Katz, 1972; Wiggins, 1997). Morris believed that, because the members had not been selected by the elected legislature, the Court of Chancery had been illegally created and the governor had no right to place the Supreme Court in the role of Exchequer Court. In fact, Morris believed this so strongly that he had already composed his decision denying the right of the Exchequer Court to hear Cosby's case prior to hearing any argument in the courtroom and had even sent an early draft of it to Alexander and Smith prior to the trial (Finkelman, 1994). It is not surprising that as soon as the lawyers' statements were finished, before either Delancey or Philipse could state their opinions, Morris declared that the court had no right to hear the case and quickly adjourned the courtroom (Buranelli, 1957; Finkelman, 1994).

For a number of years, the Morris men held positions of command and respect in New Jersey and New York. However, over the previous decade the family had lost a number of these positions; all that remained was Lewis Morris' position as chief justice. Thus, Cosby's decision to remove Lewis Morris as chief justice served as the final blow to the Morris family. Morris responded to this affront by joining Van Dam, who, due to the governor's actions in the Van Dam salary dispute, was campaigning to expel Cosby, whom they both declared incapable of guiding New York. These two men would, by 1734, form the Morrisite Party in conjunction with Gerardus Stuyvesant; Philip Livingston, second lord of Livingston Manor; James Alexander; William Smith; and Cadwallader Coden.

THE CASE OF JOHN PETER ZENGER:
TRAILBLAZING SEDITIONIST

Zenger Becomes Involved

The members of the Morrisite Party recognized the importance of the media and used pamphlets to distribute their complaints against Governor Cosby. However, they felt that a more regular and reliable political organ was needed and approached John Peter Zenger about printing the *New York Weekly Journal*, the first party newspaper in America. Evidence seems to indicate that Zenger entered into the agreement without a political agenda, though he eventually became a staunch supporter of the Morrisite Party. The *Journal* reported both domestic and foreign news; however, its intent was to disgrace Cosby and his cronies using reprinted essays and pseudonymous essays from the Morrisites themselves, which were displayed in the form of letters to the editor. The attack on Cosby and his associates was also often echoed in sham advertisements, inserted along with the legitimate paid advertisements (Buranelli, 1957; Katz, 1972; Wiggins, 1997).

For the Morrisites, the *Journal* was an unquestionable success; copies sold out and several editions had to be reprinted (Wiggins, 1997). For Cosby, the *Journal* was a thorn that needed to be removed as soon as possible. Thus, only two months after the first edition of the *Journal* was published, Cosby began a campaign to end its publication. In 1734, Cosby instructed James Delancey, whom he promoted to chief justice after dismissing Morris, to ask two separate grand juries (one in January and a second in October) to indict any seditious libels that had been published within New York. The first jury, realizing that this indictment was intended for Zenger, refused to do so; the second agreed to indict two texts, but argued it was impossible for the court to tell who had written the scandalous words.

Failing to achieve victory through the grand jury, Cosby next tried to force a public burning of four particularly libelous issues of the *Journal* to set an example. The provincial council agreed to his request and on November 2 ordered that a public burning take place. The assembly, however, refused to offer its support. This sentiment was echoed by the colonists, and so, though the burning went on as planned, it was not the public display Cosby intended.

However, the council also offered a reward for the names of the authors of the libelous texts and ordered that Zenger, as publisher of the texts, be arrested and imprisoned. In response to this decree, on November 17, the sheriff arrested Zenger. In preparation for the prosecution, the county prosecutor was ordered to find all evidence of seditious libel contained in previous issues of the *Journal* (Buranelli, 1957; Katz, 1957). This decision to prosecute Zenger instead of Alexander, who was editor and chief writer of the *Journal*, was a conscious attempt to stop the paper's publication. Cosby had every reason to assume that with Zenger in prison there would be no one to carry on the printing of the *Journal*. Though this was not the case, as Zenger's wife took over printing, a successful conviction would certainly stop Zenger from printing and it would be unlikely that his wife could carry on the practice alone or that the Morrisites would be successful in convincing another printer to take up Zenger's work. Cosby may have also assumed that convicting Zenger would prove easier than accusing a man of Alexander's power and prestige, particularly since the law held printers of libelous material as guilty of libel, if not more so, as those who composed the essays (Finkelman, 1994; Kaltenborn, 1957).

The day after Zenger's arrest, Alexander and Smith began what was one of the most brilliant defense strategies in American history. It relied heavily on gaining the public's support for Zenger and the Morrisite cause. Thus, the two lawyers were likely relatively calm when, despite their arguments that due to Zenger's station and the misdemeanor status of a serious libel charge a small, reasonable bail should be granted, Delancey set Zenger's bail at £400 (and in doing so infuriated a number of the colonists). Zenger himself certainly could not afford such a large sum of money; however, the Morrisite Party could have raised this sum. They chose to leave Zenger in prison and arguably manipulated the situation by intending to intensify the public's affronted reaction. Allowing Zenger to remain in jail also helped the Morrisite Party gain the colonists' sympathy and dramatically increased public support for Zenger. Additionally, there was some worry that if Zenger was released he would be charged with scandalous libel a second time, thus forfeiting his bail money. The Morrisites may have also refused to pay while knowing Cosby still had to convince the grand jury, who met for only two more months, to bring official charges against the printer. If Cosby were unsuccessful, as his track record indicated he might be, Zenger's stay in prison would be short.

Cosby had initially turned to the grand jury, and as the jury again refused to charge Zenger, Cosby again relied on an unconventional method of achieving his goals. On January 28, 1735, Zenger was finally charged with serious libel by Attorney General Richard Bradley. Bradley used an "information," a type of formal charge enacted by a government official without the consent of a grand jury. Unfortunately for Cosby, charging someone via an information was viewed by most colonists as arbitrary and unfair. In fact, New Yorkers were staunchly against charging via information, which they believed permitted both financial corruption (as prosecutors were paid by the number of cases they tried) and political corruption. Over ten years earlier, the assembly had passed a law prohibiting the use of information. The English government later disallowed it. After the Zenger trial, the assembly attempted to pass another bill making prosecution by information riskier for the prosecutor, who would now be responsible for all costs of the trial if the defendant were found not guilty. So, though the prosecution successfully brought Zenger to trial, its method of doing so only decreased already-waning colonist support and brought legitimacy to the Morrisites' accusations.

The Morrisite Party's success in obtaining public support against Cosby was not as successful overseas. The Morrisites used the media to continue their attack on Cosby in London, printing pamphlets describing Cosby's improper behavior. Then, in 1734, Morris left in secret for England in hopes of convincing those in authority there to remove Cosby from his governing position in New York. Yet, despite Morris being known and respected in London and the validity of his arguments, it was apparent that Cosby's connections in government were enough to guarantee no help from that front (Buranelli, 1957; Finkelman, 1994; Katz, 1972).

TRYING TIMES PRIOR TO THE COURT DATE

James Alexander and William Smith's behavior prior to their disbarment indicates they had every intention of using the courtroom to continue their attacks on Cosby. One of their first actions, despite warnings from Delancey that doing so would invoke serious consequences, was to file papers challenging the appointments of both Delancey and Philipse. The two lawyers accused Delancey and Philipse of being partial and under the control of Governor Cosby, and challenged that Delancey had not been appointed for a term "during good behavior"; instead Cosby had appointed Delancey for as long as the governor wished him to remain, or "during pleasure." This challenge, it should be noted, was not leveled against the position of chief justice; rather, Alexander and Smith were opposed specifically to Delancey holding the position. This might explain why Chief Justice Delancey responded to these accusations a few days later, on April 18, by simply disbarring both Alexander and Smith. Though disbarring the two lawyers was an imperious move by Delancey, and one Alexander and Smith never considered, it was likely done in an attempt to deny Zenger competent representation.

The very same day, Zenger petitioned the court to provide him with counsel, and the court assigned John Chambers to defend him. Chambers supported the governor. Chambers then entered Zenger a plea of not guilty and moved that a jury be struck. The process of striking jury required that the clerk of the court provide a list of forty-eight New York freeholders (landowners) from whom the defense and the prosecution would each eliminate twelve. Then, a jury of twelve men would be randomly selected from the remaining twenty-four freeholders, allowing for the appointment of an unbiased, fair, and reasonable jury. The governor and his supporters, however, attempted to manipulate this process by altering the original list of forty-eight freeholders. In fact, when Chambers arrived, the clerk presented him with a pre-chosen list that Chambers recognized contained the names of individuals under the governor's employ and those who were not freeholders. Chambers not only acknowledged this discrepancy but also, despite being a governor's man, asked the court to have a new, unbiased list struck from the Freeholders' Book in the presence of both counsels. The court agreed.

Despite Chambers' honorable and intelligent actions since being appointed defense, including avoiding the selection of a jury that would certainly have convicted Zenger, the Morrisites felt that to win his case Zenger needed representation that was superior to anything Chambers was capable of achieving. This led Alexander to recruit his associate and personal friend from Philadelphia, Andrew Hamilton, to act as defense counsel for Zenger. Hamilton's ideals and values went hand in hand with those the men in the Morrisite Party, many of whom he considered personal friends, were putting forth via Zenger's paper. In his native Pennsylvania, Hamilton was often at conflict with the governor, and he held a long-standing personal vendetta against Andrew Bradford, the son of *Gazette* publisher William Bradford. More importantly, Hamilton, in his sixties when he took the Zenger case, was older and more experienced than any other participant in the proceedings, including Delancey. In fact, Hamilton was reputed to be the best lawyer in Pennsylvania, if not all of America (Katz, 1972; Wiggins, 1997).

THE DAY OF THE TRIAL: HAMILTON TAKES OVER

Hamilton captivated the courtroom from the moment he stood and announced, much to the surprise of both the prosecution and the court, that he would assume responsibility for Zenger's defense. This declaration came as quite a surprise for Bradley and Delancey, who had expected to face the competent Chambers, not Hamilton, arguably the top lawyer in the colonies. Yet, surprisingly, Delancey did not hold Hamilton in contempt of court either during this announcement or at any point during his unorthodox defense (Wiggins, 1997).

After stunning the court by announcing his intent to defend Zenger, Hamilton once again shocked the members by stating, "I do (for my client) confess that he both printed and published the two newspapers set forth in the information—and I hope that in doing so he has committed no crime"

(Alexander, 1736, in Buranelli, 1957, p. 98). Because serious libel charges were not influenced by the level of truth in the printed documents, by admitting Zenger had printed and published the papers, Hamilton no longer had the law on his side. However, the attorney had no intention of merely pleading guilty; instead Hamilton provided a brilliant and revolutionary defense based almost solely on political arguments. Hamilton incorporated the colonists' current distrust in the governor and his party, with the writings of previous scholars such as Milton, Locke, Swift, Steele, Addison, and Defoe, whose words he used to support his argument.

Specifically, Hamilton presented a defense composed of several major points. He first set out to prove that the information Zenger printed was true; then, he argued that true information could not be considered libelous. Hamilton ended by arguing that the jury had the right to determine not only the facts, but also the law. He argued that the law should not necessarily be the same in the colonies as it was in England. To achieve this, Hamilton in some ways took advantage of Attorney General Bradley and of Delancey's inexperience, on several occasions directly challenging the court and in the end ignoring Delancey's instructions entirely and addressing the jury itself (Alexander, 1736, in Buranelli, 1957).

RESOLUTION OF THE CASE: FREEDOM OF SPEECH MUST SET YOU FREE

Upon entering the courtroom, the prosecution had no reason to believe it would not receive a sure and swift guilty verdict from both the jury and the court. In fact, if one considers both precedent and law, Zenger was guilty of seditious libel; the words published in the *New York Weekly Journal* were such that the governor of New York felt threatened. Yet, it took the jury a mere ten minutes to return with a verdict of not guilty; a verdict that, surprisingly, Delancey did not set aside (Wiggins, 1997). These twelve men essentially took away from the court its legal right to determine whether the articles printed were libelous. In effect, the jury took the power away from the court and placed it in its own hands.

Yet, how did twelve intelligent and educated men unanimously agree in less a quarter of an hour to return with a verdict that contradicted current law? How did Hamilton successfully convince twelve men to defy Delancey's final instructions to the jury, which nearly told them they must convict Zenger? Hamilton succeeded because he did not argue against the law, which was clearly against him; instead the wily lawyer chose to base his defense on politics and bet on his perception that the majority of public opinion did not agree with the law. Instead of trying to prove that Zenger did not print material critical of the government, Hamilton argued that the colonists had a right, even a responsibility, to criticize and question those in authority. He asserted that seditious libel laws were designed to protect the king of England, not the American governors, who were mere representatives of the crown and as such should be accountable for their behavior. Hamilton argued that the only way to do this was through free speech and press. The colonists' belief in Hamilton's argument was obvious in the days immediately following the trial. Even before Zenger's release, a great party was thrown for Hamilton, and he was later given a gift of an inscribed box and a certificate and made an honorary citizen of New York (Finkelman, 1994).

MEDIA AND CRIME REPORTING SEEK A BALANCE

Actions taken by the media can influence not only the general public's perception of a crime, but the final outcome of a trial and whether future generations remember that story. Although the John Peter Zenger trial took place long before radio and television, it received—the eighteenth-century equivalent of—media coverage at the same level as any major trial in America's history (Chassion, 1997; Wiggins, 1997).

The formation of America's first politically independent newspaper, the *New York Weekly Journal,* allowed members of the opposition party to send out their complaints and accusations in a more efficient and timely manner. While the idea of a free press situated itself well with the philosophy of the *Journal,* the paper's intense focus on freedom of the press may likely have been an attempt to legitimize itself. It was necessary that the people of New York view the *Journal* as an attempt to provide the colonists with a free and open paper, instead of simply the Morrisites attempting a new method of discrediting or humiliating Cosby (Buranelli, 1957; Finkelman, 1994). The *Journal* also provided the authors an assurance that their anonymity would be maintained.

James Alexander, Lewis Morris, and their comrades took full advantage of this situation and used every feature of the *Journal* to state their case against the governor and his supporters. Cosby recognized this and said that, although Alexander and Morris were trying to force him to justify his behavior in print, he would do no such thing. What Cosby did not mention was that he directly controlled what was published in Bradford's *Gazette.* The irony is that as Alexander and Morris used the anonymity provided to them by the *Journal,* the governor used the *Gazette* to print his words and defense without his name attached to it. What resulted was a full scale "paper war" that began in January 1734 and did not cease until after the Zenger verdict and Cosby's death a few years later.

Prior to the Zenger trial, the *Journal* compared the local sheriff, a governor's man, to an escaped monkey; and Harison, another Cosby supporter and the *Gazette*'s editor, to a lost spaniel. It reported any of the governor's behavior that might be viewed as questionable. In fact, the paper later described him as a monkey (Katz, 1972; Wiggins, 1997). Bradford responded by publishing articles about the governor's intelligence and honor, reprinting essays declaring the importance of the established order, and even attacking Zenger's journalistic abilities. Bradford also cited English law, which claimed that a man had the right to speak his mind but that the government had the right to punish the man for his words. The *Journal* eventually admitted to this argument, conceding that those who engaged in specific and limited types of treasonous speech were deserving of punishment; however, Zenger argued that the material published in the *Journal* did not fall within this limited category (Katz, 1972).

Cosby hoped that by arresting Zenger the publication of the *Journal* would come to a halt during his stay in prison. In this, Cosby was disappointed. He had not counted on the loyalty of Zenger's wife, Anna Catherine. She supported her husband and the Morrisite cause throughout the trial. She never once asked him to save himself by revealing the names of Alexander and the others, and she continued his work without complaint. Thus, two weeks after Zenger's arrest the *Journal* was back in publication (Buranelli, 1957; Kaltenborn, 1957; Wiggins, 1997).

Once again, the Morrisite Party used the *Journal* to sway public opinion on issues critical to the trial's outcome, and by doing so increased their chances of a not-guilty verdict. Not only did they continue their attacks against Cosby, but they also used letters written by Zenger from prison and various other articles to turn Zenger into a martyr for their cause. They timed these articles to run during the trial. For example, while Zenger's jury was being chosen, the *Journal* ran a number of articles that promoted trial by juries and encouraged jurors to rule on both law and fact. Alexander and the other Morrisites recognized the link between the media and obtaining a successful verdict. This recognition of the dramatic influence the media can have on the result of a trial is still an important part of defense strategy today.

SIGNIFICANCE OF THE CASE: WHY DID THIS TRIAL MATTER?

There is no question that the trial of John Peter Zenger holds within it the seed of later change on several fronts. In many ways, Hamilton argued his case using the "law of the future" and, in some respects, his actions enabled future generations to shape that law (Katz, 1972). However, the Zenger trial would also serve as a catalyst for social and political change.

Free Press

The Zenger case is perhaps most commonly thought of as addressing the issue of freedom of speech, specifically the right of the American people to have a free press. In many ways, this assumption is accurate. The Zenger trial may represent the beginning of the battle for a free press, and there is little doubt that it played some role in jump-starting that fight. Similarly, there is no question that, while today the press still does not have free reign to print falsehoods and Americans are still at some risk of being charged for writings against the government, America considers itself a nation with a free press.

It is the level of importance the Zenger trial held, as well as the level of genuine concern the Morrisites had for later generations' right to a free press, that is debatable. Some scholars have noted that, though the Morrisites strongly embraced the free press and declared it necessary if those who abused their authority in the colony were to be controlled, "they were hardly the radical exponents of free speech which history has held them to be" (Katz, 1972, p. 16). In fact, it was unlikely that those involved in the Zenger trial recognized the long-lasting impacts of their actions. The Morrisite Party's primary concern was to free Zenger and keep the *Journal* publishing long enough to win their battle against Cosby. The government's primary concern was stopping Zenger (Buranelli, 1957). This may be why the case did not serve as a landmark of freedom of the press and established no legal precedent in the reformation of libel law.

In fact, it was not until almost a half-century later that, following the trials of John Wilkes and the Dean of St. Asaph, the first official reforms were made in England regarding the law of seditious libel. In 1792, Fox's Libel Act gave juries the right to return a general verdict. Full reform did not come for another half-century, when Lord Campbell's Act permitted the use of truth as a defense in seditious libel cases. Interestingly, the Zenger case was not cited in the formation of either one of these reforms. The newly liberated Americans were only slightly quicker to develop reforms and also neglected to acknowledge the Zenger case (Katz, 1972, pp. 32–33).

What the Zenger trial did do was alter the legal system in New York, at least regarding serious libel charges, in a definable way. The Zenger trial substituted the former idea "the greater the truth, the greater the libel" with the notion that a valid and true criticism of the government was not only not a crime but, in fact, necessary. Thus, though the law in New York did not change, no longer could prosecutors be certain that juries would not exercise their power and return a verdict of not guilty (Buranelli, 1957; Katz, 1972; Finkelman, 1994; Guinther, 1988).

Had Cosby succeeded in convicting Zenger, the rights of American journalists would likely have been forever changed in a manner many who are not directly involved in the media do not consider. Zenger set an example for future generations of journalists when, even after being imprisoned, he refused to disclose the identities of those who wrote for his paper; his sources to this day remain unconfirmed. Zenger not only began the right to a free press but was the first individual to declare a journalist's right to have anonymous informants (Buranelli, 1957; Wiggins, 1997).

Jury Nullification

To some, the most important ramifications of the Zenger verdict may lie not outside the courtroom, but within its walls. It is the role of juries to protect against bias and unfair prosecutions. The Zenger verdict reaffirmed to the common man his ability to serve as a buffer against the unfair use of criminal charges to prosecute those at odds with the government (Jonakait, 2003). In some ways, this serves as an example of a jury's ability to champion or oppose the government by way of a verdict. Had a guilty verdict been given in this case, the government would have received a message that the people approved of a restricted press; by returning a not-guilty verdict, the jury tempered the supremacy of the government and its officials (Alder, 1994).

The Zenger trial was not a total victory for the colonists, as it also reminded England of the power a jury might invoke. This knowledge may have been one reason why prosecutions for those who protested the Stamp Act or spoke against later and much-loathed trade and revenue laws were conducted in front of an English judge instead of an American jury. Even today, the importance of jury nullification may be largely symbolic; it is very rare for any jury to use it. This may be because juries are often ignorant of their right to examine the facts and, despite legal guilt, return a verdict of not guilty (Guinther, 1988; Jonakait, 2003).

Political Impact

Although Zenger was acquitted and allowed to continue printing the *Journal* until his death in 1746, for the Morrisites the Zenger trial was a short and somewhat unremarkable victory in the war against Cosby. Due to several political losses and Morris's failure in London, the party failed to wrest control from Cosby, who remained governor of New York until his death in 1736. After Cosby's death, many Morrisite leaders scrambled to receive positions in newly appointed Governor Clark's administration, and Morris himself became governor of New Jersey. In saving their own careers, the Morrisite leaders isolated and disillusioned their followers, and New York politics remained almost as it had always been (Katz, 1972).

Despite this, scholars often refer to the Zenger trial as representing a landmark in the evolution of American politics. Finkelman (1994) even goes so far as to label the Zenger trial as "clearly the most significant political trial of the pre-Revolutionary period—perhaps of the entire colonial era" (p. 26). The recognition of the Zenger trial's status as a political landmark is due in part to its ability to serve as an excellent example of the often complex relationship between political trials and subsequent legal change. The trial also serves as an example of the importance of the public and the very real ability of the common man to influence the formation and enactment of law via public opinion. In fact, the Zenger case deserves credit for promoting an early recognition of the importance of politics and its direct connection to the law (Buranelli, 1957; Finkelman, 1994; Katz, 1972).

The Zenger trial also serves as a political landmark when one recognizes that the events surrounding the trial of John Peter Zenger illustrate the political forces vying for control in the early 1700s, forces that would later form the foundation of an independent America (Katz, 1972). Though at the time of the Zenger trial the authority of the British crown remained unquestioned, the colonists' easy acceptance of Hamilton's argument can be seen as predicting a coming revolution. The popular belief that America and Americans were sufficiently different from England and the English to require a different set of laws certainly appears to indicate the forthcoming fight for independence.

Regardless of the colonists' mind-set at the beginning of the trial, as Zenger's story was told throughout the colonies it helped to plant the seeds of dissatisfaction that would eventually result in the American Revolution. Then, as a growing sense of Americanism opened the door for others who wished to challenge the government's previously undisputed authority, resistance and criticism of governors became more acceptable. Hamilton's arguments were echoed by later generations as they sought revolution and independence, and his ideals would be considered when composing the Bill of Rights (Wiggins, 1997). Zenger's story and its message would provide motivation and guidance to a future generation as they fought for their freedom and then, while forming a new America, struggled to preserve that very freedom.

Works Honoring the Trial

Soon after the trial, James Alexander published *A Brief Narrative of the Case and Trial of John Peter Zenger, Printer of the New York Weekly Journal* to describe the victory of Zenger and the Morrisite Party. Within a year another author, calling himself "Anglo-Americanus," wrote a response to *A Brief Narrative*, criticizing the legal basis of Hamilton's case and providing serious argument against Hamilton's politics. Anglo-Americanus's article was soon followed by another letter, written by an unknown author, raising similar criticisms, and the publication of a pamphlet entitled *Remarks on Zenger's Tryal, Taken out of the Barbados Gazette for the Benefit of the Students in Law, and others in North America*. Alexander quickly responded to both these attacks in four separate letters printed in the *Pennsylvania Gazette*, once again asserting that free speech was a necessary and natural right (Finkelman, 1994; Katz, 1972). The mysterious Anglo-Americanus was not the only person interested in Alexander's *A Brief Narrative*. In fact, so many colonists wanted copies of the text that it had to be reprinted fifteen times by the century's end (Jonakait, 2003).

Then, interest in the Zenger trial waned, so much in fact that, after the flurry over *A Brief Narrative*, there were no major publications written regarding the Zenger case for over 150 years. However, the importance of the Zenger verdict was rediscovered in the past century, and a number of scholars have published works on the case. In addition to the numerous books and articles written about Zenger and his trial, the case has been honored in other ways. The University of Arizona and The New York Newspaper Publishers Association distribute awards in Zenger's honor. A weekly internet news service named in his honor, the Zenger News Service, distributes information "supporting individual liberty and other traditional values."[2] On the 200th anniversary of its publication, the *Weekly Journal* was recognized in several ceremonies. Hamilton's role in the trial is also commemorated on a tablet printed by the New York Bar Association in his honor, and in New York City tourists can view scenes from Zenger's life and hear his story in the John Peter Zenger Memorial Room.

CONCLUSION

The events written about in this chapter were never intended to have such dramatic consequences. The Morrisites were not interested in long-term reform, and Zenger was a simple man who printed the Morrisites' words to make a living. Yet it was the trial of this man that served as a catalyst for changes in both the media and the courtroom. The words spoken at his trial would years later guide and motivate revolutionaries. Perhaps this is because when John Peter Zenger was brought to trial, justice and law were forced to do battle with one another and justice won.

NOTES

1. According to Buranelli "The place of Alexander is all this is virtually unknown, and yet without him, Hamilton's fame would be cut in half, while Zenger would not merit even a footnote in the histories of America, of democracy, or of journalism" (1957, p. 1).

2. The website for the Zenger News Service is http://www.zns.com

REFERENCES

Alder, S. J. (1994). *The jury: Disorder in the courts.* New York: Doubleday.

Belknap, M. R. (Ed.). (1994). *American political trials* (Rev. ed.). Westport, CT: Praeger Publishers.

Buranelli, V. (Ed) (1957). *The trial of Peter Zenger.* Washington Square: New York University Press.

Chassion, L. Jr. (Ed.). (1997). *The press on trial: Crimes and trials as media events.* Westport, CT: Greenwood Press.

Edwart, J. E. (2003). *Zenger News Service.* Retrieved June 30, 2004, from http://www.zns.com/. Zenger News Service.

Finkelman, P. (1994). Politics, the press, and the law: The trial of John Peter Zenger. In M. R. Belknap (Ed.), *American political trials* (Rev. ed.). Westport, CT: Praeger Publishers.

Guinther, J. (1988). *The jury in America.* New York: The Roscoe Pound Foundation.

Jonakait, R. N. (2003). *The American jury system.* New Haven: The Yale University Press.

Kaltenborn, H. V. (1957). Forward. In V. Buranelli (Ed.), *The trial of Peter Zenger* (pp. v–vi). Washington Square: New York University Press.

Katz, S. N. (Ed.). (1972). *A brief narrative of the case and trial of John Peter Zenger, printer of the New York Weekly Journal* (2nd ed.). Cambridge, MA: The Belknap Press of Harvard University Press.

Wiggins, G. (1997). The case of John Peter Zenger (1735): A Monkey . . . about 4 foot high. In L. Chassion Jr. (Ed.), *The press on trial: Crimes and trials as media events* (pp. 1–14). Westport, CT: Greenwood Press.

5

The Boston Massacre: A Prelude to Revolution

Marcella Bush Trevino

The Boston Massacre, a clash between British troops and a Boston mob that resulted in five civilian deaths, occurred on the night of March 5, 1770, and was one of the most violent events of the pre-Revolutionary era. The British troops had been sent to Boston at the request of customs officials, who were charged with collecting customs duties under the Townshend Acts imposed by the British parliament on the colonies. Americans felt that the duties threatened their traditional British right to no taxation without representation in Parliament and vigorously protested them. Customs officers repeatedly complained that angry townspeople prevented them from carrying out their duties. In 1768, the new British secretary for American affairs, the Earl of Hillsborough, ordered General Thomas Gage to send four regiments to Boston to aid the beleaguered customs officials.

The first British troops arrived in Boston on October 1, 1768, to a hostile reception. Most Bostonians felt that the soldiers' duty to protect the customs collection aided the suppression of the American colonists' rights. They also shared the traditional English fear of standing armies in peacetime and viewed the soldiers as invaders. Off-duty soldiers looking to supplement their poor pay vied with unemployed workers in a tight labor market, and Boston had

Boston Massacre Monument. (Courtesy of Library of Congress)

to house the soldiers in private homes and public buildings under the Quartering Act.

Taunting of the soldiers quickly became a common occurrence as Bostonians loyal to the patriot movement made every effort to discomfort them. "Lobsterback," a derogatory term for the bright red British military uniforms, was a favorite insult. Bostonians also complained that the soldiers spent much of their time whoring and drinking. Such treatment often met with a hostile response, and witness depositions taken after the Boston Massacre included many cases of individual soldiers intimidating civilians. Although General Gage had withdrawn all but two regiments of the soldiers by the winter of 1769–1770, tensions between Boston citizens and the soldiers who remained continued to escalate in a charged atmosphere of taunts, name-calling, and fights on the Boston streets and docks.

EVENTS LEADING TO THE MASSACRE

Many historians feel that the events leading up to the Boston Massacre began at John Gray's ropewalk in the Fort Hill section of Boston on Friday March 2, 1770. It was here that ropemaker Samuel Gray entered into a dispute with a passing soldier from the 29th Regiment. Gray asked the soldier whether he was seeking employment and received a positive response. The soldier took insult when Gray then laughingly requested that the soldier clean out his privy (toilet). The soldier attacked Gray, then left to seek reinforcements. Other workers and soldiers joined in the dispute, and what began as a fistfight escalated with the use of clubs, sticks, and cutlasses. Both Gray and Matthew Kilroy, one of the soldiers involved in the fight, were later involved in the Boston Massacre.

Some of the workers involved claimed that the soldiers began stalking them and that the soldiers spread a rumor that one was missing from his regiment and presumed killed by Boston patriots. The commanding officer of the regiment involved in the fight brought a formal complaint to Lieutenant Governor Thomas Hutchinson, but the town's council could not decide what action to take. The bitterness and hostile feelings on both sides greatly intensified in the days following the fight at Gray's ropewalk. The March 12, 1770, edition of the *Boston Gazette* named this incident as a direct forerunner to the Boston Massacre (Hansen, 1970, p. 47).

Another large scuffle between Bostonians and British soldiers occurred in the hours preceding the Massacre on March 5, 1770. The details of the outbreak are unclear, but it appears that several soldiers attacked and beat a group of boys who had gathered in front of Murray's Barracks, the troops' main headquarters, to taunt them. The boys dispersed since the soldiers had clubs, cutlasses, and bayonets, but they attracted a crowd who attempted to charge the barracks. British officers had by this time ordered the men back into the barracks and barred the crowd from entering. The crowds remained outside shouting insults. Bands of colonists consisting of apprentices, day laborers, and merchant seamen protested in the streets into the clear, crisp evening.

An account of a late military massacre at Boston, or the consequences of quartering troops in a populous town, March 12, 1770. (Courtesy of Library of Congress)

THE BOSTON MASSACRE

The disturbance that became known as the Boston Massacre began in front of the customhouse on King Street later that evening when a young barber's apprentice loudly announced that a passing British officer had not paid for his master's services. Customhouse sentry Private Hugh White of the 29th Regiment argued with the boy. White roughly pushed the boy and knocked him to the ground, causing the boy to protest and noisily attracting an angry crowd. The crowd continued to grow as angry cries attracted others in the vicinity. Some of the witnesses claimed in later statements that a man in a red cloak and white wig was speaking at Dock Square, presumably against the soldiers, and that his audience soon rushed to the customhouse disturbance. Witness accounts varied as to the sentry's next actions. Some claimed that the sentry loaded his gun while others claimed that his gun was not loaded. Various accounts state that he knocked on the customhouse door for aid, although there is disagreement over whether he received a reply.

As the growing crowd threatened the lone customhouse sentry, someone from the mob began ringing the meetinghouse bells, a traditional signal for fire. The loud bells brought more crowds rushing into the streets, and the increasingly outnumbered and frightened sentry cried for the main guard. British Captain Thomas Preston, the officer of the day, sent a noncommissioned officer and six soldiers to answer the sentry's call and soon followed them in fear that the crowd's taunts would provoke the soldiers into a rash act. In a later letter written to justify his actions, Preston claimed that someone had informed him that the patriots were planning to kidnap, and possibly murder, the sentry and steal the king's money that was collected from customs duties. He also claimed that the ringing bells actually signaled that the townspeople were gathering to attack the troops so that nearby militia would rush to their aid.

Captain Preston and his men arrived at the customhouse and found an angry mob of Bostonians taunting the sentry. Witness estimates of the crowd's size varied from about a dozen people to over 100 people, with new arrivals wandering in throughout the incident. The crowd began throwing snowballs, ice chunks, oyster shells, lumps of sea coal, and garbage at the British soldiers as they joined the sentry. Some members of the crowd also began hitting the soldiers' guns with sticks and dared them to fire, taunting that the soldiers would not dare to fire.

The soldiers were backed up against the customhouse and becoming increasingly panicked as many people shouted, "Fire, damn you! Fire!" The crowd taunted that the soldiers dared not fire because they could not do so without permission from a civil magistrate. Then a stick hit Private Hugh Montgomery's gun barrel and he stepped back, or slipped on the icy street.

Montgomery quickly retrieved his gun and fired while shouting an order for the rest of the soldiers to fire. Several of the soldiers then fired six or seven erratic shots at point-blank range into the mob, killing three of the men instantly and mortally wounding two others. Another six men received less serious injuries.

Crispus Attucks, a mulatto and part Native American, was struck twice in the chest and was the first to die. He was approximately forty-seven years old at the time and was believed to be a runaway slave who became a sailor, although his contemporaries knew little of his background. Numerous witnesses claimed to have seen him lead a group of twenty to thirty sailors to the growing crowd at the customhouse. They also claimed that he carried a large stick, possibly a cord stick, and some claimed that he was among the first to strike the soldiers' weapons with his stick. Samuel Gray, the worker from Gray's ropewalk who had been involved in a fight with British soldiers a few days earlier, and James Caldwell, an apprentice ivory turner, also died instantly at the scene.

The other casualties were Samuel Maverick and Patrick Carr, who were mortally wounded and died in the days after the Massacre. Carr had heard the meetinghouse bells and expected that trouble, rather than a fire, was their true meaning. He tried to leave his landlady's house with a sword, but a neighbor persuaded him to leave the sword behind (Hansen, 1970, p. 59). Dr. John Jeffries treated Patrick Carr and later testified at the soldiers' trial. The wounded were seventeen-year-old apprentice John Clark, seventeen-year-old shipwright's apprentice Christopher Monk, wheelwright's apprentice David Parker, seafaring man Robert Patterson, merchant Edward Payne, and tailor John Green.

IMMEDIATE REACTIONS TO THE MASSACRE

Most of the crowd fled when the soldiers fired, although some stayed behind or rushed back to carry off the dead and aid the wounded. Captain Preston remained with the soldiers to prevent further trouble and later turned himself in to the sheriff. The meetinghouse bells continued to ring, joined by the drumbeat of a call to arms alerting the other British soldiers stationed near the disturbance. The 29th Regiment under Lieutenant Colonel Carr formed three divisions, and the 14th Regiment was placed under arms but remained in the barracks. Soon, angry citizens, many of them armed, refilled the streets and demanded immediate action against the soldiers. Most of the crowds dispersed only after Lieutenant Governor Thomas Hutchinson assured them that the soldiers would receive a proper punishment.

The morning after the Boston Massacre, members of the Sons of Liberty, a radical patriot society that agitated against British interference in colonial affairs, began arriving in Boston to attend a town meeting about the event. Patriot John Hancock opened the meeting, at which speakers demanded an immediate end to Boston's military occupation. The meeting then selected a committee of fifteen, chaired by Samuel Adams, which presented its demand in a resolution to Hutchinson. Hutchinson held his own meeting with the town council and Colonel William Dalrymple, commander in chief of the two regiments involved in the Massacre. In response to Adams's committee, Hutchinson replied that the commanding officer had orders from General Gage in New York to slowly remove the troops to Castle William, an island in Boston harbor. Hutchinson claimed that he did not have the power to countermand these orders. A new town committee later responded that this action was not satisfactory and again requested that all troops be immediately removed. The council advised the governor to comply for the good of the town and province. Customs officials, afraid to remain in town unprotected, joined the troops at Castle William.

The re-stationing of the troops at Castle William in Boston Harbor took eleven days to complete. However, this action prevented the outraged citizens from launching a full-scale riot. The colonel of the Boston militia also helped prevent further trouble by setting a watch to patrol the streets until the soldiers completed their evacuation. The governor later allowed the soldiers and their families to periodically enter Boston to purchase provisions, but British troops were not to return to Boston proper until four years later. The town committee also called for the immediate trial of Captain Preston and his accused men, but the government delayed the trials as long as possible to allow passions to die down. Lieutenant Governor Hutchinson hoped that this tactic would help prevent almost certain convictions. It also allowed time for Hutchinson to receive instructions from London, since mail and information could take up to four months or longer to reach America. Hutchinson eventually received word from London that if the soldiers were convicted, King George III would pardon them.

The funeral for the first four victims of the Boston Massacre was held on March 8, 1770, and attracted several thousand spectators. The whole town marked the patriotism of the solemn event, as shops closed, harbor operations ceased, and church bells rang. The hearses moved in separate processions. The bodies of Crispus Attucks and James Caldwell, who were not Bostonians, arrived from Faneuil Hall; Samuel Gray's body arrived from his brother's house on Royal Exchange Lane; and Samuel Maverick's body arrived from his mother's house on Union Street. The separate processions joined on King Street, at the site of the Boston Massacre, and proceeded to the Old Granary Burying Ground in the heart of downtown Boston. There, the four victims were buried in a common grave. Patrick Carr, who died a week after the funerals, was buried in the same common grave on March 17, 1770.

THE TRIALS OF THE BRITISH SOLDIERS
AND AMERICAN CIVILIANS

Before dawn on the day after the Boston Massacre, Captain Preston and the soldiers were remanded to jail and ordered to stand trial for murder. Two justices conducted a preliminary interrogation of Captain Preston at the town house. Their questions focused on whether or not the captain had given the order for his men to fire. Preston maintained from the beginning that he had not given such an order. The government then held separate hearings for Captain Preston and his men, with the prosecution seeking to prove that the troops "fired with malice aforethought, despite mitigating circumstances" (Martin and Lender, 1982, p. 25). A grand jury indicted Preston and eight soldiers on March 13, 1770. Attorney General Jonathan Sewall drew up indictments against thirteen men, but left Boston before the start of the trials.

There would be three separate trials: that of Captain Preston, that of his soldiers, and that of several civilians charged with firing into the crowd from the customhouse windows. The accused soldiers were Corporal William Wemms, James Hartigan, William McCauley, Hugh White, Matthew Kilroy, William Warren, John Carrol, and Hugh Montgomery. All of the accused pled not guilty at their arraignments for murder on September 7, 1770. The jailed soldiers wrote an appeal to the court asking to share the same trial with their captain, as they were only following his orders. Three soldiers, Hugh White, James Hartigan, and Matthew Kilroy, signed the petition, which the court denied. Captain Preston's trial and the soldiers' trial were two of the longest trials in colonial American history. The jurors spent the duration of their trials sequestered in the town jail, with sleeping quarters and meals provided.

All of the accused were tried before the Superior Court of the Judicature, the highest court in Massachusetts, and the three trials were all held in the Queen Street courthouse. Justices of the Superior Court were acting Chief Justice Benjamin Lynde Jr., John Cushing, Peter Oliver, and Edmund Trowbridge. Lieutenant Governor Thomas Hutchinson was chief justice, but declined to preside at the trials. Samuel Quincy, loyalist and solicitor general for Massachusetts, and Robert Treat Paine, a patriot and lawyer from Taunton, Massachusetts, served as special prosecutors when Attorney General Sewall left town. Samuel Quincy was the brother of defense attorney Josiah Quincy Jr.

Well-known and respected Boston lawyers John Adams (the future U.S. president) and Josiah Quincy Jr. defended the soldiers. Adams was Boston's foremost attorney at the time. He claimed that Boston merchant James Forrest had begged him to take the case, as Quincy otherwise refused to join the defense. Both Adams and Quincy were actively associated with the patriot cause, but also shared the conviction that the struggle against Britain must follow the rule of law and that any accused man deserved the right to a fair trial by jury. Adams knew his decision to join the defense would be unpopular with the Boston townspeople, but he detested mob actions and stuck to his principles. He later wrote in his diary entry for March 5, 1773, that his actions were "one of the most gallant, generous, manly, and disinterested actions of my whole life, and one of the best pieces of service I ever rendered my country" (McCullough, 2001, p. 68). Judge of the Vice Admiralty Robert Auchmuty would join Adams and Quincy on the defense team at the trial of Captain Preston. Simpson S. Blowers assisted during the soldiers' trial.

As both the prosecution and the defense prepared their cases, both worried about the effect the verdict would have on the townspeople as well as on general American relations with Britain. If the soldiers were convicted of murder in the first degree, they would be hanged unless the British king interfered, but if the defense gained their acquittal, the defense would have to admit the role that the townspeople's riotous behavior had on the soldiers' actions. Both sides gathered numerous depositions from witnesses, which contributed to the often-confusing picture of exactly what happened on that night. More than eighty witnesses would eventually speak at one or more of the three trials. Many of these witnesses were either loyal to the patriot movement or to the royal government, and their perspectives often colored their accounts.

Captain Preston's trial, *Rex v. Preston*, began on October 24, 1770, and lasted six days. No transcript remains, so participant accounts and witness statements from the soldiers' separate trial provide the only sources of information about Preston's trial. William Frobisher was the jury foreman. Other jury members were Joseph Trescot, Neal McIntire, Thomas Mayo, Josiah Sprague, Joseph Guild, Jonathan Parker, Gilbert DeBlois, Phillip Dumaresque, William Hill, William Wait Wallis, and James Barrick. The last five members were talesmen, or jurors selected from among the spectators at the trial because the jury pool ran out before the court could impanel a full jury.

The trial focused on the key issue of whether Captain Preston had issued the order to fire into the crowd. Preston relied on several strategies for his defense. Through his friends, he hired the best liberal lawyers in town, Adams and Quincy, and packed the jury panel with people loyal to the British government. Preston and his friends knew that even though Adams and Quincy were patriots, they also respected the rule of law. He was also aided by the facts that no witnesses could state with certainty that he had given the orders to fire and that the random nature of the soldiers' shots into the crowd showed that there was no concerted volley as would be expected after an order to fire. English common law prevented Preston from testifying on his own behalf.

Captain Preston's defense team and the sympathetic jury helped him win a quick acquittal after only a few hours of jury deliberations. Justice Peter Oliver stated that "[it] appears quite plain to me that he must be acquitted; that the person who gave the orders to fire was not the captain, and indeed if it had been he, it at present appears justifiable" (Chaffin, 2000, p. 148). The Hutchinson administration was satisfied with the outcome while radical patriots like Samuel Adams were openly critical. Preston retreated to Castle William in Boston harbor and did not return to Boston before his ship left for England that December. He received a pension of 200 pounds from the British government.

The trial of the eight soldiers of the 24th Regiment accused of firing into the Boston mob, *Rex v. Wemms et al.*, began on November 27, 1770, and lasted more than seven days. A trial transcript was later published. The jury at the soldiers' trial contained no Boston residents. The jury foreman was Joseph Mayo. The jury members were Nathaniel Davis, Edward Pierce, Abraham Wheeler, Isaiah Thayer, Benjamin Fisher, Samuel Davenport, Joseph Houghton, Consider Atherton, Jacob Cushing Jr., Josiah Lane, and Jonathan Burr. The jury not only had to determine the soldiers' guilt or innocence, it also had to determine whether any soldier found guilty had committed murder or manslaughter. Both were capital crimes, but a finding of manslaughter offered the possibility of pleading "benefit of clergy," which would circumvent the death penalty.

Witnesses agreed to the basic facts of what had occurred but varied enormously on the details. Their testimony was often confusing, and many of them were obviously biased toward one side or the other and distorted their accounts accordingly. The law prevented the soldiers from testifying on their own behalves. Confusion also occurred because there were eight defendants on trial, but only six or seven shots had been fired. There was general agreement that Private Montgomery, the sentry, had killed Crispus Attucks and that Private Matthew Kilroy had killed Samuel Gray. Some witnesses elaborated that Kilroy stated he would not miss an opportunity to fire upon the townspeople and had later run his bayonet through Gray's dead body, although others discounted such statements. Reasonable doubt remained as to which of the other six accused men had fired, and it was not ascertained at trial which soldier had shouted the order to fire.

March 5, 1770, the Boston Massacre, Crispus Attucks in center. (The Granger Collection, New York)

The prosecution emphasized the soldiers' hatred for the townspeople, highlighting witness accounts of the soldiers' drunken antics and hostile behavior since their arrival in Boston. The defense centered its case on the fact that the soldiers had acted in self-defense at a time of confusion and fear for their safety. Defense attorneys Adams and Quincy had to proceed carefully, so that they justified the soldiers' actions in the face of a threatening crowd but did not make the Boston people solely responsible for the resulting violence. Both attorneys argued that the soldiers lived in a state of constant apprehension due to the town's open hostility toward their presence and that outside agitators had provoked them into acting. The fact that many of the agitators had arrived at the customhouse with sticks and swords clearly demonstrated their hostile intent.

Adams portrayed Crispus Attucks, a runaway slave who was not a Boston resident, as the principal aggressor. He claimed that Attucks fell upon the soldiers, taking hold of a bayonet with one hand and knocking its holder down with the other. Adams concluded, "This was the behavior of Attucks, to whose mad proceedings in probability the dreadful carnage of that night was chiefly to be ascribed" (Hansen, 1970, pp. 56–57). The emphasis on outside agitators like Attucks allowed the defense to avoid openly placing sole blame on Bostonians for the mob's behavior. Adams also blamed the crowd's hostility on the British policy of quartering troops in a city.

The defense was also aided by the testimony of one of the Boston Massacre's five victims. Attending physician Dr. John Jeffries was called to give the deathbed testimony of Patrick Carr, who had been mortally wounded at the shooting and died ten days afterward. Dr. Jeffries was a British sympathizer, and his testimony reflected this viewpoint. His hearsay evidence was admitted because Carr had given it on his deathbed, where common belief held that no man would lie. He testified that after he had repeatedly questioned his patient, Carr revealed that the crowd had greatly abused the soldiers that night and some had even threatened their lives. Carr felt the soldiers showed a great amount of patience in not firing earlier and that he had no anger or hatred toward the soldier who had wounded him because the soldiers had only been acting in self-defense. Dr. Jeffries' testimony about Carr's feelings provided a powerful message to the jury, as it came from one of the martyred victims.

Both Defense Attorney John Adams and Justice Trowbridge carefully differentiated between murder and manslaughter in their closing addresses to the jury. Adams reminded them that they must base their decisions on the facts rather than their passions. Justice Oliver's final jury instructions seemed to point toward acquittal. He reminded the jury that under the rule of law, it must return a not-guilty verdict if there is any reasonable doubt. This was the first instance of a judge using the term "reasonable doubt" in an American court of law (O'Neill, 1999). The jury found six of the soldiers—Carroll, Hartegan, McCauley, Warren, Weems, and White—not guilty, and they were subsequently released.

The jury convicted Hugh Montgomery and Matthew Kilroy of the lesser charge of manslaughter, which was still a capital crime. Both Montgomery and Kilroy were later able to plead benefit of clergy, giving them the option of branding. Benefit of clergy was a medieval holdover stating that clergy, who were literate in a time when illiteracy was common, were not subject to secular courts. After medieval times, it became permissible for non-clergy to also invoke this benefit. Kilroy, who was illiterate, benefited from the fact that in 1705 the government had abolished the requirement to prove literacy by reading a psalm from the Bible. Suffolk County Sheriff Stephen Greenleaf branded Montgomery and Kilroy with an M for *murder* on their right thumbs. The brand prevented them from pleading benefit of clergy again in the future. They were subsequently discharged from the military. In 1949, historians discovered in Lieutenant Governor Hutchinson's papers that Montgomery had admitted privately to one of his counsel that he had given the order to fire after being knocked down, but this admission did not surface during the trials or their aftermath.

The third trial to follow the Boston Massacre concerned the four men accused of firing guns from the customhouse window and balcony. The four accused civilians were Hammond Green, Thomas Greenwood, Edward Manwaring, and John Munroe: all customs employees. Their trial began on December 12, 1770. The case against them was based entirely on testimony from a French servant boy named Charles Bourgatte, whose story had been repeated to the town committee by interrogated witness Samuel Drowne. Other witnesses accused Drowne of being ignorant and claimed that they had seen no firing from the customhouse, but the case proceeded. Josiah Quincy appeared for the attorney general—there is no evidence of Adams' participation or of the defense counsel's identity. The jury found Drowne's testimony to be false and acquitted the accused men without retiring to deliberate. The French boy later retracted his story and was arrested for perjury.

MEDIA COVERAGE OF THE MASSACRE AND TRIALS

In the months following March 5, 1770, the Boston Massacre became a focal point of anti-British propaganda. Its victims became martyrs to the movement for American independence. Patriot leader Samuel Adams and his followers, including the Sons of Liberty, made sure that the American colonists did not forget the Massacre. Adams' simple act of labeling the incident the "Boston Massacre" in one of his many political articles published under various pseudonyms in the *Boston Gazette* was designed to reinforce this view. In fact, some officials actually accused Adams of instigating the encounter for the sake of fueling anti-British sentiments within the American colonies. As both the British colonial leaders and the patriots worried over the impact of the coming trials, they also sought to control how Britain would learn of the events. Both the Boston town committee, organized by patriot leaders, and Lieutenant Governor Thomas Hutchinson's administration quickly rushed to prepare their accounts of the events for both British government officials and American supporters in London, England.

Prior to the trials, the town committee had written a pamphlet, titled *A Short Narrative of the Horrid Massacre in Boston*, which included ninety-six witness depositions. Many of these statements included a substantial amount of gossip and conjecture. The committee's goal was to offset the charge of mob rule in Boston that Massachusetts' royal officials had sent to

London. They also intended to show that the British troops had been on a rampage for weeks before the March 5 violence by gathering together individual incidents of soldiers swearing revenge on townspeople and making them seem like a grand conspiracy. The prosecution did not pursue this conspiracy theory during the trials. In order to avoid influencing prospective jurors, the press did not immediately publish the town committee's pamphlet. Copies were circulating in Boston as early as July 1770, however, and royal officials claimed that its circulation was an attempt to influence prospective jurors. A later committee prepared a report called *Additional Observations to a Short Narrative of the Horrid Massacre in Boston* to counteract continued bad press in Britain.

Captain Preston, the commander of the accused soldiers, wrote several publications from jail during the seven months he spent there awaiting trial. In a letter to the *Boston Gazette*, he thanked the people of Boston who had "stept forth advocates for truth, in defense of my injured innocence" (Hansen, 1970, pp. 77–78). He also sent a letter in his defense to London, which the *Public Advertiser* published there on April 28, 1770. This second letter contradicted the first by accusing the Boston townspeople of causing the Massacre and threatening his ability to receive a fair trial.

Several well-known Boston newspapers published this letter from June 21 through June 25, 1770. The Boston townspeople read his accusations that they had tormented the soldiers in the months prior to the Boston Massacre. The letter accused the mob's leaders of plotting to call out the militia, stating that they rang the meetinghouse bells to alert Bostonians to fire on the soldiers. It also accused them of plotting to murder the sentry and steal the King's revenue. Preston stated that the witnesses who claimed they heard him give orders to fire and swear at the soldiers who were not firing were confused and misrepresenting the facts. The publication of Preston's letter resulted in numerous angry public addresses, newspaper editorials, and meetings. The letter further inflamed public opinion against the captain as his trial neared.

The conclusion of the trials brought another round of publicity as patriot leaders and British officials reacted to the verdicts. Samuel Adams, angered over the acquittals of all but two soldiers, led the movement to publicize the perceived injustices and ensure that Americans would not forget the Massacre or its meanings as he saw them. He wrote to the *Boston Gazette* using classical pseudonyms such as "Vindex" to criticize the verdicts, the conduct of the cases, and the misuse of evidence. Adams was determined to free Boston from military occupation and keep the patriots ready for any further British threats to American liberty. Adams also became a principal defender of Crispus Attucks, who his brother had targeted as the principal agitator. Adams defended Attucks and the rest of the mob in order to substantiate his claim that the soldiers had no justification for firing into the crowd. Adams also argued the case's merits with Attorney General Jonathan Sewall, who submitted a series of counterarguments to the *Boston Evening Post* under the pseudonym "Philanthrop."

PAUL REVERE'S ENGRAVING

Paul Revere's engraving, "The Fruits of Arbitrary Power; or The Bloody Massacre perpetrated in King Street Boston on March 5th 1770 by a party of the 29th Reg.," was the most famous rendering of the Boston Massacre. Prints of the engraving first appeared within twenty days and circulated widely in both Britain and the American colonies. Revere created the engraving as propaganda rather than as an accurate depiction, a common occurrence in the period before photography. Revere shows a squad of British soldiers firing a point-blank volley into a crowd of unarmed and peaceful civilians. Three civilians are lying on the ground as someone in the crowd carries off another wounded man. The customhouse is labeled "Butcher's Hall," and a smoking gun barrel is shown protruding from one of its windows, even though the story of shots fired from within the building had been largely discounted.

The print published on March 25, 1770, reflected several corrections from an earlier draft. Revere corrected several errors in the text and changed the time on a house clock in the background from 8 p.m. to 10:20 p.m. so that it would be closer to the actual time of the Massacre (Hansen, 1970, p. 149). A letter from Revere associate Henry Pelham, unearthed many years later, accused Revere of appropriating Pelham's sketch to complete his engraving. Revere's response to the accusation is unknown. Pelham later engraved his sketch, which he offered for public sale in announcements in the *Boston Evening Post* and the *Boston Gazette*. He advertised his print as an eyewitness account. Other sketches based on Pelham's original, with only a few minor details changed, circulated in Britain and America, but none were able to match the popularity of Revere's.

Edes and Gill, the publishers of Revere's engraving, had earlier commissioned him to engrave four coffins with the initials of the first four victims of the Massacre and skulls and crossbones. The *Boston Gazette* published both of Revere's engravings in the weeks following March 5. The Boston Massacre engraving was a powerful propaganda tool because it reached a large audience in a time when literacy was rare. It also had an impact on the Boston Massacre trials, as Josiah Quincy remarked during the soldiers' trial that the print was prejudicial to the accused. Centuries later, Revere's rendering of the Boston Massacre remains one of the most famous American prints.

THE MASSACRE IN THE CONTEXT
OF THE PATRIOT MOVEMENT

The British and American use of the Boston Massacre as a propaganda tool was effective because Boston was the center of the patriot movement and the most turbulent of the northern American seaports. The town was the scene of repeated resistance to hated royal taxes, and mobs repeatedly hindered the performance of royal customs officials, giving Bostonians a reputation for disrespect and lawlessness among British leaders. This unstable political atmosphere had first shaped the townspeople's hostile reactions to the British troops stationed in the city. Boston events also influenced anti-imperial behavior in other American communities. Hillsborough had originally ordered the troops to Boston because he believed that political stability in the provinces depended on controlling Boston citizens (Martin and Lender, 1982, pp. 22–23). It was only natural that Boston patriots like Samuel Adams and the Sons of Liberty would utilize the Massacre's publicity to advance their cause. Adams organized a movement to create committees of correspondence in each colony to further unite the patriots to defend against British threats to American liberty like the Boston Massacre.

Boston's economy also played a role in creating the tensions that fueled the Boston Massacre. The British government sent troops to Boston to protect the customs officers who collected trade duties under the Townshend Acts, which placed duties on several English goods imported into the colonies beginning in November 1767. Bostonians protested that these acts violated their traditional British right of no taxation without representation in Parliament. It was patriot John Hancock, another strong critic of the presence of British troops in Boston, whose violation of the Acts started the disorder of which customs officials complained. His ship *Liberty* had arrived in the harbor and unloaded a shipment of Madeira wine without paying the necessary duty. When customs officials later seized the ship, the subsequent public outcry led to the decision to bring in troops to restore order. Coincidentally, Parliament repealed the offending Townshend Acts on the same day as the Boston Massacre, although word did not reach the colonies for several months.

The town's economic instability also resulted from the impoverishment of large segments of the urban population, including politically active wage-earning laborers, mariners, artisans, small shopkeepers, and struggling professionals. The poorly paid British soldiers represented a direct economic threat, as they often competed with these workers for part-time moonlighting jobs. In addition, the Quartering Act required that the town house the soldiers in private homes and public buildings at their owners' expense.

The soldiers were a political, as well as an economic, threat. Bostonians shared the traditional British fear of standing armies in peacetime and viewed the troops as invaders. Beyond that, the soldiers became an immediate focus of the colonists' general discontent. Theoretical defenses of American constitutional rights had little impact on the average illiterate Bostonian, but the soldiers were a constantly visible presence, challenging them as they moved through the streets. The soldiers symbolized all threats to American liberties; however, most Bostonians simply wanted the soldiers removed from their town. Although Samuel Adams and the Sons of Liberty used the Boston Massacre to emphasize the seriousness of the threat, the average Bostonian was not yet calling for a revolution.

COMMEMORATION OF THE MASSACRE
IN HISTORY AND CULTURE

The commemoration of the Boston Massacre made it one of the central events in the time leading up to the American Revolution. March 5 became an annual holiday in Boston until 1783, and Samuel Adams and the Sons of Liberty worked to keep the memory of the tragic event alive. They also ensured that their presence would be felt in large numbers at the annual events. Patriot leaders wanted to ensure that anti-British sentiment remained high as the American colonies moved toward revolution. They also hoped the memorials would remind citizens of the need to be ever vigilant of their liberties.

The Massacre's first anniversary remembrances included an oration with negative images of standing armies crushing innocent people. Featured speaker Dr. Joseph Warren's speech, at the 1772 commemoration, utilized vivid imagery to revive the memory of the Massacre victims when he stated, "Language is too feeble to paint the emotions of our souls, when our streets were stained with the blood of our brethren; when our ears were wounded by the groans of the dying, and our eyes were tormented with the sight of the mangled bodies of the dead" (Martin and Lender, 1982, p. 25). The anti-British rhetoric of the commemoratory speeches grew as the American Revolution grew closer. The Massacre's fourth anniversary in 1774, on the eve of war with Britain, included a memorable and vividly anti-British oration by patriot leader John Hancock. Samuel Adams ensured that numerous copies were printed and sent to the committees of correspondence in various colonies.

In 1888, the town placed a memorial on Boston Common over the objections of the Massachusetts Historical Society. The Society felt that the victims being memorialized were agitators rather than heroes. Most

Bostonians did not share their view, and the event was marked with much patriotic spirit and symbolism. Historian John Fiske made an address to the crowd and poet John Boyle O'Reilly composed a verse to commemorate the event. The site of the common grave for the first four Massacre victims, the Old Granary Burying Ground, also includes the graves of Paul Revere and Samuel Adams. It remains a central landmark of historic Boston, which many people feel is the cradle of American liberty.

The Boston Massacre continues to play a large role in America's national history and mythology as a symbol of the sacrifice necessary to achieve liberty. Paul Revere's famous engraving, based on a sketch of the Boston Massacre, has appeared in numerous schoolbooks, histories, and encyclopedias over the years, accompanying countless retellings of the events of March 5, 1770. Crispus Attucks, a mulatto and the first victim of the Boston Massacre, enjoyed renewed fame when the civil rights movement of the 1950s and 1960s placed a growing emphasis on the contributions and achievements of African Americans in U.S. history. He and the other victims continue to be memorialized as the first martyrs to the cause of American independence. The trials of the British soldiers have come to symbolize protection of the rights (such as the right to a fair trial by jury) that the American Revolution was fought to protect.

REFERENCES

Chaffin, R. J. (2000). The Townshend Acts crisis, 1767–1770. In J. P. Greene and J. R. Pole (Eds.), *A companion to the American Revolution* (pp. 134–150). Malden, MA: Blackwell Publishers.

Hansen, H. (1970). *The Boston Massacre: An episode of dissent and violence.* New York: Hastings House Publishers.

Jodziewicz, T. W. (1976). *Birth of America: The year in review 1763–1783: A chronological guide and index to the contemporary colonial press.* Glen Rock, NJ: Microfilming Corporation of America.

Leach, D. E. (2000). The British Army in America, before 1775. In J. P. Greene and J. R. Pole (Eds.), *A companion to the American Revolution* (pp. 151–156). Malden, MA: Blackwell Publishers.

Lewis, P. (1973). *The grand incendiary: A biography of Samuel Adams.* New York: Dial Press.

Maier, P. (1974). *From resistance to revolution: Colonial radicals and the development of American opposition to Britain, 1765–1776.* New York: Vintage Books.

Marcus, R. D., and Burner, D. (1997a). A British officer's description: Thomas Preston. In *America firsthand: Readings from settlement to reconstruction* (pp. 96–99). Vol. 1. Boston: Bedford Books.

Marcus, R. D., and Burner, D. (1997b). Colonial accounts: George Robert Twelves Hewes and the *Boston Gazette* and *Country Journal*. In *America firsthand:*

Readings from settlement to reconstruction (pp. 100–106). Vol. 1. Boston: Bedford Books.

Martin, J. K., and Lender, M. E. (1982). A respectable army: The military origins of the republic, 1763–1789. In J. H. Franklin and A. S. Eisenstadt (Eds.), *The American History Series*. Arlington Heights, IL: Harlan Davidson, Inc.

McCullough, D. (2001). *John Adams*. New York: Touchstone.

Nash, G. B. (1979, 1986). *The urban crucible: The northern seaports and the origins of the American Revolution*. Cambridge, MA: Harvard University Press.

O'Neill, S. C. (1999). *The Boston Massacre trials*. Supreme Judicial Court Historical Society. Retrieved October 1, 2003 from http://www.sjchs-history.org/massacre.html

Reich, J. R. (1998). *Colonial America* (4th ed.). Upper Saddle River, NJ: Prentice Hall.

Warren, J. (1998). Boston Massacre oration, March 5, 1772. In M. P. Johnson (Ed.), *Reading the American past: Selected historical documents* (pp. 78–81). Vol. 1. Boston: Bedford Books.

Zobel, H. B. (1970, 1996). *The Boston Massacre*. New York: W. W. Norton.

6

Bathsheba Spooner: The Result of a Wicked and Licentious Appetite on the Life Expectancy of Husbands

Salita S. Bryant

On Thursday, July 2, 1778, at 2:30 in the afternoon, Bathsheba Spooner, James Buchanan, Ezra Ross, and William Brooks were led from their prison cells in Worcester, Massachusetts, to begin their final passage to the gallows for the murder of Bathsheba's husband, thirty-seven-year-old Joshua Spooner. Thirty-two-year-old Bathsheba Spooner had, earlier in the year, not only become pregnant, probably by her lover Ross (Navas, 1999, p. 38), a seventeen-year-old veteran continental soldier she had first met when he was sixteen, but she had bribed British deserters Buchanan and Brooks to join Ross in ambushing and murdering her husband and tossing the body down the family's well. The number of participants, the method by which Joshua was killed, and the fact that such obvious premeditation was required caused *The Massachusetts Spy* to claim, four days after the March 1 homicide, that the murder of Joshua Spooner was "the most extraordinary crime ever perpetrated in New-England" (*The Massachusetts Spy*, 1778, March 5). On this day, however, having been discovered, found guilty of the crime, and sentenced to hang, the four were transported to the gallows under a guard of "about an hundred men"; and as the three men walked to their deaths, "Mrs. Spooner was carried in a chaise" as she "had been for a number of days, exceedingly unwell" (August 6). As this coterie made its way through a swarming crowd of 5,000 "shriek[ing]" and pushing spectators, a "black thunder cloud arose" with such "loud peals of thunder" that the August 6 edition of *The Massachusetts Spy* opined that God himself was "determined to add such terrors to the punishment of the criminals as must stagger the stoutest heart of the most abandoned."

Bathsheba Spooner, however, did not seem to be "stagger[ed]" in the least. Wearing, as legend has it, her wedding dress, she displayed the same calm and indifferent manner she had displayed throughout the trial and prehanging events (Navas, 1999, p. 105).[1] On the ride to the gallows her spiritual advisor, Reverend Thaddeus Maccarty, had asked Bathsheba "if the sight of it did not strike her? She answered not at all any more than any other object" (Maccarty, 1778a, 1778b, as quoted in Navas, p. 98). Once at the gallows, Bathsheba was noted to have bowed to acquaintances standing in the crowd in her familiar "haughty and imperious" manner (Chandler, 1844, p. 8). Numerous sources report that throughout her life, trial, and execution, Bathsheba displayed a studied casualness and arrogance in her dealings with others that bordered on manipulation. Indeed, such behavior ultimately led to her ruin as she had variously appealed to and exploited the mercenary appetites of Ezra Ross, James Buchanan, and William Brooks in order to coerce them into murdering her husband. It was perhaps partially this removed and superior attitude that had led Bathsheba to operate outside of the bounds of legality and morality in conducting her life and her affairs, for she had supposedly engaged in numerous extramarital affairs. At its best, this attitude would have been read by her fellow citizens as arrogance, at least, and perhaps treasonous, at worst. Spooner, the strong-willed and beautiful daughter of Timothy Ruggles, the wealthy Tory General, was suspect in her hometown of Brookfield due to her attitude. It was a town situated in the heart of a country embroiled in the schism of a national revolution. This national crisis, perhaps more than anything else, would ultimately prove her undoing, for not only had Bathsheba flouted the religious, civic, and moral restraints of marriage, she had committed perhaps the most scandalous of sins—she was the daughter of a renowned and despised loyalist, who shared not only her father's comportment, but also his political sympathies as well.

FAMILY ALLIANCES

The sixth child of the often volatile and passionate marriage between Bathsheba Bourne Newcomb Ruggles and Timothy Ruggles, Bathsheba was born February 15, 1746 in Sandwich, Massachusetts. To understand why Bathsheba murdered and why she was ultimately executed, it is important to understand her family history.

Her mother, Bathsheba Bourne, was the daughter of a distinguished New England family headed by Judge Melatiah and Desire Bourne of Sandwich.[2] Bathsheba Bourne was married to Harvard University graduate William Newcomb, with whom she had seven children. After William's death in 1736 when Bathsheba Bourne was thirty-four, she continued to run the Newcomb public house until she married twenty-five-year-old Timothy Ruggles on September 18, 1736. As did Bourne's first husband, Ruggles had also graduated from Harvard. After graduating in 1732, he began practicing law in Plymouth, Massachusetts, and by 1734 had embarked on a twenty-three-year career in the Massachusetts legislature with his election to the General Court from Rochester. They lived together in Sandwich, Massachusetts, from 1736 until 1753, at which point they moved themselves and their own seven children, including seven-year-old Bathsheba, with twenty-four other connected families to a 100-square-mile family compound in Hardwick, twenty miles from Worcester. Bathsheba Bourne's seven children from her previous marriage to Newcomb remained in Sandwich, and they were either married or tending to the family's businesses.

By all accounts, Ruggles and his wife were both strong-willed and forceful personalities whose marriage was a tumultuous one. Ruggles was "infamous for his profanity," humorous, "handsome," "wise," and at over six feet tall, physically imposing (Navas, 1999, p. 19; Shipton, 1933, p. 199). Ruggles had a long and distinguished legal and political career, and besides serving on the Rochester General Court between 1754 and 1759, he served his country in five campaigns during the French and Indian War. He became chief justice of Worcester's Court of Common Pleas in 1762, a position he held until 1774. Ruggles refusal to "sign the Stamp Act protest in late October 1765," and his election as president of the First Provincial Congress (or "Stamp Act Congress") in 1765 verified his standing among the loyalists; it was a stand that would eventually cost him his country (Navas, 1999, pp. 21–22, 28). Separated from his wife by 1774, Ruggles left Hardwick forever when he alone left for Boston that August to join the Mandamus Council. Appointed by royalist Governor Lieutenant General Thomas Gage, Ruggles was, in effect, run out of town and threatened with arrest by the town militia for his acceptance of this British appointment. The February 13, 1775, issue of the *Boston Evening-Post* declared the sentiments of Ruggles' neighbors, stating, "You have given the finishing stroke to your tatter'd Reputation, and are now driven out from your inheritance, the Society of your good Friends and Neighbors, and like the cursed Fratricide of old, fear that everyone who finds you shall slay you" (Shipton, 1933).

Ruggles removed himself to Boston and then later, when the British were forced to evacuate, to Nova Scotia onto land granted to him by King

George III. His wife remained for a time on the family plantation; she never rejoined her husband. Their daughter Bathsheba, Ruggles's favorite, seemed to have inherited both her mother's beauty and resolute independence and her father's brash arrogance. With these parental gifts came the threat of death at the hands of Massachusetts' citizens. It was a threat that the following events would eventually enact.

A CRIME BORN OUT OF DESPERATION

Sunday March 1, 1778, after drinking the evening away at Cooley's Tavern, Bathsheba's husband, Joshua Spooner, returned home in the darkness to his wife, his children, his servants, and a house that occasionally contained a visiting Continental soldier, Ezra Ross. Spooner had taken a liking to young Ross and, unlike some of the other soldiers his wife had taken in, he apparently had little problem with his presence. Two weeks prior to his last walk, Spooner had requested that two other wayward soldiers, Buchanan and Brooks, depart his house at once. He hadn't liked their looks, was frightened of them, and as they were no longer visible, had assumed them gone. However, Bathsheba, with the aid of various servants, had kept them hidden in the barn, tending to them when Spooner was either away from home or asleep. Ross, by this point, had returned from a visit to his parents and was also being hidden from Spooner. On this fateful night, Brooks and Buchanan, joined by a still somewhat reluctant Ross, met Spooner within his own garden gate. Struck by Brooks, Spooner fell to the ground crying out "murder." The three quickly stripped Spooner of his watch and shoes and shoved his body—head first—into the family's narrow well. They then retired to the house for their payment for services rendered.

On January 15, 1766, twelve years earlier, Bathsheba Ruggles had married Joshua Spooner and together they had had three children (two daughters and a son) who survived childhood. However, Spooner was a man whom most sources confirm Bathsheba soon loathed (Navas, 1999, p. 11). Indeed, Bathsheba's spiritual advisor noted in his "Account of the Behavior of Mrs. Spooner" that soon after the marriage, "domestic dissentions . . . went on . . . till she conceived an utter aversion to him" (p. 36).

The reasons Bathsheba had consented to such a marriage in the first place remain a mystery. She wasn't pregnant at the time of their marriage. Although quite possible, there is no proof that her father—fearing the chaotic circumstances the colonies were in—had arranged this marriage in order to situate his daughter. However, Spooner was from a prominent family and wealthy, and he provided her a means out of her turbulent childhood home. Although lacking definitive proof, most sources contend that a part of Bathsheba's animosity toward her husband was that he was believed to be an abusive alcoholic and adulterer. Another part of later explanations for their poor marriage and its deadly conclusion has been the erroneous belief there was a vast age difference between the two. Although it has often been reported that Bathsheba was thirty-seven years younger than Joshua Spooner, and that Joshua was a sixty-three-year-old "retired merchant," and "a grandfatherly man," this was not true; actually Joshua was thirty-seven years old at the time of his murder (Sifakis, 1982, p. 679; Nash, 1990, p. 2832). Neighbor and tavern owner Ephraim Cooley testified at the trial that he had heard Spooner's son call him "Old Bogus," an expression he had apparently picked up from his mother. In fact, neighbor Obediah Rice testified as well that "before the murder [he had] heard Mrs. Spooner say she wished Old Bogus was in heaven" (Navas, 1999, p. 127). The belief that he was much older than Bathsheba seems to have stemmed from these references and from accounts of his personality that certainly would not have pleased the vivacious Bathsheba, who apparently modeled her image of manly behavior on her gregarious and demanding father. Indeed, "Joshua looked and acted much older than his chronological age," and Bathsheba was thought to have believed his behavior to be "unmanly" and "prissy" (Navas, 1999, pp. 3, 4). The *Massachusetts Spy*, reporting on the trial, declared that Spooner's "only fault appears to be his not supporting a manly importance as head of his family, and not regulating the government of it" (1778, May 7).

Whatever the causes of their loveless and acrimonious marriage, his support of patriotic causes and his reputation as a staid and plodding citizen, though mitigated by a possible reputation as a philanderer and alcoholic, seem to have contributed to Bathsheba's murderous feelings. It was also eventually argued by her defense, albeit fruitlessly, that Bathsheba was certainly insane to have attempted such a desperate act. Her final insane actions, while rooted in abhorrence of her husband, were fueled by more lascivious explanations. Bathsheba reputedly had various lovers. However, it was not until she made the acquaintance of sixteen-year-old Ezra Ross and became pregnant that her desire to escape the confines of her marriage resulted in murder.

In March 1777, the year prior to the murder, Ezra Ross had met the Spooners when he passed through Brookfield. He had completed his one-year stint with Washington's army at Morristown in December 1776, and he was making the 240-mile journey to his family in the small farming village of Linebrook. Ross was unwell, and whether the cause was the foul camp conditions or the effect of such winter travel, the result was that Bathsheba offered Ross shelter and ministered to his failing health. Ross resided with the family for a time before continuing on to Linebrook. By August, Ross had reenlisted for a four-month tour of duty and had embarked for New

York. On his way, he stopped in at Brookfield to visit Mr. and Mrs. Spooner. According to his parents, Ross, encouraged "by gratitude of past favors," was moved to "call on his old benefactress" (Petition of Ross family, 1778).

Ross seems to have been an intimate friend of both the Spooners and "became a frequent and welcome visitor in the family" (Chandler, 1844, p. 9). Once his 1777 fall tour at Fort Ticonderoga, Saratoga, and Mount Independence was completed, Ross returned to the Spooner house in mid-November. Upon his return, Ross rejoined his place in this family, riding and talking with Bathsheba and accompanying Spooner on business excursions. At some point after Ross's return to the Spooner's that fall, the relationship between Bathsheba and Ross became far more precarious as "an improper intimacy grew up between them" (Chandler, p. 9). As Peleg Chandler claimed half a century later in reviewing the case in volume 2 of *American Criminal Trials*, Bathsheba "cherished a criminal regard for another person, and, in the blindness of passion, lost all self-control" (p. 9). Joshua Spooner either was amenable to the situation between Ross and his wife or was unaware of the extent of their involvement. Bathsheba would indeed lose control, and what seemed to propel that loss was her pregnancy.

Bathsheba would have become aware of her pregnancy in late January or early February, and as Navas correctly points out, "most writers who have taken up the Spooner story have assumed that Ezra Ross was the father of Bathsheba's unborn child" (1999, p. 38). Although the actual veracity of this claim is unsubstantiated, Bathsheba herself officially claimed that the child "was lawfully begotten." She would most certainly have made this claim regardless of its paternity. She also stated to "constable Elisha Hamilton, [that] it [the murder] happened by means of Ross's being sick at our house" (Navas, 1999, p. 38; Foster, 1778). The elderly Reverend Ebenezer Parkman, from nearby Westborough, recorded that while in prison Ross confided in him that Bathsheba "gave [him] an invitation to Defile her Marriage Bed" (Navas, pp. 38–39). It was an invitation Ross states he accepted. Soon, he claims, Bathsheba "proposed constantly every sheam [scheme] for her husband's death" (Navas, p. 39). With the assurance of eventual marriage, the two made at least two attempts to poison Spooner. The first came before a business trip on which Ross was to join Spooner. Ross slipped aqua fortis (nitric acid) into Spooner's beer. Nitric acid is "extremely bitter," and Spooner quickly "spit it out," stating that "if he had enemies in the house he should think they intended to poison him" (Navas, p. 43). The second attempt was on a subsequent business trip where Ross failed to find either the courage or the possibility of carrying out his intent. The pressure to commit murder apparently unnerved Ross, who did not return to Brookfield with Spooner, but instead "left on a horse borrowed from Joshua to see his father . . . [not to]

reappear in Brookfield again for nearly a month, until the night before the murder" (Navas, 1999, p. 44).

While Spooner apparently had accommodated Ross and the assortment of soldiers Bathsheba gave shelter to, he seemed to draw a line when Brooks and Buchanan took up residency. During the month of Ross's absence, Bathsheba sent servant Alexander Cummings into the street to gather Brooks and Buchanan as they ambled by on the street. Brooks and Buchanan were either escaped, deserting, or released British soldiers who, according to Cummings' later trial testimony, were known to him from his own days in Burgoyne's company. They were invited to "warm themselves by the Spooner kitchen fire and told [by Cummings that] his master was away on business, but [that] his mistress had a great regard for the British army and would be very glad to meet them" (Navas, 1999, pp. 48–49). Bathsheba treated the two as honored guests and offered them the unexpected generosity of good rum, food, and shelter. Bathsheba and "Buchanan's conversations grew increasingly personal . . . [until she] confided" to him Ross's and her plan to kill her husband (p. 49). Cummings would also later testify that "he overheard her say to Buchanan," that "they could enjoy one another . . . if her husband were out of the way" (p. 49).

When Spooner returned home without Ross, servant Jess Parker later testified that he had heard Bathsheba joke that "she never was so stumped in her life" (Foster, 1778). Though she was "stumped," she had certainly already laid the groundwork for a backup arrangement for murdering her husband, as she had perhaps already realized that the likelihood was slight that Ross would poison Spooner while they were traveling together. After several tense days of Spooner's concern over the disreputable men, the two British soldiers obliged him by leaving. They traveled around the town, returning at night to eat and drink Spooner's stores as they hid out in the house and barn. Although it appears that the soldiers attempted to leave the area, Bathsheba succeeded in playing Ross and Buchanan against one another by making each jealous of the other. While attempting to obtain poison more efficient than aqua fortis, she plied the two British soldiers with sexual attention, with gifts, and with promises of more money. Perhaps prompted by fear that Buchanan would accomplish what he had apparently promised Bathsheba he would accomplish, Ross returned to Brookfield the day before the murder with a brace of pistols. According to Buchanan in *The Dying Declaration*, when the three men finally met one another that Sunday, Bathsheba told Buchanan and Brooks that Ross "was in the house . . . [and with his pistols and that] he had promised her he would kill Mr. Spooner as he [Mr. Spooner] came home from the tavern." The lately arrived pair pointed out to Ross and Bathsheba that a gunshot "would alarm the neighbors," and the murderous party quickly devised another plan by which Brooks would attack and beat Spooner upon his return, to be joined by Ross and Buchanan at the final moment. Bathsheba's flurry of activity, letter writing, promises, and manipulation of these men's emotions had finally succeeded in garnering her what she wanted—the death of her husband (Buchanan et al., 1778).

The desperate activity of the previous few weeks had resulted in several ineffective plans. Now, a feebly constructed and poorly executed murder would have an even worse follow-through. By the next day all three men would be arrested. According to *The Dying Declaration*, after the murder, Bathsheba retrieved Spooner's moneybox, which Buchanan broke open and out of which she "gave two notes of 400 dollars each to Ross to change and give the money to Brooks" (Buchanan et al., 1778). Finding paper money, she gave them some of that, along with Spooner's clothes and shoe buckles and the promise of more to come. Ross, Buchanan, and Brooks immediately left the crime scene and traveled fewer than twenty miles to Worcester, arriving at Mrs. Walker's Inn and Tavern at four o'clock in the morning (Navas, 1999, p. 67). While Ross apparently retired to bed, Buchanan and Brooks foolishly "began drinking," and went to another "tavern; there showing Mr. Spooner's watch, and the people seeing him have [engraved] silver Buckles, became suspicious of him" (Navas, p. 68; Buchanan et al., 1778). By that Monday afternoon, Ephraim Curtis, Worcester's jailer, "Captain Whitney, and Joseph Ball went to Walker's to question Buchanan, Brooks, and Ross" (Navas, p. 69). They were found, examined briefly, and quickly arrested. All three directly accused Bathsheba as instigator of the crime.

For her part, Bathsheba woke the next morning and, acting curiously mystified about the whereabouts of her husband, sent Alexander Cummings to "go and get a horse and go to the town and inquire for him" (Sargeant's Trial Notes). As Navas reports:

Ephraim Cooley was worried about Joshua's safety and took six men with him to the Spooner house, where he found Bathsheba eating her breakfast in the kitchen with Mrs. Stratton and the family. He asked her if Joshua was home, to which she answered no and cried. Cooley then went outside and found near the gate a heap of snow covering Joshua's hat, which he brought in to be identified by Bathsheba. Shortly the body was discovered in the well and blood stains were found on the well curb. Ephraim Cooley went immediately to fetch Brookfield's coroner, Thomas Gilbert, and when they returned Joshua's corpse had been taken from the well and laid out in the east sitting room on the table. (p. 70)

As was later testified to in court, Bathsheba, upon seeing and touching Spooner's corpse, simply whispered, "poor little man"; and, despite her attempt at befuddlement concerning Spooner's location, she and three servants were taken in for questioning.

THE CRIMINAL TRIAL

A jury of inquisition was conducted March 3, 1778 and found enough evidence to bind the four over to the grand jury. The Superior Court of Judicature began that spring's term on Tuesday, April 21, and the "grand jury found a true bill against" Buchanan, Brooks, Ross, and Bathsheba Spooner (Navas, 1999, p. 75). The indictment found that "Brooks had struck Spooner down . . . and that James Buchanan and Ezra Ross were present and aiding, assisting, abetting, comforting, and maintaining William Brooks in the murder; and that Bathsheba Spooner on February 28th incited, moved, abetted, counseled, and procured in the manner and form in which the murder was to be committed" (Navas, 1999, p. 76; Superior Court Records, 1778). The three men were charged with murder, and Bathsheba was charged as an accomplice before the fact. To these capital charges, all four pled not guilty and were held over for the April 24 trial.

There were five judges on the Massachusetts Superior Court. The group, consisting of Jedediah Foster, Nathaniel Peaslee Sargeant, David Sewall, and James Sullivan, was chaired by Chief Justice William Cushing (Navas, 1999, p. 76). The prosecutor, Robert Treat Paine, member of the Continental Congress and a signer of the Declaration of Independence, was a seasoned trial lawyer who used the testimonies of Bathsheba's servants against the four, "apparently in exchange for immunity" (Navas, 1999, p. 75). The defense was led by a young patriotic lawyer, Levi Lincoln. While some critics, such as Deborah Navas, claim that Lincoln "was no match in experience to Robert Treat Paine" (p. 75) and that he was "young and untried" (p. 181, n21), he was actually more than competent and later served as U.S. attorney general during Thomas Jefferson's presidency. Navas notes as well that the prosecutor's notes indicate that a Mr. Sprague offered testimony for the defense; in actuality Sprague was a loyalist sympathizer and Harvard-trained lawyer practicing in Worcester County who was probably a member of the defense team. The court either assigned these two proficient lawyers to defend the four, or supporters of one or more members of the group hired their services. Despite sources that often paint the defense as unequal to the prosecution, the problem of the defense seems to have more to do with the fact that not only were the four so blatantly guilty, but that Bathsheba, daughter of a despised loyalist general, had enticed two ex-British soldiers to murder her patriotic husband.

Prosecution Arguments

Prosecutor Robert Treat Paine relied almost solely on the confessions of the three soldiers and on the damning statements of the witness to support his case. In his trial notes, he summarized the testimony of the witnesses and recorded the following defense arguments that he apparently would have argued against in his closing statement.[3]

Mr. Sprague argued that:

- The evidence concerning Ross "only makes him an accessory after the fact."
- Ross's defense suffered because he was tried with the other three.

Mr. Lincoln argued that:

- Ross was a man of "good Character."
- When Ross left Spooner during their business trip he borrowed a horse to ride to Linebrook. In the process of getting back to Brookfield because of a letter Bathsheba had sent him, the horse was injured. If Ross had intended to commit the murder, why wouldn't he conceal himself and the horse from Spooner once he returned?
- Enlightenment philosophies of Cesare Bonesana, Marchese di Berccaria "arguing against capital punishment and cruel treatment of criminals" (Navas, p. 134).
- "Presumptive evidence dangerous."
- The credibility of the servants offering testimony.
- Mrs. Spooner must be insane and could "expect immunity."
- If they had actually been planning a murder, would they not have "agreed upon a plan of escape?"

Defense Arguments

Lincoln had a challenging case, as the three soldiers had already formally confessed to their guilt. Bathsheba, however, never formally confessed to her guilt, but on the "night of her arrest she appears to have been relieved to admit her involvement in the crime. Justice Foster recorded that Ephraim Cooley testified, 'at Brown's [Tavern] in Worcester she spoke freely of the matter and said she was the whole means of this murder being committed'" (Navas, 1999, p. 72).

Lincoln's notes indicate that this case was "the first case of bloodshed, the first capital trial since the establishment of the government" and that for this reason, special care should be taken "to attend to, decide by, and give [their] verdict according to the fair result of the evidence" (Lincoln). Because of the aforementioned confessions and obviously pejorative testimonies, Lincoln never denied the fact that Spooner was murdered. Indeed, he argued that although there were confessions, it did not make them all guilty—indeed, he argued that only one person actually committed the murder. Everyone else either knew before or after the fact, but they didn't actually kill. In an effort to win the defendants' freedom, Lincoln wanted the jury to separate the defendants' actions by their culpability. Lincoln's trial notes demonstrate that he drew these distinctions most firmly among Bathsheba, Ross, and the two British soldiers, and expended most of his effort on presenting Bathsheba as not guilty by reason of insanity and Ross not guilty of anything but youthful turmoil and bad timing.[4]

As to Ross, the young American war hero, he argued that:

- Ross was "perfectly innocent in reference to the crime" of murder. Simply touching Spooner's leg after he was dead does not make him a murderer.
- Ross's confession should be disregarded, as he was naturally quite "anxious and pressed by leading questions."
- Ross, in returning to Brookfield, had no knowledge of the activities of the two other men.
- Ross is not even an accessory as he did not command, counsel, abet, or procure another to commit a felony.
- Ross had no "design" to injure Spooner. Indeed, if Ross were intent on killing Spooner, would he not have taken another, easier opportunity to commit the deed?
- Although he bought poison, he did not use it. The poison was not the cause of the murder and should not be considered as evidence.
- To have attempted to stop Buchanan and Brooks might have resulted in his own death.
- Ross never made any real attempt to escape when he certainly could have.

As to Bathsheba Spooner's defense, Lincoln argued that:

- He could see no advantage to Mrs. Spooner that would result from Mr. Spooner's death. She had no motive.
- All the talk of poisons in front of potential witnesses is irrelevant if he was to be attacked.
- There was no actual murder plan.
- She was insane: "disorders of the brain operate variously."

    A sane person would not give an incriminating watch, buckles, and clothing to murderers.

    No sane person would "intrust such an affair to strangers, diserters and foreigners—to women and boys."

    The murder itself was irrational and indicates a disturbed mind.

    "Conduct is only evidence of the state of a persons mind" and the aforementioned evidence all goes to prove that her behavior was irrational.

The defense for Brooks and Buchanan was slim indeed, and all of their previous confessions were used against the others in the group. Lincoln noted the following arguments to be made at trial:

- "Words may be very innocent when spoken and criminal when related."
- Can a man who is a murderer be expected to give a truthful confession? (Lincoln)

Not much energy was expended on defendants so clearly guilty. Indeed, the two previous statements would certainly have benefited Bathsheba and Ross more than they would have helped Buchanan and Brooks. Today, confessions such as these would only be used against the confessor, not his partners.

Not only was this the first capital case of the new republic, it was also the first to attempt an insanity defense. The jury discounted both the insanity plea and Lincoln's arguments that Ross was guilty of foolish, not criminal, behavior. The trial and deliberation lasted one day, and quite swiftly all four were found guilty of capital murder and sentenced to hang on June 4, 1778.

Appeals

As a group, the four appealed to the Massachusetts Council for a postponement of the June 4 execution date in order have "more time to prepare themselves for their deaths" (Navas, 1999, p. 85). The Reverend Thaddeus Maccarty, Bathsheba's spiritual advisor, "appended a note to the petition supporting it, adding 'and as to the unhappy woman . . . she declares she is several months advanced in her pregnancy, for which reason she humbly desires, that her execution may be respited till she shall have brought forth'" (Navas, p. 85). On May 28, the group's stay was allowed and a new execution day set for July 2.

Bathsheba's individual request to plead her belly, however, set off a flurry of activity. As custom and law both prohibited the execution of a pregnant woman, the Council ordered the Worcester sheriff to determine the truth of the claim. The sheriff's report to the Council claimed that he had "summoned two men midwives and twelve lawful matrons" to examine Bathsheba (Return of the Sheriff, 1778). The signed and notarized June 11 report concluded that all the male midwives and matrons, "headed by volatile patriot Elizabeth Rice," had found Spooner to "not [be] quick with child" (Nash, 1990, p. 2832; Return of the Sheriff, 1778). She was, however, four months pregnant by this time and attempting to persuade the Council of the matrons' error, attached to the sheriff's report a letter begging them to "preserve [the] life" of her unborn child. While the Council denied her request, Maccarty apparently convened another panel, "by [Bathsheba's] desire," in order to prove that she was indeed pregnant (Opinion of Midwives, 1778).

This time the decision was split four to two in favor of Bathsheba. The group still retained the two male midwives and included a third. All three of the men, and a new female midwife, found "reason to Think that she is now quick with Child" (Opinion, 1778). However, two of the female midwives, Elizabeth Rice and Molly Tattman, returned for the second examination and claimed that not only was Bathsheba "not quick with Child" when they first examined her, she, in their opinion, was "not even now Quick with Child" (Opinion, 1778). The result did not sway the council. Accepting the failure of her attempts for a stay of execution, Bathsheba sent the council a final request that an autopsy be performed upon her death. Never one to mince words, Bathsheba charged that, "the midwives who . . . examined me have taken into greater account my father's Royalist leanings than they have the stirrings in my body which should have stirred their consciences. The truth is that they want my father's daughter dead and with her my father's grandchild" (Sifakis, 1982, p. 680).

In his publication *Account of the Behaviour of Mrs. Spooner*, Maccarty let it be known that Bathsheba had indeed been telling the truth, as her autopsy revealed "a perfect male foetus of the growth of five months or near it." Unfortunately, by the time it was known, Bathsheba had already been executed. However, the facts that Bathsheba was pregnant and that the state of Massachusetts had committed murder in executing Bathsheba would cause quite a stir in the years to come.

Ross's parents, Jabez and Johana Ross, had petitioned the Council to also spare their son's life. Ross had been baptized on May 24, and he was, they argued, a boy from a patriotic and brave family that had sent four of its five sons to war to fight alongside General George Washington. Indeed, they claimed, Ross himself was an honored and brave soldier who had been seduced by the wickedness of Bathsheba Spooner, upon whose doorstep "the lot of Providence" had "cast" him (Petition of Ross family, 1778). It was not their intention, they said, to "attempt an extenuation of guilt," but to beg the "pardon" of a boy who had fallen in with "ruffians," who was a "valuable member of society," who had "fought in her cause," whose greatest crime seemed to have been his falling prey to the "alluring seducements" of a wicked woman (Petition). Ross's pardon was not granted and indeed, according to Navas, was apparently not acted on by the Council.

Ultimately, none of the petitions altered the eventual outcome of the case. All four defendants were summarily hanged July 2, 1778.

MEDIA COVERAGE: SENSATIONALISM ACROSS THE CENTURIES

Media attention to the Spooner case was relatively heavy. The titillating circumstances of an adulterous woman who persuaded three men to do her bidding, the quadruple hanging, the pregnancy, and the political intrigue were all just as exciting to seventeenth-century citizens as they are to twenty-first-century ones. This was sensation and spectacle at its best, and in a time when murder or trial narratives were published quickly and seldom reprinted, the Spooner murder garnered quite a bit of press. Despite the interest and the contemporary newspaper reports concerning the case, the media probably had little or no immediate impact on the trial or its outcome other than voicing the presumption of complete guilt of the parties involved. The Ruggles were already known and loathed, and revolutionary rhetoric and sentiment would have been as damning as anything specific about the case. the *Boston Gazette*, for instance, included small articles about the case on March 9 and July 6 and primarily highlighted the fact that Bathsheba was the daughter of the hated Timothy Ruggles. In essence, the damage to Bathsheba's case was done before the murder had been committed. Besides numerous newspaper reports, mainly in Isaiah Thomas's patriotic Worcester newspaper, *The Massachusetts Spy* (1778, March 5, May 7, June 2, June 11, June 25, July 2, July 9, August 6), there were numerous sermons, trial reports, poems, and dying declarations published in broadsheet and chapbook form after the murder.[5]

In order of publication, the Spooner case has appeared in the following print sources. The first publication (following the March 5 *Massachusetts Spy* report of the March 1 murder and the arrest of "seven capitally concerned" citizens) was the publication of Joshua Spooner's funeral sermon. The Reverend Nathan Fiske delivered, and Isaiah Thomas and Timothy Fleet published, *A Sermon Preached at Brookfield March 6, 1778*. Fiske's sermon was quite damning to Bathsheba, as he called the murder "so premeditated, so aggravated, [and] so horrid [that its like was] never perpetrated in America, and . . . [was] almost without parallel in the known world" (Fiske, 1778, p. 6). Fiske's sermon was reprinted twice that year, once by Danvers printer Ezekiel Russell and again by Norwich, Connecticut printers Green and Spooner.

Between March 2 and the July 2 execution, two ballads were published: *The Cruel Murder Or a Mournful Poem Occasioned by Sentence of Death being passe'd upon William Brooks, James Buchanan, Ezra Ross and Bathsheba Spooner*, was published by a Boston printer. A second ballad appeared in the same year, also out of Boston, under a slightly different title, and was probably a reprint. The largest production by far was *The Dying Declaration of James*

Buchanan, Ezra Ross, and William Brooks. The same basic information enjoyed publication in at least six editions. The first publication was a broadside published by Worcester printer Isaiah Thomas. It was republished as an eight-page chapbook, *The Dying Declaration of James Buchanan, Ezra Ross, and William Brooks*, probably also by Thomas. On June 11, *The Massachusetts Spy* published what amounted to an advertisement for Isaiah Thomas' broadside, "The Dying Declaration of James Buchanan, Ezra Ross, and William Brooks, Who were executed at Worcester, July 2, 1778, for the Murder of Mr. Joshua Spooner" that Thomas intended to sell the day of the execution for two shillings. Sold along with a one-shilling poem concerning the tragedy, Thomas surely had high hopes for the community interest and subsequent marketability of a quadruple hanging.

The next four editions changed the title from *The Dying Declaration* to *The Last Words and Dying Speech of James Buchanan, Ezra Ross, and William Brooks*. The first broadside, titled *The Last Words*, was published by Boston printers Draper and Folsom. With slight variations, this broadside was published again in 1778 in Boston. This version of the broadside was published twice more, probably in Boston in 1778 after July 2, as the editions now included a statement as to Bathsheba's conviction and execution.

Although Bathsheba never made a public confession or dying speech, as none appear in print, she was highlighted in Thaddeus Maccarty's published execution sermon, *The Guilt of Innocent Blood Put Away*, in the section *ACCOUNT of those PRISONERS in Their LAST STAGE*. Published by Isaiah Thomas, this account, with additions, was soon republished by Norwich, Connecticut printer John Trumbull. As well, the original section of Maccarty's *Innocent Blood* was separately published by an unknown printer as *The Rev. Mr. Maccarty's Account of the Behavior of Mrs. Spooner after her Commitment and Condemnation for being Accessory in the Murder of her Husband at Brookfield*. Reverend Ebenezer Parkman, a minister from the neighboring community of Westborough, visited the prisoners and, besides keeping a journal of his impressions, published his July 5 postexecution sermon, *The Adultress Will Hunt for the Precious Life* (1778) in which he denounces Bathsheba as the worst sort of "Evil woman."

Throughout the next century, the case would continue to garner attention. In the second volume of Peleg Chandler's *American Criminal Trials* (Boston, 1844, pp. 1–58), Chandler notes the case's importance as the first American capital trial. Bathsheba Spooner was also the subject of Samuel Swett Green's October 22, 1888, remarks to the annual meeting of the American Antiquarian Society. Green, a distant relation to Bathsheba, offered his remarks as a "defence [*sic*] of her memory" (1889, p. 2), the basic argument of which attempts to substantiate what her lawyer, Levi Lincoln, attempted to prove almost a century earlier, namely that Bathsheba was insane. Relying mainly on family lore, he places great importance on the fact that insanity ran in the family and that Bathsheba must surely have been insane to have had an affair with the young Ross.

Bathsheba Spooner is commonly believed to have been the last woman hanged in Massachusetts; however, there are at least two later cases, that of Rachel Wall in 1789 for piracy, and of Mary Johnson in 1831 for murder. This belief about Spooner seems to have stemmed from the 1899 article by feminist Elizabeth Cady Stanton, "The Fatal Mistake that Stopped the Hanging of Women in Massachusetts," that was published in the *New York World*. The fatal mistake, of course, was that Bathsheba was indeed pregnant, as she had claimed.

The twentieth century also saw an interest in the case. Editor John D. Lawson's *American State Trials* (1914) examined the case in "The Trial of Bathsheba Spooner, William Brooks, James Buchanan and Ezra Ross for the Murder of Joshua Spooner, Massachusetts, 1778" (1914, pp. 175–201). The case was fictionalized by Ester Forbes, an author of historical fiction. Her treatment of the case in *The General's Lady* (1938) was delicate, as the Bathsheba she created was innocent of not only murder but also of adultery. As well, in an era of sensationalistic examinations of historical murders, Edmund Pearson, in *Instigation of the Devil* (1930) and Edward Rowe Snow, in *Piracy, Mutiny, and Murder* (1959) each included chapters on the case.

The Spooner case has enjoyed not only legal, journalistic, religious, and fictitious treatments, but has also been explored on the airwaves as well. During the 1953–1954 broadcast season, CBS launched a new thirty-minute radio series, titled *Crime Classics*, that was broadcast on Monday evenings at 8 p.m., produced by Elliot Lewis and hosted by Lou Merrill, as the fictitious host Thomas Hyland. Although it lasted only a season, it is notable here for its audition episode, "The Crime of Bathsheba Spooner, the First Woman to be Tried in the U.S.," which was aired on December 3, 1952.

Although incorrect on several key points (such as Joshua Spooner's age), the Spooner case has been briefly examined in *Annals of Murder* (1961), *Hang By The Neck* (1967), *The Encyclopedia of American Crime* (1982), *The Encyclopedia of World Crime* (1990), and the *Dictionary of Culprits and Criminals* (1995). The most current and extensive treatment of this case is the book-length historical study by Deborah Navas, in *Murdered By His Wife: An Absorbing Tale of Crime and Punishment in Eighteenth-Century Massachusetts* (1999). A modern reprint of the first broadside publication is included in Daniel E. Williams's *Pillars of Salt: An Anthology of Early American Criminal Narratives* (1993) and includes an extensive publication history of the works in this case. Mention has been made of the Spooner case in most of the twentieth century's studies of crime and murder, for instance, in Ann Jones' *Women Who Kill* (1996) and Karen Halttunen's *Murder Most Foul: The Killer and the American Gothic Imagination* (1998).

CULTURAL CONCERNS AND SEXUALITY OF THE TIME

This case fascinated and intrigued readers almost certainly because of its blatant and feverish illicit sexuality, its daring (if foolish) murder plot, its ultimate destruction of the marriage contract, and its glance at the criminal behavior of loyalists honestly and rightly punished by independent Americans. The political connections and concerns are fairly obvious; as such, the cultural concerns about marriage and sexuality are worth further consideration here. Although some historians have proposed that "escape from an unhappy marriage was virtually impossible" (Navas, 1999, p. 29), it was certainly not unheard of. Recent studies, particularly those of Dayton (1995) and Cott (1976) offer theories of the rising acceptance of divorce in a revolutionary society that was embracing the ideology of romantic love.[6] For Bathsheba, it would, however, have been legally difficult to maintain charges of abuse or adultery against her husband when she herself was suspect on these same charges. Her remaining choice, impotency, would have been more than difficult for a pregnant woman to prove without substantiating her own adultery. Her case for possible divorce was even further injured when one considers the possibility of a hated Tory general's daughter divorcing a prominent patriot. Her pregnancy, however, threw the possibility of divorce or departure into the realm of fantasy. Her speed in accomplishing the act seems to imply that Bathsheba recognized the importance of having Spooner dead before she began to show. Although technically possible, Bathsheba certainly would not have feared for her life if convicted of adultery. The only death suffered for adultery seems have been the March 21, 1643 hanging of an eighteen-year-old Massachusetts woman, Mary Latham. Bathsheba could certainly, however, have feared "the brutal tar-and-feathering of loyalists" that was "commonplace" given the "rabid anti-Tory sentiment prevalent through Massachusetts" (Navas, 1999, p. 41). Bathsheba's punishment would likely have been thirty lashes on her bare back in the public square. Perhaps though, to a proud and arrogant woman, such public humiliations would have been more devastating than the gallows. Could she have managed to divorce her husband, Bathsheba would, however, have been dispossessed of the wealth and lifestyle she had enjoyed her entire life. Prior to the murder of her husband, Bathsheba reputedly told neighbors that she wanted to leave

Joshua to go find "her sister" or "her Daddy" (Navas, 1999, p. 127; Foster, 1778). To have been driven to plot her husband's death speaks volumes about Bathsheba's desperation and her priorities. It also reinforces concerns about the importance of marriage grounded in love and respect, and highlights the necessary concerns about female sexuality.

Although the concept of a sexual murder is mostly a twentieth-century one, the early republic was beginning to experience a degree of tension and conflict concerning sexuality. Sexual uncleanness had, of course, been a tangential matter in early American literature; however, sexual relations were generally not detailed or seen as motivation for murder. However, by the time of the Revolution, earlier familial, religious, and community control of reproduction and sexual activity began to become less regulated and enforceable. Romantic ideals, emotional intimacy, and the physical aspects of relationships began to become major issues for citizens, as did the notion that sex beyond procreation could be spiritual and pleasurable. As sex became part of the cultural discourse, it became increasingly important to understand the nature of sexuality, its origins, and its manifestations. Included in this confusion was a growing fear regarding women's sexual liability, weakness, and susceptibility. For this new country, sexuality offered "both the promise and the potential threat of sexual intimacy. And the popular literature of murder captured both" (Halttunen, 1998, p. 178).

The locus of most of this concern over power and control invariably fell on the shoulders of women. Then, even much more than now, the sexual history of a female murder victim or a female murderess was paramount. Situations in which passionless women were the chaste and innocent victims of cruel murder and were to be pitied; or where the women were prostitutes, depraved and devoid of morality and therefore completely open to mistreatment, were clear-cut. The third category, however, was where danger resided. In this category, once-innocent women, should they choose to abandon their passionless nature, ran the risk of falling into a whirlpool of vice. To submit to lust or to give into her passion catapulted Bathsheba Spooner, and others like her, into the category of "fallen woman" and into the cruel hands of fate. Such a corruption and degradation generally had but one result—death. Death came either at one's own hand, at the hand of one's seducer, or figuratively (and literally) at the hands of a society bent on expulsion and control.

The rhetoric surrounding women, sexuality, and murder was fervent and unyielding. Cautionary tales of seduction began to surface in narratives, fiction, editorials, magazine articles, and in poetry. As Halttunen has noted, "these fears [of women's sexuality] were especially loaded because of the ideological burden placed on womanhood by 'republican motherhood,' which made mothers responsible for the future of the American political system, and the doctrine of separate spheres, which affirmed and required women's moral superiority to men. The new ideals set aside earlier views of women as the 'weaker vessels,' more susceptible than men to succumbing to their own lustful passions" (p. 177). Women's virtuous moral superiority was achieved and demonstrated through self-control and restraint and resulted in the required and much lauded *passionlessness* that would keep them safe and, by extension, controlled.

The American Revolution sparked organizational, institutional, religious, and scientific shifts in thought that further secularized the culture. Exposed in this void were the crumbling community and religious sexual regulations and the deeply conflicted sexual morality. This was accompanied by a burgeoning fear that women's sexuality was at odds with the new ideal of "republican motherhood" and the accompanying vision of woman as "passionless." Accounts of sexual murder became progressively more popular as the culture struggled to define how female sexual behavior contributed to the new republic's escalating concerns over sexual order and disarray. This sexual disarray was ultimately exposed through the tales of female killers. Generally portrayed as passionate (i.e., sexual) and controlling, these women illustrated the dangers of the sexually powerful woman. Narratives such as those about Bathsheba Spooner sought to reinforce sexual order by identifying and defining appropriate roles and attributes for married women.

NOTES

1. D. Navas's book-length study of the Spooner case reveals an interesting chalk drawing discovered at the Bigelow-Temple tavern in West Boylston, Massachusetts. The drawing on the attic walls shows Bathsheba with a man (either Ross or the hangman) as she stands in her wedding dress. As Navas correctly points out, Bathsheba probably wore her high-waisted wedding dress to either "accommodate her pregnancy" or to demonstrate the irony inherent in the situation (1999, p. 105).

2. Bathsheba Bourne was born November 11, 1704. For detailed information concerning Bathsheba and Timothy Ruggles' family histories, see Navas (1999, chap. 3, pp. 14–28).

3. The following quotations are taken from court documents and trial notes primarily housed in the record books of the Superior Court of Judicature, 1775–1780, housed in Massachusetts State Archives in Boston, and published for the first time in Navas (1999).

4. The following quotations are taken from court documents and trial notes primarily housed in the record books of the Superior Court of Judicature, 1775–1780, housed in Massachusetts State Archives in Boston, and published for the first time in Navas (1999).

5. The Boston newspapers the *Independent Chronicle* and the *Continental Journal* republished *The Massachusetts Spy*'s May 7 account on April 30 and May 7, respectively. The *Boston Gazette* also mentioned the case on March 9 and July 6, primarily highlighting the fact that Bathsheba was the daughter of Timothy Ruggles.

6. In some cases, the developing value of romantic love tragically intersected with the notions of a compassionate marriage. While valued, romantic love and passion were also seen as a dangerous influence often beyond the restraint of individuals. Also, the "absence of love and affection," and its subsequent complaint of unhappiness within a marriage, was more frequently recognized as acceptable "evidence that a marriage was not a normal one," some individuals opted to avoid the court system (Kerber, 1997, p. 175).

REFERENCES

Bloch, R. H. (2003). Changing conceptions of sexuality and romance in eighteenth-century America. *William and Mary Quarterly, 60,* 13–42.

Buchanan, et al. (1778). *The dying declaration of James Buchanan, Ezra Ross and William Brooks.* Worcester, MA: I. Thomas.

Bullock, C. (1939). *The Bathsheba Spooner murder case.* Worcester, MA: American Antiquarian Society.

Chandler, P. W. (1844). Trial of Mrs. Spooner and others. In *American criminal trials* (pp. 2–58). Vol. 2. Freeport, NY: T. H. Carter.

Cohen, D. A. (1993). *Pillars of salt, monuments of grace: New England crime literature and the origins of American popular culture, 1674–1860.* Oxford: Oxford University Press. Coroner's jury report. (1778, March 3). Miscellaneous manuscript collection. Boston: American Antiquarian Society.

Cott, N. F. (1976). Divorce and the changing status of women in eighteenth-century Massachusetts. *William and Mary Quarterly, 33,* 3d Ser., 586–614.

Cushing, Chief Justice W. (1778). Notes of cases decided in the Superior and Supreme Judicial Courts of Massachusetts, from 1772–1789, Worcester, April term, A. D. 1778. MS2141, MSS bound manuscript collection. Cambridge, MA: Harvard Law School Library.

Dayton, C. H. (1995). *Women before the bar: Gender, law, and society in Connecticut, 1639–1789.* Chapel Hill: University of North Carolina Press.

Fiske, N. (1778). *Sermon on the tragical death of Mr. Spooner.* Boston: Thomas and John Fleet.

Forbes, E. (1938). *The general's lady.* New York: Harcourt Brace.

Foster, Judge J. (1778). Notes on the trial of Bathsheba Spooner, 1778. Foster family papers, box 1, folder 3. Worcester, MA: American Antiquarian Society.

Friedman, L. M. (1993). *Crime and punishment in American history.* New York: Harper Collins.

Green, S. S. (1889). *Bathsheba Spooner: Incidental remarks made at the annual meeting of the American Antiquarian Society, Worcester, October 22, 1888.* Worcester, MA: Charles Hamilton.

Halttunen, K. (1998). *Murder most foul: The killer and the American gothic imagination.* Cambridge: Harvard University Press.

Indictment. (1778). April term, 1778. Superior Court records. Boston: Massachusetts State Archives.

Kerber, L. (1997). *Women in the Republic: Intellect & ideology in Revolutionary War America.* Chapel Hill, NC: University of North Carolina Press.

Lewis, J. (1987). The republican wife: virtue and seduction in the early republic. *William and Mary Quarterly, 44,* 689–721.

Lincoln, L. Minutes in the case of the murder of Mr. Spooner. Lincoln family papers, 1776–1820, Octavo Vol. 50. Worcester, MA: American Antiquarian Society.

Maccarty, T. (1778a). The guilt of innocent blood put away. Sermon preached July 2, 1778, with appendix, "Account of the behavior of Mrs. Spooner after her commitment and condemnation fro being accessory in the Murder of her husband at Brookfield, March 1, 1778." Worcester, MA: I. Thomas.

Maccarty, T. (1778b). Reverend Maccarty's final plea to the Council supporting Bathsheba's pregnancy, 26 June 1778. Executive council records. Boston: Massachusetts State Archives.

Massachusetts General Court. (1989). *Journals of the House of Representatives of Massachusetts,* Vol. 54. Boston: Massachusetts Historical Society.

The Massachusetts Spy. (1778, March 5, May 7, June 2, 11, 25, July 2, 9, August 6). Early American newspapers collection. Worcester, MA: American Antiquarian Society.

A mournful poem: Occasioned by sentence of death being pass'd upon William Brooks, James Buchanan, Ezra Ross and Bathsheba Spooner, of Brookfield, and who were all executed at Worcester on Thursday the 2nd Day of July 1778. (1778). Boston.

Nash, J. R. (1990). *Encyclopedia of world crime* (p. 2832). Vol. 4. Wilmette, IL: CrimeBooks.

Navas, D. (1999). *Murdered by his wife: A history with documentation of the Joshua Spooner murder and execution of his wife, Bathsheba, who was hanged in Worcester, Massachusetts, 2 July 1778.* Amherst, MA: University of Massachusetts Press.

Opinion of midwives, second examination. (1778, June 27). Executive records, revolutionary council papers, 1777–1778. Boston: Massachusetts State Archives.

Order for Suspension of Sentence. (1778). May 28, 1778 to Thursday, the 2nd day of July. Executive Records, Revolutionary Council Papers, 1777–1778. Boston: Massachusetts State Archives.

Paine, R. T. (1778). Minutes of trial and law cases, 1777–1778. Robert Treat Paine papers. Boston: Massachusetts Historical Society.

Parkman, Rev. E. (1778). The adultress will hunt for precious life. Sermon preached at Westborough, 5 July 1778. Parkman family papers, Octavo Vol. 5, box 1, folder 7. Worcester, MA: American Antiquarian Society.

Petition of Ross family. (1778, May 26). Executive records, revolutionary council papers, 1777–1778. Boston: Massachusetts State Archives.

Record book of the executive council. (1778). Refusal to grant Bathsheba's petition for a stay of execution, 23 June 1778. Executive records, revolutionary council papers, 1777–1778. Boston: Massachusetts State Archives.

Record book of the Superior Court of Judicature. (1778). 1775–1780. Executive records, revolutionary council papers, 1777–1778. Boston: Massachusetts State Archives.

Return of the sheriff, first examination writ. (1778, July 6). Executive records, revolutionary council papers, 1777–1778. Boston: Massachusetts State Archives.

Sargeant, N. P. "Indictment of William Brooks, James Buchanan, & Ezra Ross for the Murder of Joshua Spooner on the 1st Day of March at Brookfield & Bathsheba Spooner as accessory before the fact." Nathaniel Sargeant Casebook. Salem: Peabody-Essex Museum.

Shipton, C. K. (1933). *Sibley's Harvard graduates*. Cambridge, MA: Harvard University Press.

Sifakis, C. (1982). *The encyclopedia of American crime*. New York: Facts On File.

Stanton, E. C. (1899). The fatal mistake that stopped the hanging of women in Massachusetts. *New York World*.

7

The Whiskey Rebellion: Western Settlers Challenge Federal Power

Brandon K. Webster and Jennifer H. Childress

In 1794, the wild, wild West was the other side of the Allegheny Mountains in Pennsylvania. That is where this account centers. For it is there that the most violent, organized, and threatening resistance to the sovereignty of the United States took shape. The residents of western Pennsylvania—who would come to take up arms against their government—were largely immigrants from Scotland and Ireland. They lived a hardscrabble life of subsistence farming and warring against French settlers and American Indians. They received little support from the national government, which was far removed from their daily lives by both the transportation of the day and the settlers' own attitudes of rigid self-reliance.

These two facts would play a major role in the crimes committed by the frontiersmen, for their isolation from the authority of the central government, both geographical and mental, led to the motive and perceived opportunity for their crime. The inhabitants of the western frontier believed the laws created in the nation's capital did not apply to them and that they could not be forced into recognizing them. They were wrong on both counts.

The law that proved the most difficult for inhabitants of the frontier to abide by was a tax placed on the manufacture, sale, and use of liquor.

The tarring and feathering of a tax collector at Pigeon Creek, Washington County, Pennsylvania, during the Whiskey Rebellion in 1794. (The Granger Collection, New York)

Advocated by Alexander Hamilton, a strong proponent of central government and the first secretary of the treasury, the law was passed by the U.S. Congress in 1791 as a means of providing revenue for the young country.

There were many reasons why the settlers in the western portion of the country found the tax odious. First, the geographical isolation of the frontiersmen made transporting their goods to market untenable. Their solution was to distill the fruit of their labor (grains) into whiskey. Since all goods had to be transported on foot or horseback over mountains and through forests back east to market, transporting the same volume of whiskey as grain was much more economical. Indeed, the farmers who raised the grains and distilled the spirits traded their goods for necessities (such as iron or salt) they could not produce on their farms (Fogelson and Rubenstein, 1969).

In addition to the tax on the settlers' only "cash crop" being a burden, the mechanism of tax collection itself was also offensive to the frontiersmen. To collect the tax, agents of the state had to visit and inspect the homes of individual people known to be, or suspected of, distilling their own liquor. This intrusion was more than many of the rugged individualists who resided on the far reaches of civilization could bear.

Finally, there was the common belief that the tax was unfair. The tax was more lenient on larger distillers who were able to make a single annual payment, while individuals had to make payments throughout the year and at a rate that was almost fifty percent higher (National Park Service, 2003). Even among farmers, the rate was based on the volume, not value, of the product, and since the cost of transporting the liquor east was so high, whiskey on the east side of the nation was worth double the price of the same whiskey on the frontier, but was nonetheless taxed at the same rate. Additionally, the tax was required to be paid in cash, which conflicted with the lifestyle of settlers who traded and bartered for all that they needed. Last, the settlers feared that revenue raised by the tax would be used to support an army that would be used against them, a worry that proved well founded.

THE PARTICIPANTS: FRONTIERSMEN OF THE EARLY WEST

In this case, as with many other entries in this volume, the crime in question did not constitute a single act. Rather, the criminal behavior was spread in space and time over years and hundreds of miles. Tax collectors were assaulted and battered, and disruptions of the peace were reported along the frontier from New York to Nashville (Slaughter, 1986). However, the defining incident of the Whiskey Rebellion occurred on July 16, 1794, in western Pennsylvania. It took place at the home of a man named John Neville, who was a member of the landed gentry and a friend of George Washington. Neville was a veteran of the French and Indian War (1754–1763) and found his way to western Pennsylvania as a member of General Edward Braddock's expedition during that conflict. After the war, Neville stayed and held the office of sheriff for years in a county along the frontier. And with the help of his son Presley, Neville acquired a great deal of land and slaves in Pennsylvania, Ohio, Kentucky, and Virginia (Slaughter, 1986).

By 1794, John Neville had become regional supervisor for the collection of tax on distilled spirits in western Pennsylvania. The leniency with which opposition to the whiskey tax had been met since its inception in 1791 was vanishing; after three years of indulging settlers and rewriting the whiskey tax law, the federal government tired of coddling dissenters. Alexander Hamilton believed enough time had passed since the enactment of the law to allow opponents of the tax to either fall in line or be identified as unrepentant subversives. Additionally, government officials faced growing criticism back east from distillers who paid the tax while the western frontiersmen dodged it. These factors lead to a renewed vigor in tax collection and prosecution of tax evaders.

In this charged atmosphere, U.S. District Attorney William Rawle garnered summons for more than fifty people suspected of tax evasion in Pennsylvania. The responsibilities of serving the summons fell to U.S. Marshal David Lenox, who at first met no opposition to the completion of his duties. However, the situation changed dramatically when Lenox reached the westernmost part of Pennsylvania and took up with John Neville.

Neville, who was still referred to as "General" by locals, was despised for his occupation of tax collector. Neville agreed to act as guide to the marshal as Lenox went about his business of delivering summons. For some settlers it was more than they could stand to be met on their doorsteps by a tax collector and a U.S. marshal who ordered them to both make payments on back taxes and report to Philadelphia for a court hearing that would cause the neglect of their family, livestock, and crops.

At this critical juncture, a false rumor influenced the further unraveling of events. When Neville and Lenox served one William Miller a summons to appear in a Philadelphia federal court, somehow the rumor got started that federal agents were forcibly taking settlers to Philadelphia. The first people to hear this rumor and act on it were a group of men working in a field near Miller's home. They rushed to what they believed was Miller's defense with muskets and pitchforks. Once there, the mob was surprised to find that no one was being kidnapped, but it was too late. The rumor that citizens were being whisked away to stand trial on the other side of the state had already spread to other ears.

Ironically, one audience to hear the rumor and respond with outrage at what they saw as a violation of the Constitution was a militia gathered in response to President Washington's plea for fighters to oppose American Indian attacks. The militia decided to pursue and capture the marshal and have him answer the accusations made against the government and him. On the basis of the false rumor, the militia converged on Neville's home, where they mistakenly believed the marshal was still staying. Unbeknownst to the militia, Lenox had already left for Pittsburgh (having completed his duties). The fact that the militia was operating on misinformation regarding both the whereabouts of the marshal and his actions in western Pennsylvania led to the tragedy of the Whiskey Rebellion.

THE CRIME: THE WHISKEY REBELLION

Near dawn on July 16, 1794, about forty armed members of the Mingo Creek militia surrounded the home of John Neville, the regional supervisor of the excise tax on distilled spirits. Neville heard people milling around outside his domicile and opened his door to confront them. While the mob had no plans for Neville (it was David Lenox they were after), they lied to Neville about their identity and purpose, saying they were friends who meant to guard him. Sensing the dishonesty of the mob, Neville ordered the crowd to disperse and fired his musket, fatally wounding Oliver Miller, son of William Miller—the same settler whose defiance of the summons had helped spark the rebellion (Bradford House, 2003). The mob returned fire and meant to take the home by force, but Neville was prepared for them. Having previously armed the slaves on his estate, he commanded them as he had soldiers in the French and Indian War. The slaves were in positions behind the mob, where the slave quarters stood. Realizing they were surrounded, the mob fled the scene, but not before sustaining more casualties.

After being routed at Neville's home, the militiamen regrouped at nearby Couche's Fort. The slaying of Oliver Miller had the effect of polarizing the feelings of both antitax zealots and middle-of-the-road bystanders against the government, which had come to be personified by General Neville. It was this change in dynamics, from a situation where tax evasion was largely the stuff of middle-class immigrants to a cause supported by the most respected members of frontier society and backed by popular support, that posed the most menacing threat to the rule of the U.S. government.

Meanwhile, General Neville knew that while the battle may have been won, he was in danger of losing the war for his livelihood and his life. After the beaten militiamen fled from his home, Neville sent urgent requests for reinforcements to the county sheriff, local militia, and other government officials. The only one to heed his call was Major James Kirkpatrick, who arrived at Neville's estate with ten soldiers from Fort Pitt (located in the center of the village of Pittsburgh).

The next day (July 17, 1794), the rebels returned to Neville's home, increased in strength tenfold (with reports varying from 400 to 800 people). The nature of the crowd had also changed from a hastily gathered mob to a military force complete with drummers and color bearers. The manner of their arrival—in military parade—spoke volumes of both the contempt settlers held for "easterners" (people living in the more developed eastern side of the country) and the competition for legitimacy that antiestablishment views posed to the laws written by eastern leaders.

At the cessation of their parade, the militiamen ordered Neville to surrender himself and his office as tax collector. But Neville had already been smuggled out of his residence by Major Kirkpatrick. When the chief rebel leader, James McFarlane, was informed by Kirkpatrick that General Neville had fled, McFarlane ordered the Neville household to be evacuated and the soldiers to surrender their arms. The major offered to allow the home to be searched and to surrender any government documents relating to tax code violations, in order to prevent further violence.

But this was not enough for McFarlane and the rebels, and with their swollen numbers and swollen pride they began to set fire to the out-buildings surrounding the Neville home. Major Kirkpatrick first acted to evacuate the rest of General Neville's family, and then with ten soldiers and a small number of armed slaves, took up defensive positions against the larger rebel force. The militia members continued to burn barns, dairies, and slave quarters, while being fired upon by the defenders.

At some point McFarlane heard, or thought he heard, pleas to restart the negotiations from the soldiers occupying the Neville residence. When McFarlane approached the house to ascertain whether the defenders were ready to meet the militia's demands, he was shot and killed by someone from within the home. This infuriated the insurgents who were sure that McFarlane had been killed under a false banner of truce.

James McFarlane was a veteran of the Revolutionary War and an impor-tant member of western/frontier society. With his death, especially under such circumstances, the rebels surged forward and set fire to the kitchen, the closest building to the house proper. At this point, the soldiers and slaves inside the Neville homestead felt the heat (metaphorically and literally) and subsequently surrendered.

The insurgents' victory over the federal troops and James McFarlane's martyrdom had the effect of again changing the dynamics of the conflict. The victory reenergized the radical faction of settlers who wanted to secede from the East, and silenced or swayed voices of opposition in their rank. Also, the ironic death of James McFarlane, a man who had fought against unfair taxation in the Revolutionary War, was not lost on any Westerner.

While some rebels besieged the Neville homestead, others pursued Marshal Lenox on his way to the village of Pittsburgh. Lenox, unaware of the central role the false rumor about his kidnapping of settlers had had on the frontier, was seized outside of Pittsburgh. Once taken prisoner, Lenox was led to Couche's Fort, the base of the rebels and the place where James McFarlane's body lay in state. At Couche's Fort, the rebels threatened the marshal's life and forced him to swear an oath on McFarlane's beard to never inform against the rebels, to never support the whiskey tax, and to never return to the western side of the Allegany Mountains (Slaughter, 1986).

This forced oath-taking and allegiance-making was a tactic that would be used repeatedly by the mob. When members of the western intellectual elite refused to endorse the rebellion or seemed lukewarm about its objectives, they were threatened and ordered to speak at rallies in favor of the rebels' actions. Even dissenters among common settlers and distillers found themselves threatened in open letters signed "Tom the Tinker" (meaning *gypsy* or *wanderer* to the Scots-Irish).

Despite these fissures in their base, the radical antigovernment rebels made plans to expand their insurrection and to raid Pittsburgh. To accomplish their objective, the rebel leaders called for volunteers to come forward and join their militia. The response of almost 7,000 desperately poor frontier people would again change the dynamic of the conflict and shift the focus of the opposition.

Originally the civil disobedience and outright criminal behavior that had confronted the whiskey tax (since its passage three years earlier) had been the work of land-owning and still-owning settlers. In 1794, owning property and the machinery necessary to distill liquor distinguished someone as being middle class. However, after General Neville's home was sacked and a U.S. marshal taken prisoner, 7,000 disenfranchised, landless laborers responded to the call to arms against the eastern establishment.

In order to arm their agrarian army, rebel leaders decided they must take Fort Fayette and its store of weapons and munitions. However, Fort Fayette proved a much harder target than the Neville household. Faced with a serious fight, the rebel leaders lost their nerve, and their followers began to scatter. Unfortunately, the communication and intelligence-gathering technology of the late eighteenth century left the leaders of the eastern United States with the impression that the Whiskey Rebellion was just getting underway. In fact, the rebellion had already reached its high-water mark and would only diminish further with time.

THE RESPONSE OF THE STATE: THE WATERMELON ARMY

The Whiskey Rebellion must be understood as an event of international significance. Attempts to characterize it as a backwoods rebellion or isolated insurrection are simply wrong. Not only was rebellion spread up and down the frontier, but the rebels also courted alliances with England and Spain, deadly rivals of the United States with landholdings of their own in North America. In this context of armed confrontations centering in western Pennsylvania and rebels making overtures to the nation's enemies, President Washington and other members of the federal government had reason to be concerned. The true brilliance on the part of the nation's leadership was to see the Whiskey Rebellion as an opportunity—an opportunity to change the negative image it had garnered by failing to both protect settlers from Native American attacks and to secure land and water navigation rights from foreign powers.

Washington now had a chance to prove the federal government capable of executing its laws within its territory. The first step in demonstrating the national government's sovereignty was to be granted certification by a U.S. Supreme Court justice that the use of federal troops against American citizens was justified. Nineteen days after the first attack by militiamen on John Neville's home, Justice James Wilson made legal the use of U.S. soldiers to put down the rebellion in western Pennsylvania. However, this first step only made military action against settlers and frontiersmen a legal possibility. Washington, as any other leader who had to answer to the electorate, had also to concern himself with making military action politically feasible. His administration accomplished this by sending an envoy of negotiators into rebel territory.

The envoy was made up of Pennsylvania Supreme Court Justice Jasper Yates, Pennsylvania Senator James Ross, and U.S. Attorney General William Bradford. These men were granted the power to confer amnesty for all offenses committed against the United States thus far, if only the rebels laid down their arms and swore to no longer protest the whiskey tax. However, everyone involved on the federal government's side feared that dragging out the negotiation might only give the revolutionaries more time to plot, prepare, and to court foreign powers.

Once in western Pennsylvania, the envoy found that opinions were divided among moderates (who opposed the whiskey tax to varying degrees) and radicals (who called for a violent separation from the Union). The talks proceeded at a labored pace. The negotiators for the federal government were more comfortable preparing to meet the challenge of the radicals than waiting for peace with the moderates. In fact, the correspondence between government negotiator William Bradford and Secretary Hamilton illustrates that Bradford believed the United States should be prepared to make war in western Pennsylvania no matter what conclusion the peace talks came to.

Indeed, many were making the case to Washington that the federal government had to act and act immediately. One final factor that probably helped the president make his decision was his personal knowledge of the people and territory of the frontier. He had served in that part of the country during the French and Indian War and knew that the frontiersmen would not be swayed by negotiators, and that if he delayed any longer the U.S. forces could be cut off for months by bad weather in the wilderness.

The government set a goal of garnering and equipping an army of 13,000 from the eastern portion of the United States. However, the army was severely divided by class, ethnicity, and citizenship status. This division was so discernible that the federal government's foray into the frontier resembled both a king's crusade and a peasant's crusade, with well-equipped middle- and upper-class men joining to further their personal objectives or political ideology and recent immigrants joining out of economic desperation or because they were drafted. The upper-class leadership of the federal army led to the rebels giving it a pejorative nickname—the Watermelon Army—so named because the frontiersmen considered watermelon an eastern delicacy.

To help heal what ailed the army, and to further demonstrate the government's decisiveness, George Washington himself headed up the march toward western Pennsylvania. It would be the only time in American history that a sitting president led troops in military action. Washington hoped to boost morale, unite the army, and show not only Americans (east to west), but also foreign powers (who at the time still held part of modern-day America) that the young country was capable of self-governance and self-defense.

Almost three months after the confrontation between General Neville and Marshal Lenox with William Miller, representatives of the rebels met with the president as he and the army marched west and tried to persuade Washington that order was returning to western Pennsylvania and the situation did not require his or the army's presence. However, Washington believed events had gone too far, and that only a show of force could save the government's legitimacy. The rebels' representatives returned home to await the army's arrival. Washington, confident that the army was reasonably well prepared, left command to Harry Lee, father of future U.S. officer and Confederate General Robert E. Lee.

Upon arriving on the other side of the Allegheny Mountains, it became clear to the U.S. troops that no rebel army was going to meet them. This realization brought out the worst in some of the military personnel, with General "Blackbeard" White a notable example. White had frontiersmen pulled from their homes in the middle of the night, corralling them into an unfinished structure that provided no roof to shield the prisoners from falling sleet. The inmates were housed like this for several days without food or heat, then marched more than ten miles so that the process of determining who was a traitor and who was a patriot could begin.

Having already suffered much, the suspects (and witnesses) were brought before Secretary of the Treasury Alexander Hamilton and federal judges who had accompanied the army to the frontier. Hamilton and the other government officials hoped to capture and transport the leaders of the rebellion back east for prosecution. Fortuitously for themselves, the leaders of the most radical elements had not waited for the army's arrival, choosing instead to fade deeper back into the woods (and further encroach on Indian territory). Other subversives had signed the amnesty offers of the peace commission that was sent in before the army and thus were not available for prosecution. Ironically, this left the leaders of the moderate wing of the frontiersmen, who felt they had not wronged their country and therefore never bothered to take advantage of the amnesty offers.

One such leader of the settlers was Hugo M. Brackenridge, who before the rebellion was an attorney and prominent member of frontier society. In another twist of fate, he suggested to U.S. Marshal Lenox that he not accept help from General Neville, because Brackenridge believed it was unwise to associate federal law enforcement with the collection of taxes. However, Lenox had not heeded Brackenridge's advice, and both men would be taken prisoner because of it, though by different sides in the conflict.

Brackenridge's trial was a serious ordeal for the man, and after days of harsh questioning by Hamilton and others, he was sure he would be the fall guy for the entire Whiskey Rebellion. However, friends and family of John Neville testified that Brackenridge had been forced to support the rebellion under duress and had made attempts to quit the rebellion at risk to his life. Brackenridge's acquittal left the government without any insurrection leaders to make examples of; all had either escaped or accepted amnesty.

However, Hamilton and the other federal judges still tried to give a face to the insurgents. Only two of the thousands who participated in the unrest were found guilty of treason: John Mitchell and Philip Vigol. Mitchell had a very small farm and no distillery, while Vigol was completely without property. Neither man possessed the mental, social, or financial wherewithal to plot and organize a rebellion against the federal government, but nonetheless faced the death penalty because of their convictions. It was only a pardon from President Washington that saved them.

THE ACTIONS OF THE MEDIA

The media of the day played an important role in the unraveling of events surrounding the insurrection and the fame accorded to the Whiskey Rebellion. Before the rebellion began, local newspapers made sure that Congressional representatives from Pennsylvania followed popular sentiment and tried to defeat any domestic tax on whiskey by characterizing proponents of the tax as unpatriotic. It is important to note that newspapers of the day made no claim to impartiality; rather, papers marketed themselves to people of certain opinions and spun (slanted) the news according to their audience and/or the editors' political objectives.

While newspapers were unabashedly biased, they did serve as sounding boards for important debates of the day. The new republic wrestled with issues that we still have not resolved today (and probably will never definitively resolve). For instance, newspapers debated whether it was better to have more liberty at the expense of order, or more crime control to the detriment of due process. News correspondents, whether reporting from the frontier or the city, gave themselves pen names based on their stances on this continuing issue. Pseudonyms like "Peregrine Peaceable," "Order," and "A Friend of Liberty" were common for newspaper reporters to adopt (Slaughter, 1986, p. 194). So, a debate that had raged since the inception of the union found a new sticking point in the Whiskey Rebellion.

Were the insurgents liberty-loving patriots like those who fought and died in the Revolutionary War, or were they criminal subversives and anarchists bent on destroying the United States? The people who favored law and order saw the rebels as backstabbing immigrants who were not fit to live in a democratic society. Pro-government newspapers were full of descriptions of frontiersmen as indolent and ignorant animals.

Anti-federalist, pro-liberty papers lambasted the government as a tool of the upper class, who governed not for the commonwealth but for the benefit of the eastern elite. During the rebellion, western newspapers reported that the forced draft of poor immigrants living in the east to fight the immigrants who had settled west of the Alleghenies was the ultimate irony and insult to freedom. Pro-liberty newspapers questioned the legitimacy of the national government and the patriotism of the men who served in it. What is important to understand about the role of newspapers, both pro-order and pro-liberty, is that they questioned the motives of their opponents and painted them in a light that made detesting them possible. One of the most relevant social and political issues to come out of the Whiskey Rebellion is the recognition that characterizing people who hold contrary political views as animal-like or bearing ill-intention is disastrous to political dialogue, a necessity in a democratic form of government.

Another popular form of media from the late 1700s was the broadside. A broadside was like the front page of a newspaper with less text and more headlines. They were often printed anonymously or under pen names and attacked someone or something with very inflammatory rhetoric. Broadsides were posted in gathering places (such as taverns) and intersections of roads; or sometimes on private property if they were meant for an individual or family. This was done because broadsides were used not only to inform or convince, but also to threaten and harass. Broadsides were printed very early in the debates over taxation, and some antitax advocates printed "wanted" posters (broadsides) for tax collectors. One such broadside posted a decade before the open rebellion of 1794 offered a reward for the local taxman's scalp (Fogelson and Rubenstein, 1969).

As mentioned earlier, "Tom the Tinker" came onto the western scene during the rebellion. He was meant as a metaphorical big brother who would watch the settlers along the frontier to make sure they were united in opposing the whiskey tax. Any failure to bear arms against the government agents was sufficient cause for "Tom the Tinker" (or rather the men who used this pseudonym) to post a broadside threatening to destroy the distillery, burn the home, or take the life of the man who failed to yield the call for assistance.

EFFECTS OF THE WHISKEY REBELLION ON THE "WEST"

In this charged atmosphere of hatred and distrust, the Whiskey Rebellion both took shape and dissipated within several weeks. It may not have occurred in exactly this manner but for several stunning misconceptions and fatal coincidences. First of all, U.S. Marshal Lenox met no trouble in serving his summons until he took up with General Neville. If Lenox had not solicited or accepted Neville's help, the encounter with Miller wouldn't have spurred the rumor that government authorities were kidnapping settlers for trial in Philadelphia. If this false rumor had not been started at the same time that so many armed men were gathered for a meeting of the Mingo Creek militia, then tempers could have cooled and accurate information could have been gathered before the militia marched on Neville's home. If Neville had given into the militia's demands in order to clear up the misunderstandings, instead of firing into the crowd and killing a man, then the Whiskey Rebellion most likely could have been adverted. If upon the rebels' return the next day, they had been satisfied with searching the house for Lenox and taking papers associated with tax collection, the rebellion could have been limited to one day and one fatality. Instead, the rebellion lasted for weeks, with many lives ruined by either mob violence or the army's response to it.

However, it is misleading to purport that no insurrection would have occurred but for these bewildering set of circumstances. For indeed, some clash of ideologies between East and West was inevitable, considering the level of distrust and the vast differences in values and priorities. Any solution to the Whiskey Rebellion had to entail a mending of relations between Americans.

The détente between East and West was made possible by the changing social context on the frontier. If the social context had not changed, then surely some other matter of disagreement between East and West would have sparked another rebellion and required another military intervention. The factors that allowed the change in social context are as American as the Whiskey Rebellion. First, settlers and frontiersmen who chafed under the dominance of central government simply moved further west beyond its reach. This solution was not possible in the Old World (Europe) because there was no unexplored, uninhabited territory on the continent. The vast expanse of land that lay beyond the American nation's bounds in 1794 allowed rugged individualists to move further away from the encroaching civilization and lead life as they saw fit.

The drive of people westward meant that the frontier was also pushed west. Native Americans and foreign nationals who had made life so toilsome for the inhabitants of western Pennsylvania were repulsed by the migrating settlers. This meant that people who stayed in the counties of the far side of the state no longer had the burden of upholding the westernmost boundary of the nation.

The government remedied (although unintentionally) another major complaint of Westerners. The march against the whiskey rebels caused a great deal of government spending in that part of the country in support of the troops. The influx of cash helped introduce farmers living there to the modern cash market, instead of relying on trade and bartering.

Finally, just as the French and Indian War had introduced people to western Pennsylvania who decided to stay there after the conflict, so did the Whiskey Rebellion. Many members of the federal army sent to crush the insurrection fell in love with the countryside and decided it was a better place to raise a family than the urban squalor they had known on the eastern side of the country. So a new influx of settlers, who had more in common with the people they were sent to police than the people who marshaled their services, moved to areas formerly in turmoil.

BUILDING A UNIFIED COUNTRY THROUGH FAILURE AND RECONCILIATION

As mentioned previously, the most relevant social/political issue to come out of the Whiskey Rebellion was an understanding of the failure of political discourse. To be sure, the Whiskey Rebellion was sandwiched between two more notable failures of political discourse, the Revolutionary War (1775–1783) and the War between the States (1861–1865). These other conflicts have captured much of our attention, but instead of being distractions from the Whiskey Rebellion, they should be understood as parts of the larger context of insurrection.

The same type of suspicion and intolerance of different political ideas that led to the Whiskey Rebellion was also the cause of the War of Independence from England and the American Civil War. Indeed, while the casual observer may consider any one of these events an aberration, when taken as a whole we see that in American history, failure of the political process, followed by contentious (and potentially ruinous) infighting, followed in turn by reconciliation, is the norm. The only part of this statement that may seem presumptuous is the part referring to reconciliation.

Perhaps because this country was born out of the failure to reach peaceful compromise, or because of some greater failing of the human character, Americans have been damned to constantly repeating the above-mentioned cycle of violence. Indeed, more recent examples of the failure of the political process can be found. The tumult of the 1960s and the protests against the Vietnam War and in favor of civil rights, followed by the response of the state, are examples of political disagreements turning to political violence.

This cycle continued into the late twentieth century and early twenty-first century, with the government assault on David Koresh's followers in Waco, Texas, and the attack on Randy Weaver's family, who were survivalists involved in an eleven-day standoff with federal agents in Ruby Ridge, Idaho. Similarly, fear and distrust of the central government prompted Timothy McVeigh to bomb the Murrah Federal Building in Oklahoma City, killing 168 people on the two-year anniversary of the government attack on Waco. These are further examples of how a loss of faith in the political system can result in what has been called a Hobbesian state of nature, or an environment where might makes right and life is "nasty, brutish, and short" (Ebenstein and Ebenstein, 1991, p. 399).

To avoid this fate, the government must seek to avoid disenfranchisement of its people. If the body politic believes that laws and not people rule, then opposition is more likely to be peaceful, and ideas can exist in an open market where they are traded freely and without fear of repercussions. That President Washington and his administration were mindful of this fact is illustrated by their seeking of both judicial and popular approval and by first sending negotiators, not soldiers, to the frontier.

These last two facts are probably the most relevant legal issues to come out of the Whiskey Rebellion. History has recorded that the state tried to maintain a sense of legitimacy and conformity to the Constitution when confronted with outlaw insurgency. As Alexander Hamilton said when two civilians were mistakenly killed as the Watermelon Army moved east, "It is a very precious and important idea that those who are called out in support and defense of the laws should not give occasion or even pretext to impute to them infractions of the laws" (Slaughter, 1985, p. 206).

THE IMPACT ON LEGAL AND POPULAR CULTURE

The impact of the Whiskey Rebellion on legal culture is twofold. First is the tenet that law must also apply to those who seek to enforce it. The second is that the government should be firm with citizens while they are insurgent, but gentle after they have been brought back into line. The government's move to put down the rebellion would have surely failed if it had seemed the army was operating outside the law. Instead, the government tried to compensate those who helped feed the army and conducted fair trials of suspects. While suspects were rounded up in a harsh manner, the people on the frontier realized that the soldiers could not easily double as policemen; as such, the settlers expected a military rather than civil handling by authorities. Similarly, crops were trampled and stolen by marauding soldiers, but the government tried to make amends. This helped to reestablish goodwill where little had existed.

The other legal legacy of the Whiskey Rebellion was heeded in the next major internal conflict, the Civil War. The reconstruction of the South was much different than defeated insurgents could expect in other parts of the world. This made reconciliation between the former foes possible and ultimately led to a stronger union. The impact of the Whiskey Rebellion on legal culture in the United States may easily (and mistakenly) be attributed solely to the conflicts that followed it. The interregional conflicts that precipitated the rebellion and the solutions the government found (if only by happenstance) continue to inform legal thinking to this day.

The impact of the Whiskey Rebellion on popular culture had both positive and negative results. On the positive side, the immigrants who made western Pennsylvania their home contributed invaluably to the melting pot (or montage) that is the United States. The rebellion can also point to us the fact that in its impact, the frontier was not so far away for people who lived in the eastern United States. Indeed, this western insurrection illustrates that each part of the country was once a frontier for European settlers, who left behind a legacy of hard work and self-reliance.

One negative impact of the Whiskey Rebellion on popular culture is the persistent stereotype that people who live far from major cities are somehow less cultured or humane. This prejudice by easterners in the late 1700s made it possible for them to call up the army against their fellow citizens. And unfortunately in today's politically correct climate it is still (for some reason) more acceptable to ridicule the rural poor than their urban counterparts. Perhaps due in part to this stereotype, some residents of rural areas are very suspicious of outsiders. In turn, the closed nature of some rural communities has worked to stifle the economic development of these places, and thus the enterprising offspring of the inhabitants must move elsewhere to find success. This cycle is probably the biggest negative impact on popular culture of the Whiskey Rebellion.

One impact that has both positive and negative aspects is the earlier-mentioned migration of some settlers out of Pennsylvania and further west. Many of these farmers and distillers who desired to distance themselves from the central government moved to Kentucky and Tennessee, giving these states their rich tradition in whiskey-making. And when members of the French monarchy desired to see the American frontier (which at that time was Kentucky), the visit so impressed the whiskey distillers of that state that they gave their product the royal family's name, Bourbon (but that is another story).

REFERENCES

Boyd, S. R. (Ed.). (1985). *The Whiskey Rebellion: Past and present perspectives.* Westport, CT: Greenwood Press.

Bradford House. (2003). *The "murder" of Oliver Miller.* Retrieved from http://www.bradfordhouse.org/miller.htm

Castro, W. R. (1995). *The Supreme Court in the early republic: The chief of John Jay and Oliver Ellsworth.* Columbia, SC: University of South Carolina Press.

Ebenstein, W., and Ebenstein, A. O. (1991). *Great political thinkers: Plato to the present* (5th ed.). Fort Worth, TX: Harcourt Brace College Publishers.

Fogelson, R. M., and Rubenstein, R. E. (Eds.). (1969). *History of the western insurrection, 1794.* New York: Arno Press and the *New York Times.*

National Park Service. (2003). *The Whiskey Rebellion.* Retrieved from http://www.nps.gov/frhi/whiskreb.htm

Slaughter, T. P. (1986). *The Whiskey Rebellion: Frontier epilogue to the American Revolution.* New York: Oxford University Press.

8

The Treason Trial
of Aaron Burr:
America's Would-be Caesar

Joanne Barker

The trial of Aaron Burr for treason and high misdemeanor began in a Richmond, Virginia, courtroom on May 22, 1807, and ended on September 1, 1807, when the jury acquitted him. The foreman delivered the jury's conclusion by stating that "[w]e of the jury say that Aaron Burr is not proved to be guilty under this indictment by any evidence submitted to us. We therefore find him not guilty." The jury's unusual step of including its first qualified sentence—that the submitted evidence did not prove the charge—echoed the form of the traditional Scottish verdict "not proven." This carefully limited conclusion has been reflected in the ongoing and unresolved historical debate about Burr's guilt or innocence. Public opinion at the time, however, despite the judicial acquittal, convicted him of being a scoundrel and a wrongdoer, whatever the court's definition of treason. Because Burr's own letters from the time of the alleged conspiracy have been lost (Lomask, 1982, pp. xiii–xiv), it may not be possible ever to resolve decisively the question of Burr's intentions when he began his western adventure.

BACKGROUND: POLITICAL HISTORY
AND THE FAMOUS DUEL WITH HAMILTON

The trial was inevitably the focus of tremendous public attention. In addition to the charge of the notorious crime of treason, the characters

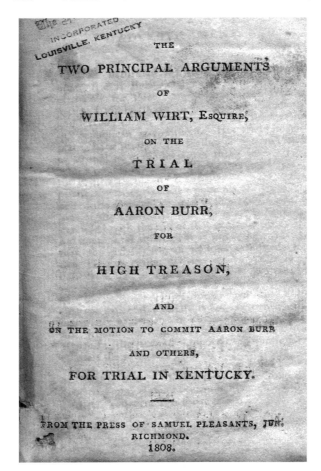

The two principal arguments of William Wirt, Esquire, on the trial of Aaron Burr for high treason and on the motion to commit Aaron Burr and others for trial in Kentucky. (Courtesy of Library of Congress)

involved were notable figures in American politics and government in the early nineteenth century, and the newspapers of the time followed the entire course of events closely. Aaron Burr, the central figure, had been vice president of the United States from 1801 to March 1805. He came from a prosperous and prominent New York family; his maternal grandfather was Jonathan Edwards, the famous Calvinist minister whose conversions in Northampton, Massachusetts, began the Great Awakening and who had been a president of the College of New Jersey (later renamed Princeton).

Burr's father, also named Aaron, had also been a president of the College of New Jersey, which Aaron Burr attended. Burr served with distinction in the American army during the American Revolution, earning the title "colonel," by which the newspapers referred to him. Burr was an extremely effective lawyer, but despite his professional success and family connections, he frequently was short of funds and needed to borrow from friends. He possessed great charm and sociability; his manner was almost always calm and equable. However, he revealed to few his emotions or innermost thoughts (Melton, 2002, pp. 8, 55; Chidsey, 1967, p. 17).

When the alleged conspiracy began, Burr was a highly controversial figure. In the presidential election of 1800, the Democrat-Republicans had put Burr forward as the vice presidential candidate on a ticket with Thomas Jefferson as the candidate for president. The Democrat-Republican ticket decisively defeated Federalist candidate John Adams. However, at that time, the members of the electoral college would each cast two ballots, which were not distinguished by office; the candidate with the highest number of votes became president, and the one with the second highest became vice president.[1] Because every Democrat-Republican elector voted for both Jefferson and Burr, they received the same number of votes, and therefore the election went for decision to the House of Representatives, still dominated by the lame duck Federalist Party. It had been decisively voted out of office in the 1800 elections, but the members' terms did not expire until March 1801 (Malone, 1962, pp. 495–499).

Although everyone understood that Jefferson was the intended presidential candidate, Burr did not step aside. Many Federalists sought to elect Burr instead of the ideologically unacceptable Jefferson, and it was widely rumored that Burr was negotiating with the Federalists to win their support. It took thirty-six ballots in the House before Jefferson won the election. Jefferson's victory was attributed in part to the efforts of Alexander Hamilton, a leader of the Federalists and Jefferson's political opponent during Washington's administration when both served in the president's cabinet. Hamilton feared Jefferson's politics but regarded Burr as unprincipled and untrustworthy, calling him the "Catiline of America" (referring to the Roman conspirator who sought to seize power by force in the Roman Republic, and who was defeated by Cicero), and therefore urged Burr's defeat (Malone, 1962, pp. 493–505). Due to his conduct during this electoral crisis, Burr forfeited the trust of most Democrat-Republicans, including Jefferson. He was frozen out of most decisions, including patronage appointments, made by the new administration. When Jefferson ran for reelection in 1804, he replaced Burr with Governor George Clinton of New York as his vice presidential running mate (Melton, 2002, p. 38).

In 1804, Burr ran for governor of New York against a fellow Democrat-Republican. Again there was widespread speculation that Burr was negotiating with Federalists for support, perhaps expressing a willingness to cooperate in the secessionist schemes of New England Federalists, who were extremely unhappy with Jefferson's foreign policy of hostility to England, New England's primary trading partner. Burr lost the election, in part due to the strenuous opposition of Alexander Hamilton, at this point practicing law in New York but still influential within some Federalist circles (Melton, 2002, pp. 38, 45–46).

Hamilton, according to an Albany newspaper, had uttered a "despicable" opinion about Burr. After an exchange of letters through which Burr failed to obtain a retraction or explanation to his satisfaction, Burr challenged Hamilton to a duel. On July 11, 1804, Burr and Hamilton met at Weehauken, New Jersey, and Burr shot Hamilton in the abdomen. Hamilton died the next day. A huge outpouring of grief, especially in the Federalist newspapers, followed. Burr removed himself from New York to Philadelphia; after he left, a grand jury in New York State indicted him for violating the state's anti-dueling statute. New Jersey subsequently indicted him for murder (Chidsey, 1967, pp. 18–20, 26–27). At this point, Burr's focus turned to the western part of the United States.

EVENTS IN THE CONSPIRACY

The events on which the charges of treason and misdemeanor were based began shortly before Burr's duel with Hamilton. General James Wilkinson, the commander of the U.S. army, visited Burr in New York City in May 1804 and invited Burr to his lodgings to meet some of his friends and see maps of the western territories (Lomask, 1982, pp. 26–27). Wilkinson would figure prominently in the Burr conspiracy, as the chief witness against Burr as well as apparently one of his closest collaborators.

In August 1804, while Burr was still vice president, Anthony Merry, the British ambassador to the United States, reported to Lord Harrowby, the British secretary of state, that Burr had offered to assist the British government in an effort to separate the western part of the United States from the east. At this time, the American Revolution had ended only twenty-one years earlier, and another war between the United States and Great Britain, the War of 1812, was eight years in the future. Although technically at peace, tensions were high between the two nations, and Britain still viewed the United States as an experiment that could easily fail. In exchange for his efforts to achieve this separation, Burr sought financing from Britain. Merry recommended to his superiors that in light of the "profligacy" of

Burr's character, his great ambition, and his spirit of revenge against the current federal administration, Britain might expect fidelity from Burr. Charles Williamson, a British agent in the United States who was a friend of Burr and who also met with Burr at this time, however, reported to the British government that Burr intended his expedition to be a march to Mexico to free Mexico and the Floridas from Spain. Burr approached Merry again in March 1805 and proposed a dual operation consisting of both an expedition against Mexico and the separation of the western half of the United States. Burr and Wilkinson also met again in Washington during the winter of Burr's last year in office (Lomask, 1982, pp. 34–35, 37–39, 49–50).[2]

On April 24, 1805, Burr left on the first of two trips he would take to the states west of the Appalachian Mountains. His departure was noted by the *Philadelphia Gazette*, which presumed that his visit to the West was principally related to his ties to a company formed to open a canal at Louisville (Lomask, 1982, p. 57). Burr's movements throughout the next two years were widely reported in the press, as were speculations regarding his purposes and rumors of his connection to Wilkinson. The idea of intrigue on the western frontier was not a novel one at the time. Jefferson had acquired the Louisiana Purchase in 1803 and with it New Orleans, thereby meeting the demands of American settlers in Ohio, Kentucky, Tennessee, and along the Mississippi River for secure access to the port of New Orleans through which to ship their produce. Prior to the Louisiana Purchase, there had been speculation that western settlers would secede from the United States and put themselves under the protection of Spain, then the owner of New Orleans, in order to ensure the use of the port. James Wilkinson was widely believed to have been involved in one of these plots, known as the Spanish Conspiracy; he secretly continued to be employed as a Spanish agent, receiving a yearly pension of $2,000, even as an officer in the U.S. military and although this connection was widely rumored (Chidsey, 1967, p. 36; *Poughkeepsie Journal*, 1806a, p. 3).

After the Louisiana Purchase, tension with Spain developed over the determination of the correct boundaries of the two countries. France had conveyed to the United States all the interest it had recently acquired from Spain, but there were no precisely drawn borders. The United States believed it had acquired West Florida (a strip that now runs along the coast of Alabama) and land in the west up to the Rio Grande River. Spain claimed it still owned West Florida as well as East Florida (the current state of Florida) and the land (now part of Texas) from the Rio Grande to the Sabine River. The United States itself was less than thirty years old, and many still believed its continued unity was an uncertain proposition.

Burr reached Pittsburgh in late April 1805 and continued onward by boat. In Marietta, Ohio, he received a letter of introduction to Harman Blennerhassett, an Anglo-Irish immigrant. In early May, Burr arrived at Blennerhassett's Island, which would become the geographic center of Burr's later expeditionary force and the events on which the 1807 treason trial was based. Blennerhassett had arrived in America with a small fortune, much of which he had consumed building an elegant house on the island. It was in the Ohio River and within the jurisdiction of what is now West Virginia, but in 1805 was part of the Commonwealth of Virginia. Burr stayed only a day or two on the island and then continued his journey (Lomask, 1982, pp. 57–59, 63–64).

Burr visited Cincinnati, where he met with Senator John Smith of Ohio and Jonathan Dayton. In Louisville, Burr met General John Adair. All three were subsequently accused of being part of Burr's conspiracy. While in Cincinnati, Burr drafted the papers to establish a canal company, which sold stock to the general public by promising to build a canal outside Louisville that in fact was never dug. Burr obtained a bank line of $25,000 from this transaction. He visited Nashville and spent three weeks in New Orleans. He then returned through Natchez and reached St. Louis in September, where he and Wilkinson again met. Wilkinson subsequently claimed that at this time he wrote to Robert Smith, the secretary of the navy, that Burr was "about something" but that he could not determine whether it was internal or external. Major James Bruff, Wilkinson's principal military aide, however, suspected both Wilkinson and Burr and believed they had a "grand scheme" in mind, but Bruff was unable to learn what the scheme was (Lomask, 1982, pp. 64–66, 70, 78–84).

Burr returned to Washington in November 1805. He again conferred with Anthony Merry, who reported to London that Burr had stated to him that the revolution was well-commenced and suggested that the proceeds of American bonds purchased in London be channeled to Burr through Daniel Clark of New Orleans (Lomask, 1982, p. 99). In fact, the government in London never committed to any support of Burr's project. While in Washington, Burr visited Thomas Jefferson at the White House and certainly learned from administration officials that there would be no war with Spain. Jefferson had ordered his ministers to pursue the acquisition of Florida through diplomatic means (Lomask, 1982, pp. 89, 91–92, 95).

During Burr's time in Washington, he, in cooperation with Jonathan Dayton, also attempted to obtain financing from Spain's representative in the United States. In early December, Dayton visited Marques de Casa Yrujo in Philadelphia and stated that in exchange for a reward he would reveal Burr's plans. Dayton described Burr's conferences with Merry and stated that Burr planned to take the Floridas, incite the western states to separate from the United States, and then unite them into a new federated republic. In return for its support, Britain would receive commercial and navigational preferences. Dayton returned to Yrujo in late December and confessed that in reality he had come as an agent of Burr, who was offering to sell his services to Spain. Burr's real intention was to seize Washington and control of the U.S. government. Yrujo wrote to his superiors that, although to an outsider the plan would sound insane, the government of the United States was so weak that it could work. He recommended that Spain give Burr between $500,000 and $1,000,000. Madrid, however, rejected this advice; Yrujo gave Dayton and Burr only approximately $2,500 to encourage the communications (Lomask, 1982, pp. 102–105).

During this period, Burr invited Commodore Thomas Truxton to join an expedition against Mexico. Truxton, a naval hero, had resigned from the U.S. navy with a grievance against the administration. Truxton inquired of Burr whether the government approved Burr's project and, when informed it had not, said he would have nothing to do with it (Lomask, 1982, p. 109). Burr also extended an invitation to General William Eaton, who had gained public acclaim for his involvement in the war against the Barbary pirates. Eaton, like Truxton, had complaints about the federal government, because it was slow to reimburse him promptly for expenses he incurred during the Barbary war.

Eaton later gave a deposition in which he claimed that Burr described his project as one to separate the western country from the Union and establish a monarchy with New Orleans as the capital. Burr claimed to have ten to twelve thousand men. Wilkinson would have the chief command of the army. Burr offered Eaton the second command. According to Eaton, Burr further claimed if he could gain the marines and the navy, he would assassinate the president, turn Congress out of doors, and declare himself the protector of an energetic government. Eaton claimed to have expressed horror at the idea. Some weeks later, Eaton visited Jefferson and warned him to beware of Burr, as he was dangerous and might incite insurrection on the western frontier. According to Eaton, Jefferson expressed confidence in the integrity of the westerners and in their attachment to the Union, the administration, and himself. Eaton then returned to his farm in Massachusetts but, according to Eaton, in the fall of 1806, he was alarmed by a letter from an acquaintance in Marietta, Ohio, stating that Burr had commenced preparatory operations. Eaton then forwarded to the president through Postmaster General Gideon Granger a full statement of his conversation with Burr (Lomask, 1982, pp. 109–111; *Providence Gazette*, 1807b, p. 2).

In late July 1806, Burr sent a letter in cipher to James Wilkinson. The copy of the letter that Wilkinson made and translated stated, in part,

"I have obtained funds, and have actually commenced. The Eastern detachments, from different points and under different pretences, will rendezvous on the Ohio first of November." The letter also (falsely) stated that Truxton would go to Jamaica to arrange English naval protection. While the letter appeared to describe a military expedition, it failed to name its ultimate object (Chidsey, 1967, pp. 152–153). Samuel Swartwout, a young associate of Burr, stated that Burr wrote a letter, Swartwout put it in cipher form, and Burr gave it to Swartwout to carry overland to Wilkinson. Dr. Erich Bollman, another friend of Burr, subsequently took a duplicate by sea to New Orleans. However, Peter Ogden, a nephew of Jonathan Dayton, overtook Swartwout in Pittsburgh and told him on behalf of Burr to destroy the first letter and instead take a sealed letter, given to Swartwout by Ogden, to Wilkinson. Swartwout did as he was told. It is still disputed whether the letter delivered to Wilkinson was drafted by Burr or Dayton. Wilkinson in any case attempted to obliterate references to earlier letters between Burr and him (Lomask, 1982, pp. 115–117, 119–120).

In August 1806, Burr began his second and final trip to the western states. Outside of Pittsburgh, he visited George Morgan and his sons, John and Thomas. As the Morgans later testified at trial, Burr suggested in conversations that the western states would leave the union within five years and contended that the eastern states' preparedness was so poor that he could seize Washington with a force of 200 men and New York with 500. The Morgans expressed shock at the idea that the western states would secede, and Burr did not pursue the idea further. The tone of the conversation, however, left the Morgans with the impression that Burr was arranging a plan for separation and sufficiently alarmed George Morgan that he contacted a local judge and with him wrote to President Jefferson to warn him that Burr appeared to be up to something (Coombs, 1992, pp. 175–185).

Burr then went to Blennerhassett Island. Harman Blennerhassett and his wife had fully committed to follow Burr in his plans. They agreed to use the island as the gathering point for men recruited by Comfort Tyler and Israel Smith in the east. Burr and Blennerhassett made a contract in Marietta, Ohio, for the construction of fifteen boats for delivery on December 9. After Burr departed on September 1, Blennerhassett wrote articles published in the *Ohio Gazette* on the benefits likely to accrue if the western states withdrew from the Union. Blennerhassett also sought local recruits for Burr's venture. This led him imprudently to talk to two local Federalists, John and Alexander Henderson, who claimed that Blennerhassett told them Burr had contemplated the separation of the Union and the seizure of New Orleans. The Hendersons subsequently alerted the local Wood County, Virginia, militia, which resolved to oppose any such action and denounced Burr and Blennerhassett as enemies to the republic (Lomask, 1982, pp. 127–131, 139, 186; *Poughkeepsie Journal*, 1806e, p. 2).

Burr, meanwhile, set up his headquarters in Lexington, Kentucky. During this autumn, the hostile rumors were such that Burr felt compelled to deny them to certain individuals. Andrew Jackson, then-commander of the Tennessee militia, confronted Burr after Captain John Fort informed Jackson that he had learned from Samuel Swartwout that Burr and Wilkinson planned to divide the Union, seize New Orleans, conquer Mexico, and create a new country. Jackson was satisfied with Burr's account and continued to defend him against subsequent accusations, believing that Burr had the support of the government for his expedition. Burr also wrote to Senator John Smith of Ohio denying intentions to break up the Union (Lomask, 1982, pp. 135–136, 140–141).

Joseph Hamilton Daviess, the Federalist U.S. attorney for Kentucky, however, decided to act on the rumors. He had written to the president, informing him of the rumors. To Daviess's dissatisfaction, Jefferson had responded merely by thanking him for the information but had not directed Daviess to take any action. On November 4, Daviess requested a warrant for Burr's arrest on high misdemeanor charges for planning war against a country with which the United States was at peace. (Daviess discovered that there was no law prohibiting a plan to disunite the states.) The court denied the request because Daviess had no evidence. When Burr heard of this request, he voluntarily went to Frankfurt. Daviess convened a grand jury, which on December 5 refused to issue an indictment (Lomask, 1982, pp. 126, 142–149; Chidsey, 1967, pp. 61–62).

On October 8, 1806, while Burr was in Kentucky, the cipher letter finally arrived in the hands of General James Wilkinson. Wilkinson informed a colonel under his command, who was with Wilkinson in his camp at Natchitoches, that he had received information that Burr was intending to attack U.S. territory. Wilkinson wrote two letters to Jefferson to explain his actions. Although Wilkinson identified a threat to the Union, he disclaimed knowledge of the person behind it. On November 7, Wilkinson received a second copy of the cipher letter and in addition a letter from James L. Donaldson, who claimed he had learned from Michael Myers, who had heard from someone close to Burr, that Burr intended to revolutionize the western country. Kentucky, Ohio, Tennessee, New Orleans, and Indiana were to declare themselves independent on November 15. Wilkinson sent officers ahead of him to New Orleans to prepare the defense of that city; he also sent a further report to Jefferson enclosing the Donaldson letter (Lomask, 1982, pp. 163–168, 170–173).[3]

In early October, Jefferson received the communication from Gideon Granger containing William Eaton's affidavit and summoned his cabinet. The administration planned to send a naval detachment to New Orleans and alert the militia commanders. However, when an October 24 packet arrived from the western states with no word of any disturbances or any overt acts of disloyalty, it rescinded the naval orders and instead sent an officer to check on Burr's movements and to alert the western governors. When Wilkinson's courier arrived on November 25 with Wilkinson's first packet of letters, however, Jefferson and his cabinet took immediate action. On the 27th, Jefferson issued a proclamation announcing that "certain persons" were planning an "enterprize" against the dominions of Spain and that such actions were without the authority of the government. Although Jefferson did not name Burr, everyone who read the proclamation knew to whom it referred. On January 22, 1807, Jefferson sent a message to Congress denouncing the conspiracy and naming Burr (Lomask, 1982, pp. 176–180; Malone, 1974, pp. 244–245, 247–251, 264–265).

From the moment Jefferson's proclamation was issued, Burr's enterprise was doomed. Upon reading the proclamation, citizens in Nashville, who had feted Burr, burned him in effigy (Lomask, 1982, p. 181). The *Lexington Gazette*, which had formerly supported Burr, immediately shifted its position. Wilkinson, now energetically positioning himself in opposition to Burr in New Orleans, attempted to impose martial law in that city, despite the reluctance of Governor William C. C. Claiborne and the opposition of the local courts. Wilkinson arrested Swartwout, Bollman, and Ogden and put them on ships bound for Washington, despite an order of *habeas corpus* (an order to produce the prisoners so the court could review the legality of the arrests) from a New Orleans court (Lomask, 1982, pp. 184–185).

Meanwhile in Ohio, before Jefferson's proclamation arrived, Gov. Edward Tiffin learned of the order for boats to be constructed in Marietta and heard of the belief of Woods County residents that 1,200 stands of arms had been sent downriver, that Andrew Jackson was raising 1,000 men for Burr, and that another 800 from Kentucky and 2,000–3,000 from Pittsburgh were expected. Tiffin summoned the General Assembly, which authorized calling out the militia. On December 2, 1806, the militia seized most of the boats that had been constructed and raided Blennerhassett Island. But Comfort Tyler and the assembled men had learned of the movement of the Ohio militia and left the island shortly before the raid (Lomask, 1982, pp. 187–191).

Burr and approximately 100 men met on Bayou Pierre near Natchez in the Mississippi Territory. On January 19, 1807, acting Governor Cowles Mead of the Mississippi Territory, at the head of the local militia, demanded the surrender of Burr, who submitted without resistance. Mead wrote to the

Department of War that Burr had nine boats and about 100 men, most of whom were "just boys or young men just from school." They expressed ignorance of Burr's designs, and Mead sent them on their way. A search of the boats found thirty to forty rifles and muskets, three or four pounds of powder, two hundred barrels of pork, and trunks of books (although Burr apparently sank or hid some of his weapons) (Melton, 2002, pp. 139, 140–142; Lomask, 1982, p. 214; *Poughkeepsie Journal*, 1807a, p. 2).

Burr was arraigned in Natchez, but the grand jury opined that he was not guilty of any crime or misdemeanor within the jurisdiction of the Mississippi Territory and deplored the government persecution of him. The court ordered the accused to be conveyed to a tribunal competent to try him and refused to release Burr from his obligation to appear in court the next day. During the night, Burr fled. He was arrested by troops from Fort Stoddert, near the Florida line, after being recognized by a local tavernkeeper from whom he asked directions. The commander of the Fort Stoddert troops arranged to transport Burr overland to Richmond (*Poughkeepsie Journal*, 1807b, p. 2).

THE NATION'S NEWSPAPERS TAKE SIDES

The newspapers of the time not only covered the incidents of Burr's western expeditions, but in fact significantly influenced the course of events. From the time Burr left Washington on his first trip in 1805, newspapers tracked his movements. National and international news were prominently featured in the papers of the time, and the papers freely borrowed from each other. Therefore, for example, articles printed in the Washington *National Intelligencer*, the Richmond *Enquirer*, and the Kentucky *Western World* reappeared in local papers, such as the *Providence Gazette*, the *Poughkeepsie Journal*, and the *Raleigh Register*, weekly papers typical of the news available to Americans in the early nineteenth century. The editors felt free to comment within the articles on the information that appeared therein. They also reprinted letters from correspondents in other states, offering the information in the letters for what it was worth without attempting to verify it. By the time Burr appeared before Chief Justice John Marshall on March 30, 1807 to be examined, any reader of the newspapers probably had obtained a definite idea about what Burr's activities had been for the previous two years.

On August 2, 1805, less than four months after Burr's departure from Philadelphia, the *Gazette of the United States*, the largest Federalist paper in Philadelphia, printed an article on its front page titled "Queries." Among the questions it posed was, "How long will it be before we shall hear of

Col. Burr being at the head of a *revolution* party on the western waters?" and "Is it one of the inducements [to attract young men to Louisiana] that an *immediate convention* will be called from the *states* bordering on the Ohio and Mississippi, to form a separate government?" The article was reprinted in the *Kentucky Gazette* and the Philadelphia *Aurora*, but the latter, a prominent Jeffersonian newspaper, described it as the "ravings of a concealed traitor, or perhaps of some emissary of a foreign government." Burr himself believed it had been planted by Yrujo (Lomask, 1982, pp. 75–77).

The *Western World*, a newly formed Federalist paper published in Kentucky, frequently repeated charges that Burr and Wilkinson were involved in a revival of the Spanish Conspiracy, which contributed to the uproar in Kentucky when Burr was there (Lomask, 1982, p. 138). Articles from the *Western World* were republished in the *Providence Gazette* (1807d, p. 2) and in the *Poughkeepsie Journal* (1806a, p. 3; 1806c, p. 2), which also printed a history of the Spanish Conspiracy and the belief that Wilkinson had been implicated and was still receiving Spanish payments, as well as speculation about Burr's trip to Kentucky and New Orleans and his relationship with Wilkinson (*Poughkeepsie Journal*, 1806b, p. 2). After printing an article from the *Western World*, the *Poughkeepsie* editors commented that they had "formed no opinion on the subject of these various reports. We have seen nothing which could justify a belief that any of them are true." But they promised to give any forthcoming information to their readers (*Poughkeepsie Journal*, 1806c, p. 2).

The affidavit of William Eaton was printed in full, as was Jefferson's proclamation (*Poughkeepsie Journal*, 1806f, p. 3; 1806g, p. 2; *Providence Gazette*, 1807b, p. 2). The *Poughkeepsie Journal*, which had mourned Hamilton's death for weeks when it occurred, noted in October 1806 when commenting on the fact that Burr had engaged several young men to accompany him in a secret expedition that "the late embarrassed situation of his pecuniary affairs, renders somewhat mysterious the means by which he is enabled to defray his enormous expense" (1806c, p. 2).

Letters from correspondents in the West provided alarming statements. When the Ohio militia seized Burr's boats, it was reported that two boats loaded with artillery and with officers on board who spoke French had passed down the Ohio River. Another letter from Washington stated that Burr had 1,500 men, arms, and ammunition. A letter from St. Louis reported that military commissions from Colonel Burr had been seen. A letter from the brother of a marine lieutenant in Marietta wrote that Burr's actions were suspicious and so the brother had moved his family back from the river, although he himself intended to remain and protect his property. The resolutions of the inhabitants of Wood County expressing their resolve in "this alarming crisis" to counteract the "ambitious and disorganizing views of Aaron Burr and his partizans" were reprinted from the *Monongahela Gazette*. An express from Natchez reported that Burr had a following of 6,000 men and that General Adair was within a three-day march with 2,000 men (*Poughkeepsie Journal*, 1806d, p. 3; 1806, November 25, p. 2; *Providence Gazette*, 1807a, p. 2; 1807c, p. 3).

Such papers also reported the Kentucky and Mississippi grand juries refusing to find any wrongdoing on the part of Burr. The editors of the *Poughkeepsie Journal* commented on the puzzling contrast between those decisions and the vigorous actions of the governor of Ohio. However, until Burr was arrested and it was determined he had only one hundred men, this Federalist paper took the threat seriously; its articles on the Burr conspiracy did not contain the same negative editorial comments on the Jefferson administration as did the articles on, for example, the administration's foreign policy. Only after Burr was acquitted did the *Providence Gazette* reprint an article from the *Norfolk Journal* complaining about "all this mighty fuss" and the suspension of *habeas corpus* and regular due process in New Orleans (*Providence Gazette*, 1807c, p. 3).

After Burr's arrest, however, the partisan nature of newspaper comments became more intense. Federalist papers denounced Jefferson's involvement in advising the preparation of the prosecution and accused the administration of pursuing a political vendetta. The *Virginia Gazette* referred to the trial as "King Tom's Puppet Show." After the verdict, Republican journals responded by denouncing both Marshall and the Federalist lawyers who defended Burr (Malone, 1974, p. 347).

COURT PROCEEDINGS IN THE TRIAL
OF AARON BURR

The presiding judge at the treason trial was John Marshall, the chief justice of the U.S. Supreme Court. Marshall was the justice who would largely shape the role of the court in the American political system and articulate many of its enduring doctrines, such as the court's authority to review the constitutionality of legislation. Marshall, one of President John Adams' "midnight appointments" made during the waning days of his administration, was a Federalist and by 1807 one of the few effective obstacles to the democratic policies of President Thomas Jefferson. (Jefferson and Marshall were cousins but shared an intense mutual dislike.) Marshall served as the trial judge in the Burr case because the trial was heard in the federal circuit court in Virginia; Supreme Court justices served with the various circuit courts in addition to hearing the court's appellate cases. In 1807, the existing system of federal district courts had not yet been created, and so the circuit courts heard trials (Judiciary Act of 1789). Although sitting as a trial judge rather than as an appellate judge, Marshall rendered legal opinions during the Burr trial that determined the American law on treason until the Civil War. Marshall's decisions essentially mandated the acquittal of Burr.

Burr's team of counsel at the trial included Edmund Randolph, a former governor of Virginia and delegate to the Constitutional Convention; and Luther Martin, a rabid Federalist and also a delegate to the Convention. Martin was regarded as one of the most brilliant lawyers in America at that time, although he also was a renowned drunkard. In addition, the team included prominent lawyers John Wickham, Benjamin Botts, John Baker, and Charles Lee. Despite this team of lawyers, Burr acted as his own counsel during the trial as often as he relied on his lawyers. The government team consisted of George Hay, William Wirt, and Alexander MacRae. Wirt, a young lawyer at the time, would go on to an illustrious career, but the prosecution did not boast as many luminaries of the bar as did the defense. Behind the government lawyers was another major player, President Thomas Jefferson. He appeared in the trial only by letter in response to a demand for documents by the defense. However, he was in regular contact with the U.S. attorneys trying the case and firmly believed in the guilt of the defendant.

The proceedings in Richmond against Burr began with an examination by Chief Justice Marshall regarding whether to send the case to the grand jury. The prosecution introduced the record of earlier proceedings against Bollman and Swartwout, including affidavits of Eaton and Wilkinson, and the testimony of Major Perkins, who apprehended Burr in Mississippi after he fled. The defense denied that there was evidence of any overt act of treason or that there was probable cause to submit the case to the grand jury.

Marshall, therefore, was compelled to issue the first of his opinions analyzing the law of treason in the United States, a legal analysis that in the end determined the outcome of the trial. He concluded that the cipher letter to Wilkinson obviously described a military enterprise, which must have been intended against the United States or against some other power on the continent, with all of whom the United States was at peace. Therefore, the Wilkinson affidavit furnished probable cause for the charge of high misdemeanor, based on the allegation that Burr had organized an unauthorized action against a nation with whom the United States was at peace. Marshall, however, refused to endorse the charge of treason. He noted that as treason "is the most notorious offence which can be committed against the political body, so is it the charge which is most capable of being employed as the instrument of those malignant and vindictive passions which may rage in the bosoms of contending parties struggling for power." He cited the fact that it was the only crime defined in the Constitution, rather than left to legislation to define. The crime must consist of an overt act. Marshall concluded that the intention to commit treason is entirely distinct from the actual commission of the crime. Actual force must be employed. Burr's statements summarized in Eaton's affidavit and Swartwout's statement to Wilkinson, attributable to Burr, that "this territory must be revolutionized" could at most provide probable cause for treasonable designs. As there were no affidavits showing that men had actually assembled, Marshall declined to insert a charge of treason. However, that decision did not detract from the prosecution's right to prefer such a charge before the grand jury if it could produce the appropriate evidence (Coombs, 1992, pp. 6–11).

The grand jury proceedings began on May 22, 1807. Both these proceedings and the subsequent trial were characterized by prolonged arguments by both sides' lawyers on challenging evidence and procedural decisions. For example, the prosecution offered a presidential pardon to Dr. Erich Bollman, one of Burr's confederates, but Bollman refused to accept it, so he continued to assert his right to refuse to answer questions on the ground that the answer might incriminate him. (This situation would not occur in a modern criminal trial, where the offer of unconditional immunity from prosecution voids the Fifth Amendment right to refuse to testify.) The attorneys argued over that and other issues, such as Burr's subpoena *duces tecum* (a demand for documents) to the president for Wilkinson's communications to the executive regarding Burr. This demand was eventually met. As these arguments continued, the grand jury heard witnesses and returned an indictment against Burr and Harman Blennerhassett for both treason and misdemeanor. Burr objected that the indictment was obtained through perjury, thereby anticipating one of his major trial tactics of attempting to put the character of Wilkinson, the chief witness against him, on trial. Marshall, however, rejected the defense theory that a grand jury indictment could be undermined on the ground that the evidence on which it relied was suspect (Coombs, 1992, pp. 13, 37–39, 54–56, 60–62, 93–94). The case, therefore, was set for trial.

The focus of the trial was the specific charge that Burr had levied war against the United States on Blennerhassett Island on December 13, 1806. As Marshall had observed in his response to pretrial motions, the U.S. Constitution, Article III, Section 3, defined treason to, "consist only in levying War against [the United States], or in adhering to their Enemies, giving them Aid and Comfort. No person shall be convicted of Treason unless on the Testimony of two Witnesses to the same overt Act, or on Confession in open Court." The American legal concept of treason drew on English precedents. However, the precisely drawn language of the Constitution retained only two of the three English criteria for treason. In addition to levying war and giving aid and comfort to the nation's enemies, the historic English law of treason included the concept of "compassing the king's death." This approach was the most elastic and could be stretched to capture, within the meaning of treason, lawlessness or hostility to the government.

It was the concept most likely to include a conspiracy that in fact had little chance of success. English courts had recognized the constructive levying of war if one made an effort by violence to fix or enforce public policy. However, by the end of the eighteenth century, English juries had acquitted several notable defendants who really had incited riots, rather than launched wars (Hurst, 1945, pp. 5–6). Americans during the Revolutionary period had been critical of the political use of the charge of treason in England. Marshall argued that the wording of section three of Article III reflected the American fear of concentrated power in the hands of the state, a fear that exceeded concern over the risk of disloyal citizens.

The limitation of the Richmond trial to the events on Blennerhassett Island stemmed in part from a restricted view that the court's jurisdiction was limited to acts within its geographic territory. However, the prosecution was really defeated by the limitations in communications of the time. Although the Federalists criticized the Jefferson administration for waiting too long to act against Burr, from the point of view of the prosecution, the administration acted too soon, before Burr had committed any action that would decisively reveal whether he intended to use his men to attack American territory or Spain or merely settle some western lands that he had purchased. In a situation where it could take weeks for a letter to travel from the Mississippi region to Washington, the administration, when deciding whether the safety of the western states required intervention by the militia, had to rely on Wilkinson's communications, reports of alarming conversations individuals had with Burr or his associates, and rumors about the number of men Burr could raise. Only after Governor Mead had broken up Burr's expedition was it clear that Burr had little support for whatever he planned and posed little threat.

The trial began on June 26, 1807, when Burr pled not guilty to the charges. Several days were occupied with examining potential jurors. Out of the first pool of forty-eight potential jurors, only four were chosen. Most of the remainder had been successfully challenged by Burr, because they had already expressed a negative opinion about him. It was clear that there were few, if any, residents in Virginia who had not followed events in the paper. For example, one potential juror, Hezekiah Bucky, argued that he had never said Burr was guilty of treason. "I only declared that the man who acted as Colonel Burr was said to have done, deserved to be hung." Bucky was dismissed as a juror. Another candidate, Hamilton Morrison, joked that perhaps Burr was in terror of his name, Hamilton. Burr used a peremptory challenge to discharge Morrison (Coombs, 1992, pp. 98–100, 107–134).

George Hay, the chief prosecutor, expressed extreme frustration with the process, arguing that no one who was interested in matters of concern to the nation could have failed to take an interest in the conspiracy. He argued that "a man need only do enough to draw down the public attention upon him, and he would immediately effect his discharge." But the court granted Burr's challenges. During the second pool, Burr picked eight men who had also expressed doubts about his innocence; in an effort to speed the process, Burr accepted the potential jurors' claims of open-mindedness regarding the evidence (Coombs, 1992, pp. 107, 134–138).

Witnesses finally were called on August 17. In addition to William Eaton and the Morgans, the prosecution called a series of witnesses who testified to the gathering of men on Blennerhassett Island, the construction of a kiln, the laying in of provisions, the running of bullets, the presence of rifles, and the coming and going of a large number of boats. However, none of the witnesses could place Burr on the island at the same time that these preparations were being made (Coombs, 1992, pp. 150–215). On August 20, the defense moved to exclude further testimony on the ground that the prosecution's case could not prove that Burr was guilty of treason, because Burr was not present on the island at the time in question. No evidence showed an overt act of levying war (Coombs, 1992, pp. 216–231).

Essentially the defense contended that American law did not recognize "constructive treason" in which the wrongful acts of one person could be attributed to another. The prosecution argued that each action had to be put into the larger context of stated intentions and the pattern of all of the actions and communications of Burr and his associates. The arguments on this motion lasted eight days (Coombs, 1992, pp. 216–306).

On August 31, Marshall rendered his opinion. He concluded, based on English precedent and the Supreme Court's reasoning in the cases of Bollman and Swartwout, Burr's closest associates, that where a body of men assembled for the purpose of making war against the government and were in a condition to make war, the assemblage was an act of levying war, even if no shots were fired. But war was an appeal to force, which must be proved by open deed. The deed had to be unequivocal in its warlike appearance. Marshall concluded that if Burr were not personally present on the island, the actions on the island could not prove an overt act on his part. The government had to name a date and place where Burr personally committed an overt act. The United States, unlike England, did not treat accessories as principals in treason cases.[4] After receiving this opinion, the prosecution declared that it had no further witnesses to offer, as its theory regarding the connection between the events on Blennerhassett Island and its accusation against Burr had been vitiated by Marshall's decision. The jury therefore acquitted Burr (Coombs, 1992, pp. 307–354). Marshall committed Burr for a trial in Ohio on a violation of the Neutrality Act. Burr, however, never appeared, and the federal government did not pursue him (Lomask, 1982, p. 289).

BURR'S LEGACY IN AMERICA

Burr left the United States shortly after the trial concluded, under pressure from his creditors, including Harman Blennerhassett, who was financially ruined by his involvement with Burr. Burr lived in England until 1809, when the English government required him to leave because he was attempting to interest officials in schemes involving Cuba and South America. He traveled to Sweden and then France. In 1812, he returned to New York and resumed the practice of law, where he remained undisturbed by the government, although his creditors continued to pursue him (Melton, 2002, pp. 225–227).

The mystery that surrounded Burr's motives invites fictional treatment, because fact runs out before the questions about the case are answered. Burr told such different stories to various people that one can only speculate which version, if any, was the true one. While Gore Vidal's novel *Burr* is perhaps the most famous fictionalization, by 1982, Burr had appeared as a character in forty-nine novels and short stories and in thirty-three plays (Lomask, 1982, p. xvii). (Vidal presented a fictional representation of events from Burr's point of view, an entertainingly cynical if idiosyncratic account of early American history.)

Although historians will continue to debate the intriguing evidence, perhaps the real significance of the Burr case lies in what did not happen. No uprising in the West occurred, and Burr found almost no support among the western residents for his schemes. In fact, Jefferson's sanguinity regarding the loyalty of the westerners was fully justified. Despite the dubious constitutionality of Wilkinson's conduct in declaring martial law in New Orleans, no one was hanged for disloyalty and, in the end, the accused received civil trials and acquittals. Although the president was outraged at the acquittals, the government acquiesced in the court decisions and did not use its control over the country's military to molest Burr further or even to force him to go to Ohio and face yet another trial. The rule of law prevailed both on the frontier and in Richmond.

NOTES

1. This system was changed in 1804 by the 12th Amendment to the U.S. Constitution.

2. These conversations with the British government and subsequent conversations with a representative of Spain were not known to Americans at the time of the trial. Had they been, such knowledge could only have intensified public condemnation of Burr.

3. One may speculate, as many historians have done, that if Wilkinson had at one point collaborated with Burr, by this time Wilkinson would have concluded that Burr would fail and it was safer to continue serving the existing administration and be seen as an opponent of Burr.

4. For an interpretation that disagrees with Hurst and Marshall's interpretation, and which argues that the American law of treason in the eighteenth century (involving the Fries Rebellion and the Whiskey Rebellion) was no more restricted than that of England, see Chapin, 1964. Although Jefferson was outraged at Burr's acquittal, Marshall arguably did Jefferson a favor in limiting the definition of treason in a way that assured that result. Federalist attacks on Jefferson complaining of "tyranny," which carried little weight with the American public, might have gained significance if the administration had executed one of Jefferson's political rivals, especially on ambiguous evidence.

REFERENCES

Chapin, B. (1964). *The American law of treason.* Seattle: University of Washington Press.

Chidsey, D. B. (1967). *The great conspiracy.* New York: Crown Publishers, Inc.

Coombs, J. J. (1992). *The trial of Aaron Burr for high treason.* New York: The Notable Trials Library.

Hurst, J. W. (1945). *The law of treason in the United States.* Westport, CT: Greenwood Publishing Corp.

Lomask, M. (1979). *Aaron Burr: The years from Princeton to vice president 1756–1805.* New York: Farrar–Straus–Giroux.

Lomask, M. (1982). *Aaron Burr: The conspiracy and years of exile 1805–1836.* New York: Farrar–Straus–Giroux.

Malone, D. (1962). *Jefferson and the ordeal of liberty.* Boston: Little, Brown.

Malone, D. (1970). *Jefferson the president. First term, 1801–1805.* Boston: Little, Brown.

Malone, D. (1974). *Jefferson the president. Second term, 1805–1809.* Boston: Little, Brown.

Melton, B. F., Jr. (2002). *Aaron Burr: Conspiracy to treason.* New York: John Wiley & Sons, Inc.

Poughkeepsie Journal. (1806a, August 26). p. 3.

Poughkeepsie Journal. (1806b, September 16). p. 2.

Poughkeepsie Journal. (1806c, October 28). p. 2.

Poughkeepsie Journal. (1806d, November 11). p. 3.

Poughkeepsie Journal. (1806e, November 25). p. 2.

Poughkeepsie Journal. (1806f, December 2). p. 2.

Poughkeepsie Journal. (1806g, December 9). p. 2.

Poughkeepsie Journal. (1807a, March 10). p. 2.

Poughkeepsie Journal. (1807b, April 14). p. 2.

Providence Gazette. (1807a, January 3). p. 2.

Providence Gazette. (1807b, February 7). pp. 2–3.

Providence Gazette. (1807c, November 21). p. 3.

Providence Gazette. (1807d, December 6). p. 2.

Vidal, G. (1973). *Burr: A novel.* New York: Random House.

9

The Tragic Murder
of Helen Jewett:
Sin and Sensationalism

Andrea L. Kordzek and Carolyn Levy

Helen Jewett was twenty-two at the time of her death on a snowy April
night in 1836 in New York City. As it is with many crimes, the exact details
of the evening of April 10 have never been established with certainty. Factual
information on the crime and the events that followed is difficult to obtain
given the lack of official crime records in early America. Patricia Cline
Cohen's book *The Murder of Helen Jewett* (1998) pieces together newspaper
articles, published commentaries, and local government documents to create
the authoritative book on the events surrounding this crime. The following
description of the night in question conforms to Cohen's depiction of the
crime and the events immediately preceding and following it.

It is a fact that Jewett worked as a highly paid prostitute in a brothel at
41 Thomas Street (located mere steps from where the World Trade Center
would stand in the twentieth century). Although she had lived and worked
at Thomas Street in the past, she had left for a while, returning only three
weeks prior to her death. On that fateful evening Jewett had asked the brothel
madam, Rosina Townsend, not to admit her usual Saturday evening date, a man
known about 41 Thomas Street as Bill Easy. Jewett had already made plans
with another guest.

Between 9 and 10 p.m., Townsend admitted a man she believed to be another paramour of Jewett, a man she knew as Frank Rivers. His actual name was Richard P. Robinson, and he had just finished celebrating his nineteenth birthday with friends before stopping by to see Jewett, his on again, off again companion. Jewett and he had had something of a tempestuous relationship in the year past. Letters between the two painted a picture of intensely shared feelings, consisting of clever flirtations, dark moods, and manipulation. Unbeknown to Townsend, or to anyone else, Robinson had sent Jewett a letter announcing his intent to visit that night and requesting that Jewett admit him herself and that she not mention their plans to meet. Indeed, when it was Townsend and not Jewett who answered the door, Robinson covered his face with his cloak. She recognized him by his voice and stature, as did other women in the brothel. Furthermore, several people heard Jewett greet him by name after he scurried quickly up the steps to her room.

At 11 p.m., Townsend delivered champagne to the room. Although Robinson's back was to her, she recognized the patch of thinning hair on his head. A number of hours later she was awakened by a knock on her bedroom door. A customer was locked within the brothel—the door was secured from the inside after a certain hour for both safety and to prevent theft. Townsend informed the customer that he would have to get his girl to let him out. Another client arrived at 3 a.m. Townsend awoke to admit him and observed some strange details. The back door to the house was open, yet no one was out back. A lamp from one of two upstairs bedrooms was sitting downstairs in the lobby. She took the lamp upstairs, intending to return it to Jewett, its likely owner. When she opened the door to Jewett's room, smoke rushed out. Jewett's body was on the bed. There were three gashes from an axe on her forehead, and the bed had been set on fire (Cohen, 1998).

THE PROSTITUTE AND THE CLERK: A CONTRAST IN WEALTH AND STATUS

While prostitutes were considered by many to be among the lowest classes of citizen, Helen Jewett did not live the life of a low-status woman. In fact, her life was quite comfortable even when compared to that of many women of high social standing. She wore beautiful dresses with extravagant jewels and lived in a room in a high-class brothel, where she had the services of a maid who took care of her laundry, helped her dress, and laid the fire in her room (Cohen, 1998). Jewett spent her days writing letters to friends and lovers and attended the theater on many evenings. She had more freedom in her activities than most women of her day. Jewett was not so desperate that she had to give herself to any man who could afford her services; she had her choice among many. Respectable members of the society, such as judges, were rumored to have been her clients. The mayor visited her room after her death, and it is rumored that he, too, had been one of Jewett's lovers (Cohen, 1998).

While Jewett likely made fifty dollars a week, based on a fee of five dollars per client, Robinson made sixty dollars a year (Cohen, 1998). Robinson was from a well-respected Connecticut family. He came to New York to clerk for Joseph Hoxie, a distant relation, who owned a dry goods store and was a highly regarded businessman in the town. Although Hoxie was strongly against drinking, sexual misbehavior, and other forms of vice, he did not seem to strictly supervise his own clerks who did not hold the same ideals. Based on evidence revealed after the murder, Robinson may have been embezzling money from Hoxie's business (Cohen, 1998), and Robinson had lambasted his employer in his journal for his meager salary (Day, 1836a). Despite this history, Hoxie not only stood by Robinson's side throughout his arrest and trial, he also paid a substantial sum for his defense.

THE INVESTIGATION AND THE EVIDENCE

On the night of the murder, George Noble and Dennis Brink, two local watchmen, responded immediately to Townsend's cries for help. After putting out the fire in Jewett's room, they directed other watchmen to search the backyard. Nothing was found. However, when the sun rose, a bloody hatchet was found in the yard and a man's black cloth cloak was found on the other side of the tall fence bordering the property. The hatchet had a string attached to it. A matching piece of string was found tied to the cloak, indicating that Jewett's killer had tied the hatchet to the inside of the cloak in order to disguise it until it was needed (Cohen, 1998).

Around sunrise, police officers arrived at the boardinghouse where Robinson rented a room. He was asleep, and his roommate, James Tew, who admitted the officers, had to shake him awake. James Tew was also a regular visitor to the brothel at 41 Thomas Street. Jewett's friend and coworker Elizabeth Salters had been intimate with both Robinson and Tew, but she knew each of the men by the name Frank Rivers. Cohen (1998) implies that this was a cover, in the event that Salters mentioned Rivers as her client in conversation with the possessive Jewett.

After he awoke, Robinson seemed calm and did not even question the officers about why he was asked to accompany them. The officers noted a white stain on his pant leg; perhaps, it was later surmised, coming from the fence behind Townsend's property that had recently been whitewashed (Cohen, 1998). When they asked him if he owned a cloth cloak, he claimed that he did not. Robinson was brought to the brothel, shown the body of Jewett, and then told he was under arrest. He maintained his cool demeanor throughout this process. An autopsy was performed in Jewett's room, and two doctors determined that the axe blows had led to a quick death (Cohen, 1998).

Following the autopsy, the coroner next rounded up twelve individuals from the gathering crowd of onlookers to form a coroner's jury, a group of individuals who reviewed evidence to assist the coroner in establishing the official cause of death. Ten witnesses, including the watchmen and the women in the brothel, testified as to the evidence found, Robinson's presence at the brothel the previous evening, and his longtime involvement with Jewett (Cohen, 1998). The jury concluded that Jewett had been killed with a hatchet by Robinson, who was then brought to Bridewell, the city jail, where he was observed as being "clear, calm and unruffled" (Bennett, 1836a). To the large crowd of onlookers gathered below his window, including "several young women of tolerable personal appearance" (Bennett, 1836b) and reporters, Robinson tossed a note that read "I am innocent and I shall prove it tomorrow" (Cohen, 1998).

Meanwhile, the police searched Robinson's room and turned up several interesting pieces of evidence. Robinson's journal, a wallet fat with bills of exchange made out to Mr. Hoxie, and a miniature of Robinson deemed to have been in Jewett's possession the previous Friday, were seized (Cohen, 1998). Small portraits, referred to as miniatures, were somewhat expensive personal portrait drawings that individuals had made. Sweethearts often exchanged them as tokens of affection (Cohen, 1998).

A grand jury was convened on April 18, 1836. In contrast to grand jury proceedings of today, Robinson, in the company of his counsel, was brought to the grand jury room where he was questioned by the coroner and a judge. Robinson, on the advice of his attorney, invoked his right against self-incrimination and refused to answer any questions about the charges against him (Day, 1836b). Excerpts from the letters exchanged between Robinson and Jewett were introduced, as were excerpts from Robinson's journal.

A number of women testified about Robinson's unfaithfulness to Helen Jewett. He was involved with at least two other prostitutes, including Jewett's friend Elizabeth Salters. He was also involved with a teenager, runaway Imogene Chancellor, who claimed to be his wife (Cohen, 1998). It came out that Robinson threatened to kill an acquaintance of Jewett, who knew of Robinson's relationship with the teenager, if she ever divulged this information to Jewett. One might think that there is no such thing as unfaithfulness to a prostitute, but Jewett demanded faithfulness of her suitors (Cohen, 1998). On April 20, Robinson was indicted on a single charge of willful and deliberate murder (Day, 1836c) and moved from Bridewell to Bellevue, a combination prison, workhouse, and almshouse. At Bellevue he was permitted cigars, reading materials and frequent visits from friends, family and supporters, including a grocer who reminded Robinson that he had been at the grocer's shop on the evening of Jewett's death (Cohen, 1998). Robinson had borrowed the now-infamous cloak, and ironically enough, its rightful owner, Thomas Gray, was incarcerated on a theft charge at the same time. The two men exchanged frequent letters, which would later return to haunt Robinson after the trial (Cohen, 1998).

MEDIA: THE FRENZY BEGINS

In an unusual move, the police, after they finished exploring the crime scene, allowed James Gordon Bennett, editor of the *New York Herald*, to view the body. Bennett took full advantage of this opportunity to glamorize what must have been a disturbing scene. He wrote about the beauty of Jewett's corpse and how pale and pure it appeared, even while describing how her burned skin was "bronzed like a statue" (Bennett, 1836a). He described her bosom as beautiful, even though the physician had already been there and she was most likely already cut open and disfigured (Cohen, 1998). The picture that Bennett painted for his readers was both erotic and gruesome, comparing her corpse to a statue of Venus. His portrayal of Jewett was quite romantic, describing her as talented and of remarkable character. He described the books and poetry that Jewett was reading, furthering the image of an educated woman with romantic thoughts. While Cohen (1998) accepts the legitimacy of this account, if not the romanticism, there is speculation that this entire editorial was fictional and that Bennett had neither seen Jewett nor visited the scene. Tucher (1990) suggests Bennett may have been trying to sell as many papers as possible, using his imagination of what a high-class prostitute's room would look like. This would explain the romanticizing and the lack of any detailed description of Jewett such as eye or hair color (Tucher, 1990). At any rate, Bennett was not entirely sympathetic in his characterizations of Jewett, lest young girls see her as a person to be emulated. He commented on her moral wretchedness. He wrote an editorial in which he stated that those acquainted with Jewett proclaimed that she was filled with an antipathy to the male sex and that she wanted to ruin them all for ruining her (Bennett, 1836b). He took this opportunity to call for a moral reformation of New York.

The usual types of stories covered in the newspapers during this period were political speeches and religious lessons, not murder mysteries. The penny presses diverged from what was considered "legitimate news" by reporting human-interest stories. Penny presses were smaller and cheaper than other newspapers, making them media for the people, not just the elite. These papers went in and out of business with great frequency in Jacksonian America, creating vigorous competition among them. After Bennett's depiction of the murder scene was published, the media attention to the murder skyrocketed. The massive coverage is indicated by the fact that the siege of the Alamo was overshadowed and not the top story because of this murder and the public's desire to learn more about it. Newspaper sales rose by the thousands within the first week of the murder. According to Bennett, dishonest paperboys were selling the *Herald* for up to ten times its price. He, furthermore, was incapable of printing enough papers to keep up with the demand (Bennett, 1836c). Over 3,000 papers were added to the *Herald's* daily circulation during the first week following the murder (April 14). The frenzy was not limited to New York. Attention was being given to this crime all over the East Coast; even Montreal papers were covering the story (April 30). Articles from New York newspapers were being reprinted as far west as Mississippi and Ohio. Everyone wanted to know about the beautiful Jewett and how she came to such a tragic end.

HELEN JEWETT'S EARLY YEARS

Accurate information about Jewett's life prior to her move to New York City was extremely difficult to acquire. This was mainly due to Jewett's own less-than-forthright accounts of her past. Jewett knew how to tell a story that would entice a man. In her narrative, given years before her murder, she described to a journalist how she was orphaned and taken in by a judge's family in Massachusetts, where she was a playmate for his daughter. She was later sent to boarding school for education. It was there that she was seduced by a respectable merchant and forever tainted. Because this original interview was for the *Transcript*, that newspaper was the first to print this version ("The Murder in Thomas Street," 1836, April 12) of Jewett's past. The next day the *Herald* also printed this version but added to it a letter sent to Jewett supposedly by the reporter who conducted the interview (Bennett, 1836c). In his letter expressing his deep appreciation for Jewett's beauty and mind, he stated that he envied her seducer and wished that he could have been the one to take her innocence. This letter was possibly a fraud, invented by Bennett to discredit a rival reporter and sell more papers at the same time (Tucher, 1990).

By the Friday following the murder, the *Boston Post* had published a letter from the judge whom Jewett had lived with, allegedly giving a more accurate account of Jewett's upbringing ("The Murder," 1836, April 18). This version put her upbringing in Augusta, Maine, where she was employed as a servant rather than a playmate to the judge's daughter. The judge also stated that Jewett never went to boarding school but instead had a common school education. The judge had no knowledge of her being seduced while being employed in his home, at which she remained until her eighteenth birthday. Helen Jewett's name was actually Dorcas Doyen, and she was the daughter of "poor and destitute" parents (Cohen, 1998).

Patricia Cline Cohen (1998) makes an argument that Jewett's self-described account of her upbringing was deliberately designed in order to make her more attractive to men. By stating that she was orphaned and a playmate to a judge's daughter, instead of a poor servant, she diminished the class difference between her suitors and herself. This is also true of her claim to have had a boarding school education. Jewett's seduction story may have also been fabricated in order to increase her appeal. Seduction by a respectable gentleman who then betrayed her, but awakened her hidden desires, is more enticing than having a romp with a person of low class and then having no way to live but to resort to prostitution.

The newspapers in Maine were more critical of Jewett than the New York papers, portraying her as depraved in youth. This may have been in an effort to show that it was not through any lack of moral upbringing in the judge's residence that led to her indecent status, but instead that she was born of that disposition (Cohen, 1998). They did not lavish praise on her accomplishments as the New York papers did, stating that these must have been attributes later acquired because they certainly were not true of Jewett while she resided in Maine ("The Murder," 1836, April 18). The *Boston Post*'s response to the accounts of Jewett's supposed beauty described her as being "short and full" and "not at all extraordinary" ("The Murder," 1836, April 18). According to Cohen, it was likely that the *Post* had a source from Augusta who was looking to protect a certain gentleman from speculation about him being the infamous seducer. By making Jewett seem less desirable, it became less likely that a man of high standing would have seduced her. It would be more likely that she would have chased after such a man than the other way around.

Bennett took to defending Jewett's character from these attacks on her physical and intellectual attributes. He accused the Maine papers of reducing the liability of its citizens by printing defamatory articles in an attempt to "diminish their own wickedness of having been the cause of her original fall" (Bennett, 1836f). He went on to say that the destruction of her character was merely attempts to alleviate the enormity of the guilt for Augusta's failure to protect her from seduction (Bennett). Bennett sympathized with Jewett's situation and wrote in his paper, "Ye base seducers, prepare for the next world—you may escape in this, but you cannot escape the next" (Bennett).

MORALITY AND DEPRAVITY IN NEW YORK SOCIETY

Newspapers took the opportunity of Jewett's death to discuss and express outrage about the state of morality in New York. Tucher (1990) describes Jewett as "an archetype, a symbol, a myth, a heroine of popular tradition . . . the frail flawed female dead because of sex" (p. 131). According to the *Herald*, Jewett's death was the natural result of the immoral state of the society, where young passions were going unregulated (Bennett, 1836c). Many moral reform groups were formed because of increased concern about the morality of young people in the city, especially the illicit acts of young men. Ironically, these groups were sometimes chastised for bringing indelicate topics, such as prostitution, to public attention (Cohen, 1998). In the week following the murder, an article was printed in the *Transcript* about a doctor who refused to treat pregnant women who were unmarried. The paper applauded the doctor for "confining his charity to chaste women" ("Matrimony Encouraged," 1836, April 19). There was little sympathy for a woman who allowed herself to fall into ruin, but not all of the papers blamed women for society's immorality. Other papers defended the right of these women who had been "ruined and abandoned by worthless men" to have medical care (April 19).

Pregnancy outside of marriage was not always the shame that it had become in the 1830s. When mobility was low, there was little likelihood that the father of a child could run off and escape responsibility. However, this changed as young men left rural areas and small towns to seek work in the cities. This change in mobility occurred at about the time of, and may have fueled, the Second Great Awakening, a religious revival that was sweeping through New England and other northern states. The Awakening valued chastity and sobriety, among other Christian virtues. Robinson's behavior both challenged and mocked this Christian morality (Gilfoyle, 1992).

ROBINSON: A RESPECTABLE GENTLEMAN

Robinson's past was not subjected to the scrutiny that Jewett's had been. This may be because Robinson did not create a mysterious past for himself or because the life of a clerk was ordinary, especially when compared to Jewett's scandalous but captivating life. The world of prostitution was not a common topic: most members of polite society pretended that it did not exist. Jewett's death was an opportunity to learn about and discuss a taboo topic. Most of the articles on Robinson were either factual accounts of his contact with the justice system or dealt with whether or not he was the actual murderer. On the first day of publication after the murder, it was assumed that Rosina Townsend's narrative of that night was accurate. Originally Bennett went along with the others in assuming Robinson's guilt, making statements about the substantial strength of the facts against him (Bennett, 1836b). Bennett even went as far as to label him a villain whose "intentions could not be in doubt" (Bennett, 1836a). A few days after the murder, in an effort to distinguish the *Herald* from the other penny presses, Bennett began to proclaim that Robinson, a young man of potential from a good, well-respected family, very possibly was not the killer. Instead he postulated that it must have been a desperate woman from the brothel, bringing both class and gender bias into his conjecture. Bennett asked his readers how a young man such as Robinson could act with such brutality, surmising that the attack and arson seemed much more like the acts of a woman. He urged the public to pause before it condemned a man of unblemished reputation, conveniently forgetting the fact that he kept a prostitute, which had already served to soil his character in the eyes of many. He accused Townsend, the brothel's proprietress, and asked why she was not in custody of the police. Given her business, she obviously lacked morals, so how, he asked, could her word be taken over Robinson's? He promised his readers to get to the bottom of this "mystery" (April 13). The *Transcript* was less kind to Robinson. The editor commented on the "reckless falsehoods" and the "absurd speculations" that were spread by Robinson's supporters ("Thomas Street Tragedy," 1836, April 16). The paper described the attempts to implicate someone else for this murder as contemptible (April 14).

THE PRESS AND ETHICS

This trial brought out many ethical questions for the press that had never been dealt with before. Instead of just copying the police reports, editors were seeking out their own leads and making commentaries on those implicated in the crime. The overriding concern was that the editors could circumvent the trial proceedings and influence Robinson's verdict. Should the press be making its own pronouncements of guilt or innocence? The *Transcript* ("The Late Horrid Murder," 1836, April 14) and the *Sun* (Day, 1836a) were unequivocal in their declaration of Robinson's guilt, Bennett equally staunch in his assertion of innocence.

One question that was raised by the case was whether it was up to editors to differentiate between fabricated and genuine evidence. When the editor of the *Herald* printed an obviously false confession letter (1836, April 15), the other editors censured him for doing so (Cohen, 1998). Newspapers questioned whether or not prejudicial evidence ought to be printed at all. Both the *Evening Post* (1836, April 13) and the *Transcript* ("Late Horrid Murder,"1836, April 14) wrote in their columns that new information had become available but that they would refrain from printing it because it might be detrimental to Robinson. The public might have become even more convinced of Robinson's guilt by the assertion that there was secret evidence that was even more damning than what already lay before them. Given the void of journalistic integrity, it is likely that this new "proof" was nonexistent.

Another ethical issue was whether or not it was acceptable for the press to have access to and publish police evidence. The *Transcript* was willing to publish a brief excerpt of Robinson's diary that showed him to be of less-than-impeccable character. Robinson wrote of his sexual exploits in his journal, noting that while he did not boast aloud, he could tell of things that would shock even his grandmother because of his so very innocent appearance (1836, April 16). Bennett, meanwhile, suggested that there must have been some kind of conspiracy between the *Transcript* editor and the police (Tucher, 1990). As he described Robinson in jail, Bennett still referred to him as handsome, gentlemanly, and philosophical (1836g).

Given the baseness of the crime and its participants, one ethical reservation was whether or not the papers should have been writing about this murder at all. On April 30, 1836, Bennett published an article from a Montreal paper that attacked the New York City press and the *Herald* specifically. The Montreal paper stated that the papers were catering to the worst of human depravity with all the attention that was being focused on this crime. Bennett defended his coverage of the tragedy by stating that the penny presses had created a way to view the morals of the society (1836h). He then went on to state that if Robinson's trial were properly conducted, it would bring about an incredible change in society's contaminated morals.

AN ACCOUNT OF THE TRIAL

The capital trial was presided over by the wealthy and highly esteemed Judge Ogden Edwards. Ogden Hoffman, Hugh Maxwell, and William Price together created Richard Robinson's "dream team" of high-profile attorneys. Hoffman, the lead attorney, hired by Robinson's employer Mr. Hoxie for the sizeable sum of $1,500, had been a district attorney until shortly before the crime (Cohen, 1998). He was known as a splendid orator who held his audiences in awe. According to the *Sun*, "it is the opinion of every person who heard Mr. Hoffman's address to the jury in closing the trial of

Robinson, that it was the most magnificent production of mind, eloquence and rhetoric that ever resounded in a hall of justice. Our own opinion is that it was never equaled by any orator that ever lived" (Day, 1836d).

On the prosecution side was neophyte attorney Thomas Phoenix, assisted by Robert Morris. While the members of the defense team were schooled in Ivy League universities and were well-established attorneys, the prosecutors were unknown and inexperienced relative to their defense counterparts (Cohen, 1998). The difference in the experience level of the two sides contributed substantially to the evidence introduced, the witnesses called, and the persuasiveness of the opening and closing statements.

The trial was very well attended. The courthouse had seating for approximately one thousand individuals, and for each of the five days of the trial, thousands more congregated outside in hopes of gaining entry. Indeed, on the second day surging crowds broke down court railings and had to be subdued by fifty extra court marshals brought in for the trial. Many of the young clerks in New York City identified with Robinson and attended his trial as supporters. This was not a quiet crowd. When testimony was given in favor of Robinson, the crowd cheered (Day, 1836e), meanwhile jeering at the prostitutes called by the prosecution. There was a belief that even if Robinson did indeed kill Jewett, she was only a prostitute and therefore not worth this young man's life. These supporters copied Robinson's attire and wore identical cloaks and matching caps. A fashion trend began (Cohen, 1998).

Trial juries at the time were drawn from lists of leading male citizens. Fifty-nine citizens were called for jury duty that first day. Only twenty-one showed up, and of those only seven were accepted. All of the ten excused for peremptory challenges were excused by the defense. To fill the remaining jury spots, the judge had to resort to using "talesmen," whereby random men who happened to be in the area were rounded up and brought into court to act as potential jurors (Cohen, 1998). After the trial ended, some charged that this practice led to a jury of men who could relate to Robinson— men younger and less professional than the men ordinarily summoned to be jurors. In a composite sketch of the jury, it did seem that the jurors resembled Robinson in youth (Cohen, 1998).

The trial itself would primarily focus on Robinson's actions on the evening of April 9 and alternate explanations for the evidence gathered by the watchmen (*Murder Most Foul*, 1836).

The Evidence

The cloak was one of the most important pieces of evidence in Robinson's trial. According to friends of Robinson, he had been wearing the cloak earlier in the evening of the murder (Cohen, 1998). Salters was able to identify the cloak found behind the brothel as the one Robinson frequently wore, based on a finely repaired tear in the fabric that Robinson had once pointed out to her (Cohen, 1998). The prosecution furthermore pointed out that the cloak had not been seen since, and that Robinson had lied about having a cloak in the initial investigation (*Murder Most Foul*, 1836). The defense attacked the fact that Mr. Gray, the alleged owner of the cloak, had not been presented to the jury. In an attempt to find any possible explanation for the damning cloak, the idea was suggested by the defense that perhaps it was Mr. Gray and not Robinson who went to Thomas Street that night and left the cloak behind (*Murder Most Foul*, 1836).

Another important piece of evidence, the hatchet, was identified by one of Hoxie's employees, based upon its markings, as coming from Hoxie's business (Cohen, 1998). The importance of the paint observed on the leg of Robinson's pants was left open to interpretation. While a fence behind Townsend's property had been whitewashed shortly before the crime, evidence was presented that the clerks at Hoxie's store had been doing some painting on the day before the crime (Cohen, 1998).

The miniature portrait of Robinson, seized from his room following his arrest, contributed as a final piece of important circumstantial evidence. Jewett's personal maid, Sarah Dunscombe, testified that while dusting Jewett's room on the evening before her death, she had observed a miniature portrait and asked Jewett who it was. Jewett responded that it was Robinson. The miniature, in Jewett's room on Friday, was back in Robinson's possession when his room was searched on Sunday.

Also detrimental to Robinson was a lie he told the friends he had been with earlier in the evening. Robinson stated that he was going to the Clinton Hotel, but a friend later stopped by. Robinson was not there (Cohen, 1998).

Factors that Worked in Robinson's Favor

Robinson's alibi came in the form of a respectable grocer, Mr. Furlong. Indeed, in contrast to trial proceedings of today, many of the jurors knew Furlong, the star witness for the defense, in a personal and/or professional context and therefore could vouch for his honest character (Cohen, 1998). Furlong stated that Robinson regularly frequented his store and was there on the night of the murder until 10:15 p.m., smoking a cigar and jokingly flicking his ashes on a sleeping porter. He therefore could not have arrived at the brothel at the time Townsend claimed. The prosecution challenged this by stating that it was possible Furlong was mistaken about the day of

Robinson's visit (Cohen, 1998). The porter was never called to refute or corroborate these statements ("For the Evening Post," 1836, June 10). Furthermore, Furlong did not provide Robinson with this alibi until quite awhile after the murder (*Murder Most Foul*, 1836). Robinson, however, had never offered his visit to Furlong's shop as an alibi.

While the prosecution had many witnesses of good character as well, Hoffman and his defense team were very adept at discounting the testimony of witnesses considered to be credible. When watchman Brink took the stand, Hoffman questioned him about his friendship with prostitutes at 41 Thomas Street and instances where he had interceded with the district attorney on their behalf. Although Brink denied this, and there is no evidence supporting Hoffman's assertions, this line of questioning may have placed traces of doubt about his credibility in the minds of the jurors. Prosecutors and Judge Edwards sat silently by as Hoffman continued badgering Brink (Cohen, 1998).

The prosecution called a surprise witness, Frederick Gourgons. Gourgons worked in an apothecary shop and testified that Robinson attempted to purchase arsenic from him under an assumed name shortly before Jewett's death. Maxwell attacked Gourgons' credibility, and Judge Edwards blocked corroborating testimony, determining that murder by arsenic was not relevant to the trial (Cohen, 1998).

If credible witnesses had troubles when examined by the defense team, those with faltering credibility were destroyed. The credibility of the prostitutes, especially that of Townsend, was frequently challenged by the defense counsel. In the mid-nineteenth century it was common for individuals to drink out of the same glass. A juror, however, refused to drink out of a glass that touched the lips of Townsend (Cohen, 1998), showing a prejudice that was not limited to the jury and certainly would not diminish through the days of the trial. At the start of the defense summary, Mr. Price began by reiterating the possibility that Townsend was in fact the murderer. At this suggestion the court broke out in applause (*Murder Most Foul*, 1836). The defense referred to Townsend as "the old bag who had murdered dozens before . . . [by] consigning them to an ignominious life" (*Murder Most Foul*). Robinson's attorney went on to speak of the heartbroken parents of the girls Townsend employed and her decision to become involved with prostitution despite the fact that she had had a husband. Even the fact that Townsend had an insurance policy on the house was brought as evidence against her, suggesting the arson was all a moneymaking scheme (*Murder Most Foul*). Jewett's friend and coworker Elizabeth Salters was speculated to be involved in Jewett's death as well. The defense team reminded the jurors that Robinson had been involved with Salters until Jewett moved into the house, reminding them that "a woman's pride once wounded, a woman never forgets—a prostitute, when once her pride is injured, will pursue her victim to the grave. . . . It is contrary to a woman's character, to bear such a thing without feelings of revenge" (p. 10). The Thomas Street residence was referred to as "a pest house, where young men sicken" while Robinson, the jurors were reminded, was "From one of yourselves . . . still an infant—a boy surrounded by respectable connexions [*sic*]" (p. 11). At the time, the law stated that doubtful testimony should be backed up with other evidence. The prosecution addressed the credibility issues of the women, noting that the testimony of the women was corroborated by other evidence, namely the cloak and the hatchet (*Murder Most Foul*). The fact that the main witnesses, however, were both women and prostitutes proved to be a nearly insurmountable problem for the prosecution.

Who Did Not Testify

Perhaps more interesting to the trial is not who testified and what evidence was presented, but who did not testify and what evidence was withheld. Letters between Robinson and Jewett demonstrated that she knew something of an illegal or unsavory act committed by Robinson. Robinson hinted that he had been told that Jewett would betray him. As noted earlier when Robinson's room was searched after the crime, police found a number of bills of exchange made out to Mr. Hoxie. The prosecution did not pursue this important evidence. Furthermore, the judge would not let the prosecutor question Mr. Hoxie about Robinson's salary, thus preempting Hoxie's questions regarding embezzlement of store funds contributing to Robinson's extravagant lifestyle (Cohen, 1998).

According to Cohen, in the weekend before the murder, Jewett threatened Robinson in a letter claiming "you have known how I have loved, do not . . . provoke the experiment of seeing how I can hate" (Cohen, 1998). In his response, Robinson asserted that women were foolish to threaten, and told Jewett that he would be over on Saturday and she was to let him in herself and not mention his plans to visit to anybody. The letters between Robinson and Jewett, when read together, painted a portrait of a relationship strained with jealousy, secrets, and suggestions of betrayal. These letters, however, were not admissible during the trial proceedings. Of issue was the possibility that they were not written by Robinson. Numerous friends and colleagues of Robinson were called forth to testify about whether or not the letters were indeed representative of Robinson's handwriting, but on the whole, they were equivocal, and therefore the judge refused to allow them into admittance (Cohen, 1998). The district attorney tried to introduce them along with an excerpt from Robinson's diary; the judge allowed only one. This solitary letter that was admitted made reference to Robinson's desire to end the relationship and accused Jewett of betrayal. After prosecutor Phoenix read that letter, he provided no discussion of meaning or context (Cohen, 1998). For the most part, neither the prosecution nor the defense appeared to express great interest in delving into the emotional aspects and complexities of the relationship between the two, instead focusing mainly on the more immediate events surrounding the murder.

Also absent from discussion and/or appearance at the trial were Imogene Chancellor, Robinson's balding head, and the men who were in the brothel on the night of the crime. It had been established at the grand jury proceeding that Robinson was involved with runaway teenager Chancellor. Chancellor had reportedly vanished, and there was grumbling that Robinson had murdered Chancellor, and Jewett knew this (Tucher, 1990). Despite Townsend's assertions that she knew Robinson was in Jewett's room at 11 p.m., recognized by the bald spot on the back of his head, Robinson wore—and no one questioned his wearing of—a curly wig during his trial. Also odd was that none of the men who had been in the brothel on the evening of Jewett's death were called to testify. Townsend's bedmate, especially, could have corroborated her account of being awakened by a customer trapped inside the brothel. After the trial, prosecutor Phoenix defended his actions in not calling forth the clients of the brothel on the fateful evening. A couple, he announced, had vanished into the night. Of those who were known to the prosecutor, they were respectable citizens who begged to maintain their anonymity. Phoenix deduced that they had no valuable information to add. Even if Townsend's bedmate and the 3 a.m. arrival could verify her lack of involvement in the crime, Phoenix determined that she was not the one on trial (Cohen, 1998).

The Verdict

After a mere fifteen minutes of jury deliberation, the jury returned with its verdict. Robinson was not guilty of the murder of Helen Jewett. As he sobbed in relief, word of the verdict quickly spread. As discussed below, the court was frequently and publicly criticized for the manner in which the trial had been handled.

The trial of Robinson confirmed that even in antebellum America it was possible to avoid a murder conviction by hiring a skilled attorney. While we make no judgment as to Robinson's guilt or innocence, the facts at our disposal provide strong circumstantial evidence suggesting guilt. Mr. Hoffman and his associates took this abundance of damning evidence and skillfully planted doubt in the minds of the jurors as to its relevance. They also skillfully appealed to the emotions of the jurors, making frequent references to the heartbreaking effect a guilty verdict would have on Robinson's parents and citing cases where innocent people were put to death only to be exonerated after their deaths (*Murder Most Foul*).

Judge Ogden Edwards likely had some influence on the outcome of the trial as well. He blatantly favored the defense in his rulings, allowing them to endlessly grill prosecution witnesses and admit third-person testimony while denying the prosecution these privileges. He sustained most of the defense's objections and excluded a significant amount of the evidence held by the prosecution. Perhaps most importantly, he urged the jurors to discount the testimony of the prostitutes and mused about Robinson's actions on the evening in question, offering defense-friendly suggestions as to how the cloak and the hatchet ended up at 41 Thomas Street (*Murder Most Foul*, 1836). The prosecution, too, was somewhat equivocal in its closing statements, frequently admonishing the jurors to acquit Robinson if they weren't completely comfortable with the evidence presented (*Murder Most Foul*). Not long after the trial, a joke began making the rounds regarding Robinson's six attorneys: Mr. Hoffman, Mr. Price, Mr. Maxwell, Mr. Morris, Mr. Phoenix, and Judge Edwards (Cohen, 1998).

THE GREAT JURY OF THE PUBLIC

The legal verdict of not guilty did not mean that Robinson was not guilty in the minds of the public and the press. After the acquittal, the *Sun* described the circumstantial evidence step-by-step and determined "calmly and dispassionately" that Robinson was "guilty of the willful and peculiarly atrocious murder of Helen Jewett." The *Sun* further stated that any good-looking young man of privilege enough to hire such a defense team would have been acquitted (Day, 1836d). According to Tucher (1990), this account in the *Sun* was the most accurate and reasoned depiction produced by any of the papers. The editor of the *Transcript* also believed in Robinson's guilt and criticized the jury as well as the judge for allowing this obviously guilty defendant to go free (1836, June 10). The *Transcript* then printed letters from readers who disapproved of the newspaper's reluctance to accept the jury's verdict (1836, June 14). Following the acquittal, an *Evening Post* (1836, June 10) reporter attempted to be impartial and to not deny Robinson's innocence but felt that he had a "public duty" to explore the issue further. The article eventually denounced the trial and the secrecy that existed on both sides as a "farce" and a "mockery of the forms of justice." The mystery of the trial was a bigger mystery than that of the murder. The most interesting part of the posttrial coverage was Bennett, as he was Robinson's lone supporter in the penny presses. Immediately following the trial, Bennett proclaimed, "Robinson is innocent" and that every bit of evidence against him could be explained (1836i). Bennett then launched a tirade against the other editors, accusing them of advocating "prostitution and wickedness" and of having received bribes to make it appear that Robinson was guilty (1836i). For the next couple of days the *Herald* featured articles calling for the discovery of the true murderer. On June 15 Bennett, in a complete turnaround, wrote that "Robinson indeed may have murdered (Helen) Jewett," given that the circumstances were against him (1836). Bennett wrote that the jury's verdict should be accepted and Robinson's punishment would be the internal suffering of his guilty conscious (1836k). Tucher (1990) hypothesized that Bennett had been receiving bribes from Hoxie, Robinson's employer since a few days after the murder. After the acquittal, according to Tucher, Hoxie no longer felt the need to pay Bennett to gain public sympathy. A sudden and disappointing halt of funds would explain Bennett's complete reversal in the articles following the verdict. Bennett had been accused of bribery in the past, and it is not difficult to imagine money being more important than journalistic integrity (Tucher, 1990).

Public sentiment against Robinson intensified when letters he had exchanged with Gray, while both were in jail, became public knowledge. With Gray he discussed, among other things, the possibility of seducing Gray's fiancée if after marriage Gray should want grounds for divorce, and of assaulting his jailhouse maid if she betrayed him. In the end, Hoxie publicly withdrew his support of Robinson, and even Hoffman is said to have spoken of his famous trial whereby he helped a man get away with murder (Cohen, 1998).

WHAT WE KNOW OF MORALS AND FASCINATION

While we may never discover the truth about Jewett's past, or which of the media details of the case were complete fabrications, we can look at the norms and morals of the day. Tucher describes two ways in which Jewett was depicted: "the Unfortunate" and "the Siren." While both types are doomed to suffer, which type an editor chose and which paper the people chose to read says a lot about their views of sin, justice, and gender (Tucher, 1990). Fear for the state of morals of the young brought about the formation of groups opposing prostitution, which had blossomed under anonymity before. While prostitution remained a loosely enforced crime of vagrancy or disorderly conduct, its controversy in New York society was escalating.

We also learn about the public by looking at its seemingly unparalleled fascination with this gruesome crime. Thousands flocked to both the trial and to where Robinson was jailed. Public interest was so great that the police had to be called to preserve order. Miniatures of both Jewett and Robinson were created and sold to the public (Bennett, 1836i). This fascination did not desist with time. More than ten years after the crime, Wilkes published an account in the *National Police Gazette,* his new paper. Fictionalized accounts were published based on the story for years after the tragedy (Ingraham, 1843; Wilkes, 1849; Paul, 1982). This story has also become a point of scholarly research. Patricia Cline Cohen, author of the book *The Murder of Helen Jewett,* has analyzed the newspaper coverage and the public records pertaining to this trial, theorizing about the link between sex and violence. Andie Tucher, author of *Froth and Scum: Truth, Beauty, Goodness and the Axe Murderer in the First Years of the New York Penny Press,* focuses on the penny press as an institution and specifically comments on the motivations of each of the major editors throughout this affair. The ethical dilemmas that this story created for journalists, and the changes it invoked in how the public received its news, made this crime one of the most important in America's history.

After the acquittal, Robinson moved west to Texas. He changed his name and became a property owner and prominent citizen. He married a young widow with children, though never had any children of his own. On the coffee table in his Texas parlor he kept a book telling the story of the murder of Helen Jewett (Cohen, 1998).

REFERENCES

Bennett, J. G. (1836a, April 11). The recent tragedy. *New York Herald.*

Bennett, J. G. (1836b, April 12). Most atrocious murder. *New York Herald.*

Bennett, J. G. (1836c, April 13). Still further on the tragedy. *New York Herald.*

Bennett, J. G. (1836d, April 14). Rapid increase. *New York Herald.*

Bennett, J. G. (1836e, April 15). Progress of the case. *New York Herald.*

Bennett, J. G. (1836f, April 25). Ellen Jewett—progress of the sensation. *New York Herald.*

Bennett, J. G. (1836g, April 27). The culprits. *New York Herald.*

Bennett, J. G. (1836h, April 30). *New York Herald.*

Bennett, J. G. (1836i, June 10). Who is the murderer! Still say I. *New York Herald.*

Bennett, J. G. (1836j, June 15). Robinson's case: Another hoax. *New York Herald.*

Bennett, J. G. (1836k, June 21). Robinson's case. *New York Herald.*

Cohen, P. C. (1998). *The murder of Helen Jewett: The life and death of a prostitute in nineteenth-century New York.* New York: Alfred A. Knopf, Inc.

Day, B. (1836a, April 13). Young Robinson, the supposed murderer. *The New York Sun.*

Day, B. (1836b, April 18). The examination of Robinson. *The New York Sun.*

Day, B. (1836c, April 21). The indictment of Robinson. *The New York Sun.*

Day, B. (1836d, June 9). The trial of Robinson. *The New York Sun.*

Day, B. (1836e, June 10). Further remarks upon the trial of Robinson. *The New York Sun.*

Evening Post. (1836, June 21).

For the evening post. (1836, June 10). *Evening Post.*

Gilfoyle, T. J. (1992). *City of Eros: New York City prostitution and the commercialization of sex, 1790–1920.* New York: W.W. Norton and Company, Inc.

Ingraham, J. H. (1843). *Frank Rivers, or, the dangers of the town.* New York: M. J. Ivers & Co.

The late horrid murder. (1836, April 14). *Transcript.*

Letter to the editor. (1836, June 14). *Transcript.*

Matrimony encouraged. (1836, April 19). *Transcript.*

The murder. (1836, April 18). *Transcript.*

Murder most foul. (1836). New York: R. H. Elton.

The murder in Thomas Street. (1836, April 12). *Transcript.*

Paul, R. (1982). *The Thomas Street horror: An historical novel of murder.* New York: Ballantine Books.

Richard P. Robinson: The suspected murderer of Ellen Jewett. (1836, April 13). *Evening Post.*

The Thomas Street tragedy (1836, April 16). *Transcript.*

Transcript. (1836, June 10).

Tucher, A. (1990). *Froth and scum: Truth, beauty, goodness, and the axe-murder in the first years of the New York penny press.* Ann Arbor, MI: Dissertation Services.

Wilkes, G. (1849). Lives of Helen Jewett. *National Police Gazette.* New York: Camp & Wilkes.

10

Amistad:
Slavery's Northern
Dred Scott Decision

Kathy Warnes

Four men took me on the road. Came from Mendi to Lomboko. Three moons from Africa to Havana; ten nights in Havana. The cook told us they carry us to some place, and kill and eat us.
— Joseph Cinque (Transcript of the *Amistad* Trials, p. 2)

The astounding voyage of the schooner *Amistad*, the Africans who shaped its destiny, and the court cases and diplomatic battles resulting from the voyage are among the most riveting human rights stories of the nineteenth century. The *Amistad* case dramatically demonstrated that Africans were not ignorant savages and could effectively act on their own behalf, one even suing the two Spaniards who had imprisoned them. After the American translators had learned the Mende language, they were able to recognize the Africans as sympathetic human beings longing for freedom and home.

The *Amistad* case focused the abolitionist movement and polarized the conflict over slavery, as well as underscoring the fact that slavery existed in 1839 in northern states like Connecticut, just as in the South. The *Amistad* issue forced the U.S. judicial system to confront and adjudicate the human and legal questions involving slavery.

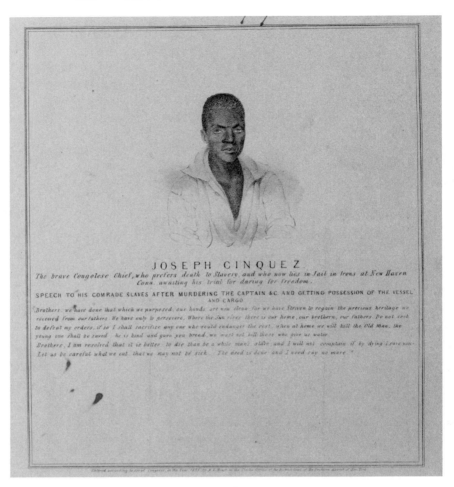

Joseph Cinque. (Courtesy of Library of Congress)

The *Amistad* case spanned three presidencies. President Martin van Buren lost his bid for reelection before the case was resolved, losing the election to William Henry Harrison. After a short forty-three days in office, Harrison died of pneumonia. John Tyler sat in the White House when the ship's captives finally set sail for Sierra Leone in November 1841. The *Amistad* case also involved former President John Quincy Adams, who argued and condemned the policies of Martin van Buren's incumbent administration before the U.S. Supreme Court. The disposition of the case tainted diplomatic relations between the United States and Spain for decades and created a movement to send Christian missionaries to Africa.

BEGINNINGS: THE HERO'S CAPTURE IN AFRICA

The *Amistad* story begins with Joseph Cinque, who is the common thread weaving the African, Spanish, and American threads of the story together. Twenty-five-year-old Cinque had been working on a road between villages in his Mende homeland in Sierra Leone, West Africa, early in 1839, when four black strangers seized him. Strong and agile, taller than most of his fellow tribesmen at five feet eight inches, he still could not prevail against the combined superior force of his captors. His captors chained him by the neck to other blacks, including a few whom he recognized, and forcibly marched him and the others to the West African coast. His situation puzzled Cinque. Even though his own Mende people were peace-loving, he knew that many African towns and villages made war on each other to capture and sell captives to slave dealers. He also knew that some people were sentenced to slavery for committing crimes punishable by death and that some people were captured in the jungle and sold to pay off debts. He suspected that he had been captured as the payoff to a debt that he owed a business acquaintance. However it happened, Cinque had gone from a free man to a slave, captured by strangers. When they reached the coastal slave factory called Lomboko, strange and hostile white people loaded Cinque and his fellow captives, about 500 people, into the slaver *Tecora*.

Cinque and the other captives spent two months on the *Tecora*, enduring the long Middle Passage to Cuba. Over a third of the captives died from sickness and disease caused by lack of food and inadequate sanitary conditions. The white men had provided sufficient rice for the captives, but not enough water. If the blacks did not eat all of their rice, their captors whipped them and rubbed vinegar into their wounds. The survivors would never be physically or emotionally the same people they had been before their capture.

Finally, the *Tecora* approached Cuba, the place that Cinque thought would mark the end of the journey, but the ship halted some distance offshore. The *Tecora* would not nose into shore until after dark, because the captain and crew and officers knew that British cruisers patrolled the waters surrounding Cuba on the lookout for slavers and their cargo. The *Tecora* operated in violation of an Anglo-Spanish treaty, originally written in 1809, which prohibited the African slave trade and promised death to its violators. Spain officially ignored the treaty and continued to deal in African slaves, setting up a hub for this trade in Havana, Cuba, on the theory that the African slaves fresh from Africa made better breeding stock and better field hands. By 1819, Spain, Britain, and the United States had signed the treaty, and the United States and Britain attempted to enforce its provisions (Jones, 1987, p. 16).

After nightfall, the captain and crew of the *Tecora* unloaded the slaves in a secluded inlet along the Cuban shore. The crew pushed the blacks into the jungle, marched them for three miles, and finally jammed them into crude huts where they subsisted for two weeks. Then one night in June, the captain and crew again marched the blacks through the brush to the outskirts of Havana. When morning came, Cinque and the other blacks were put into a barracoon—an oblong pen without a roof—that served as a slave market during the day and a holding pen at night.

After the captives had spent about ten days in the barracoon, in mid-June 1839, Jose Ruiz, a twenty-four-year old Cuban, bought Cinque and forty-eight other adult male Africans for $450 each. On June 26, 1839, Ruiz secured phony passports for the men that authorized transporting them to his plantation near Puerto Principe, a two-day sail on the northwest coast of Cuba. He listed the Africans as "black Ladinos." One of the three classes of Negroes in Cuba, Ladinos were blacks who had lived in Cuba for a long period of time and who owed their allegiance to Spain. The *Amistad* Africans were really Bozals, the name given to those recently arrived from Africa. Pedro Montes, a wealthy fifty-eight-year-old businessman, bought four children, including three girls. He, too, got phony passports that approved the transfer of his new slaves to his plantation at Puerto Principe. In a later memoir, Cinque said that when he and the others who had been sold to Montes and Ruiz were taken from the barracoon, the Africans were in tears. They had been captured from the same country and now were being torn apart and taken into the unknown again.

On the night of June 28, 1839, Pedro Montes and Jose Ruiz led their fifty-three captive Africans through Havana to the ship they had chartered: the *Amistad*. Built and fitted in Baltimore for the coastal slave trade, the small and sleek black schooner featured two masts. The two Spaniards knew that the British anywhere in the Caribbean could search the *Amistad*, and despite the signed passports, they could not afford to have a British search pinpoint the discrepancies. Their captives were not Ladinos. All spoke only African tongues and knew no Spanish. The four children were too young to have been slaves in Cuba before the antislave trade law became effective in 1820. But the passports contained descriptions of each black and the false Spanish names that their purchasers had assigned to them.

The *Amistad* departed for Puerto Principe at midnight, commanded by Ramon Ferrer, its captain and owner. It carried Ruiz and Montes, their fifty-three captives, two sailors as crew members, the captain's sixteen-year-old cabin boy and slave Antonio, a mulatto cook named Celestino, $250 in cash, and cargo and provisions worth about $40,000 (Jones, 1987, p. 23).

Captain Ferrer and his two Spanish crewmembers believed that the trip would be a routine one. The tropical heat and humidity covered them like a heavy wool blanket, and the next day the winds shifted and the sails drooped. The voyage stretched longer than the captain had originally planned, and he decided not to make any more shore trips for provisions. This meant that each black's ration would be only one banana, two potatoes, and a small cup of water per day.

MUTINY ON THE *AMISTAD*

The Africans grew restless and worried about their fate. During one of his periods on deck, Cinque asked the cook what would happen to them. In a cruel joke, Celestino grinned, pointed to the barrels of beef across the room, then to an empty barrel behind them. Using sign language, he told Cinque that when they arrived in Puerto Principe, the Spaniards planned to slit all the slaves' throats, chop their bodies into pieces, salt them down, and eat them as dried meat (Jones, 1987, p. 24).

Cinque decided he would not allow himself to be eaten. He found a nail and hid it under his arm, determined to pick the lock on the iron collar around his neck and make a run for freedom. On July 1, 1839, the third night at sea, Cinque and a fellow captive named Grabeau prepared to mutiny. They freed themselves and the other captives from the irons and found boxes in the hold that contained weapons—sugar cane knives. They stole up the hatchway and attacked Captain Ferrer where he slept on deck.

Cinque, along with Grabeau and another man named Burnah, took command of the *Amistad*. Captain Ferrer and the cook Celestino were dead. Ruiz surrendered after suffering several minor wounds. The cabin boy Antonio had begged for mercy and the blacks had tied him alive to the anchor. The two sailors had disappeared, probably drowning after jumping overboard and trying to swim to shore. Only Montes was missing.

The sun arose and Cinque and Burnah crept below to look for Montes. When they found him cowering under a blanket, Cinque attempted to kill him with the cane knife. After a long and heated argument with Burnah, Cinque finally dragged Montes on deck. Cinque tied Ruiz and Montes together and communicated to them by signs that he expected them to sail the ship to Africa. The two Spaniards, talking in Spanish, which none of the blacks understood, concocted a plan that during the day Montes would steer the *Amistad* in the right direction, but at night turn it west, hoping to land in the southern United States.

Using these methods, Ruiz and Montes managed to keep the *Amistad* in the Caribbean and then the Bahamas for a time. At one point Cinque risked landing in the Bahamas for food and water and maybe a pilot, but since the Africans did not speak enough English to communicate effectively, they assumed that the people on land wished to enslave them again. Quickly, they took their provisions to the schooner and set sail.

Eventually, the *Amistad* made her way into the Atlantic Ocean toward the United States. The Atlantic currents carried the *Amistad* up the coastline past the slave states of the South to the coastline of New England. Supplies aboard ship dwindled. The *Amistad* passed merchantmen and other vessels, but Montes could not send distress signals. Supplies were almost gone, rough winds nearly destroyed the sails, and ten blacks had already died.

The days melted into late August. By now the *Amistad* had caused such a stir along the North American coast that commanding officers at the Brooklyn Navy Yard ordered two vessels to search for the ship. *The New London Gazette* reported what happened next:

Much excitement has been created in New York for the past week, from the report of several Pilot Boats having seen a clipper-built schooner off the Hook, full of Negroes, and in such condition as to lead to the suspicion that she was a pirate. Several Cutters and navel vessels are said to have been dispatched in pursuit of her, but she has been most providentially captured in the Sound by Capt. Gedney, of the surveying Brig Washington. (Barber, 1840, p. 1)

There are several variations of the story of the *Amistad*'s capture, and Cinque, Burnah, and Grabeau and five of their companions figure prominently in all of them. One version of the story says that two sea captains, Peletiah Fordham and Henry Green, were shooting birds on the dunes of Culloden Point on the eastern tip of Long Island on the morning of August 26, 1839, when they encountered four black men wearing only blankets. After a sign language conversation in which Fordham and Green assured the blacks that they had not landed in a slaveholding country, the Africans led them to a high point of land where they could see a black schooner anchored about a mile off the beach. Another smaller boat sat on the beach, guarded by more black men wearing necklaces and bracelets of gold doubloons. The black man who seemed to be the leader of the group told Fordham and Green that he would give them two trunks full of gold if they would outfit them with provisions and help them sail back to Sierra Leone (Transcript of the *Amistad* Trials).

After anchoring the *Amistad* off Culloden Point on the tip of Long Island, Cinque and seven others jumped into the small boat and headed ashore to find provisions. They wandered around frightening most of the people who lived on isolated farms, but managing to buy two dogs, a bottle of gin, and some sweet potatoes with Spanish gold doubloons from the *Amistad*.

By late afternoon, five white men who had seen the *Amistad* offshore arrived in wagons, approaching Cinque and his companions on the beach. Henry Green and his friends were seamen from the area and communicated with Cinque and his fellow blacks with sign language. Burnah told the whites that they would pay them in gold doubloons for taking them to Sierra Leone. The offer caused Green to speculate about the value of the cargo aboard the *Amistad*, and he decided to try to seize it as a prize. But Cinque became suspicious of their motives and decided to get the *Amistad* underway the next morning (Jones, 1987, p. 28).

Then Green saw an American naval vessel on the horizon. Fearing that the navy would get to the *Amistad* before he could, he told the blacks who were preparing to leave that the Americans would capture and enslave them. As Green watched, the USS *Washington*, a naval brig survey ship, intercepted the rowboat as the black men headed away toward the *Amistad*. Lieutenant Thomas Gedney, the commander of the brig, boarded the *Amistad* and sent the hands below deck at gunpoint. Two Spaniards came on deck— Mendes, in his fifties, gray-haired, bearded, and sobbing; and Ruiz, in his mid-twenties, haggard but much calmer. In English, Ruiz told the Americans the tale of mutiny aboard the *Amistad*.

Suddenly, a husky black man, naked but for a gold necklace, appeared from below, leaped off the boat, and attempted to swim away. Finally, crew-members captured the man, who turned out to be Cinque, and put him in chains. The *Washington* towed the *Amistad* to New London, Connecticut, just across the sound from Long Island. The Africans were captive once again, and this time their fate rested in the hands of the Americans.

THE *AMISTAD* CAPTIVES IN AMERICA

Since the *Amistad* Africans were captured about a mile off Montauk Point, Long Island, historians speculate that Lieutenant Thomas Gedney towed the ship to a New London, Connecticut harbor instead of a closer New York port because slavery was still legal in Connecticut in 1839 and he intended to claim the ship and the slaves as a prize. Ironically and tragically for the *Amistad* Africans, they had sailed past the Southern slaveholding states, only to land across the sound from one of the remaining Northern slavery states. Slavery did not end in Connecticut until the mid-1840s, so it would seem that Lieutenant Gedney had a valid salvage claim on the *Amistad* and its cargo. In the state of New York, this claim totaled about $40,000 in a time when the average working person made about three dollars a week. By taking the *Amistad* to Connecticut, a slave state, Gedney could claim the Africans as cargo, too, which doubled his claim to about $80,000.

One of the telling facts about the *Amistad* capture and trial of its Africans that is not emphasized much in the history books or in the Steven Spielberg movie *Amistad* is that Connecticut, not Washington, DC, or New York, is essential to the case. Lieutenant Gedney had the *Amistad* towed to New London in August 1839. The first two trials were held in Connecticut: one in Hartford and one in New Haven, with only the Supreme Court case heard in Washington, DC.

The *New York Commercial Advertiser* highlighted the location of the first trial:

On Wednesday night, Captain Gedney dispatched an express to the U. S. Marshal at New Haven, who gave information to his Honor A. T. Judson, U. S. District Judge. On Thursday morning, both these gentleman arrived, and after careful deliberation, concluded to hold their Court on board the Washington, then lying off the Fort, within musket shot of the schooner. Lieut. Wolcott kindly offered the services to the U. S. cutter Experiment to take all interested on board The Washington. The U. S. Marshal politely took us under his protection. (1839, August 26)

Judge Andrew T. Judson would play a crucial role in the lives of the African captives. Born in Ashford, Connecticut, Judson was the son of a poor minister and did not have much formal education. Unable to afford college, he studied law in the office of an attorney and became a member of the bar in 1806. He practiced law in Vermont for a few years and then returned to Connecticut, where he was elected to the General Assembly. In 1816, he became a Democrat and from 1819 to 1834 played an active role in state politics. He held the post of state attorney for Windham County and served in both the state House of Representatives and Senate. In 1835, Judson was elected to the U.S. House of Representatives, clearly one of the richest and most powerful men in the state. In that same year he took on the controversial prosecution of Prudence Crandall for operating a school for black girls in Canterbury, Connecticut. In 1831, Crandall had established an elite finishing school for white girls in Canterbury; and her neighbor Andrew Judson became a member of the board and, from all accounts, her great friend and supporter.

Then Prudence Crandall decided to teach a black girl, Sarah Harris, at the school, and Judson and many other people in Canterbury objected. When Crandall refused to expel Sarah, people began withdrawing their daughters from the school, and she countered by expelling the white girls and converting the school to one exclusively for black girls. Judson responded by getting elected to the state legislature and passing the Black Law. The Black Law stated that black people could not attend school in the state without the written consent of the townspeople and town council in the school district. A series of court trials resulted, a mob burned the school, and Prudence Crandall left Connecticut.

Shortly after this—some people thought as a reward for his actions—President Andrew Jackson appointed Judson to be a federal judge in the Sixth District of Connecticut. He would turn out to be the judge in the second pivotal *Amistad* trial, the one with no jury.

On August 29, 1839, only four days after Lieutenant Gedney captured the *Amistad*, Judge Judson convened a special session of the U.S. District Court of the District of Connecticut. The African captives, the Spaniards Ruiz and Montes, and the American captors gathered on board the U.S. cutter *Washington* to hear the story of the *Amistad*, with District Judge Judson presiding. Pedro Montes and Jose Ruiz swore out a complaint against Joseph Cinque and thirty-eight other Africans, charging them with murder and piracy on board the Spanish schooner *Amistad*. The marshal brought Cinque, the leader of the Africans, into the cabin heavily manacled. He wore a cord around his neck with a snuffbox suspended from it, a red flannel shirt, and duck pantaloons.

Lieutenant R. W. Meade, who spoke fluent Spanish, acted as an interpreter between the Spaniards and the court. Lieutenant Meade testified that he had been in the boat that boarded the *Amistad*. Senors Ruiz and Montes claimed protection for themselves as the only two white men on board. Lieutenant Meade had demanded documents, and the Spanish owners readily gave him the false papers for the Africans. Then the navy towed the *Amistad* to New London.

Next, Ruiz was sworn in and he testified that he had bought forty-nine slaves in Havana and shipped them aboard the *Amistad*. About the fifth day out, the slaves mutinied and killed Captain Ferrer and Selestina, the cook. Two sailors, Manuel Pagilla and Yacinto, were missing. The slaves, led by Cinque, forced Ruiz and Montes to navigate, and despite their efforts to return to Havana, the *Amistad* eventually reached the New York coast.

Montes testified in Spanish, with Lieutenant Meade interpreting. He related the same story as Ruiz about the mutiny, and said that Cinque treated him harshly and would have killed him if some of the other Africans had not interfered.

The court adjourned to the *Amistad* to inspect her, and took along Antonio so that he might identify the Africans who murdered the captain and his mulatto cook. Antonio testified that one of the slaves who attacked the captain had died and Joseph Cinque and two of the others had been on the *Amistad*. He went below deck and picked out the two Africans who had conspired to kill the captain and his cook.

After hearing the testimony, Judge Judson allowed Lieutenant Gedney to submit his claim for a salvage award and heard testimony about the mutiny on the *Amistad*. Judson ordered the marshal to take the Africans on board the *Amistad* into custody with a warrant of arrest, while a warrant of seizure authorized holding all of the Mende, pending determination of the salvage claim.

The navy loaded the Africans on board a sloop with Lieutenant Holcomb of the *Washington* in charge, accompanied by Colonel Pendleton of the New Haven prison. They arrived in New Haven on Sunday morning, September 1, 1839, and Cinque, the leader, was separated from the rest and transported to jail in irons.

Throngs of curious visitors crowded cell windows of the New Haven jail to see the exotic captives, so many that the jailers charged admission. Josiah W. Gibbs, linguistics professor at Yale College, visited the Africans at the jail. He began to communicate with them by holding up one finger and saying, "one." He held up a single coin and said the same thing. Finally, Grabeau sensed what the professor meant and shouted "eta," the Mende word for *one*. Gradually, Professor Gibbs built up a limited Mende vocabulary and realized that although some of the captives spoke other African languages, most of them spoke Mende.

Professor Gibbs began to search the waterfronts of New Haven and New York for English-speaking Mende. He would approach blacks and count from one to ten in Mende, listening for someone who understood. Along the New York waterfront, Professor Gibbs found James Covey, who had been stolen from his Sierra Leone village at the age of twelve, taken to the slave factory of Lomboko, and placed on a slave ship bound for Cuba. A British cruiser intercepted the slave ship, Covey and the other Africans were freed, and later Covey enlisted as a sailor on the *Buzzard*, a British man of war. The captain of the *Buzzard* gave Professor Gibbs permission to take Covey to meet the Africans, and soon the captives began to tell their stories. The professor questioned Cinque extensively, and Cinque asked him to arrange English language lessons for the Africans. Professor Gibbs gladly arranged them. Covey, too, became extensively involved with the people in the New Haven abolitionist movement.

As a result of the work of Professor Gibbs and James Covey, the stories of kidnap, terror, and mutiny that the Africans told were translated into English so that Americans could understand them. The Africans were revealed as intelligent people with names and personalities, not savage brutes from an uncivilized land. Cinque told them his story. A Mende rice planter who never owned or sold slaves, Cinque had a wife and three children, one son and two daughters. One day as he traveled on the road, four men seized him and tied his right hand to his neck. They took him to the slave factory at Lomboko. From there he was sold to the Portuguese slave traders on the

Tecora, taken to Havana, and sold to Cuban planters, who transported him on the *Amistad*. He desperately wanted to return to his homeland.

Grabeau, the second in command of the *Amistad* after Cinque, was four feet eleven inches tall and very energetic. Born in Mende country, two moons' journey into the interior, he also was a rice planter. He was married with no children. In his country he saw people write—they wrote from right to left. They had cows, sheep, and goats and wore cotton cloth. Smoking tobacco was a common practice. None but the rich used salt, because it cost too much. He was caught on the road when going to Taurang, in the Bandi country, to buy clothes. His uncle had bought two slaves in Bandi and gave them in payment for a debt. One of them ran away, and Grabeau was taken for him.

Fuliwa and his five brothers were born at Mano, a town in the Mende country, where his king, Tikba, lived. Soldiers surrounded his town, and some of the Mende were killed. Fuliwa and the survivors were taken prisoner. He passed through the Vai country, then was taken to Lomboko on a one-month journey. He was in middle life, five feet three inches high, face broad in the middle, and with a slight beard. It was Fuliwa who instituted the suit against Ruiz and Montes (Barber, 1840, pp. 11–12).

Professor Gibbs translated the stories of the remaining Africans into English, and John Warner Barber published them in 1840. Professor Gibbs and Covey also built bridges to the New Haven abolitionist community, which in turn appealed to its fellow New York abolitionists to help the *Amistad* Africans. Soon after the *Amistad* was towed into port, the Connecticut abolitionists contacted New York abolitionist Lewis Tappan. Tappan joined with Simeon Jocelyn and Joshua Leavitt to form what he called the *Amistad* Committee. The *Amistad* Committee hired lawyers to represent the captives, raised money for their defense and upkeep, increased public support for their cause, recruited teachers to teach them, and eventually arranged for their return to Africa.

Tappan and his committee decided to file civil suits in New York against Montes and Ruiz for assault, battery, and false imprisonment. The civil suits created much anger and adverse publicity, but did succeed in focusing public attention on the broader moral issues that the *Amistad* affair highlighted. Tappan attended each day of the *Amistad* trial and wrote daily accounts of the proceedings for the abolitionist paper *Emancipator*.

The abolitionists hired Roger S. Baldwin to argue for the Africans. When abolitionists asked Yale-educated Baldwin to represent the Africans of the *Amistad*, he was a forty-six-year-old New Haven lawyer with a reputation for defending the unfortunate. He first represented abolitionist causes in 1831, when he confronted a mob seeking to block the building of a training school for blacks in New Haven.

Theodore Sedgwick and Seth Staples joined Baldwin on the *Amistad* defense team. Baldwin's primary legal goal called for winning the freedom of the Africans, and the arguments he stressed were those he thought to be the most successful. Often, these were narrow arguments based on property law instead of moralistic attacks on slavery. Baldwin argued that Ruiz and Montes were the criminals, not the Africans who fought for their freedom, and that the two Cubans deserved to be put to death for piracy. He constructed a case claiming that the Africans had been illegally kidnapped and enslaved because Spain had by treaty outlawed the African slave trade, and the captives had the right to free themselves however they could.

On September 14, 1839, all of the captured Africans except Burna, who was left ill at New Haven, were moved to Hartford, Connecticut, for their trials.

THE CRIMINAL TRIAL

On Wednesday, September 17, 1839, the circuit court impaneled a grand jury to consider the U.S. attorney's indictment of the Mende on charges of piracy and murder. In 1839, circuit courts heard criminal trials, presided over by a justice of the U.S. Supreme Court. Civil trials were usually heard by the district court. The first *Amistad* trial addressed the criminal charges of murder, mutiny, and piracy that the Cubans Montes and Ruiz had brought against the Africans of the *Amistad*. Judge Smith Thompson presided over the criminal trial that began on September 19, 1839.

Born in New York in 1768, Thompson graduated from Princeton in 1788 and taught school for several years. After clerking in the law firm of Gilbert Livingston and James Kent, he became a lawyer and married Sarah Livingston, his boss's daughter. Livingston's connections with powerful Jeffersonian politicians in New York probably contributed to Thompson's quick political success.

Eventually, Thompson served in the state legislature and accepted a seat on the New York Supreme Court, which he held until President James Monroe named him secretary of the navy in 1818. He served in that position until 1823, when he was appointed to the U.S. Supreme Court. He also enjoyed close ties with President Martin van Buren. He remained on the Supreme Court until his death in 1843.

The abolitionists pressed the judge to issue a writ of *habeas corpus* that would have freed the Mende, pending any formal charges against them. Judge Thompson of the U.S. Supreme Court denied the writ but also refused to indict the Mende for piracy or murder. He returned the case to the federal district court in Connecticut.

In the meantime, the Spanish government demanded custody of the Africans so that they could try them in Cuba for murder and piracy. In effect, Spain and the United States were calling upon the Pinckney Treaty and the 1819 treaty between Spain, Great Britain, and the United States to decide the status of the Mende. The Mende were being depicted as pirates, property, or innocent victims, depending on how American or European law interpreted the situation.

On September 18, 1839, Judge A. T. Judson opened the district court session to consider the claims filed in response to Lieutenant Gedney's suit for salvage. William Holabird, the U.S. attorney, asked the court to consider the Spanish ambassador's request for the return of all property on the *Amistad*, with no deduction for salvage. As an alternative, Holabird requested that the court order the return of the Mende to Africa if it determined that they were not slave property.

President van Buren had appointed William Holabird, the U.S. attorney for the District of Connecticut, a position that forced Holabird to decide what to do initially with the *Amistad*, its passengers, and its cargo. Holabird did not approve of the abolitionist movement, and his personal sympathies lay with Montes and Ruiz. At first he viewed the case as an open-and-shut matter of mutiny and murder, but he hoped that the case could be handled through diplomatic channels instead of by trying the *Amistad* Africans. Holabird believed that the courts should put the *Amistad* matter in the hands of the president, who in turn should deliver the captives to Spain. In a letter to Secretary of State John Forsyth as the trial began in Hartford, Holabird wrote, "I should regret extremely if the rascally blacks should fall into the hands of the abolitionists, with whom Hartford is filled" (Transcript of the *Amistad* Trials, p. 13).

A group of men who gave provisions to the Mende on the New York shore submitted their own claim for a salvage award. Judge Judson ordered a panel of attorneys in the case to determine the precise location where the navy crew seized the *Amistad*, so that he could establish which district court had jurisdiction. The district court adjourned on September 23, 1839, with Judge Judson directing it to meet in Hartford on the third Tuesday in November, after the judge had directed the U.S. marshal "to see that the prisoners should be comfortably provided for, with regard to food, clothing & c." In pursuance of this direction, the Africans were remanded back to the prison in New Haven (Transcript of the *Amistad* Trials, p. 16).

On October 17, 1839, Ruiz and Montes were arrested in New York, based on the suits of Cinque and Fuliwa for assault and battery and false imprisonment. The Spaniards were unable or unwilling to post the $1,000 bail, so they were imprisoned. The judge hearing the case decided that

Montes should be discharged on nominal bail and that the amount of bail for Ruiz should be reduced to $250.

THE CIVIL TRIAL

The district court for the District of Connecticut met on Tuesday, November 19, 1839, and the examination of witnesses occupied the entire day. Several claims asserted that the Mende were slaves. A lawyer for the Mende asked the court to dismiss the case for lack of jurisdiction, on the grounds that the Mende had arrived as free persons in the district of New York. U.S. Attorney Holabird presented the claim of the Spanish ambassador to the court. The Spanish ambassador had sent the claim to Secretary of State John Forsyth, a slaveholder from Georgia, asking for the return of all the Spanish property on the *Amistad*. The Spanish consul from Boston asked the court to order the return of the slave Antonio to the heirs of Ramon Ferrer, the dead captain of the *Amistad*.

On Wednesday, November 20, seven of the Africans were brought to court and after more testimony regarding the place where the *Amistad* was captured, Judge Judson found that the translator for the Mende was ill. He adjourned the district court on November 21, 1839, ruling that it would reconvene in New Haven on January 7, 1840.

In the meantime, President Martin van Buren, after consulting with his cabinet, decided that his administration would honor the Spanish claims. From the time that the first whisper of the *Amistad*'s capture in the United States reached his ear, President Van Buren understood its implications for his reelection and for race relations in the United States. At one point he even conspired with Secretary of State Forsyth to use the marines to kidnap the Africans after the second trial and sail them back to Cuba. U.S. Marines waited at the courthouse door in New Haven in January 1840 with a signed presidential order to "escort" the Africans to the USS *Grampus* once Judge Judson had ruled for the government and before the defense team could file an appeal.

While the *Grampus* waited in New Haven Harbor to take the Africans back to Cuba, the trial resumed on January 7, 1840. The court opened its session in New Haven, with Judge Andrew T. Judson presiding. At the opening of this session, the owners of part of the *Amistad*'s cargo submitted their request for the return of their goods. Judge Judson heard testimony for five days. The witnesses included three of the Mende: Cinque, Grabeau, and Fuliwa. James Covey, the interpreter, and Professor Gibbs of Yale College testified that the *Amistad* captives were recently from Africa. The evidence on this point was so clear that on the second day of the trial, Judge Judson said that he was fully convinced that the men were recently from Africa and that it was unnecessary to take up time in establishing that fact.

Cinque, the leader of the Africans, was called as a witness, and Covey repeated the oath to Cinque in the Mende tongue. Cinque testified that at the time of their capture by Lieutenant Gedney, a large number of them were on shore on Long Island. He also gave an account of the voyage to and from Havana, described their captivity, and demonstrated the way that Ruiz examined the Africans to ascertain whether they were healthy and sound. He also showed the position that they were forced to lie in when packed on board the slaver. Grabeau and Fuliwa were sworn and examined and testified to the same facts.

On January 13, 1840, Judge Judson rendered his decision about the *Amistad* and asked the two most important questions that still needed answering:

Shall these Africans, by a decree of this Court, be delivered over to the Government of Spain, upon the demand of her Minister as the property of Don Pedro Montes and Don Jose Ruiz? But if not, what ultimate disposition shall the Government of the United States make of them? (Transcript of the *Amistad* Trials, p. 22)

Judge Judson ruled that the Mende were not slaves under Spanish law and that he could not order their return to Cuba. On January 23, Judson issued a decree ordering the delivery of the Mende to the president for return to Africa and granting an award of salvage of the ship and its cargo to Lt. Gendey and his crew. The judge also ordered that Antonio be delivered to the heirs of the captain of the *Amistad*. U.S. Attorney Holabird cited the Spanish ambassador's demand for the return of all property and immediately appealed every part of the decree except the part about the slave Antonio. The owners of the goods on the *Amistad* appealed the portion of the decree that ordered payment of a salvage award.

An important legal question addressed and answered in the Connecticut and district courts involved the Pinckney Treaty of 1795 and the Anglo-Spanish Treaty of 1819. The 1795 Pinckney Treaty between Spain and the United States required the return of all Spanish property if the people who claimed it had proper proof of ownership. Judge Judson agreed that the Pinckney Treaty obligated the United States to return lawfully held Spanish property, but he emphasized the right of the federal courts to investigate how valid the property claims were. His review of the testimony and evidence in the district court trial established that the Spanish planters had produced no title to the enslaved Mende, only passes for their transportation. The passes incorrectly stated that the Mende were longtime inhabitants of Spanish territory when, in truth, they were recent arrivals in Cuba and free under Spanish law.

Judge Judson's opinion for the U.S. district court also stated that if the Mende were legally the slaves of the Spanish planters, the court would return them just as they would other merchandise that the planters owned. The Spanish-English-American treaty called for proof of ownership, and the courts were obligated to determine whether the foreign government's documents had been subject to fraud. The fraudulent origin of the passes for the Mende captives invalidated the planters' claims of slave property.

Two questions pierced the heart of the *Amistad* case: Were the Mende slaves from the *Amistad*, and if the Mende from the *Amistad* were not slaves, what authority did the federal courts have over them? Each federal court decided that the Mende were not slaves. The Spanish planters Ruiz and Montes claimed that they had legally purchased the *Amistad* Africans in Cuba, and they asked the U.S. district court to order the return of the slaves and the other property that they had left on the *Amistad*. Judge Judson decided that the Africans were not slaves under Spanish law and could not be returned to the planters without valid proof of ownership. Testimony in the district court trial proved that the Mende on the *Amistad* had arrived in Cuba in June 1839, and under Spanish law no Africans transported to Spanish territory after 1820 could be enslaved. The circuit court affirmed this decision.

The judicial decision that the Mende were not slaves under Spanish law did not provide the Africans' release from federal custody. The judge ordered that custody of the Mende be transferred from the federal courts to the president. Under the provisions of the 1819 Act, any enslaved Africans transported into the United States were to be delivered to the president for return to Africa at government expense. Judge Judson acknowledged that the Mende arrived in command of the *Amistad* rather than as enslaved persons, but he thought that the humanitarian objectives of the act called for a broad interpretation of its provisions. The circuit court decree upheld this part of Judson's decision.

On April 29, 1840, Judge Thompson presided over the two appeals of the district court decree, while also considering a motion from the Mende's lawyers to dismiss the appeal of the U.S. attorney. Thompson denied the motion for dismissal and affirmed the district court's decree. Immediately following Thompson's decree, Attorney Holabird filed an appeal to the Supreme Court. Judge Thompson granted that appeal to the next term of the Supreme Court, which would begin in January 1841.

APPEALING TO THE SUPREME COURT

Oral arguments in the *Amistad* case began in the Supreme Court in Washington, DC, on February 22, 1841. The Court suspended arguments after Justice Barbour died on February 25, but arguments resumed on March 1. Congressman and former President John Quincy Adams joined Roger S. Baldwin to argue the Africans' cause. Adams severely criticized Secretary of State Forsyth's handing of the *Amistad* affair. Adams argued that Forsyth was guilty of deception in his interpretation of the Spanish claims as an obligation to return slaves, rather than as a demand that the captives be returned for trial and executions in Cuba. On the other side, Attorney General Henry D. Gilpin presented the administration's case, underscoring that Spain's demands for the return of the *Amistad* captives to Cuba based on Pinckney's Treaty of 1795 were valid.

It took the Supreme Court about a month to decide the case. Associate Justice Joseph Story read the Court's ruling. The Court reversed Judge Judson's order to the executive to return the Africans to their homeland, but essentially upheld Judson's finding that the Africans had been illegally enslaved and had thus exercised a natural right to fight for their freedom. The Court had found Roger Baldwin's arguments more convincing than those of John Quincy Adams. On March 9, 1841, Justice Story delivered the opinion of the Supreme Court. The Court agreed that it was clear "beyond controversy" that the Mende were never the lawful property of Ruiz or Montes or any other Spanish subjects. By the laws of Spain, the Mende were declared to be free. The federal courts of the United States had no authority to detain the Mende once they determined that the Africans were not slaves and that they had entered the United States as free individuals.

The Court ordered the U.S. Circuit Court in Connecticut to free the Mende held in custody. Justice Thompson, as circuit justice for the District of Connecticut, subsequently ordered the release of the Mende. Upon learning of the Court's seven to one vote to recognize the status of the Africans as free persons, Baldwin praised the abolitionist cause.

GOING HOME

The Supreme Court ruling set the Africans free, but it revoked their tickets home when it struck down the district court's order to return them to Africa. The Van Buren administration waspishly refused to help; so, overjoyed with their freedom but frustrated at their lack of means to return home, the Africans relocated to Farmington, Connecticut. There, a number of Yale College students taught them to read English and converted them to Christianity.

In this laudable object, they received much assistance from James Covey, the interpreter. By his aid and that of John Ferry, a native of the Gissi country, Mendi and Gissi vocabularies were made by Professor Gibbs and published in the thirty-eighth volume of the *American Journal of Science* (Transcript of the *Amistad* Trials, p. 23).

Now that it had helped win the freedom of the Africans, the *Amistad* Committee worked to raise funds to pay for their return voyage to Africa. The Africans told their stories in local churches and demonstrated their education and conversion to Christianity. Through its representatives, the Committee located Mende country, and finally in October 1841, Lt. Governor Fergusson of Sierra Leone responded with information about Mendeland and an offer to accept the Africans. After eight months, the fund drive had raised $1,840, and this enabled the *Amistad* Committee to charter the barque *Gentleman* for the return voyage to Sierra Leone. By November 1841, she was ready to sail with thirty-five African freemen aboard.

The *Gentleman* carried more than the African freemen. It carried the dreams of the abolitionists to abolish U.S. slavery and the Atlantic slave trade. It carried the vision of the missionary transformation of African society. Several ministers and their families took the return journey to Africa with the *Amistad* Africans, including Mr. and Mrs. Raymond and Rev. James Steele, who were white; and Mr. Henry Wilson and Miss Tamor Clark, who were black. They planned to set up a Mende mission near Cinque's home and preach not only the Gospel but also American commerce, dress, and morality.

In mid-January 1842, the *Gentleman* arrived in Freetown—just about three years after Cinque had been kidnapped into slavery. The Africans were excited to be back home, and a welcoming crowd greeted them. In a bittersweet homecoming, Cinque learned that his village and most of his family had been wiped out in slaving wars. Once back home, most of the *Amistad* Africans drifted away from the American missionaries, until all that remained were ten adults and four children. Cinque himself lost contact with the mission and disappeared into the African interior. Of the fifty-three captives originally taken in chains onto the *Amistad*, only thirty-five lived to return to African shores.

NEWSPAPER COVERAGE OF *AMISTAD*

Newspapers played an important part in the *Amistad* trials. *The New London Gazette* reported that a "long black schooner" was sighted near Long Island, New York, in late August 1839. The newspapers followed the story of the African fugitives as they adapted to their surroundings, learned the language of their captors, and struggled for the right to return to their homeland. Some newspapers unsympathetically portrayed the Africans as savages. For example, the New York *Daily Express* described them as, "hardly above the apes and monkeys of their own Africa" (Jones, 1987). However, the *Emancipator*, the abolitionist paper of William Lloyd Garrison, provided extensive coverage of the case, as did the *New York America*. After students from Yale College began teaching the Mendi English and the Christian religion, the abolitionist newspapers recounted the harrowing experiences of the enslaved Africans. However, such coverage occurred in a political environment in which slavery as an institution created sharp divisions. Some non-abolitionist newspapers commented not only on the legal issues of the case, but on what was perceived as the radical antislavery stance of the abolitionists (Jones, 1987, pp. 48–49).

After the Supreme Court had ruled in favor of the Mendi and they returned to their home villages in Africa, the *Amistad* trials continued to impact America. The newspaper stories provided a rallying point for abolitionists who were often divided. They focused public attention on the inconsistencies between slavery and religious/political views that were important foundations of American culture, and they revealed the humanity of the Africans. The abolitionist newspaper the *Emancipator* prophesied in 1841, "Cinque will continue to be an object of interest and his name will be the watchword of freedom to America and her enslaved sons throughout the world."

AMISTAD, THE MOVIE

When Steven Spielberg made the feature film *Amistad* in 1997, he focused long-overdue attention on the case. His dramatic unfolding of the events is both vivid and riveting, and for the most part accurately recaptures most of the true story. When Spielberg retold the *Amistad* story in movie version, he rightly used dramatic license and created composite characters and representative scenes when documentary evidence did not exist or featured a maze of complicated twists and turns. Spielberg made an interesting movie that exposed many people to a story that they otherwise would not have ferreted out of the history books.

There are just a few glaring examples of dramatic license where the actual happenings in the story would have made a lasting historical impression. One such scene is the Supreme Court trial in Washington, DC, where Cinque and some of his fellow Africans sit, then stand in court and cry, "Give us free." This is a poignant scene, but the historical fact is even more poignant. A black man would not have been allowed inside the U.S. Supreme Court, much less be present while the justices heard a case. An imagination of the caliber of Steven Spielberg's could have created a scene to illustrate this great irony.

The movie portrays the character of Roger S. Baldwin, the attorney for the Africans, as a down-at-the-heels ambulance chaser. Baldwin was much more honorable and principled than he is shown to be in the movie. He defended the *Amistad* case without a fee because he was an abolitionist and believed in the *Amistad* cause. Later, he became the governor of Connecticut and then a U.S. senator from that state.

Perhaps the saddest commentary on the disparity between American ideals and American reality is embodied in the character of the black abolitionist played by Morgan Freeman in the movie. The Connecticut of the 1830s and 1840s paralleled the segregation in any southern state. Freeman's character could possess money, fame, freedom—any attribute—but as long as he had black skin, he would not have been allowed to sit and eat with white people. He would have been sent to an all-black tavern or out in the back room to eat. Spielberg could have communicated that terrible irony in an effective scene as well. The specter of Freeman's character working so hard to free the Africans but being denied such a basic freedom himself is even more horrible than the movie's opening scenes where Cinque and his fellow mutineers cut the throats of the captain and the cook.

In a unique example of the past reconciling with the future, the Freedom Schooner *Amistad*, a replica of the original ship and ambassador of New Haven, Connecticut, sails with her crew and the *Amistad* story from St. Petersburg, Florida, to Portland, Maine, and ports on the Great Lakes and Canada.[1]

NOTE

1. For more information about the schooner *Amistad*, visit the website http://www.amistadamerica.org/

REFERENCES

Barber, J. W. (1840). *History of the Amistad captives*. New Haven, CT: E. L. and J. W. Barber.

Jones, H. (1987). *Mutiny on the Amistad: The saga of a slave revolt and its impact on American abolition, law and diplomacy*. New York: Oxford University Press.

New York Commercial Advertiser. (1839, August 26).

Transcript of the *Amistad* trials. (n.d.). Retrieved October 11, 2003, from http://www.law.umkc.edu/faculty/projects/ftrials/amistad/AMISTD.HTM

11

The Bickford Murder of 1845: The Somnambulist and the Fallen Woman

Karen Elizabeth Chaney

Mr. and Mrs. Joel Lawrence got more than they bargained for on October 27, 1845. For eighteen months, they had owned a boardinghouse at 56 Charles Street off Cedar Lane on Boston's Beacon Hill. The couple soon discovered that running a boardinghouse was no easy task. If it wasn't the drunken woman pounding on the door, then it was the rowdy couples whose behavior often disrupted the household. The other night had been no exception. The drunken woman had returned and raised such a ruckus that the police arrested her for disorderly conduct. In addition to the occasional transient, the Lawrences currently rented rooms on the third floor to two female tenants, Mary Ann Bickford and Priscilla Blood. Both women often entertained gentleman friends and at times disturbed the peace.

Mrs. Bickford and her friend, Albert J. Tirrell, were especially disruptive. Their fights had become increasingly violent until they finally ended in tragedy. On October 26, 1845, Mr. Lawrence locked up the house at 9 p.m. and retired for the night. At approximately 5 a.m., a loud noise and the smell of smoke awakened the tenants. The Lawrences soon realized that the disturbances came from the third floor. After Mr. Lawrence called for help, he hurried upstairs and discovered fire in Mrs. Bickford's room and in front of Priscilla Blood's door. As the Lawrences extinguished the fire, they stumbled over Mrs. Bickford's badly burned corpse. She lay in a pool of blood, sparsely dressed with her throat cut from ear to ear. Several minutes earlier, the tenants had heard someone running down the stairs and outside the building. Since Lawrence had locked the house earlier, no one could have entered the building. The tenants immediately suspected Tirrell because they had seen him in her room after 9 p.m.

After setting the fire, Tirrell escaped the house and made his way to Mr. Fullam's stables in Bowdoin Square. He hired a carriage and a driver to take him to his wife's home in Weymouth. With his family's help, he purchased passage on the *Sultana*, which first sailed to Montreal and then south to New Orleans. As Albert Tirrell hid in a safe house, a beautiful young woman lay murdered in a Boston boardinghouse. Why did Mrs. Bickford die such a violent, unseemly death? What events led to this tragic end? What urban reality did this case expose? A reality that the Boston elite preferred hidden in the shadows because it tarnished Boston's reputation as a "religious and moral city."

THE TEMPESTUOUS LIFE OF MARY ANN BICKFORD

Mary Ann Dunn was born into a working-class family in Bath, Maine, on June 19, 1824. After her father's death, the family moved to Bangor. When Mary Ann was fifteen, she served as a domestic in Bangor and also worked in a cigar factory in Oldtown. At that time, she met James Bickford, a local cordwainer, or shoemaker, who fell in love with the young woman and paid court. The middle-aged Bickford was a hardworking, pious gentleman who offered an attractive alternative to life as a factory worker and domestic. In March 1840, the couple married in Brewer, Maine, and then moved to Bangor. Everything went well in the beginning. Then Mary Ann, now seventeen, gave birth to a daughter, Mary Elizabeth, on January 7, 1841. The child died from undisclosed causes on April 7, 1842. After the child's death, Mary Ann suffered subsequent bouts of depression that, according to some critics, triggered her moral decline. Her friends thought that a change of scenery would brighten her spirits. They persuaded her to visit Boston with them in May 1842.

The holiday in Boston changed Mary Ann's life forever. The beautiful clothes, magnificent shops on Washington Street, and the attentions of handsome young men overwhelmed her. She admitted to her friends that she wanted to live in Boston. After a few weeks, she reluctantly returned to her husband in Bangor. The couple set up housekeeping with a widow, but Mary Ann quickly grew restless. At that time she met John Johnson, a young man who promised her the adventurous life she longed for.

Desperate to escape her restrictive marriage, Mary Ann jumped at the man's proposition, and the couple boarded a ship in December 1842 and sailed to Newburyport. Mary Ann wrote to one of her friends on December 6, 1842, to explain her decision to leave. She realized that her actions had disgraced her sister and ruined her reputation. However, she could no longer live with a man whom she claimed was her "enemy." She felt trapped and regretted the day she had married Bickford.

Unfortunately, Mr. Johnson soon dashed Mary Ann's dreams. A few weeks after leaving Bangor, he deserted her in a Boston brothel. Destitute, she thought nothing of asking her husband for support and wrote to him from a boardinghouse in Boston. She pleaded for money to buy clothes and pay rent. She appealed to his emotions, complaining about serious illnesses that included pleurisy, a swollen stomach, and chronic toothache. The pain was often so severe that she could not move without screaming. It is unclear whether she suffered from venereal disease or had undergone an abortion.

On January 4, 1843, she wrote Bickford that she had moved to more pleasant housing but again needed money to pay her rent. She described her new landlady as a motherly figure who provided medicine and comfort. However, something happened at the house that forced her to move. By January 7, 1843, under the alias Maria Welch, she had relocated to the North End, to 16 North Margin Street, which she described as a very genteel house. She often vacillated between the security of her marriage and the excitement of her new life. Her thoughts of reconciliation often coincided with her need for money. In January 1843, she promised to live with Bickford on the condition that he move to Boston. Before the move, Mary Ann rented rooms on Endicott Street in the North End. Mary Ann and Bickford viewed the move differently. To Bickford, the relocation promised reconciliation, but to Mary Ann it provided the financial stability and the legitimate cover she needed to continue her new life. While he agreed to her request, he also acknowledged that the move was not wise economically. New England was suffering from a severe economic depression, and the job market in Boston was worse than in Bangor. However, he was eager to reconcile with Mary Ann at any cost: "I shall be happy in poverty, if you will only return to my fireside with reformation upon your brow" (Bickford, 1846, p. 13). His rhetoric, however, had the opposite effect on Mary Ann, who had no intention of living with him in poverty. Even while promising to set up house with Bickford, she continued to entertain young men. In a letter to a female friend dated January 24, 1843, she briefly mentioned reconciliation but in the next breath described the night she had spent with two handsome naval officers from the warship *Somers*. With the rare exception, she received gifts rather than money from her suitors. Timothy Gilfoyle, in *City of Eros*, distinguishes between prostitutes and "treaters": prostitutes accepted money for sex while treaters simply took gifts. Mary Ann knew the values of the gifts, itemizing the dollar values to her friends. The evidence suggests that Mary Ann fell into the latter category of treater. Needless to say, the move to Endicott Street never materialized.

As Mary Ann's reputation as "a woman about town" grew, she attracted the attention of various moral reformers. Mrs. Emeline Hovey, a self-proclaimed "friend of virtue," exposed Mary Ann's activities to Bickford, who was still in Bangor. Mary Ann had lied about the house on Margin Street. It was not a genteel boardinghouse but a notorious brothel. This explains her reason for discouraging Bickford from visiting the house. In February 1843, the concerned husband traveled to Boston to persuade his wife to return to Bangor. He went to North Margin Street, but the owner told him that Mary Ann had recently moved to Washington Street, but was expected to visit on February 9, 1843. During that visit, Bickford once again used moral persuasion. If she promised to practice monogamy, he would forgive her past sins. After Mary Ann agreed, Bickford took the first steps to establish a respectable home. After renting a house on Suffolk Street, he accepted a job as a shoemaker for Thomas Boot Manufacturer on Cambridge Street. Mary Ann, however, had second thoughts. She wrote her friend E. S. that her husband's limited finances and his inability to pay her large debts concerned her. In the next breath, she talked about the new man in her life and the exciting sleigh rides on Washington Street that were in vogue. She described the splendid robes, the magnificent fur muff, the grand horses, and the elegant sleigh. In contrast to Bickford, this new man was "the richest man's son" in Boston and they "made Washington Street tremble" (Bickford, 1846, p. 17). She confessed that she entertained the man and his brother even while discussing reconciliation with Bickford. Apparently, this new man dissuaded her from returning to her husband.

Mary Ann, therefore, confessed to Bickford that she could not give up her new life, but instead proposed a shocking compromise. She offered to live with him in exchange for some liberty, essentially proposing an open marriage. Bickford refused, appealing to her conscience, to her sense of family, and to the memory of their dead child. He accused her of confusing money with respectability. These men, he argued, "corrupt the morals of the city they claim to promote" (Bickford, 1846, p. 18). He warned her that these men would desert her once "their lust is satisfied and leave you to beg on the highway" (Bickford, p. 18). He, however, would remain constant.

Bickford's predictions were sadly realized. Her sleighing partner reneged on his promise to pay her bills, leaving her once again destitute. By March 26, 1843, she had moved from Washington Street to Canton Street and then back to the brothel on North Margin Street. By that time, her reputation as a prostitute was firmly established. It was not until June 1843 that Mary Ann and Bickford actually shared a house. In June, Mary Ann's limited finances forced her to once again consider living with Bickford. They actually moved into hired rooms on Townsend Place. Because she continued to entertain young men while Bickford was at work, they were forced to vacate the house after a month. Her behavior not only ruined her reputation, but tarnished her husband's as well. It could have opened him up to prosecution for running a brothel. He expressed his concerns to "Friend E.," fearing that Mary Ann was "lost to society, honor, and friends" (Bickford, 1846, p. 19). While Mary Ann was perfectly content with the situation, Bickford could not accept conditions that "would disgrace any man" (Bickford, p. 19). He had unwisely trusted his wife, but could no longer live with a woman who violated the natural laws of decency and honor.

In July 1843, Mary Ann moved to Sudbury Street with Emma L. and then in August rented her own tenement at 3 Fruit Street Place under her legal name, Mrs. Mary A. Bickford. During that time, she entertained several men, who reciprocated with various gifts, including some sheeting for the house. At one point, an older gentleman offered Bickford sixty-five dollars to "give up his claim. Comment is unnecessary" (Bickford, 1846, p. 21). Although the man paid her bills, he tempered his generosity by taking out a mortgage on her furniture and soon deserted her for unspecified reasons. She was forced to leave the house on March 1, 1844, because she suspected the police would arrest her, suggesting that the house doubled as a brothel. Apparently, Bickford was still working in Boston, but they lived separately.

After that, Mary Ann boarded for short periods in various parts of the city, but in July 1844, she went to New Bedford, notoriously known as New England's Sodom and Gomorrah. She lived in the notorious Hard Dig that consisted of five "bad houses" in which the tenants drank, fought, danced, and fornicated all night. She described the Hard Dig as the most vile area she had ever seen. She once again turned to Bickford for help. Although she desperately wanted to return to Boston, she needed six dollars to pay her board. Bickford once again capitulated and sent her seven dollars, primarily because she promised to leave New Bedford. But once she received the money, she reneged on her promise and decided to remain in New Bedford. Under the alias Maria Welch, she moved from the Hard Dig to more respectable housing. Bickford was furious. He refused to support her lifestyle in New Bedford, especially since she lied to extort money. In spite of his anger, he sent her five dollars when she once again appealed to his sympathy, complaining about recurring illness.

Although she refused to live with Bickford, she continually turned to him for protection. Bickford was more a father figure than a husband. On October 24, 1844, she asked him to protect her from a former lover, Frank C., who had been jailed for undisclosed offenses. After his release from jail, he was determined to reconcile with Mary Ann. She was concerned not because Frank C. was violent, but because he would threaten her newest relationship. She told Bickford that she had found a new "first-rate friend," Albert J. Tirrell. She admitted to Bickford that it was better for her "to be steady with one, than to be with every one." Bickford never understood why he as her lawful husband could not be her one steady man.

In spite of Mary Ann's growing promiscuity, Bickford took his role as moral reformer seriously and was determined to save his wife from herself. When he went to New Bedford, he found her living with Tirrell at the Railroad House as man and wife. In spite of Tirrell's concerns, Mary Ann assured him that Bickford would not file an indictment against him for adultery. Tirrell's father had been a respected and wealthy shoe manufacturer in Weymouth. At nineteen, Albert married Orient Humphrey Tirrell, possibly a cousin, on February 6, 1843, and they had two children, Catherine and Abbie. Tirrell had gone through the motions of respectability but was often unfaithful with numerous women, including Mary Ann.

In February 1845, Mary Ann realized that a seemingly respectable marriage would be the perfect front for her adulterous affair with Tirrell. She asked Bickford to act as her agent and to rent rooms in a respectable house. The couple would then masquerade as a happily married couple, but occupy separate rooms. Tirrell would visit weekly and pass as her brother. Bickford was appalled at such "a vile proposition. I fear your mind is sadly debased" (Bickford, p. 26). Mary Ann's plan fell through when Bickford refused to aid and abet her adulterous behavior. His earlier experiences on Townsend Street had not only humiliated him, but opened him up to possible prosecution.

When Tirrell and Mary Ann arrived in Boston on February 20, 1845, they boarded first at the Pembroke House and then for three weeks at the North American House. Tirrell's depravity reached a new low when he openly flaunted his relationship in front of his wife and family. He persuaded Mary Ann to accompany him to his wife Orient's house in Weymouth. He planned to force Orient to accept his paramour as part of the family. Although Mary Ann had made a similar proposal to Bickford, Tirrell's plan offended her sensibilities, perhaps because she sympathized with the woman. To openly live with his family surpassed the boundaries of decency even for Mary Ann. This marked a turning point in her relationship with Tirrell. Subsequently, they left New Bedford and traveled to Albany and Saratoga Springs before returning to Boston to the Hanover House under the name Jackson.

The relationship grew increasingly violent, and at one point Tirrell savagely ripped her dress. When the hotel management discovered the real nature of their relationship, it evicted them on April 24, 1845. In May, the hotel filed an indictment against Tirrell for adultery.

Tirrell then rented a house on London Street under the name Miss Welch because of the indictment. Because of Tirrell's illegal activities, other criminals recognized him as an easy target. Two men called at the house, posing as police officers. They told him that they had a warrant for his arrest but would dismiss it if he paid them $100. Tirrell soon realized that two "spongers" had successfully conned him because he was as an easy mark. The "spongers" knew that because of his own legal problems, Tirrell could not file a police report.

On June 16, 1845, Tirrell and Mary Ann left the house because of a disagreement and the constant fear of arrest. At this time, Mary Ann decided to leave him and went to her mother's house in Guilford, Maine. Tirrell, desperate to win her back, followed her from one place to another. She eventually returned to New Bedford and stayed at the Hard Dig because the Railroad House was closed. She wrote to Bickford, expressing her growing concerns to him about Tirrell's violent temper: "I expect to get killed when he does come" (Bickford, 1846, p. 28). She assured Bickford that Tirrell and she were separated. Mary Ann was concerned about three trunks filled with clothes and jewelry that represented her entire estate. She left them with her husband and begged him not to give them to Tirrell. She knew that he would sell the contents for instant cash, once again leaving her destitute and at his mercy. In spite of her fears, Tirrell convinced her to reconcile on June 22, 1845, sealing the deal with a gold watch. They traveled to Albany and then to New York and stayed at the Lorillard House until they were once again evicted for misbehavior. In July 1845, they returned to Boston and moved to the United States Hotel under the name of Hale. She wrote to Bickford, asking him to bring clean shirts and her accordion to the hotel. When he arrived, she asked him to accompany her to the South End to visit some mutual friends from Bangor. She confessed to Bickford that she knew Tirrell would kill her. When they were living in Newport, Tirrell demanded some of her more valuable dresses to sell because he needed instant cash. When she refused, he struck her, knocking her to the ground. To save her life, she promised to do whatever he wanted.

When Bickford called at her hotel on July 24, 1845, he witnessed Tirrell's violent temper. When Mary Ann told him that she was going shopping with her husband, Tirrell threatened her life, forbidding her to leave: "You shall not go out alive by G-d" (Bickford, 1846, p. 31). He eventually acquiesced if she promised to return, but forced her to leave the gold watch. Bickford accompanied his wife as far as Hanover Street. She eventually met her female friend E. W., who took her to Joel Lawrence's boardinghouse on Mt. Vernon Avenue. On July 25, 1845, Mary Ann packed her bags and left Boston alone. In September, she returned from Attleboro to Boston to check the police register for a possible indictment against her.

In September, the police arrested Tirrell in New Bedford for the adultery indictment that the Hanover House had filed in May. He appeared in Boston Municipal Court and was then sent to the Leverett Street Jail. Mr. Bayley, a family friend, posted Tirrell's bail. Numerous people, including Tirrell's family, a Boston merchant, and a Weymouth selectman appealed to District Attorney Samuel Parker for a stay of the proceedings. Parker agreed to postpone them for six months if Tirrell paid costs and promised to amend his behavior and keep the peace. The hotel, not the family, filed the charge because it needed to distance itself from scandal for economic reasons. Neither Mary Ann's nor Tirrell's family ever considered such a move.

Immediately after Tirrell's release, he violated the court order and searched for Mary Ann. During Tirrell's brief imprisonment, she went into hiding in the North End. About three weeks before the murder, Mary Ann moved from the North End to the Lawrences at 56 Charles Street off Cedar Lane. After Tirrell's release from jail, he rented a room at 9 Elm Street under the alias Albert DeWolfe. He subsequently found Mary Ann at the Lawrences and visited her nightly while maintaining his room on Elm Street. He grew increasingly jealous, possessive, and abusive. He often purchased clothing and shoes for her, but then destroyed them in front of her. Why did Mary Ann repeatedly reconcile with a man she obviously feared? Priscilla Blood testified at the trial that Mary Ann "liked to quarrel with him, as he had such a good time making up" (Weeks, 1846, p. 11). The altercations soon escalated into physical violence and culminated in murder. On October 27, 1845, Tirrell cut Mary Ann's throat and set the room on fire. Thomas Smith, Bickford's employer at the shoe factory, sent a cursory note to Bickford in Bangor, informing him that "your wife had her throat cut this morning and died, and I want you to come up without delay" (Bickford, 1846, p. 34). For whatever reason, the coroner buried Mary Ann's charred body before Bickford arrived to reclaim her.

THE ARREST

Immediately after the murder, Tirrell went to Fullam's Stable in Bowdoin Square. He rented a carriage and driver, who promptly took him to his family's house in Weymouth. With his family's help, he boarded a ship and sailed first to Montreal and then south to New Orleans. Some sources suggest that he intended to escape west to California. Officials eventually arrested him in New Orleans on December 6, 1845, and extradited him back to Boston, where he was arraigned on February 26, 1846. Tirrell's family hired Rufus Choate and A. B. Merrill, two distinguished Boston attorneys, to defend him. The team based its subsequent defense on somnambulism, or sleepwalking. Because of the overwhelming amount of circumstantial evidence against him, a mental illness defense was the logical choice.

THE PRESS COVERAGE

According to Mrs. Mary Ann B. Brown in her speech on moral reform to the Worcester Female Reform Society, there were 500 brothels in Boston in 1839 that were filled with women whose seducers had deserted them. Prostitution and houses of ill fame were the stuff of court calendar and crime reports published in the penny presses. These newspapers chronicled countless indiscretions involving street trotters and disturbances at brothels that ranged from petty larceny to drunken and disorderly behavior. Massachusetts statute Chapter 130, Section 8 sentenced anyone who kept a house of ill fame for the purposes of prostitution or lewdness to two years in the county jail and a fine of $300. In these statutes, moral misbehavior spilled over into the legal arena and made its way into the press. The Bickford case provided titillating fodder for the penny press because it involved sex, adultery, arson, and murder. It was the perfect opportunity for the press to assume its role as the public's moral arbiter and decry the corruptness of city life while preaching its consequences.

As soon at the story hit the papers, the reports emphasized the murder's sensationalism and the victim's questionable character. The *Boston Bee* compared the case to the Helen Jewett homicide in New York City in 1836. Richard Robinson had been accused of brutally murdering his lover, Helen Jewett, a well-known prostitute in a brothel. The press immediately attacked Mary Ann's character and condemned Lawrence's house as a brothel. Although the Lawrences denied the charge, the city never granted them a boardinghouse license. The press reported that Julia King, a notorious prostitute, had previously used the house as a brothel. The *Bee* reported that "the premises have been used a house of assignation—rooms being kept for the accommodations of those in the habit of visiting them" ("Horrible Murder," 1845). The papers then moved to the graphic description of the corpse. The *Bee* referred to Mary Ann as "a young and beautiful female of 23" who lay half-naked on the floor covered by a blood-soaked sheet ("Horrible Murder"). Her "head was thrown back, exposing a ghastly and terrible cut from ear to ear, the jugular vein and windpipe being entirely severed" ("Horrible

Murder"). According to the *Boston Post*, her throat was "cut from ear to ear" and the "skin around her mouth burnt to a crisp" ("Awful Murder," 1845).

The New York papers also picked up the story. George Wilkes, the editor of the *National Police Gazette*, also compared the murder to the Helen Jewett tragedy. The Jewett murder had fascinated Wilkes. He eventually published a novel in 1849 that had been serialized in the *Gazette*. In the Bickford coverage, Wilkes published several detailed drawings depicting both the murder and the arson. One drawing portrayed a well-dressed male leaning over a woman's prostrate body as he cut her throat. Her head hung over the bed, her long hair touching the floor. The second graphic showed Tirrell's escape from the burning room. Wilkes sentimentalized Mary Ann, referring to her as "a paragon of virtue and an irreproachable wife" ("Destiny of Crime," 1845). This more sympathetic and romantic portrait differed from those of the Boston papers, which excoriated her character. Wilkes attributed the crime to unbridled passion and the effects of lust on the human psyche. He argued that this murder "speaks a portentous warning to every victim of misguided lust" ("Destiny of Crime," 1845).

For the most part, the pretrial coverage portrayed Mary Ann as a wanton young woman who was in part responsible for her own murder. The *Mail* suggested that she fell under the spell of an older woman who introduced her to a world that prized the material over the spiritual. The editorial was a diatribe against a young woman's susceptibility to vanity. The pretrial coverage so completely ruined Mrs. Bickford's character that it turned Tirrell into more a victim than a cold-blooded murderer who cut her throat.

The second phase of coverage began with the trial on March 24, 1846, in Boston's court house. The *Daily Times* suggested that interest in the case had subsided, due perhaps to little pretrial coverage. Because the couple were not Bostonians, the public had no vested interest. Mary Ann and Tirrell were transients who escaped to Boston to avoid the legal consequences of their crimes. They belonged to the criminal element that was an unwelcome but unavoidable part of urban reality. Other pennies, however, disagreed. Capital trials, by their very nature, excited interest. The Bickford murder provided the public with a titillating glimpse into the seedy underbelly of conventional society. This was a different reality than the one that defined the elite on Beacon Hill. The two existed simultaneously: the boardinghouses and brothels stood within blocks of the elite homes on Beacon Hill. Urban life was a constantly changing landscape in which boundaries were blurred and no longer delineated.

As the trial began, the spectators gathered to watch this reality played out in a Boston courtroom. The readers who could not attend the trial lived vicariously through the press. The papers described everything in great detail, including Tirrell's appearance. According to the *Boston Mail*, men were innately curious about the appearance of men who committed violent acts. The press focused on the shape of his head and mouth, because according to physiognomy, these features revealed much about a person's character. Tirrell was six feet tall, muscular, and clean-shaven. He had a high forehead and an unusually large mouth. The corners were turned down, suggesting either grief or violent passion. In spite of his gentlemanly attire, his facial features reminded the press more of a mechanic (workman) or farmer than of a well-bred gentleman. Throughout the proceedings, the defendant sat emotionless and appeared unconcerned about what he had done or about the verdict. The papers suggested that his calm demeanor reflected a firm nerve and strong will.

In addition to the trial's sensationalism, the public attended the trial to hear Rufus Choate, who was known as much for his rhetorical skills as for his legal knowledge. On March 26, 1846, the crowd gathered for a pivotal moment in the trial—Choate's closing statement. The *Boston Mail* described the intense excitement, comparing the atmosphere in the courtroom to a galvanic battery. The crowd stood packed so closely that the energy passed between them as a conduit. The *Boston Mail* described Choate "as the great galvanic battery of human oratory" ("Trial of Albert," 1846). The electric energy passed through the brains of the closest observers and into their spinal columns and then from heart to heart. The crowd hushed as Choate rose to speak. What he lacked in conventional masculine beauty, he made up with his charismatic command of the audience. The reporters described his trademark curly dark hair, his brilliant black eyes, and the trembling hands that showed "that this great battery was highly charged with Heaven's own fire" ("Trial of Albert," 1846). The crowd stood mesmerized "cheek to breast and shoulder to shoulder, listening intensely" and "forming a chain for the electric fluid to do its work on the soul" ("Trial of Albert"). Choate, the consummate showman, understood the persuasive power of language. He spoke in calculated sentences, pointing his finger at the "weeping, trembling prisoner." He then wiped his brow and ran his fingers through his hair. The *Boston Mail* reporter compared the fingers to electrical charges that he shook over the judges, jury, lawyers, and audience, much like a "Roman Catholic Priest scatters the holy water upon his devout and worshipping audience" ("Trial of Albert," 1846). Choate's skills and his dynamic personality transcended the ordinary into the realm of the supernatural.

THE QUICK VERDICT

On Saturday, March 28, 1846, the case went to the jury. It deliberated for fewer than two hours and returned a verdict of not guilty. When questioned, the jury admitted that it had never considered the somnambulism argument, but based its verdict on the prosecution's failure to prove its burden. In the posttrial coverage, the press criticized the verdict. While the *Boston Mail's* editor did not dispute the jury's integrity, it questioned its wisdom. The overwhelming amount of circumstantial evidence was more than enough to convince any reasonable man of Tirrell's guilt. George Wilkes condemned the verdict as perverted. While everyone eagerly condemned Mary Ann, Wilkes reminded the reader that Tirrell was not an innocent victim. He was an adulterer, a spendthrift, an abusive husband, and an uncaring father who had abrogated his family responsibility for his "abandoned and degraded paramour" ("Boston Tragedy," 1846). To Wilkes, arson was the more serious crime because it endangered innocent people and private property.

Wilkes argued that Choate's defense strategy was flawed. While he did not doubt the existence of somnambulism, he suggested that Choate had manipulated the facts to his end. He referred to several famous men, including Alexander the Great and Benjamin Franklin, who purportedly suffered from this disorder. However, neither of these men was violent when in that state. Since no evidence proved that somnambulists committed murder, to use it as a defense strategy was preposterous. How could anyone in a state of somnambulism overpower a woman, throw her on the floor, cut her throat, and then escape after setting strategically placed fires? Any genuine somnambulist awakens before committing acts that violate his conscience. This defense strategy was pure humbug intended to divert the jury from the real issue.

The *Boston Bee* criticized other pennies, including the *Courier*, the *Mercantile Journal*, and the *Transcript* for their response to the verdict. The *Bee* defended the decision, arguing that a legally sworn jury had weighed the evidence and come to a verdict based on the rule of law. It criticized the press and public who disagreed with the decision and who insisted on trying Tirrell "extra-judicially" ("Case of Tirrell," 1846). If, however, the trial were unfair, the pennies were obligated "to haul Tirrell over the coals of public opinion from which he suffered so much before his side of the story was told" ("Case of Tirrell," 1846). Everyone agreed, however, that both the prosecution and the defense had conducted an impartial trial. The public apparently agreed with the verdict. The *Bee* reported that as Tirrell left the courtroom a vindicated man, the public cheered.

LEGAL ISSUES—SOMNAMBULISM

The defense team's decision to argue somnambulism was controversial. The public was increasingly skeptical of any defense that delved into the shadowy realm of mental disorder. To most people, the insanity defense was humbug, a convenient ploy that protected murderers who abrogated individual responsibility. The team based its strategy in part on Tirrell's alleged history as a somnambulist. A. B. Merrill's opening set the stage for a scientific explanation of the disorder. After distinguishing among various types of somnambulism, he moved to a theory of sleep and dreaming. According to this theory, numerous delicate and sensitive fibers cover the body's surface. These fibers originate in the brain, branch out and adapt to sensory perception such as sight, sound, and taste. These fibers act as conduits through which the brain communicates with the body. After a certain amount of external stimuli, these fibers become exhausted. This exhaustion results in inertia, called sleep, that "render to the mind no account of what is going on around us" (Weeks, 1846, p. 21). Disease also affects normal sleep patterns. In sleepwalking or somnambulism, a disease overstimulates certain senses such as hearing and sight while leaving others inactive. If intense enough, the stimulation overpowers the will. The mind focuses on its own impressions and lacks the reason to correct erroneous perceptions. People in this state can perform various normal activities with no consciousness of the situation. Thus, the theory suggests a serious disconnect between involuntary biological activity and the conscience or the will.

After Merrill's opening, Choate introduced expert medical witnesses to support this argument, including Dr. William Channing, who cited numerous documented cases, including that of Lord Culbertson. In 1686, Culbertson murdered a member of the Life Guard but was acquitted because he was in a state of somnambulism. Channing then cited numerous authorities on the scientific theory of sleep. While sleeping, the individual breathes normally and involuntarily, while the memory and imagination create acute visions in the dream state. He acknowledged a distinct disparity in sleep between the will to act and the conscience to prevent certain actions. Physical powers increase during sleep while the moral agency decreases. Thus, people perform acts in sleep that they would never commit while in a conscious waking state. Dr. Woodward, the well-respected superintendent of the Lunatic Hospital in Worcester, confirmed Channing's theories. He testified that many sleepwalkers perform normal, daily functions such as dressing and eating. Claustrophobia was an important component of this disorder. The somnambulist experienced fits more commonly in a closed room than in open areas. He concluded that Tirrell's actions during the murder were perfectly consistent with those of somnambulism.

The defense team then moved from theory to the concrete. They called several family members who testified that Tirrell had suffered from symptoms in childhood. As a child, he often awakened at night in the winter and wandered to his neighbors. Tirrell often emitted strange, smothered sounds and screams that frightened those around him. While in this state, he also committed several violent acts. Tirrell often rushed to the window, tore the curtains, and broke the glass. At times, he suffered paranoia, convinced that an assassin was chasing him around the house. After Tirrell's marriage, he attempted to murder his mother and wife. The incidents increased after he met Mary Ann. According to the testimony, she had confided to several people that he often beat her while in this state. Mary Ann, at one point in New York, allegedly prevented Tirrell from jumping out a third-story window. Mary Ann herself, however, never alluded to such aberrant behavior. Her letters suggested that he was fully awake and cognizant when he abused her.

SOCIAL ISSUES: THE UNDERMINING ENTICEMENTS OF URBAN LIFE

The Bickford murder case dramatized the central role of women in nineteenth-century society. Women's journals, weekly papers, and advice books addressed the importance of marriage, the woman's role in raising moral children, and her role in providing a well-run home. The *Boston Saturday Evening Gazette* referred to the family as the nursery of the state and church that educated children to serve society and strengthen the nation. The morality tales in the advice manuals and papers often pictured a pious woman holding the Bible and attending church weekly, if not daily. These stories emphasized the power of a submissive and pious Christian woman to convert her doubting husband through the power of scripture and moral example. Society placed the woman on a pedestal, suggesting that the mother performed the highest service for the state.

Mary Ann rejected this conventional image of proper womanhood. Rather than provide stability, marriage stifled her. She and Albert Tirrell chose to live outside the boundaries of traditional society. This behavior not only destroyed their characters but had far-reaching consequences. Their promiscuity mocked the family as a moral, religious, and economic unit. The couple's crimes were not just moral indiscretions but legal ones as well. Adultery undermined the integrity of the family and violated the financial contract between man and woman. Marriage was a business arrangement that connected families, resulting in economic and social power. The law sanctioned the union because it enhanced the economic and moral well-being of society and, by extension, the nation. Some critics suggested that if Mary Ann had received a better religious education, she would not have compromised her morals and made such destructive choices.

The murder also dramatized the anonymity of the city. It was a Darwinian environment in which people used any means to survive, regardless of the consequences. In the city, the end justified the means. The criminal read his environment well, luring gullible young men into the gambling dens and seducing financially destitute women into prostitution. For some, the city represented upward mobility while to others it offered anonymity that protected them from authorities. Mary Ann and Albert understood the value of anonymity as a safety net and used it to their advantage. Under various aliases, they moved from one hotel to another every few weeks, keeping one step ahead of the authorities. Hotel managements often evicted the couple for their rowdy and adulterous behavior. This behavior damaged the hotels' reputations and affected their profit margins as well. In order to protect their good names and attract better customers, hotels could not afford any exposure to scandal.

IMPACT ON LAW AND POPULAR CULTURE

The jury admitted that its verdict was not based on somnambulism. Was there another plausible explanation? One possible answer rests with Mary Ann herself. Was it possible that Mrs. Bickford's character had influenced the verdict and outweighed the prosecution's case? If the jury were society's conscience, then was this verdict an indictment of all fallen women or of society for tolerating immoral behavior? Bickford sat at the center of this case, not just as victim but also as cause. Both the prosecution and the defense portrayed her as an evil force who overpowered Tirrell's reason and drove him to commit unspeakable acts. Mary Ann, therefore, was the instrument of her own demise. The jury ignored the evidence of Tirrell's character—his open adultery, his cruelty, and the abrogation of his responsibility to family, community, and ultimately to society. Was justice lopsided in this case? Had Mary Ann paid for her sins because of her reputation while the man who murdered her went free?

CULTURAL IMPACT

Several individuals and newspapers published pamphlets that were either trial reports or semi-biographical sketches. The *Boston Mail* and the *Times* published fairly accurate documents that recreated the daily activities during the trial. Some of these pamphlets had specific moral agendas. In H. B. Skinner's report of the trial, the portrait on the cover portrayed Tirrell as a well-dressed, clean-shaven young man. The caption cautioned young men against beautiful women who would seduce them with language and sexual advances. Skinner suggested that immoral women caused men's downfall.

In addition to the trial pamphlets, other authors published works that were allegedly more biographical. These pamphlets for the most part emphasized the consequences of immoral behavior. The work titled "The Authentic Life of Mrs. Mary Ann Bickford" was the most credible. Mrs. Bickford's husband, James, sanctioned the pamphlet to counter the blatant misconceptions in other publications. It included several letters and first-hand accounts that enhanced its credibility. Mary Ann's portrait on the title page depicted a well-groomed, respectable woman dressed in an elegant gown. Her dress cost $100 and symbolized her love for the material over the spiritual. The author poignantly stated that the officials found the dress in her trunk on the day of the murder, sublimely linking the murder to the dress and then to her vanity. The work convincingly chronicled Mary Ann's life up to the murder. Bickford published it in response to what he called the "wholly fictitious" work attributed to a clergyman from Brunswick, Maine.

The clergyman's agenda was ultimately more religious and political than biographical. The pamphlet began as a cautionary tale about illicit sex. As part of his religious agenda, he incorporated literary motifs such as the dream sequence, in which the main character experiences an epiphany and seeks redemption. One graphic metaphorically depicted the consequences of sin, portraying Mary Ann sleeping amid dancing devils. The position of the body recalled the graphic of Mary Ann lying in a pool of blood. As Mary Ann struggled with demons, she confessed her sins and found forgiveness. The author's ultimate goal, however, was a political attack on the South and the institution of slavery. He introduced a Southern gentleman, a fictional character, who first seduced Mary Ann and introduced her to a life of sin. He then compared the slaveholder to the seducer. The author described the young sons of Southern slaveholders attending a slave auction and purchasing "a beautiful and accomplished female" for sex much as the male purchased a prostitute in a brothel. Thus, the abolitionist linked the wanton sex trade to slavery, suggesting that both were responsible for the nation's moral decline.

In another pamphlet, described as a "snapper-upper," the author, a widow from Weymouth, Massachusetts, chronicled Tirrell's various eccentricities. The author blended some fact with fiction, using a hodgepodge of literary devices. While the widow claimed to have known Tirrell, the fantastical narrative undercut her credibility. Like the clergyman, the widow incorporated an elaborate dream sequence. Tirrell's journey began within the context of a letter to his mother written while imprisoned in New Orleans. In the dream, a violent storm shipwrecked him on an island. As he struggled to return to the mainland, he continually encountered Mary Ann's ghost. While he attempted to escape the ghost, he never accepted responsibility for her murder. The narration moved from the repentant sinner to Tirrell as a Paul Bunyanesque character who performed incredible acts of strength and possessed supernatural powers over animals. His behavior became more bizarre and immoral. Ultimately, his depravity led him to New Bedford, the Sodom and Gomorrah of New England, where he continued his "career" as "rake and libertine." The author condemned the city not only for its licentiousness but also for its extremely high murder rate. In five months, the sextons secretly buried thirty-four "young and beautiful creatures who had been betrayed and abandoned by heartless men in houses of ill fame" ("Widow of Weymouth," 1846, p. 24). She suggested that most of these women committed suicide with prussic acid mixed with minute soda. She then compared these unfortunate, ruined women to the "fair-haired children of promise" who lived in the "country districts" sheltered by loving parents, underscoring the importance of family as a moral shelter. She also pitted the bucolic countryside against the dangerous and immoral city. The pamphlet evolved into a diatribe against the whaling industry of New Bedford. The author linked the whaling magnates to the moral corruption of the city and society. The merchants catered to the sailors' inherently weak characters. These men, who were more susceptible to women and liquor after months at sea, immediately headed for the brothels and taverns. The merchants controlled the taverns and the brothels. Thus, the money that the sailors spent in these establishments immediately went back to the merchants. The sailors were then forced to sign onto more voyages. While the merchants grew richer, the sailors grew poorer. Like the slaveholder-prostitute in the clergyman's diatribe, the merchant permanently indentured the sailor, perpetuating a vicious cycle.

Ultimately, these authors were concerned with the character of American society. Did America want a society based on solid republican values or one that valued the almighty dollar at an untenable moral cost?

After Tirrell's trial, the murder receded into memory. Mary Ann was buried unceremoniously in an undisclosed grave while Tirrell was acquitted of arson. Tragically, many young women came from an economically depressed Bangor to Boston to pursue better lives. These young women were exposed to the dangers of the city and, like Mary Ann, ended up in brothels. Many suffered the deadly consequences of their indiscretions in the clinics of practitioners like Madame Restell in New York. Many abortionists like Restell advertised certain abortive medications in the classifieds that were disguised as legitimate cures for female disorders. In 1848, a young mill girl, Sarah Furber, died from a bungled abortion. To shift suspicion, the doctors brought the body to Boston, hoping to sell it to the medical community as a legitimate corpse for dissection. However, when the physicians examined her body, they quickly realized that Sarah had not died from natural causes but had been murdered in a back alley abortion clinic. Whether the death was from a botched abortion or from a murderous paramour, the outcome was the same. These deaths were the tragic results of a counterculture that traded money for sex and prized the almighty dollar over virtue and respectability. Abortion clinics and brothels were parts of an economic subculture that made its living off the sins of others. The unfortunate ended up in the crime reports and the county lockup or died in back alley clinics or were dragged from the Charles River. In contrast, the urban survivor read the landscape, avoided the pitfalls, and lived within the accepted boundaries of social conduct that promised upward mobility and economic success. Some people, like Mary Ann and Albert Tirrell, suffered the tragic consequences of devious behavior and forever fell into the cracks of urban anonymity.

REFERENCES

Awful murder of a female and attempted arson. (1845, October 28). *Boston Post.*

Bickford, J. (1846). *The authentic life of Mrs. Mary Ann Bickford.* Boston: Published by the Compiler.

The Boston tragedy. (1846, April 4). *National Police Gazette.*

The case of Tirrell. (1846, April 7). *Boston Bee.*

Clergyman of Brunswick. (1846). *Life and death of Mrs. Maria Bickford.* Boston.

The destiny of crime. (1845, November 15). *National Police Gazette.*

Gilfoyle, T. J. (1992). *City of Eros: New York City prostitution and the commercialization of sex, 1790–1920.* New York: Norton & Co.

The horrible murder and attempted arson yesterday morning. (1845, October 28). *Boston Bee.*

Skinner, H. B. (1846). *The trial of Albert John Tirrell.* Boston.

Trial of Albert J. Tirrell. (1846). Boston: Daily Mail.

The trial of Albert J. Tirrell for the murder of Maria A. Bickford. Fourth Day. (1846, March 28). *Boston Mail.*

Weeks, J. E. P., Esq. (1846). *Trial of Albert John Tirrell.* Boston: Daily Times.

Widow of Weymouth. (1846). *Eccentricities and anecdotes of Albert J. Tirrell.* Boston.

12

The Parkman Murder of 1849: *The Commonwealth v. John White Webster*

Karen Elizabeth Chaney

No one could have predicted the tragic events that unfolded on November 23, 1849, in Boston, Massachusetts, or smell the hint of murder in the brisk air. The day began like any other autumn day. Newsboys hawked the dailies on Washington Street to a news-hungry public while merchants opened their stores to a pre-Thanksgiving crowd, and omnibuses carried passengers to and from Cambridge. Stonemasons carted granite to the New Jail site, located on the banks of the Charles River near the Boston Medical College. Young children hurried off to school while Harvard University medical students crowded into the medical college to attend the lectures of Oliver Wendell Holmes on medicine and Professor John White Webster on chemistry. Across the river in Cambridge, Dr. Webster's three daughters happily anticipated a party later that evening. As they chose the perfect dress, their father nervously prepared for his 1:30 p.m. meeting with Dr. George Parkman, a childhood-friend-turned-creditor. For weeks, Webster had avoided Parkman, dodging his notes and postponing appointments. But he had run out of excuses and now prepared to face him.

THE MURDER OF GEORGE PARKMAN

Dr. Parkman left his house at 8 Walnut Street on Beacon Hill in mid-morning and walked down the bustling city streets toward the college. He turned left on Cambridge Street and continued to the green grocers at Vine and Blossom to reserve a head of lettuce for his invalid daughter's dinner. When he reached Grove Street, he acknowledged the owner of the iron foundry that stood on the corner. Parkman then turned right and walked up the steps and into the college. Ephraim Littlefield, the college janitor, saw him for the last time as Parkman entered the building.

Once inside, Parkman immediately turned left and entered Webster's lecture room, which contained two small offices in the back. A nervous Webster faced his angry adversary, hoping to once again sidestep Parkman. While the meeting began as a civil but cautious discussion, it soon erupted into a contentious altercation. Parkman was furious with Webster for refusing to repay a long-standing loan and for fraudulently mortgaging his mineralogical collection to both Parkman and Parkman's brother-in-law, Robert Gould Shaw. Webster never intended to repay the loan but simply hoped to negotiate an extension. Parkman threatened to expose him to the college and the police. As the argument escalated, Webster grew more agitated, not just for his own sake but for his family's as well. Parkman shouted threats and insults, waving his finger in Webster's face. In one rash moment, Webster panicked, grabbed a large piece of wood and struck Parkman fatally across the head. According to Webster, he "stooped down over him, and he seemed to be lifeless. Blood flowed from his mouth and I got a sponge and wiped it away" ("Parkman Tragedy," 1850).

Webster thought about calling for help, but realized that it was fruitless. Even if Parkman were still alive, Webster had nonetheless attacked a colleague. Not only would the violence ruin his reputation, but it would catapult the college and his family into scandal. What could he do? He had only one logical choice. He must destroy the evidence. He therefore concocted an elaborate cover-up that began once he locked the door. He dragged the corpse through the lecture room to one of his private rooms in back. The room contained a sink, a small furnace, and the chemicals Webster used in his experiments. He then calmly undressed the body and threw everything except the watch into the small furnace. After he propped the corpse up against the wall, he climbed into the sink and pulled the body up after him. He positioned the corpse so that the blood would flow downward. As he systematically dissected the body, the water carried blood through the pipe into the lower laboratory, directly under the lecture room. He then threw Parkman's head and viscera into the furnace and hid the rest of the remains throughout rooms and in the crawl space under the privy that was encased in the back stairwell. After cleaning the rooms, he tossed the weapon into the fire and locked the doors. He left the college at approximately 6 p.m., and on his way to the omnibus threw the victim's watch into the Charles River. Webster then spent the evening in Cambridge playing whist with his good friend Dr. Samuel Fay.

Many critics questioned Webster's decision to dissect the body. Why not just throw the body into the Charles River along with suicides and murder victims or into the lime vats that would have destroyed the body instantly? Dr. Fettes, a character in Robert Louis Stevenson's story "The Body Snatcher," suggested, "when we dislike a dead friend of ours, we dissect him" (Stevenson, 1992, p. 23).

PARKMAN AND WEBSTER: TO HAVE AND HAVE NOT

How did these two men come to the breaking point? What turned a competent, rational businessman into a frenzied debt collector, and a bookish academic into a cold-blooded murderer? How could a childhood friendship deteriorate into such contempt and acrimony? After graduating from Harvard in 1809, Parkman chose a medical career and studied psychiatry with Phillipe Pinel in France. When he returned to America, he wrote several psychiatric papers that reflected Pinel's more liberal concepts, and he treated patients at the Boston Lunatic Asylum. Although the board at the prestigious McLean Asylum considered Parkman for the directorship, it ultimately rejected him. Some critics argued that the board denied him because he lacked the emotional warmth to treat patients. Others suggested that the board opposed his liberal views. This decision devastated Parkman, who saw it as a professional betrayal. He subsequently shifted his focus from medicine to managing his family's business concerns, which included extensive land holdings throughout the West End. The Massachusetts General Hospital, Boston Medical College, and the New Jail stood on Parkman land. Parkman also rented apartments in his tenement buildings to the working class and floated loans to several people, including John White Webster.

Both Parkman and Webster's genealogy included Boston's elite families. Parkman's father, Samuel, had made his fortune as a merchant. Parkman's brother, Francis, was a distinguished clergyman who had baptized Webster's children at his North End parish. In 1848, Parkman was worth over $250,000. Although his ancestry included King Edward I and his grandfather was Grant Webster, a successful merchant, Webster had not amassed a fortune. He did not own property nor make it into the tax rolls. In spite of his illustrious ancestry, he was nonetheless the son of an apothecary and dressmaker, a middle-class family from the North End. His father, Redford, was not just an excellent businessman, but a minor city official as well. He had amassed a substantial fortune during the American Revolution and retired early to the life of a gentleman. To fulfill his fatherly obligations, he sent his only son,

John, to Harvard, hoping the prestigious education would ensure the boy's future. While the elder Webster lived within the boundaries of proper social behavior, his son rebelliously pushed these limits. While at Harvard, he committed numerous minor infractions that included unauthorized absence from the college and from Sunday services. At one point, the faculty temporarily suspended him and sent him down to study with the Reverend Mr. Flint in Bridgewater for a term. He successfully fulfilled these obligations and graduated from Harvard in 1811 and then sat for his medical degree. He continued his studies at Guy's Medical College in London and then, like most young men, toured Europe. Fascinated with anatomy, he observed autopsies at the morgue in Paris.

In addition to medicine, Webster's other interests included chemistry, mineralogy, and geology. From Paris, he traveled to the Portuguese Azore Islands to study their geology. In 1816 he met Harriet Hickling. Her father, Thomas Hickling Jr., had left Boston in 1789, made his fortune in trade, and subsequently served as America's first consul to the Azores. Thomas Hickling married twice and produced seventeen children, including five daughters: Sarah, Harriet, Amelia, Maryanne, and Catherine. These daughters, except for Catherine and Harriet, married prominent merchants. Catherine married the prominent Boston lawyer William Prescott, and their son, William H., pursued more academic interests in history. Amelia married Thomas Nye, an influential New Bedford merchant and local politician.

After a brief courtship, Webster married Harriet in 1816. Eventually, Webster's daughters married into the Dabney family, who inherited the Hickling consul posts to the Azores and solidified its economic link to the New England merchant community. Thus, through marriage, the Hickling family maintained its hegemony in American-Azores trade.

On paper, Webster was the perfect match. He had an impressive genealogy, a successful father, and a promising academic career at Harvard. After the wedding, the couple returned to Cambridge, where he resumed his position as a chemistry professor. Although Webster hoped to pursue a medical career, he never found a proper sponsor. He then shifted his focus from medicine to chemistry and mineralogy. In addition to his annual salary of $1,200, Webster earned revenue from ticket sales to his lectures. While he enjoyed the trappings of the gentleman, he lacked the funds to support them. He had a penchant for fine Madeira wine, rare books, and music. An accomplished musician, Webster orchestrated musical recitals in his drawing room with his family. He owned a large sheet music collection and planned various musical events with his friend Henry Wadsworth Longfellow. As a result of his lavish lifestyle, he amassed an enormous debt.

In 1834, he inherited approximately $50,000 from his father's estate. He immediately transferred his deceased family members from the Copps Hill Burying Ground in the North End to the more fashionable Mt. Auburn Cemetery in Cambridge. He purchased a plot for $600 on Narcissus Lane near Judge Story's tomb. He also built a lavish house on Harvard Street in Cambridge that his detractors dubbed "Webster's Folly." The expense eventually forced him to sell the property and lease a house on Garden Street near the Harvard campus in 1836.

Webster's financial situation worsened. He admitted to his friend, John A. Lowell, Esq., that he had never managed money well. Amelia Nye, his sister-in-law, suggested that his financial irresponsibility affected his ability to support his family. To supplement his income, Webster earned seventy-five dollars for performing an occasional autopsy or testifying as an expert witness at capital trials. In spite of these efforts, Webster constantly faced bankruptcy. He continually borrowed money from family and friends just before the creditors repossessed his property. In 1848, debt forced him to reduce his household staff and cancel social events. To protect his wife, he never discussed their economic situation with her. By 1849, his debt had increased to $4,500, and his creditors included George Parkman. While his family members often forgave the debts for his wife's sake, Parkman was not as charitable. As the creditors knocked on his door, Webster mortgaged his prized mineralogical collection to both Parkman and Parkman's brother-in-law, Robert Gould Shaw. In November 1849, the situation was out of control. Parkman forced the November 23, 1849, meeting that had such tragic consequences. Webster had committed the ultimate act, not just against an individual but against the community as well. He had violated the social code that governed the community and had allowed scandal to touch him, the family, and the community. The scandal undermined the community's reputation, credibility, and authority as society's self-appointed moral guardian.

THE ARREST

The janitor, Ephraim Littlefield, suspected Webster from the beginning. He had worked for the medical college for eight years and shared quarters with his family next to Webster's laboratory in the basement. Immediately after Parkman's disappearance, Littlefield noticed that Webster's behavior grew more erratic. He kept odd hours and locked himself behind closed doors. The police had searched the college premises but found nothing. Littlefield, who knew the building well, decided to conduct his own investigation, and on November 30, 1849, unearthed suspicious remains in the crawl space under Webster's laboratory and privy. He reported his discovery to the medical faculty and the police, who subsequently found additional remains throughout the laboratory. Because of the large amount of circumstantial evidence, the police arrested Webster on December 1, 1849, and incarcerated him at the Leverett Street Jail. Webster hired Edward Sohier and Pliny Merrick to defend him while the court appointed District Attorney John Clifford and the young George Bemis for the prosecution.

THE PRESS COVERAGE: MADAME RUMOR TAKES FLIGHT

When Parkman never returned home for dinner on November 23, 1849, the family was concerned because this was uncharacteristic behavior. As a devoted husband and father, Parkman never missed family dinners. The day after Parkman's disappearance, Robert Gould Shaw posted flyers and published notices in the daily papers offering rewards that ranged from $300 to $1,000. While these notices were fairly common, this one sparked more interest because of Parkman's prominence. The language suggested that Parkman had possibly suffered from a sudden mental illness or perhaps been murdered. To publish the notice among the classifieds acknowledged the power of the press to reach a broad audience quickly.

What began as a missing person's notice soon mushroomed into a major news event. The editors of the penny press understood the importance of this event. Crime reports were an important staple of the daily pennies. George Roberts, the editor of the *Daily Times*, argued that these reports deterred crime and were far more effective than the Sunday homily. The dailies had replaced the church and the elite as the moral governors of society. These editors immediately recognized the value and social implications of the Parkman murder. Scandal and crime touched all classes, from the Irish mechanic to the Beacon Hill elite. A Harvard professor had allegedly murdered a member of one of Boston's most elite families. What was "normal" behavior in the lower classes in the North End had spilled over into the hallowed halls of Harvard Medical College. The editors realized that this case was highly marketable and would increase subscription numbers. As showmen, the publishers knew how to position stories, attract audiences, and sell their products.

The press coverage unfolded in three acts, each with distinct concerns. In the first phase, reports captured the tumultuous excitement immediately following Parkman's disappearance. They described the police department's vigorous efforts to canvass the neighborhood, question residents, search vacant buildings, and drag the Charles River. The papers constantly reminded readers of the dangers of urban life. In addition to Parkman's unexplained disappearance, the police had discovered a dead infant on the New Jail grounds while a young servant girl who worked in the vicinity had suddenly gone missing.

As the story broke, the papers religiously reported the unfolding events as soon as they happened. The press not only responded to the public's growing interest, but manipulated it as well. The *Daily Times* probably broke the story first with its 4 a.m. edition on November 24, 1849. The *Transcript's* rhetoric not only appealed to the nineteenth-century appetite for sensationalism, but also underscored the event's importance. The reporter compared the tragedy to a thunderbolt striking the statehouse dome, implying that the crime was a serious attack on the city's social, political, and moral order. The hyperbole underscored the disbelief that Webster, a Harvard professor, could murder anyone, much less a colleague.

The *Boston Herald's* aggressive approach set the tone for the press in general. Both the Boston *Herald* and the *Mail* published drawings of the participants and of the crime scene that allowed the reader a glimpse into areas previously off limits to the average reader. On December 4, 1849, the *Herald* printed the first drawing of Webster, which portrayed him as a demonic figure with sunken cheeks and an exaggerated head. A reader from Lowell criticized the artist, writing that the picture looked no more like Dr. Webster than it did Queen Victoria. The *Herald* defended the artist as one of the best in the city and argued that it had correctly captured Webster's emotional state at the time of the arrest. Nonetheless, the paper pulled the drawing and replaced it with a more flattering portrait that became the standard depiction. It emphasized Webster's patrician features and portrayed him as a well-dressed, bookish gentleman.

Rumors dominated the pretrial coverage. They functioned to impose order on chaos, to calm an agitated public, and to provide meaning. They often ranged from the ludicrous to the somewhat plausible. Since the officials had discovered only remains, many rumors focused on Parkman sightings. On November 28, 1849, the *Herald* reported that several people had seen Dr. Parkman in East Cambridge while others saw him in Tremont Street and in Merchant's Block. According to a drover in Brighton, someone spotted the doctor wandering in the woods near Woburn. The sightings were reported as far away as New York. The *New York Tribune* claimed that numerous witnesses saw a person, supposedly Dr. Parkman, in Manhattanville and at a Harlem police station. The *Bee*, after consulting Madame Rumour and Court Square gossip, reported that an Irishman had "entered Webster's private rooms and caught him packing the remains of a dead person into the tea chest" ("Local Matters," 1850).

The dailies focused on certain important issues, including the role of a free press. The papers butted heads with Coroner Jabez Pratt over his decision to close the inquest to the public and to the press. The press argued that this decision violated its rights and prevented public access to an important judicial proceeding. It compared the coroner to the Spanish Inquisition, which had conducted closed-door proceedings for nefarious reasons. Did the coroner as the government's representative have the right to prevent public access to a judicial proceeding that was traditionally open to the public? Pratt argued that the decision best served the interests of the defendant and the respective families. He was concerned that the findings would bias the public against Webster, upset the families, and compromise a fair trial. The press, however, was unsympathetic, interpreting this decision as a smokescreen to protect the interests of the elite. The press argued that this closing violated fundamental constitutional law and that open proceedings benefited both the defendant and society. After the coroner barred the press, reporters often went to illegal means to break the news, ranging from bribery to breaking and entering. Two enterprising reporters broke into the dead room (morgue) under the courthouse during jury deliberation. According to the *Transcript*, these young men "applied their ears to the air hole that ran up to the room" ("Case of Dr. Parkman," 1849). They inadvertently locked themselves in the room, but the sheriff soon discovered their unwelcome presence. After the sheriff unlocked the door, one of the reporters quickly escaped while the "remainder [*sic*] man was taken before the jury, and coroner mauled" ("Case of Dr. Parkman," 1849).

Before the trial began, a rumor circulated that officials planned to conduct the trial in the Tremont Street Temple to accommodate large crowds. The press was appalled, arguing that the trial would then become a Barnumesque sideshow and compromise the judicial process. The government soon dispelled this rumor and scheduled the trial for the courthouse. The police issued rules that governed crowd placement and determined precisely the entrances for the press, the public, and the witnesses. To help control the large audience, spectators purchased tickets for five dollars for fifteen minutes in the courtroom, which disrupted the proceedings at least four times an hour.

The coverage entered the second phase when the trial began on March 19, 1850. The crowd, approximately 300 deep, waited at the courthouse in a severe snowstorm to purchase tickets. The press grumbled that the conditions within the courtroom hindered its effectiveness. The *Bee* complained that it had been relegated "to the rear of the witnesses close to the deafening vibration of the wall, at the front next to the Railroad Exchange and half a thousand express wagons. Where a window must be constantly open or the audience be smothered for want of ventilation" ("Word from Reporter,"

1850). The *Herald* blamed its inadequate coverage on its location as well, while several other pennies filed fairly accurate accounts. The readers experienced the trial vicariously through the press coverage. Each day the reporters prefaced the narratives with a description of the spectators and other events. The prominence of some of the visitors underscored the trial's importance. John C. Calhoun, the eminent southern statesman, attended the trial on March 25, six days before his death. Other spectators included Lieutenant Governor John Reed of Massachusetts and the Honorable E. H. Kellogg, the speaker of the House, as well as respected clergy and other public officials. In addition to the distinguished guests, the common folk, including well-dressed ladies and rowdy boys, filled the galley. A surreal sense of old-boy camaraderie also filled the courtroom. Each morning, Webster shook hands and exchanged pleasantries as he warmly greeted his friends, reminiscent more of a gentleman's club than of a courtroom. Several of Webster's community refused to attend the trial because of the embarrassing public exposure. John Sibley, Harvard's librarian, had not doubted Webster's innocence at first. He visited the family and offered his full support, but as the evidence unfolded he turned his back on his old friend. He never visited Webster in jail or attended the trial. Edward Everett, Harvard's former president, asked the prosecution to excuse him as a character witness because of poor health.

The press also reported incidents outside the courtroom that added nuance and color to the events. A fire in the Tremont House on March 21 briefly delayed the proceedings so that John Clifford, a guest, could secure his property. On March 23, 1850, the Black Maria, the prison van, broke down on Green Street. While the accident badly jostled a manacled Webster, he nonetheless survived the incident with grace.

The press also focused on Webster's appearance. In a pre-Freudian era, an individual's demeanor reflected his mental state. The press interpreted every movement and each nuance that it believed would either confirm his guilt or innocence. The *Bee* stressed the apparent discrepancy between two conflicting realities of the intellectual academic and passionate killer. The *Bee* suggested that Webster looked more like a scientist than a murderer. Webster often jeopardized his own case with inappropriate and disrespectful behavior. At one point, he forcefully shook hands with the victim's brother, the Rev. Francis Parkman, who attended the trial daily and never wavered from his belief in Webster's guilt. Webster's behavior not only embarrassed the reverend but placed him in an awkward position, forcing him to engage hypocritically in civil behavior. Webster also joked about the medical exhibits. When Dr. Jeffries Wyman illustrated his testimony with a skeleton, Webster quipped that the college should add it to its collection. As the trial progressed,

Webster's cavalier attitude gradually changed. During the prosecution's closing statement, the stress showed on Webster's face as beads of perspiration ran down his forehead.

On April 1, 1850, the case went to the jury. After a two-hour deliberation, it returned a verdict of guilty of homicide with malice that brought an automatic death sentence. The press focused on Webster's reaction as he stood in the prisoner's dock. The *Boston Post* reported that as Webster left "the courtroom, he bent forward and leaned upon the officer like a crushed wreck of humanity" ("Trial of Prof.," 1850). According to the *Bee*, Webster held "a white handkerchief to his face, and that immediately following it he nerved himself up and rose upon his feet and seemed to have perfect command of his limbs" ("The Verdict," 1850). The *Transcript*'s hyperbole emphasized Webster's heart-wrenching reaction that dramatized his profound disbelief. He "clenched for support for a moment, and then sank gradually into the chair." As his "trembling" hand dislodged his spectacles, "his whole frame shook, and he remained in that position about a minute, during which there was a dead silence in the Court, and every eye was turned upon him" ("The Trial," 1850). The rhetoric captured the tragedy of a man whose assumption did not conform to reality: he had been so convinced of acquittal that he ordered oysters from Parker's Restaurant and sent a note to his wife to expect him in the morning.

The verdict not only shocked Webster but the community as well. Many people, like Webster, automatically assumed that the jury would acquit him. The *Transcript* compared the public's reaction to an electrical shock wave "that passed shudderingly from mouth to mouth, from those in the gallery to the crowd on the stairs, from the crowd on the stairs to the multitude gathered at that unreasonable hour in the street, the reverberations of the fatal word were brought back to the jury, and the Court, and must have fallen like the knell of hope on the ears of the prisoner" ("The Trial," 1850). While the verdict surprised the public, the Cambridge community was relieved. Harvard librarian John Sibley, Harvard's former president Edward Everett, and Webster's sister-in-law Amelia Nye accepted the verdict as just and proper.

The press now entered the third phase, in which it emphasized the tragic consequence of the crime on the family. A crime that affected the family, as the moral center of society, affected society. In the dailies, everything except the family was fair game. The family now became the *cause celebre*. The press respected the family's privacy and became its self-proclaimed protector after the trial. Thus, the press championed the family as the ultimate victim. It moved Mrs. Webster from the shadows to the light. The press sentimentalized her as a strong matriarch who nurtured her children. It followed her to the governor's office as she pleaded for leniency and kept its respectful distance during her daily visits with her husband. The press reinforced the image of the devoted, courageous wife during profound crisis. The *Bee* emphasized her role as an excellent mother who raised her daughters to lead virtuous and productive lives. The press also underscored the importance of male protection and contrasted the harried family to the vulgar spectators who gathered outside the jail daily to see the family. These rowdy crowds shouted insults at the women as they left the jail. The press compared the crowds to vultures who fed off the wife's misery. Officer Andrews and Turnkey Holmes willingly filled the role that Webster abrogated. They chivalrously hurried the family outside the jail to the carriage and ultimately to the safety of its Cambridge home. The dailies heightened the pathos, ultimately suggesting that Webster's greatest crime was not against Parkman but against the family. His role as father and husband obligated him to protect them, but he betrayed this obligation while subjecting his wife to unspeakable humiliation. The wife of Henry Wadsworth Longfellow suggested that the scandal itself was enough to force the family to leave Cambridge and perhaps return to the Azores.

The *New York Star* referred to the Webster women as "the real sufferers in this unhappy case" and concluded that Webster's "poor family die a long living death—poor, without means of support, well educated, grown daughters, and children plunged into the abyss of misery by the crimes of the father. They are indeed entitled to the commiserations of the world, and to the aid of the charitable and kindly disposed" ("Opinions of the Press," 1850). While this perception created sympathy, it did not conform to reality. While the women took in sewing and other respectable jobs to supplement their income, they were not destitute. Edward Sohier handled any legal work *pro bono* while numerous family and friends provided financial and emotional support. The Appletons collected approximately $5,000 for the family's benefit. Ironically, Mrs. Parkman, the victim's widow, contributed substantially to the fund because she believed that Mrs. Webster had also been victimized. Common widowhood linked them. After the execution, Samuel Cunningham, a personal friend, purchased a house for Mrs. Webster at the corner of Mt. Auburn and Ash streets in Cambridge.

To add to the family's misery, some editors attacked Webster's character. The *Bee* criticized Webster's study of the Azores as unimaginative and his chemistry experiments as academically inconsequential. In response to these criticisms, the *Herald* did an about-face. It now emerged as the underdog's champion, more for the family's sake than for Webster's. It criticized the *Bee* for a mean-spirited attack against a man who could no longer defend himself. More importantly, it implied that the *Bee* had crossed the boundaries of appropriate behavior because the attack on Webster ultimately harmed the family. According to the *Herald*, the *Bee's* editors deserved hanging and belonged to a despicable class that unnecessarily tortured the family to sell papers. The *Bee* defended its article, arguing that it had not intended to hurt the family but simply to strip the mask from Webster and reveal his true character.

In spite of Mrs. Webster's efforts, the pleas for leniency failed, and the governor scheduled the execution for August 30, 1850. In the final months, Webster's wife and children visited him daily. He also wrote letters to his friends, wrote a forced apology to the Parkman family, and read scriptures with his religious advisor the Rev. George Putnam. While Webster's newfound piety impressed the public, it did not move Mrs. Amelia Nye, his sister-in-law, or Mrs. Catherine Prescott, who read it as another ploy. They were both disgusted that Webster continued to manipulate the family. While Mrs. Nye loved her sister Harriet deeply, she grew more impatient with her refusal to accept the truth about Webster.

As a last-minute effort to win sympathy, Webster surprised everyone with a confession that appeared in the dailies on July 3, 1850. The strategy backfired. Rather than create sympathy, it angered the public. The confession did more to confuse the issue than clarify it, especially since Webster had recently declared his innocence. Now suddenly a few days later, he did an about-face. George Wilkes condemned the confession as a last minute, self-serving effort to win leniency. He also argued that Webster had further betrayed his family's trust, thus abrogating his familial responsibility.

FINAL RESOLUTION: THE EXECUTION

On August 30, 1850, before 8 a.m., the officials prepared the scaffold in the Leverett Street Jail yard. As the Rev. Putnam solemnly prayed with Webster in his cell, the raucous crowd gathered on the rooftops in the neighborhood. In spite of the police's efforts to discourage it, spectators had rented space on neighboring rooftops to view the event. Shortly after the invited dignitaries and officials arrived, Rev. Putnam and Sheriff Everliff escorted Webster, dressed in black, to the courtyard amidst the jeers and obscenities of the crowd. After stepping up to the scaffold, the sheriff placed the noose around his neck. The pennies recreated the event, often in graphic detail. According to the *Transcript*, the sheriff pulled the rope around Webster's neck so tightly that "the culprit's countenance became flushed and eyes filled with tears." When the sheriff's foot hit the drop, "the prisoner fell some seven and one-half feet and his mortal career came to an end" ("The Execution," 1850). To some, the *Transcript's* narrative surpassed the boundaries of good taste, as it described Webster's death throes: "The body swayed slightly to and fro; and in a few seconds after the fall, there was a spasmodic drawing up of the legs once or twice. Beyond this, there was no observable struggle; nor was there any subsequent agitation or quivering of the body" ("The Execution," 1850). After the court physicians pronounced Webster dead, they placed his corpse in a plain wood casket that then remained in the jail for several hours to avoid the gawking crowds. During the night, Webster's friends took the body and buried it in some undisclosed location. He had hoped his family would inter him in his family plot in Mt. Auburn. However, Ned Sohier had told him that Mt. Auburn had denied the request since it did not inter executed felons on sacred grounds. Some later suggested that his friends secretly buried him in Copps Hill Burying Ground in the North End or in the mud flats along the Charles River.

THE CASE'S CULTURAL SIGNIFICANCE

The Parkman murder significantly impacted all levels of nineteenth-century Boston society. It reflected the importance of the press and its ability to create news as well as report it. The penny editors immediately recognized the marketability of this case and exploited every aspect of it. With the Webster case, the papers honed their crime reporting. The editors placed it on the front page, pushing aside other important stories. While the crime reports usually focused on the mishaps of the Irish immigrant and the common drunkard, this report chronicled the tragedy of an upper-class gentleman who should have known better. The unthinkable had happened. The violent underworld had intruded on the upper class, which religiously avoided scandal and guarded its privacy. A Harvard professor had murdered and dissected one of its own in a prestigious public institution intended to protect human life rather than end it. Well-respected men were forced into the public arena and were linked by association to a sordid scandal.

This case underscored the tension between the working class and the elite. Ephraim Littlefield, the prosecution's key witness, had worked as a janitor for the medical college for eight years. Littlefield's demeanor during his testimony quickly ended any suspicions regarding his involvement in the crime. The trial questioned certain assumptions about the definitions of "gentleman." Nathan Capun, a well-respected attorney, argued that Webster could never commit murder because statistics proved that mature, well-educated, and well-bred men were immune to criminal behavior. Education refined a man's sensibilities, honed his moral character, and protected him from his baser instincts. This case turned these assumptions topsy-turvy and underscored the complexities of human nature. Appearance and reality did not always conform. What were the criteria that defined the gentleman? Was it a product of birth or behavior? Etiquette manuals flooded the market and promised to teach manners to a working class who desperately wanted to move upward in society. However, the ultimate prize for success—marriage into the upper class—was off limits without breeding and family connections. Jacksonian equality thus only went so far.

The posttrial press coverage also reflected the growing discrepancy between the working class and the intellectual. Unlike the intellectual, the mechanic or workingman produced practical items that benefited society and added to the economic stability of a burgeoning market economy. The jury trusted both Clifford and Littlefield because, as "plain talkers," they spoke directly to them, unlike the scholars who spoke an esoteric language that few understood.

The political atmosphere in the mid-nineteenth century grew increasingly volatile as the abolitionists and prison reformers gained momentum. The prison reform movement had lobbied for the innovative New Jail that would eventually replace the dilapidated Leverett Street Jail. Webster's impending execution added fodder to the anti-death penalty debate. The critics had labeled capital punishment "legal homicide." A few months earlier, Washington Goode, a black sailor who stabbed a romantic rival in a drunken brawl, was executed in spite of the efforts of the reform movement. Charles Dickens, the English darling of the Boston intelligentsia, had published a letter in the English and American newspapers denouncing the circus atmosphere that defined public executions. He had witnessed the Manning hanging in London in December 1849 and focused on the crowd behavior. He argued that capital punishment catered to man's baser instincts. Controversial executions in the Boston area had occurred recently, including that of Daniel Pearson, the mentally ill man who had brutally murdered his wife and children in Worcester. In spite of the insanity plea, he was nonetheless hanged in July 1850. In this heated political environment, Governor George Briggs carefully weighed his options. He closely examined the petitions and the legal arguments and met with Mrs. Webster. In spite of these pleas, he made a prudent decision that considered the political implications as well as the social. Furthermore, as the properly elected representative of the people, he had to follow the letter of the law. The guilty verdict mandated the death penalty. He would abrogate his responsibility to his constituency and undermine the integrity of the jury if he overturned the verdict. He would commit political suicide if he granted leniency to an upper-class murderer, especially when the government had recently executed a black sailor and a mentally ill laborer. His critics could charge class bias, suggesting that the upper class used him as a political puppet.

Other legal issues included the rights of a free press and the matter of circumstantial evidence. Coroner Pratt set an unwelcome precedent when he closed the December 6 inquest to the press and the public. He argued that it was in the best interest of the families of the defendant. He was concerned that the preliminary evidence would bias the prospective jury against Webster. The press, however, accused Pratt of violating the public's fundamental constitutional rights.

Lawyers and the press debated the nature of circumstantial evidence throughout the nineteenth century. Debate focused on the nature of constituted circumstantial evidence and its preference over direct or positive evidence. Circumstantial evidence consisted of linked circumstances that led to a possible conclusion. However, what happened if a link was missing? The body of evidence or *corpus delicti* formed an essential part of this link. In murder cases, the corpse was the *corpus delicti*, because as positive evidence it proved that some agent had committed a crime. But what if part of this evidence had gone missing? Did this weaken the case? Critics argued that in the Webster case the prosecution's argument was seriously flawed because of missing evidence. Without a complete body or weapon, no direct evidence existed that Webster murdered Parkman or that Parkman was even dead. The body parts that Littlefield found could belong to anyone. What if at some point Parkman returned alive and well after Webster's execution? The critics cited the Boorne case of 1812, in which a jury had convicted the Boorne brothers of murdering Russell Colvin even though officials had found no body. After one of the boys was executed, Colvin returned alive just before the other boy's scheduled hanging. What if the same thing were to happen in the Webster case? Would this not represent a tragic miscarriage of justice? The critics argued that the circumstantial evidence was too weak to convict Webster because it was based on the inferences of a biased janitor and on body parts that were common to the medical college.

The defense team based its strategy on alibi and character. Judge Lemuel Shaw's charge to the jury created much controversy because he negated the defense team's strategy. Shaw criticized Sohier's reinterpretation of "alibi." Traditionally, an alibi was an account of the defendant's whereabouts at the time of the crime that would preclude the person's involvement. Sohier shifted the focus away from Webster to Parkman. He based Webster's alibi not on his actions but on Parkman's. Sohier called numerous witnesses who testified that they had seen Parkman after the murder had allegedly occurred. Shaw essentially argued that Sohier's reinterpretation was inept lawyering and reflected a poor understanding of the law.

Shaw also challenged Sohier's use of character. The defense called numerous witnesses, including Oliver Wendell Holmes and Jared Sparks, Harvard's president, who testified about Webster's excellent reputation in the community as a scholar and family man. They argued that while Webster was at times irascible, he was not homicidal. While character was a legitimate defense in most cases, it had no bearing in this trial because the severity of the crime outweighed the character issue.

This case reflected the complexity of the nineteenth-century urban environment. Cambridge was the intellectual counterpart to Boston's rough-and-tumble world of business. While a strict but unwritten code governed behavior in Webster's community, the urban environment was less structured. Both these worlds intersected uncomfortably at the trial. It further underscored the dangers of the ever-changing landscape that was filled with burglars, prostitutes, drunkards, and back-alley abortionists. In spite of its claims to moral superiority, the reality was far different. Like other large cities, Boston was a deadly environment filled with unsavory strangers.

The press emerged as a major force in the tragedy. With new technology like the magnetic telegraph, news spread more rapidly throughout the country. Citizens in California were instantly connected to those in Chicago and New York. Thus, a local murder soon mushroomed into a national and even international event. The English and German papers referred to it briefly. It even made a commercial copy for toothache ads and influenced testimony in legal proceedings, including an incendiary trial in Charlestown. Advances in printing technology and aggressive reporting produced more papers and created a vibrant, exciting, and indispensable read.

The trial dramatized the growing tension between the classes and underscored a basic tenet of Jacksonian America. Would Webster's class and connections influence the jury's decision, regardless of the evidence? In spite of concerns, the working-class jury fulfilled its role within the judicial process. The jury put aside questions of class and based its verdict on the evidence. However, some press criticized the jury for spending only two hours examining the tremendous amount of evidence. It also attacked the jury's piety, suggesting that had it spent less time praying and more time deliberating, it would perhaps have decided a different verdict.

The trial influenced popular culture as well. The papers published numerous accounts that rehashed the trial coverage. George Bemis, one of the prosecutors, published the best-selling version of the report, which became the definitive study. Dr. Stone also produced a version, but Bemis condemned him as a hack who plagiarized the newspapers. The murder embedded itself in the public psyche and occupied the public's interest for more than a year. Ephraim Littlefield became a minor celebrity after the trial and used the case to his advantage. He not only accepted the reward but also joined the sideshow circuit. He created lifelike wax figures of

Webster and Parkman and toured the East retelling his story. The New York papers criticized the display as unseemly and amateurish. The interest in Littlefield's Barnumesque show quickly waned as the public focused on the next, latest scandal.

Spiritualism, the newest fad that allegedly connected the spirit world to the living, also exploited the case. The notorious spiritualists Mrs. Fish and her Rochester Knockers conducted several séances that attracted "half-believers," including Horace Greeley and William Cullen Bryant. However, the spiritualists did not convince everyone, including George Wilkes and the New York Police Department. Wilkes, who condemned the group as frauds, pressured Mrs. Fish to leave New York for Rochester. The *Boston Evening Gazette* reported that at one of the séances Mrs. Fish had successfully conjured up the spirits of Dr. Parkman and Dr. Webster. The spirits assured the audience that they were once again friends and had gone to a happier place. Wilkes condemned the séance as disgusting and blasphemous and attacked these women as charlatans who preyed on the gullible and credulous.

The tragedy had played itself out, residing now in the distant recesses of memory. The murder quickly became old news, as the press moved on to a new murder and scandalous divorce. However, for Webster's community, the tragedy lingered for years. The press coverage confirmed the community's worst fears about the terrible consequences of public scandal. The dailies had invaded the community's privacy and challenged its integrity. The press epitomized the best and worst of Jacksonian society. Did the press unduly influence public opinion and impact the verdict? Or was it fulfilling its obligation in a democracy to inform the public? In response to this public noise, the community regrouped, clung to its value system, and emerged scathed but intact.

While Webster's friends hurried his body to some secret location, Dr. Parkman's remains rest alone in the family tomb nestled in the hillside, isolated from the rest of the family. Edward Sohier lies buried near Longfellow's grave, while George Bemis rests on Mimosa Lane. The names boldly etched into the marble attest to the power inherent within the name itself as the family's most enduring legacy. The family's insistence on erasing Webster's name from books at a public sale poignantly underscored the significance of this legacy. A good name transcended death, honored the descendants, and maintained the continuity of the past, present, and future.

These elegant monuments not only pay tribute to Boston's elite but also reflect the community's value system. The murder tested the elite's code of behavior. Previously, education, birthright, and connections had protected the community, the family, and the family name. But what happened in the

Webster tragedy? Had the world turned topsy-turvy, was the ethic flawed, or was Webster an aberration? Webster as the ultimate doppelganger (double) dramatized the paradox between seeming and being, and between pretense and truth. The elite had failed to read its own landscape and allowed the renegade Webster to avoid his financial responsibility for the sake of his family. The tragedy forced the elite into the unwanted limelight and subjected it to the scrutiny of the penny press with its known bias against the upper class. As the press vented its bias, Webster's community pulled back into Cambridge, regrouped, and clung to the values that anchored it. Whereas the daily papers represented the rough-and-tumble world of the working class, the elite had created a code that emphasized restraint, decorum, and civilized behavior in an increasingly uncivilized world. The community struggled to understand Webster's crime, not just against Parkman but against the community. The tragedy forced it to confront an incomprehensible evil within its midst. Webster had humiliated his friends and mocked the community that provided him with a safe haven to pursue musical and scholarly endeavors. They struggled to understand the discrepancy between seeming and being, which now dominated urban life. Previous conceptions and definitions were no longer safeguards against evil. Like the seemingly innocuous art unions and coffee shops that hid licentious behavior, Webster's bookish appearance masked an ugly reality.

Vulgarity, the province of the lower classes, had now inexplicably touched the elite. It was inconceivable that a Harvard professor could have murdered anyone. Given the anti-immigrant bias, it was for some more comfortable to assume that a drunken Irishman had committed the act. The *Pennsylvania Journal of Prison Discipline* in 1845 fueled this prejudice by demanding government protection against German convicts who had committed murder. In Webster's case, many people assumed that a drunken Irishman, a body snatcher, or a disgruntled tenant had murdered Parkman. The homicide itself questioned these assumptions, blurred the distinction between classes, and turned the society upside down. It suggested that social status, privilege, and education no longer indicated good character. Webster's professional inferior, a janitor, had exposed his social superior, a Harvard academic. Ultimately, a jury composed of predominantly blue-collar men sent a member of Boston's elite to the gallows.

In spite of the attack on its integrity, the elite's value system provided its strength. While the ephemeral newspapers quickly disappeared, the monuments at Mt. Auburn served as constant reminders of a society that survived a devastating scandal with its values intact. The monuments reflect the enduring and fundamental strength of the Founding Fathers' republican values.

REFERENCES

Bemis, G. (1850). *Report of the case of John White Webster.* Boston: Little, Brown.

Case of Dr. Parkman—Funeral of the remains. (1849, December 7). *Boston Transcript.*

The execution of Prof. John White Webster for the murder of Dr. George Parkman. (1850, August 30). *Boston Transcript.*

Halttunen, K. (1998). *Murder most foul.* Cambridge, MA: Harvard University Press.

Local matters, Professor Webster—The evidence, etc. (1850, February 6). *Boston Bee.*

Lost man. (1849, November 30). *New York Tribune.*

Opinions of the press on the verdict in the Webster case. (1850, April 2). *Boston Herald.*

The Parkman tragedy. Confession of Prof. John White Webster. (1850, July 3). *Boston Mail.*

Stevenson, R. L. (1992). *The strange case of Dr. Jekyll & Mr. Hyde and other stories.* London: Everyman.

Stone, Dr. J. (1850). *Report of the trial of John White Webster.* Boston: Phillips, Sampson.

Sullivan, R. (1971). *The disappearance of Dr. Parkman.* Boston: Little, Brown.

Thomas, H. (1971). *Murder at Harvard.* Boston: Houghton Mifflin.

Trial of Prof. John W. Webster, M.D. Charge to the jury. (1850, April 1). *Boston Post.*

The trial and the verdict. (1850, April 1). *Boston Transcript.*

The verdict. (1850, April 1). *Boston Bee.*

Wilkes, G. (Ed.). (1850a, July 13). Webster and his confession. *National Police Gazette.*

Wilkes, G. (Ed.). (1850b, October 12). Webster and Parkman in the spirit world. *National Police Gazette.*

A word from the reporter. (1850, March 27). *Boston Bee.*

13

The Shadrach Courtroom Rescue: Abolitionists Free Fugitive Slave

Kathryn Mudgett

The arrest and subsequent rescue of the fugitive slave Shadrach (Frederic Minkins)[1] took place in February 1851 in Boston, Massachusetts, in the charged atmosphere created by the passage of the Fugitive Slave Act of 1850. The act, signed into law by President Millard Fillmore on September 18, 1850, amended the Fugitive Slave Act of 1793 by expanding federal power over the rendition of fugitive slaves. The Act of 1793 implemented the fugitive slave clause of the Constitution (Article IV, Section 2, Clause 3), which provided that no person "held to service or labor" in one state and escaping into another was discharged from service but was to be delivered up to the claimant. The fugitive slave clause provided no mechanism for re-capture; it merely stated the claimant's right to recapture the fugitive despite any conflicting law of the state into which the fugitive had escaped. The Act of 1793, signed into law by President George Washington, contained provisions empowering both state and federal judges to issue certificates of removal of the fugitive and imposing fines on any person impeding recovery of the fugitive. Following its passage, free states attempted to circumvent the Act of 1793 by passing laws against the kidnapping of free blacks and alleged fugitives residing within state borders, and laws prohibiting the use of state officials or facilities to recapture fugitive slaves (Campbell, 1970, pp. 11, 14).

The Act of 1850 created a new mechanism for recapture, authorizing the U.S. circuit courts to appoint commissioners empowered to grant certificates of removal to claimants seeking extradition of escaped fugitives.[2] Proof of ownership of a fugitive was made by deposition, affidavit, or testimony under oath. Testimony of the alleged fugitive was inadmissible in court. The act also required all marshals and their deputies to execute the provisions of the act or be held liable for the financial loss of the claimant. In the provision most distasteful to those opposed to slavery, the act also authorized duly appointed commissioners and their subordinates "to summon and call to their aid the bystanders, or posse comitatus of the proper county," as "necessary to ensure a faithful observance" of the law of recapture. Thus, private citizens could be summoned to assist in enforcement of fugitive slave law. The law explicitly stated: "[A]ll good citizens are hereby commanded to aid and assist in the prompt and efficient execution of this law, whenever their services may be required" (Fugitive Slave Act of 1850, Section 5). Fines of up to $1,000 and imprisonment for up to six months could result from any willful hindrance of enforcement.

The first test of the act in Boston came in October 1850, when the Southern owner of the fugitives William and Ellen Craft sent an agent, Willis Hughes, to Boston to seek a warrant for their return to Georgia. The Crafts' escape from slavery had been daring—the light-skinned Ellen Craft disguised herself as a Southern gentleman accompanied by her black "servant," William, and traveled north by train. Once in Boston (several years after their escape), the Crafts came under the protection of the local vigilance committee and were spirited out of the city when it became clear that a warrant had issued pursuant to the Act of 1850 and would be served on them.

Southerners were aroused by what was perceived as Northern flouting of federal law, setting the stage for the events the following year when first Shadrach and then a second fugitive, Thomas Sims, would be seized under fugitive slave warrants. Charles Sumner, U.S. senator from Massachusetts, spoke for many Northerners in a speech made at Boston's Faneuil Hall in November 1850 when he decried the "legalized outrage" permitted by an act he considered unconstitutional. He declared, "Should any Court, sitting here in Massachusetts, for the first time in her history, become the agent of slave-hunters, the very images of our fathers would frown from the walls" (*Boston Commonwealth*, 1851, February 28). The state was to be tested only three months later. With the Crafts safely in Canada, Shadrach was to become the first fugitive slave in Massachusetts on whom a warrant was served following the passage of the act, and the first to be rescued from imprisonment and certain return to bondage.

ARREST OF THE FUGITIVE SLAVE
AND COURTROOM RESCUE

Shadrach, a young black man in his late twenties,[3] was a waiter at the Cornhill Coffee House near the courthouse in Boston when he was arrested on February 15, 1851, on a fugitive slave warrant issued by George T. Curtis, commissioner of the U.S. Circuit Court for the District of Massachusetts. John Caphart of Norfolk, Virginia, had sought the warrant on February 13 as the agent of Shadrach's alleged owner, John Debree, a purser in the U.S. Navy. Caphart, a slave catcher, presented documents to Commissioner Curtis alleging Shadrach's escape from Debree's service on May 3, 1850. Also appearing for Debree was Seth J. Thomas, a Boston attorney who had assisted Hughes, the slave catcher, in obtaining the warrant for return of the Crafts in October 1850. Following an *ex parte* hearing (that is, a hearing of which the alleged fugitive slave was not given notice), the commissioner signed a warrant ordering the marshal of the District of Massachusetts, or his deputies, "forthwith to apprehend one Shadrach, now commorant in Boston, in said district, a colored person, who is alleged to be a fugitive from service or labor in the state of Virginia (if he may be found in your precinct), and have him forthwith before me" (*Report of Proceedings*, 1851, p. 3).

The warrant was given to Charles Sawin, a deputy marshal, on Friday evening, February 14. On Saturday, February 15, Sawin arranged to meet a man who would point out Shadrach to him at the Cornhill Coffee House. Accompanying Sawin to Shadrach's place of employment were nine deputies, including Patrick Riley, principal deputy of the U.S. marshal, Frederick Warren, John H. Riley, and Frederick Byrnes. Just before 11 a.m., Patrick Riley and Warren entered the restaurant and ordered coffee while awaiting the person who would point out Shadrach. The alleged fugitive waited on the two deputy marshals, although they did not know his identity at the time. As Riley and Warren left the dining hall to check on their compatriots, Sawin and Byrne appeared in the passageway leading to the barroom, where Shadrach was headed with the money for the marshals' bill. Without a word, Sawin and Byrne each took one of Shadrach's arms and walked him out the back of the building to the square beside the courthouse and directly in to the U.S. courtroom on the second floor (*Report of Proceedings*, 1851, p. 5).[4]

Anticipating crowds, if not violence, Patrick Riley went to Boston City Hall and asked Francis Tukey, the city marshal, for help in keeping the peace. Riley also appealed to John P. Bigelow, mayor of Boston, who allegedly responded indifferently, "I am sorry for it" (1851, p. 5). On returning to the courthouse, Riley found the alleged fugitive and the deputy marshals in the U.S. courtroom awaiting the arrival of Commissioner Curtis. When Shadrach was first brought into the courtroom, he was still in his waiter's apron and his shirtsleeves, but someone found his coat and brought it to him (1851, p. 11). The commissioner explained the proceedings to Shadrach and asked if he wanted counsel. He replied that he did. Word of Shadrach's capture spread quickly, and soon there were six attorneys in the courtroom willing and ready to provide Shadrach with counsel *pro bono* (that is, without compensation): Samuel E. Sewell, Ellis G. Loring, Charles G. Davis, Charles List, Robert Morris, John G. King, and Richard Henry Dana Jr. (1851, pp. 9, 17). Dana rushed to the courthouse after being informed of the arrest and saw "a good looking black fellow, sitting between" two special deputies (Dana, 1968, p. 410). The crowds Riley anticipated were already forming. Dana wrote in his journal: "The arrest had been so sudden & unexpected that few knew [of] it, & it was half an hour before the crowd assembled, but it was increasing every minute & there was great excitement" (1968, p. 410).

Dana immediately prepared both a writ of personal replevin and a petition for *habeas corpus* to present to Lemuel Shaw, chief justice of the Massachusetts Supreme Judicial Court. Personal replevin is a common-law action to recover a person out of another's custody (Garner, 1999, p. 1302). A writ of *habeas corpus* challenges the legal authority under which a person is detained (1999, p. 715). Both test the legality of a person's detention. Shadrach consented to the actions on his behalf, and Dana presented the documents to Justice Shaw in the lobby of the superior courtroom.[5] As he stated to the judge, Dana's purpose in presenting the petition was to "test the constitutional power of the Commissioner to issue a warrant" (Dana, 1968, p. 411). The Act of 1850 provided that a certificate of removal granted to the claimant was "conclusive" proof of the claimant's right to return the fugitive to the state or territory from which he escaped, and prevented "all molestation" of the claimant "by any process issued by any court, judge, magistrate, or other person whomsoever" (Fugitive Slave Act of 1850, Section 6). This provision was interpreted as suspending the right of *habeas corpus* in fugitive slave rendition cases (Campbell, 1970, p. 24). Shaw objected to the petitions on the grounds that "the man [Shadrach] is in legal custody, of a U. S. Marshal," and refused to consider Dana's arguments further (Dana, 1968, p. 411). Dana returned to the courtroom determined to cure the defects in the petition alleged by Shaw, whose objections he found "frivolous & invalid" (1968, p. 411).

In Dana's absence, the hearing before Commissioner Curtis went forward, with Shadrach's attorneys Sewall, Loring, Davis, and List arguing for more time in which to challenge the arrest and detention (*Report of Proceedings*, 1851, p. 4). The commissioner agreed to adjourn until Tuesday, February 18, and granted the defense counsel's request to remain in the courtroom to consult with Shadrach about his defense. Dana returned to the courtroom from his failed audience with Justice Shaw just as the room was being cleared. He found Shadrach still sitting between the deputies, and Patrick Riley "making the most absurd exhibition of pomposity, in ordering people about, & clearing the Court room, & Mr. Curtis, dressed in a little brief authority . . . swelling into the dignity of an arbiter of life & death, with a pomposity as ludicrous as that of Riley" (Dana, 1968, p. 412). Riley had sent deputy marshal Warren to the Charlestown Navy Yard to ask Commodore Downes whether the fugitive could be jailed at the navy yard during the duration of the proceedings against him (*Report of Proceedings*, 1851, p. 5). The request was necessitated by the "Latimer Law," M. L. c. 69, §2, which prohibited the assistance of state officials in the detention of fugitives and the imprisonment of any person claimed as a fugitive slave in any jail or other building owned by the Commonwealth (Tiffany, 1890, p. 281).[6] Downes refused to grant the request, and Curtis issued an order for the deputy marshal to retain Shadrach in custody "at the court house in Boston" until Tuesday morning at 10 a.m. (*Report of Proceedings*, 1851, p. 4). The U.S. courtroom was to be Shadrach's jail.

Riley proceeded to clear the courtroom of all unnecessary people. Dana recalled the scene: "At the order of the Marshal, all left the Court room, quietly, except the officers & counsel, & when I left there were none else in the room, & the crowd in the entries & stairways & outside, though large & chiefly negroes, was perfectly peaceable" (Dana, 1968, p. 412). Dana left the building and returned to his law office nearby. Fifteen officers remained to guard the room and prisoner. Riley later testified that "crowds of negroes and others began to gather about the court room, and in the passage ways leading to the court house" (*Report of Proceedings*, 1851, p. 6). At 1 p.m., Riley made a second request to the city marshal, Tukey, to send men to the courthouse to keep the peace. Tukey was purportedly noncommittal, but agreed to send men if and when they became available. At 2 p.m., attorney Davis, who had remained to talk with Shadrach after the other attorneys had retired, got up to leave. Mr. Elizur Wright, a reporter and editor for the *Boston Commonwealth*, was one of the few other people remaining in the courtroom. He too rose to leave. As Davis approached the door, Carl Hutchins, an officer stationed at the door, pushed it open just enough to allow the attorney to pass. As Hutchins did so, people filling the passageway outside the courtroom grabbed at the door and attempted to pull it open wide. Hutchins described the scene: "I saw the stairway all filled. The stairs leading up were all filled also. When [Davis] stepped round, he got his back against the side of the door, and clapped his left hand up against the door. There was a cry to go in. I should suppose by the fingers on the door that five or six got hold of it to pull it round" (*Report of Proceedings*, 1851, p. 12). In the ensuing struggle, the officers tried to pull the door shut from the inside and the crowd continued to force its way in.

Suddenly, the way was clear and the insurgents rushed in. Eyewitness accounts of the number of people who succeeded in trespassing into the room vary widely, from claims of "a score of men" to several hundred (Tiffany, 1890, p. 282; Collison, 1997, p. 134). Riley characterized the people gathered outside the door as a "mob" who succeeded in rushing into the room "in great numbers" (*Report of Proceedings*, 1851, p. 6). Much to Riley's chagrin, one of the trespassers grabbed a symbolic sword of justice Riley kept at his desk and carried it off in the confusion. Other men hurried to Shadrach, surrounded him, and carried him out of the courtroom, down the stairs, out the door to the street, and away. The rescue, as described by Henry Homer, assistant clerk of the municipal court, was swift and unexpected, giving officers little time to react: "All done in ten seconds, I should think. Never saw anything done so quick before. Saw two men take hold of Shadrach and fetch him out, about twenty other men following. The stairs were clear when they brought Shadrach out, and they kind of threw him down the stairs. . . . In passing him out into the street, they tore his coat off, and took his hat off. His coat laid in the mud, and his hat laid there. A woman seized him by the hair and said—'God-bless you. Have they got you?' Shadrach was very much frightened,—did not seem to know whether he had got among his friends or enemies. I saw this from the window at the head of the stairs" (1851, p. 15).

Dana, whose law office was close to the courthouse, witnessed and recorded the moments immediately after the rescue:

[W]e heard a shout from the Court House, continued into a yell of triumph, & in an instant after, down the steps came two huge negroes, bearing the prisoner between them, with his clothes half torn off, & so stupefied by the sudden rescue & the violence of his dragging off that he sat almost down, & I thought had fainted; but the men seised him, & being powerful fellows, hurried him through the Square into Court st., where he found the use of feet, & they went off toward Cambridge, like a black squall, the crowd driving along with them & cheering as they went. It was all done in an instant, too quick to be believed, & so successful was it that not only was no negro arrested, but no attempt was made at pursuit. (Dana, 1968, p. 412)

Still in the hands of his rescuers, Shadrach was taken through the streets and, according to some witnesses, placed into a cab with two of his rescuers; however, the cab never moved from its place, the passengers soon exited, and the cab remained at its station with at least one broken window, shattered by an excited bystander. The cab incident may have been a ruse to throw authorities off the fugitive's trail. Lewis Hayden, one of the defendants in the ensuing rescue trials, revealed years later that he had hidden Shadrach in a neighbor's house on Southac (now Phillips) Street, not far from the scene of the rescue (Robboy and Robboy, 1973, p. 603; Collison, 1997, p. 130). In the evening, Shadrach, Hayden, and a third man took a cab driven by Thomas Murray into Cambridge, where the fugitive was received into the home of the Reverend Joseph C. Lovejoy. Shadrach then made his way to Leominster, where he found shelter in the home of an abolitionist on Sunday morning, February 16. That evening, Shadrach is alleged to have attended an antislavery meeting while "disguised in the habiliments of a woman," but this story cannot be verified (Tiffany, 1890, p. 283). He soon made his way to Canada, settling in Montreal where he worked in the restaurant business, and eventually marrying an Irish woman and raising two children (Tiffany, 1890, p. 283; Collison, 1997, p. 197).

The authorities seeking Shadrach in Boston were unable to trace his escape route. On Tuesday, February 18, the day on which Shadrach's hearing was to have continued, Patrick Riley, the deputy U.S. marshal, appeared before Commissioner Curtis and informed him that Shadrach was unavailable because the door of the U.S. courtroom, "which was being used as a prison, was forced open by a mob, and the said 'Shadrach' [was] forcibly rescued from my custody" (*Report of Proceedings*, 1851, p. 4). Riley also offered a deposition recounting the events of Shadrach's arrest and rescue as witnessed by him. In his deposition, Riley chastised city officials for failing to provide troops to assist the U.S. marshals in controlling the crowds that gathered following Shadrach's arrest. Riley saw their failure to help as calculated: "[F]rom the time of the first notice to the mayor and city marshal . . . [neither] has appeared, nor has a single officer under their direction appeared, or aided in attempting to disperse the mob, or in keeping the peace; and . . . in my opinion, it was the predetermined purpose of both not to do their duty in keeping the peace in and about their court house" (1851, p. 6). Riley then referred to the time of the Craft case the previous fall, a period of excitement in the city during which the city marshal had refused to provide law officers on "orders not to meddle in the matter" (p. 6).

Riley's deposition testimony about security concerns exemplified the clear rift between state and federal authorities in Boston arising from the Fugitive Slave Act of 1850 and exacerbated by the Craft incident in October of that year. Federal officials' failure to serve warrants on the Crafts made them even more determined to secure Shadrach's arrest and remand to Virginia. His rescue was another indication to the federal government that Massachusetts officials had no intention of honoring federal law.

POLITICAL REACTION AND MEDIA RESPONSE

Political reaction to the rescue was swift. The federal authorities made clear they would brook no defiance of the fugitive slave law by the citizenry. A cabinet meeting was called hurriedly in the executive branch, and on February 18, 1851, President Millard Fillmore issued a proclamation denouncing the rescue in Boston, calling on "all well-disposed citizens [of the city] to support the laws of their country," and commanding all civil and military officers to assist in enforcing the fugitive slave law against the fugitive and his rescuers. The president also commanded the U.S. district attorney to arrest and prosecute anyone involved in "this flagitious offence" ("Proclamation of the President," 1851). Below the president's signature, the proclamation also bore the imprimatur of Daniel Webster, secretary of state and formerly U.S. senator from Massachusetts. His reputation in his home state suffered following his support of the enactment of the Fugitive Slave Act of 1850, under which Shadrach was arrested. Webster equated the Boston rescue with "levying war against the United States, and . . . nothing less than treason" (Fehrenbacher, 2001, p. 417, n. 13). Meanwhile in the Senate, Henry Clay of Virginia, a strong proponent of slaveholders' rights, proposed an inquiry into the Boston rescue, and his resolution was passed by the Senate and forwarded to the president. Fillmore responded on February 21 with a message informing the senators of the steps taken to contain the crisis and offering his opinion of the necessity of amending existing law to permit the president to call out the militia to execute the law without first issuing a proclamation, as he had been compelled to do in the aftermath of the Boston rescue ("President Fillmore's Answer," 1851).

Boston and regional newspapers closely followed the responses of the executive and legislative branches of the federal government to the Shadrach rescue. Depending on a newspaper's political bent, reports and editorials either denigrated government actions or rallied behind the president and Congress. *The Liberator*, William Lloyd Garrison's weekly abolitionist newspaper, reprinted an editorial from the *Essex County Freeman* calling Fillmore's proclamation yet "another proof of the servility of the administration to the slave power and its hostility to freedom" ("The Rescue Again," 1851, March 7). The same editorial dared the Fillmore administration to "go on in its mad" plan to pursue Shadrach's rescuers in court, and likened the president to George III of England, late oppressor of the American colonies. A *Portland Inquirer* editorial dubbed Fillmore's proclamation a "ukase" (an authoritative decree considered arbitrary), and voiced the suspicion that the president's secretary of state, Webster—"that corrupt betrayer of his country" for supporting the Fugitive Slave Act of 1850—was its actual author ("Presidential Ukase," 1851, March 7). A column in *The Liberator* suggested that Fillmore's "Proclamation of Terror convey[ed] to us in tones of thunder, and on wings of lightning" would have the opposite of its intended effect; the Massachusetts citizenry would not be cowed into silent acceptance of the Fugitive Slave Act ("The Arrest—," 1851, February 21).

Of course, there was not a consensus of opinion about the fugitive slave law in Boston. For example, Boston merchants had an economic interest in mollifying the southern states by acquiescing to enforcement of the act. The newspapers reflected the differences of opinion. Local newspapers identified as members of the "cotton press," sympathetic to the South and supportive of the Fugitive Slave Act, included the *Boston Courier* and the *Boston Daily Mail* (Mayer, 1998, p. 411).

At the same time that federal authorities were issuing edicts, local officials were working to tighten security within the city, as well as to regain credibility with the federal government. Local newspapers published the city's official responses to the rescue crisis. On February 18, the board of aldermen passed an ordinance requiring the city marshal to respond "in the most energetic manner possible" to any request for assistance in mob containment made by a state or federal officer (Ordinance, 1851, February 21). The ordinance was both a response to federal concerns about lax enforcement of the fugitive slave law and to the perceived failure of City Marshal Tukey and Mayor Bigelow to respond to requests for aid allegedly made repeatedly by Deputy Marshal Patrick Riley before the Shadrach rescue. Both Tukey and Bigelow disputed any such claim.

Responding to Riley's deposition testimony, Bigelow forwarded a letter to the newspapers, dated February 17, recounting his interactions with Riley on the day of the rescue. According to the mayor, Riley visited Bigelow at City Hall and informed him, "We have got a negro, and I thought I would call and let you know." Bigelow took Riley's information as a "kindly hint to look out for street disturbances," not as an urgent request for security forces. The mayor claimed to have "not the shadow of suspicion that Mr. Riley was wanting in ample means to retain his prisoner against unarmed assailants." Bigelow also explained that a remark made by him to Riley had been mischaracterized in Riley's deposition testimony. Riley claimed that Bigelow responded to his request for a police presence at the courthouse with an indifferent, "I am sorry for it." Bigelow disputed that claim, stating that he had not dismissed Riley's security concerns, but rather had merely answered, "I was 'sorry for *him*,'" when Riley complained of shortness of breath during their conversation ("A Card," 1851; emphasis added).

Tukey also offered a letter to the newspapers for publication. Addressed to the mayor, it recounted Riley's visit to Tukey's office and his message to the city marshal: "We have got a nigger [*sic*]. I merely notify you, so that if they make trouble, you may be about." Following Riley's notification, Tukey went to the mayor's office, where Bigelow "directed me to prevent any breach of the peace outside the Court House." Tukey stated that he performed his duty, "sen[ding] out officers from time to time to see all was quiet." According to Tukey, one city officer sent to the courthouse shortly before 2 p.m. (the time of the rescue) was turned away by a deputy at the door ("Letter from the City Marshal," 1851, February 21).

As to reportage of the rescue itself, the sharp division in public opinion between those who favored the Fugitive Slave Act and those who sought its abolishment was reflected in the city's rival newspapers. An editorial in *The Liberator* lamented the "utter corruption of the Boston press" in supporting the slave catchers and proponents of the fugitive slave law: "The *Courier, Daily Advertiser, Mercantile Journal, Traveller, Post, Transcript,* &c &c, distort, falsify, rave, foam, in a manner not to be surpassed by any Southern journals" ("The Arrest—," 1851). An article in the same newspaper outlined press distortions in the description of the rescue, including alleged violence toward the peace officers and exaggerations of the number of rescuers. As an example, the reporter quoted the *Traveller's* description of officers at the courtroom door being "kicked, cuffed, and knocked about in every direction," when there was no evidence of such violence ("Arrest of a Man," 1851, February 21). An editorial in *The Liberator* found the Boston newspaper coverage of the rescue to be largely unprincipled and inflammatory: "The comments of the Boston press generally have been vile and profligate to the last degree. Under the pretence of a regard for the law, they set at defiance every sentiment of humanity, and libel every principle which characterizes and justifies the struggler for liberty both in America and in Europe. Prominent among these pro-slavery sheets, in venom and in falsehood, are to be named the *Courier* and the *Traveller*" ("The Arrest—," 1851).

The Shadrach rescue was not merely a matter of local concern; it was an event of national significance. While the renewed debate over slavery, catalyzed by the rescue, played out in the local press, the national government moved forward to prosecute those who had dared to defy federally mandated law.

THE RESCUE TRIALS

With Shadrach beyond the reach of the court, the authorities moved quickly to indict those alleged to have helped him to escape. The charge was aiding and abetting a fugitive slave under the Fugitive Slave Act of 1850. Section 7 of the Act criminalized the actions of any person who "knowingly and willingly" hindered a claimant from recovering a fugitive slave, or rescued or otherwise aided and abetted the escape of a fugitive. A person convicted under the Act was subject to a $1,000 fine and up to six months in prison and was liable for civil damages of $1,000 for each fugitive lost to the claimant.

Nine men were indicted for aiding Shadrach's escape: Charles G. Davis, Shadrach's counsel; Robert Morris, also Shadrach's counsel and the first black attorney in Massachusetts; Elizur Wright, an editor and reporter for the *Boston Commonwealth*; Lewis Hayden, a former slave, a clothier, and a future Massachusetts legislator; John Foye, a black man; James Scott, a black man; Joseph K. Hayes, a white member of the Boston Vigilance Committee;[7] Thomas P. Smith, a black man and a dealer in secondhand clothes; and John P. Coburn, a black clothier ("Arrest on a Charge," 1851; von Frank, 1998, p. 42; Collison, 1997, pp. 141–147; Campbell, 1970, p. 150). The charges against a tenth man, black barber Alexander P. Burton, were quickly dismissed when it was discovered he was not the man named in the warrant sworn out against an "Andrew J." Burton (Collison, 1997, p. 147). All the men brought to trial were acquitted or had the case pending against them dismissed. The "rescue trials," as they were headlined in contemporary Boston newspapers, were reported extensively, with redacted testimony appearing daily along with editorials, public commentary, reprints of proclamations of the executive branch of the federal government, and reports on Congressional statesmen's actions in response to the violation of federal law in Boston. The cases receiving the most media attention were *U.S. v. Davis, Esq.*; *U.S. v. Scott*; *U.S. v. Hayden*; *U.S. v. Morris, Esq.*; and *U.S. v. Wright*. Contemporary reportage of these trials provides the most vivid descriptions of the actual rescue, details of which emerged only during the court proceedings against Shadrach's alleged liberators. The individual rescue trials are discussed in more detail below.

U.S. V. CHARLES G. DAVIS, ESQ.

Charles Davis was indicted and brought to trial only days after the rescue. The trial opened on Thursday, February 20, in the U.S. circuit courtroom, with George Lunt, district attorney, appearing for the United States; and Richard Henry Dana Jr., and Davis himself appearing for the defense. Commissioner Benjamin F. Hallett presided at trial. The government alleged Davis's complicity in the rescue on the ground that his actions at the courtroom door had permitted, and possibly encouraged, the ingress of people who carried Shadrach away. The prosecution first tried to establish Davis's animus toward the Fugitive Slave Act of 1850. Charles Sawin, who had assisted in the arrest of Shadrach at the coffee house, testified that before the commencement of proceedings against Shadrach in the courtroom, Davis had said to him, "This is a damned dirty piece of business." Davis later allegedly said to Sawin and to Frederick Byrnes, another deputy marshal, "Well, you ought all to have your throats cut" (*Report of Proceedings*, 1851, pp. 10, 11). Byrnes testified to the same general comments allegedly made by Davis. He also claimed to have heard Davis say, "Take him out, boys— take him out," as Davis stood at the open door (1851, p. 11). On the stand, Byrnes admitted to being "somewhat hard of hearing," but believed that the day of the rescue "was one of my hearing days" (1851, p. 11). Calvin Hutchins, another prosecution witness and an officer on the day of the rescue, addressed the defendant in court, questioning Davis's method of exiting the door: "To go out the best way to clear the crowd, you ought to have turned right; but you faced round to the door, putting your left hand upon it, and opening it more than was necessary. Some one had hold of the knob of the door at the time, and there were fingers on the edges. I was holding on to the door to give you space enough to get out, and was contending with the negroes by keeping the door from being opened more than sufficient to let you out" (1851, p. 12). Hutchins then demonstrated Davis's stance at the door and testified that his "back was against the door jam, or door post on the right, when his hand was on the door" (1851, p. 12).

After the prosecution rested its case, Dana moved for discharge of the defendant for lack of proof, but the motion was denied. Witnesses for the defense, including officers of the court, testified to Byrnes's general reputation for truth and veracity, all stating that it was "bad." Constable Alonzo Neale testified to his annoyance at the lack of initiative taken by officers during the rescue. Specifically, he "felt rather vexed" that neither Patrick Riley nor John Riley had made any effort to "come to the door attacked, to assist in closing it" (*Report of Proceedings*, 1851, p. 18). Neale believed that Davis, Wright, and another man had exited the courtroom at the same time, but he did not see their departure. Attorney George Minns gave context to the allegedly inflammatory statement Davis had made to Byrnes and another officer. Minns testified that sometime before 2 p.m., a person he thought could be Byrnes said, "Kill the negroes!" to which Davis responded, "Then, on that principle, you ought to have your throats cut" (1851, p. 18). To Dana's surprise, Davis called him as a defense witness. Dana testified to his own actions in service to Shadrach on the day of the rescue, then stated in response to a question from D. A. Lunt that he could say "most positively, that I never heard one of the gentlemen who acted as counsel here, say any thing in the way of advising or planning a resort to violence, or that indicated any knowledge or belief on their part that it would take place" (1851, p. 20).

In his closing argument for the defense, Dana not only focused on the lack of evidence of Davis's assistance in the rescue, but emphasized the great "political weight" attached to the trial because of the government's interest in enforcing the fugitive slave law (1851, p. 23). On the evidence, Dana suggested the flimsiness of a government case based on nothing but "an exclamation on a staircase, sworn to, not very confidently, by a deaf man, who was too far off to hear well at any rate of hearing, denied by three officers, with good hearing" (1851, p. 35).[8] He asked: "If such evidence is sufficient, who can be safe? Who would dare to act as counsel in any case of public excitement, with a suspicious and angry government watching every motion, served by officers of broken down reputations?" (1851, p. 35). As to the trial's political nature, Dana suggested there was calculation on the government's part in so swiftly bringing to trial a man "sworn to sustain the laws, a counsellor of this court and of all the courts of the United States in this State, sworn doubly to sustain the laws." The "political State trial" now in progress was meant to intimidate Davis and to dissuade him—and others—from working as "the counsellor for a poor, unprotected fugitive from captivity" in the future (1851, p. 24).

Davis's trial would only increase the reluctance of attorneys to represent the neediest clients: "I think that two years ago no man could have stood before this bar, with perpetual servitude impending over him, but almost the entire bar would have come forward for his defense. No man would have dared to decline" (1851, p. 28). It was "a monstrous thing" to proceed against the fugitive's counsel, in a public trial that would go out to "the profession, the press, and into the private records of the country" (1851, p. 29). Dana acknowledged Davis's belief that "the dreadful [fugitive slave] statute" was "unconstitutional, a violation of our moral sense, a great breach upon the safeguards of freedom every where." Davis would not betray his duty as an officer of the court but rather would "oppose it legally, by speech, by the pen, and in Court"; he would not "yield to it any voluntary obedience," but likewise he would not "use force, or counsel citizens to use force to set aside the laws" (1851, p. 36). Dana ended with a rhetorical flourish directed toward both the court and the public who would read his argument in the local newspapers:

The doings of these last few days are now part of history. If there has been a hasty and a needless arrest of a respectable gentleman; if counsel have been intimidated, or witnesses threatened; if liberty of speech and action have been periled; if the dignity and duty of office have been yielded to the unreasonable demands of political agents, and the commands of a misinformed Executive,—the Inquest of public opinion is to sit upon the whole transaction, and it will be held up to the world. (*Report of Proceedings*, 1851, p. 37)

Lunt, in his closing argument, accused Dana of grandstanding and assured the court that he would not spend his own time "for popular effect" (*Report of Proceedings*, 1851, p. 37). Dana's remarks were made with "ill grace," and Lunt predicted that the "sentiments he has uttered here place *him* in peril." This was a suggestion that Dana would lose legal business based on his imprudent remarks: "He will find it *so, to his cost*, unless he changes the tone of his remarks, on this and future occasions" (1851, p. 37). In fact, during the rescue trials Dana was attacked in the newspapers by anonymous sources who warned the public not to hire him as an attorney. As part of his closing argument, Lunt received permission from the court to read an article from the *Boston Post*, dated October 15, 1850, that recounted a fugitive slave law meeting held by the law's opponents. Lunt's purpose was to show Davis's animus toward the Fugitive Slave Act. Among the people listed in attendance at the meeting were Samuel E. Sewall, a vice president of the group, and Richard Henry Dana Jr., who made remarks at the meeting. Charles G. Davis, though not present, was listed as a member of a vigilance committee set up to protect fugitives from slave catchers acting under the provisions of the fugitive slave law. Lunt argued that by his assent to volunteer as a member, Davis "more or less implicated" himself in the opinions expressed at the meeting and showed a predisposition to assist in an extemporaneous rescue when he found himself at the open courtroom door (*Report of Proceedings*, 1851, p. 39). In Davis's "excited state of mind," according to Lunt, the defendant verbally abused court officers and encouraged the insurgents to take Shadrach from the room (1851, p. 40). In summing up his evidentiary case, Lunt relied on Byrnes's identification of Davis's alleged cry to take the prisoner out, testimony that was uncorroborated by any other witness.

On Wednesday, February 26, the day after closing arguments, Commissioner Hallett issued his decision. Despite Dana's opinion of Hallett as a "slangwhanging radical" with an "almost incredible ignorance of law," the commissioner ordered the defendant discharged (Dana, 1968, p. 414). Hallett found "no evidence which connects [Davis] criminally with a preconcerted plan of rescue" (1851, p. 41). The commissioner conceded that the district attorney had probable cause to bring the case to trial, but found no legal, as distinct from moral, aiding and abetting of the rescue by Davis.

The Davis trial was the first and most highly publicized of the rescue trials. Begun only days after the rescue of Shadrach, when emotions were still high in the city, the trial attracted the fixed attention of the public and the press. Newspapers reported witness testimony and the arguments of counsel. With satisfaction, Dana recorded in his journal the publication of his closing argument in the *Boston Commonwealth* (Dana, 1968, p. 415). The entire case, together with documents relating to Shadrach's arrest, was published in a pamphlet called *Report of the Proceedings at the Examination of Charles G. Davis, Esq., on a charge of aiding and abetting in the rescue of a fugitive slave*. In a "Note" preceding the *Report*, the anonymous redactor explained that the pamphlet was published "at the request of numerous persons" to "spread before the public" the true nature and operation of the fugitive slave law. The *Report* was intended to inform both the legal profession and the public in the application of the statute to the facts of the instant case. Readers could form their own judgments "of the temper, and manner, as to parties and witnesses, in which the prosecution was pressed, and the judicial duties performed" (*Report of Proceedings*, 1851, p. 2). There is a possibility that Elizur Wright, journalist for the *Commonwealth*, prepared the report (Collison, 1997, p. 256, n. 44). He would soon be a defendant himself.

U.S. V. JAMES SCOTT

James Scott's trial on the charge of aiding and abetting the rescue of Shadrach began in May 1851. John P. Hale and Dana served as defense counsel. Lunt once again served as prosecuting attorney. The case was tried before Judge William Buell Sprague. Witnesses who had appeared in Davis's trial once again took the stand, offering conflicting testimony about Scott's presence or absence at the scene of the rescue. Henry Homer, assistant clerk, did not see Scott during the melee in the courtroom. Frederick Warren, deputy marshal, failed to recognize Scott as a member of the crowd. Charles Sawin testified that he saw Scott pushing his way into the courtroom with [th]e other interlopers. Constable Neale also saw Scott in the thick of the [stru]ggle. One acquaintance of Scott, George Washington, testified that near [the ti]me of the rescue he saw Scott in his shop cutting cloth ("Trial of James [Scott,]" 1851, June 2; "Rescue Trials—Continued," 1851, June 5).

[After] a week of trial, Judge Sprague delivered what Dana termed an [unfair] charge on the law, sustaining the constitutionality of the Act of [1850] [(Dan]a, 1968, p. 430). Sprague gave a lengthy disquisition on the Act [declar]ing that its constitutionality had been "acquiesced in by the [people f]or fifty-seven years" (*U.S. v. Scott*, 1851, p. 994). The matter [of va]lid[i]ty, of both the Act of 1793 and its amending act of 1850, [is settled] by contemporaneous exposition, by practice, and acquies-[cence fo]r fifty years, by the opinions and decisions of courts and [judges n]ational, and especially by the supreme court of the [U.S. [*Pri]gg v. Pennsylvania*, 41 U.S. 559 (1842)]" (*U.S. v.* [*Scott*]. [D]ana found Sprague's jury charge heavy-handed and [declared] "the neutrality of the bench at all events" (Dana, [1968). Given] the judge's seeming bias toward the government, the jurors, after deliberating for twenty-one hours, deadlocked at six to six and were discharged (Dana, p. 430). An attempt to impanel another jury failed when the jury pool was exhausted during questioning of prospective jurors as to opinions or bias in the case (p. 431). Scott remained liable for retrial.

Despite stronger eyewitness evidence in this case, the government was unable to obtain a conviction. A *Tribune* article quoted in the *Boston Commonwealth* expressed the opinion of a number of observers of the trial: "This result, considering the strenuous efforts of the Government and the care taken to exclude from the Jury every man suspected of being opposed to slave-catching, surprised us" ("Boston Rescue Cases," 1851). The article also charged judicial bias, suggesting that Sprague, "*if he had been a South Carolina Hotspur, could hardly have manifested a stronger determination to procure a conviction*" (1851; emphasis in original).

U.S. V. LEWIS HAYDEN

The trial of Lewis Hayden began in June 1851. Hale and Dana again served as counsel for the defense, and Lunt prosecuted the case, joined by Nathaniel Lord. Judge Peleg Sprague, a respected jurist who was blind, presided. He is not to be confused with William Buell Sprague, who presided Scott's rescue trial. Unlike the previous cases, the evidence against was strong, with credible eyewitness accounts at various stages of Hayden, born into slavery in Kentucky, was a well-known Boston Vigilance Committee. He had hidden William Cr the authorities were attempting to serve an arrest in October 1850.

The most compelling evidence at trial was that they had seen Hayden with the fu Henry Emerson, a resident of C seeing Hayden "on the day Court-house; saw him a from Court street, w Hayden had hol wester hat" (" dressed in foul-w Wright, a bowling a stationary cab parke Cabdriver Thomas Mu and a third, unidentified dropped the passengers off fare by Hayden, although the usual charge was $1.50 ("Trial of Lewis Hayden"). Before resting its case, the prosecution sought to present evidence tending to show that the defendant "had made threats against the execution of the law" by attending an antifugitive-slave-law meeting ("Hayden's Case," 1851). While the court ruled that evidence of such threats was admissible, the prosecution's proffer of hearsay testimony was ruled out, and the government rested its case.

In his opening argument for the defense, Dana was dismissive of the prosecution's futile attempt to prove Hayden's "seditious and treasonable" nature through the witness testimony of a reporter for the *Boston Courier*— "a *Webster Whig organ!*"—who had attended an antislavery meeting but relied on another's synopsis of events to implicate Hayden ("Hayden's Case," 1851; emphasis in original). Dana then declared that the defense would prove that Hayden, "one of the most respectable men in Boston," did not assist in the rescue but rather was "at home at dinner a few minutes past two on the day of the rescue." Dana then introduced three witnesses who testified to seeing Hayden on the street around the time of the rescue, but not near the crowd nor participating in the event. One witness testified that Hayden was walking quickly down the street in his foul-weather gear, not because he was involved with the rescue, but because it was raining. S. W. Beale, a stable owner, shed some light on the stationary cab incident testified to in a previous trial. According to Beale, three men entered the cab as it waited at a street corner. While they were inside the vehicle, two of its windows were broken by the crowd outside, and the passengers exited the cab within two minutes. Beale stated that Lewis Hayden was not one of the men in the cab, nor was he in the street crowd. Several other witnesses disputed Hayden's presence during the rescue and escape, with John Randolph, a boarder in Hayden's house, further testifying that the defendant was at home at dinner "about fifteen minutes past two o'clock on the day of the rescue" and did not shelter Shadrach under his roof ("Rescue Trials— Hayden's Case," 1851).

Hale gave the closing argument for the defense, emphasizing the political nature of the trial: "It would be idle to attempt to wink out of sight the fact that this case stands connected with a subject of widespread political agitation, a subject on which from one extremity of the land to the other there have been the most extreme opinions" ("Mr. Hale's Closing," 1851). These were show trials, Hale suggested, calling the fugitive slave law the "sole religion of a great portion of the country." It was therefore necessary for "somebody to be convicted to show the vitality of the law, to show that it will be executed without reserve" (1851). Turning to the evidence offered against Hayden, Hale "confessed" that he found the prosecution witnesses, whom he referred to as "dealers in junk," not believable, and argued that defense witnesses countered the alleged sightings of Hayden in the crowd of rescuers ("Mr. Hale's Closing—Concluded," 1851).

In closing for the government, Lunt said that he refused to insult the jury by arguing the constitutionality of the fugitive slave law, "since they have sworn that they believe it to be constitutional" ("Mr. Lunt's Argument," 1851). Lunt then attested to the respectability of the prosecution witnesses disparaged by Hale, and suggested it was the defense witnesses who could more properly be labeled "liars and perjurers" (1851).

Judge Sprague's charge to the jury instructed the members to decide whether Lewis Hayden "had any share in taking" Shadrach from custody, that is, whether Hayden "participated in, aided, or encouraged the rescue, at any time or at any place—whether in the Court House or out of it, in Boston, or in Cambridge." Sprague also cautioned the jurors that the "humanity or inhumanity" of the Act of 1850 had "nothing to do with the matter" before them ("Trial of Lewis Hayden," 1851). As in the James Scott case, the jury deadlocked, and the government failed for a third time in its trials of alleged rescuers to obtain a conviction. The government, however, reserved the right to retry Hayden.

U.S. V. ROBERT MORRIS, ESQ.

Immediately after the close of the Hayden trial in mid-June, the government called the Morris case to trial. Hale and Dana again served as defense counsel, and Lunt and Lord prosecuted the government's case. Judge Peleg Sprague presided. Morris, a member of the Massachusetts Bar, was the second attorney to be a defendant in the rescue trials.[9] A jury of twelve men was impaneled, and Lord opened the government's case. He stated that the government would prove that Morris conferred with blacks gathered at the courtroom door before the rescue, intimidated a court officer while participating in the rescue, and assisted Shadrach in his flight through the streets of Boston. Because of Morris's stature as a member of the bar, Lord told the jury, his violation of the law was "inexcusable" ("Morris's Case," 1851).

When Lord concluded his opening remarks, Lunt rose and informed the court that he had learned that one of the jurors was biased and should be removed. He named Dana D. Walker and asked the court to stay the proceedings. Hale, for the defense, protested and demanded proof. Lunt said he could say on "good authority" that the juror was ardently opposed to the fugitive slave law. Finding Lunt's assurance insufficient, the court ordered the prosecution to present its case. After three witnesses testified, court adjourned for the day. The following morning, Lunt called witnesses to the stand to testify to Walker's participation in antislavery meetings, his past comments about the Fugitive Slave Act, and his alleged communications with the defendant Morris ("Trial of Robert Morris," 1851). Hale cross-examined the witnesses on Walker's behalf. The court decided to discharge Walker, and the prosecution then made a motion to retry the case in the next court term. The motion was granted, according to Dana, "without our consent" (1968, p. 432).[10] Morris's first trial was over.

Shortly after the trial was suspended, Walker wrote a piece published in the local newspapers under the title "The rejected juror." Walker informed the public that his words were taken out of context, and he assured readers that he understood his duty as a juror to decide the case based on the law and evidence. He would not have betrayed his "solemn oath" as a juror, but the judge was swayed by "evidence of partial conversations, told by political opponents, and held in times of excitement several months ago" ("Rejected Juror," 1851). Walker claimed he now feared indictment for perjury based on the distorted testimony presented against him.

When Morris was again called to trial in the October term, his case was moved from the district court to the circuit court. His counsel, Hale and Dana, protested the remittal, but Circuit Judge Benjamin R. Curtis, presiding over the second trial, ruled that federal law permitted indictment for a misdemeanor to be remitted to the circuit court even if the defendant had already entered a plea in the district court and proceedings had begun against him (U.S. v. Morris, 1851, p. 1323). While the indictment for aiding and abetting the rescue of Shadrach was transferred to the circuit court, none of the evidence presented before the juror was discharged in the first trial was a part of the record. The trial began anew. Evidence in the Morris trial mirrored the evidence presented in the previous rescue trials, with prosecution witnesses claiming to have seen the defendant in the courtroom assisting in the rescue and getting into a cab with the fugitive, and defense witnesses contradicting the sightings or claims of Morris's active participation in the rescue. Once again, because of contradictory evidence creating doubt in the jurors' minds, the government failed to gain a conviction. Morris was acquitted and could not be tried again. Dana wrote in his journal, "I hope this will end the Rescue Cases" (1968, p. 469). It was a false hope: the last cases pending would not be resolved until 1853.

U.S. V. ELIZUR WRIGHT

Elizur Wright, the *Boston Commonwealth* reporter and editor who was leaving the courtroom with Charles Davis at the time of the Shadrach rescue, was not tried until 1852. Wright always maintained his complete innocence in the affair. At the time of Wright's arrest, Dana noted that the evidence against him was "nothing, except that one or two officers swore that, as the negroes were rushing in, he uttered an exclamation of encouragement. . . . It is clear that he knew nothing of the attempt at rescue until it took place" (1968, p. 414). In the rescue trial of James Scott, Wright testified that he was leaving the courtroom with Charles Davis when he paused to ask Patrick Riley a question. Wright was "ten or fifteen feet from the door" when he heard a "tremendous shout." As the rescue began, Riley said, "Shoot him," referring to Shadrach, and Wright responded by exclaiming, "Don't shoot a man in the courtroom" ("Trial of James Scott," 1851). This is the only "participation" in the rescue Wright ever admitted to. When Wright himself was first brought to trial in June 1852, he chose to represent himself despite his lack of legal training. The jury voted eleven to one for conviction, and the government, still without a conviction in any of its rescue trials, vowed to retry Wright. In the second trial, held in October 1852, Wright was represented by Dana, with a Mr. Farley assisting. Judge Benjamin R. Curtis presided. This time, Wright was acquitted, and Dana commented that "[t]he bar ought to vote Farley & me a service of plate, for demonstrating the importance of professional services" (1968, p. 513). Wright was the last defendant to be tried for the rescue of Shadrach, although other defendants would have charges pending against them for another year.

RESOLUTION OF THE REMAINING RESCUE TRIALS

The cases against the remaining defendants in the rescue trials, Lewis Hayden, James Scott, John Foye, Joseph K. Hayes, Thomas P. Smith, and John P. Coburn, remained unresolved. In February 1853, Dana met with Lunt to request that the cases be nol-prossed, that is, discontinued by entry of a *nolle prosequi* in the court docket. Lunt remained intractable, and Dana vented his frustration in a journal entry dated February 13, 1853: "I called on [George] Lunt, (U. S. D. Att'y) to induce him to Nol Pros. the remaining Rescue Cases, cases of men who for nearly two years have not been brot to trial, & of [James] Scott who has been tried once, the jury disagreeing & has not been brot to trial again, tho' 20 months have elapsed. I told him that such a course was unprecedented in criminal, & especially in political trials. His reply was that these were not political trials, that perhaps 'the fellows had been punished enough' (what right had he to punish?); & lastly, that he supposed I knew that the late Sec. of State, (Mr. Webster), had taken these cases into his own hands, & that he (Lunt) had been obliged to do as Mr. Webster said & not as he wished &c." (1968, pp. 531–532).[11] Lunt even suggested he might try one of the pending cases in May, and Dana resolved privately to bring the matter before Judge Peleg Sprague (1968, p. 532). Lunt must have finally relented, because the remaining cases were nol-prossed in May 1853 (Collison, 1997, p.195).

SIGNIFICANCE OF THE COURTROOM RESCUE AND TRIALS

Shadrach Minkins was the first fugitive slave rescued from federal custody following the passage of the Fugitive Slave Act of 1850. It was imperative for the U.S. government to show the nation, as well as Massachusetts, that federal law would be enforced despite some citizens' opposition to the Act. As a component of the Compromise of 1850, which controlled the expansion of slavery into the western territories while strengthening the law of recapture for the slaveholding states, the Fugitive Slave Act was considered necessary to the political survival of the Union. Federal authorities decided to make an example of the Boston community, in part to appease southerners fearful they would not be able to recover their slaves in northern courts, and in part to intimidate state and local authorities into enforcing federal law. So the government moved forward with the rescue trials.

Also involved in the decision to press the cases against the rescuers was Secretary of State Daniel Webster's political ambition. Webster hoped to gain the nomination for president, and he believed convictions of the Shadrach rescuers would increase his standing with proponents of the Fugitive Slave Act. U.S. District Attorney Lunt, who prosecuted the trials for the federal government, informed defense counsel that Webster had "taken these cases into his own hands" (Dana, 1968, p. 531). Webster's "deep interest & efforts in these Rescue Cases" was confirmed by another member of the district attorney's staff, who disagreed with the pursuit of the defendants and felt that if Webster "had common sense, with all his greatness, he would not press" for trials (Dana, 1968, p. 532). In the end, Webster's efforts proved futile, and all the defendants went free.

The rescue trials, intended to showcase the supremacy of federal law, failed to dissuade abolitionists from continuing attempts to thwart the law or to inhibit members of the bar from representing fugitive slaves before the court. One immediate effect of the courtroom rescue, however, was a tightening of security in the vicinity of the courthouse. This affected the outcome of the next fugitive slave arrest. In April 1851, after the conclusion of the Davis trial but before commencement of the remaining rescue trials, Thomas Sims, a fugitive from Georgia, was arrested in Boston and imprisoned in the federal courtroom to await a hearing. Vigilance Committee members, including Lewis Hayden, planned a more daring escape for Sims than the spontaneous rescue of Shadrach: they planned to place mattresses under a third-floor courthouse window for Sims to jump into (von Frank, 1998, p. 29). However, because of Shadrach's escape, authorities took no chances with the new fugitive and quickly barred the window and wrapped the courthouse in chains. Lawyers and judges entering the building were forced to stoop under or climb over the chains (Dana, 1968, pp. 420, 424). Sims was ultimately remanded into the custody of his owner under heavy security, and Webster had the satisfaction of seeing the Fugitive Slave Act enforced in the midst of the rescue trials.

The government argued that the defendants in the rescue trials were prosecuted "for violating the laws of the country; for this and nothing else," but the trials were clearly political as well ("Mr. Lunt's Argument," 1851). Their effect was to galvanize the positions of both abolitionists and supporters of the Fugitive Slave Act. Neither side backed down, but after the first summer of the rescue trials, the tension raised by Shadrach's rescue dissipated. Boston would not be tested nor see such civic strain and moral indignation again until the capture and trial of Anthony Burns, fugitive slave from Virginia, in 1854.

NOTES

1. Minkins was apparently the fugitive's surname, but he also used the surnames Wilkins and Jenkins during his time in Boston (Collison, 1997, p. i). Newspapers recounting the rescue and subsequent trials of his liberators most often referred to him as Frederic Wilkins. In his journals, Richard Henry Dana Jr., one of Shadrach's attorneys, identifies him as "Fred. Jenkins" (Dana, 1968, p. 411).

2. A commissioner granting a certificate of removal was entitled to a ten-dollar fee; a commissioner finding insufficient proof to grant a certificate was entitled to a five-dollar fee.

3. Shadrach's alleged owner, John Debree, described him as a "house servant . . . about 27 years of age when he left me," and "darker than a mulatto" ("Morris's Case," 1851).

4. The Boston courthouse contained both state and federal courtrooms.

5. At the same time, yet another attorney, Marcus Morton Jr., went to attorney Seth Thomas's office to discuss the possibility of purchasing Shadrach's freedom, but "[n]othing resulted from the conversation" (*Report of Proceedings*, 1851, p. 17).

6. The Latimer Law was enacted in 1843 following the detention of the fugitive slave George Latimer in the city jail in Boston while awaiting trial. The jailer took Latimer into custody at the request of the person claiming him. Latimer's freedom was purchased while he was imprisoned, and he was released from custody, but citizens protested the assistance of state officials and the use of state property to

detain fugitives. The legislature, acting on the public discontent, passed what became known as the Latimer Law the year following the fugitive's incarceration.

7. Vigilance committees in Boston and elsewhere assisted fugitive slaves to evade the fugitive slave law, and otherwise worked in the antislavery cause.

8. In his private journal, Dana wrote: "The whole thing wd. be a farce, were it not that the purblind obstinacy of Lunt (D. Atty.) & of B. F. Hallett, the Commissioner, magnifies it into a great affair. Any other man than Lunt, wd. withdraw the complaint ag. Davis. But Lunt is the oddest mixture of obstinacy, ignorance of legal principles, vanity & irritability I ever met with in such a place" (1968, p. 414).

9. During the Davis trial, a prosecution witness had pointed Morris out as "the little darkey lawyer." Dana was prompted to say, "The remark seems to amuse the district attorney," to which Lunt responded, "I cannot always control my muscles" (*Report of Proceedings*, 1851, p. 11).

10. Dana noted in his journal: "Qu[estion]. If the setting aside of Walker was illegal, is not Morris discharged?" (1968, p. 432).

11. Daniel Webster died in October 1852.

REFERENCES

The arrest—. (1851, February 21). *The Liberator.*

Arrest on a charge of aiding in the escape of the slave Shadrach. (1851, February 21). *The Liberator.*

Arrest of a man in Boston as a slave—rescue of the prisoner. (1851, February 21). *The Liberator.*

Boston rescue cases. (1851, June 10). *Boston Commonwealth.*

Campbell, S. W. (1970). *The slave catchers: Enforcement of the fugitive slave law, 1850–1860.* Chapel Hill, NC: University of North Carolina Press.

A card. (1851, February 21). *The Liberator.*

Collison, G. (1997). *Shadrach Minkins: From fugitive slave to citizen.* Cambridge, MA: Harvard University Press.

Dana, R. H., Jr. (1968). *The journal of Richard Henry Dana, Jr.*, Vol. 2 (R. F. Lucid, Ed.). Cambridge, MA: Belknap Press of Harvard University Press.

Fehrenbacher, D. (2001). *The slaveholding republic.* W. M. McAfee (Ed.). New York: Oxford University Press.

Fugitive Slave Act of 1850, *U.S. Statutes at Large, 9,* 462–465.

Garner, B. A. (Ed.). (1999). *Black's law dictionary* (7th ed.). St. Paul, MN: West Publishing Group.

Hayden's case. (1851, June 12). *Boston Commonwealth.*

Letter from the city marshal to the mayor. (1851, February 21). *The Liberator.*

Mayer, H. (1998). *All on fire: William Lloyd Garrison and the abolition of slavery.* New York: St. Martin's Press.

Morris's case. (1851, June 17). *Boston Commonwealth.*

Mr. Hale's closing argument for the prisoner. (1851, June 14). *Boston Commonwealth.*

Mr. Hale's closing argument for the prisoner—concluded. (1851, June 16). *Boston Commonwealth*.

Mr. Lunt's argument for government. (1851, June 16). *Boston Commonwealth*.

Mr. Sumner's speech. (1851, February 28). *Boston Commonwealth*.

Ordinance passed by the board of aldermen on Tuesday last. (1851, February 21). *The Liberator*.

President Fillmore's answer to Mr. Clay's resolution. (1851, March 7). *The Liberator*.

Presidential ukase. (1851, March 7). *The Liberator*, reprinted from the *Portland Inquirer*.

Proclamation by the president of the United States. (1851, February 21). *The Liberator*.

The rejected juror. (1851, July 11). *Boston Commonwealth*, reprinted from the *Boston Traveller*.

Report of the proceedings at the examination of Charles G. Davis, Esq., on a charge of aiding and abetting in the rescue of a fugitive slave. (1851). Boston: White and Potter.

The rescue again. (1851, March 7). *The Liberator*, reprinted from the *Essex County Freeman*.

Rescue trials—continued. (1851, June 5). *Boston Commonwealth*.

Rescue trials—Hayden's case. (1851, June 13). *Boston Commonwealth*.

Robboy, S. J., and Robboy, A. W. (1973). Lewis Hayden: From fugitive slave to statesman. *The New England Quarterly, 46*, 591–613.

Tiffany, N. M. (1890). Stories of the fugitive slaves. II. Shadrach. *The New England Magazine 8* (3), 280–283.

Trial of James Scott. (1851, June 2). *Boston Commonwealth*.

Trial of Lewis Hayden. (1851, June 11). *Boston Commonwealth*.

Trial of Robert Morris. (1851, June 19). *Boston Commonwealth*.

U.S. CONST. Art. IV, §2, cl. 3.

U.S. v. Morris, 26 F. Cas. 1323 (C.C.D. Ma. 1851) (No. 15,815).

U.S. v. Scott, 27 F. Cas. 990 (D.C.D. Ma. 1851) (No. 16,240b).

von Frank, A. J. (1998). *The trials of Anthony Burns*. Cambridge, MA: Harvard University Press.

14

The Daniel Sickles
Murder Trial:
A Husband's Vengeance

John McClymer

On March 5, 1859, the following front-page illustration was what the more than 150,000 subscribers of *Harper's Weekly*, plus tens of thousands of others who looked at the issue, saw: New York City Congressman Daniel Edgar Sickles shooting an unarmed and prostrate Philip Barton Key, U.S. attorney for the District of Columbia, while a witness, Samuel F. Butterworth, looks on. The other major national weekly, *Frank Leslie's Illustrated*, published a similar drawing on the same date, but it shows the witness nonchalantly leaning against a fence some distance away. *Harper's* has Butterworth standing close enough to have grabbed Sickles's arm had he wished. *Harper's* suggested the witness's complicity, and *Leslie's* his indifference, to Key's death. Both emphasized Sickles's implacable resolve.

Readers had already heard of "The Washington Tragedy," as Sickles's shooting of Key came to be called. The story flew across the telegraph lines almost as soon as it happened. The initial newspaper pieces, usually no more than a paragraph, already contained all the salient facts. Sickles shot Key, his friend of several years, because he had just learned that Key had carried on a yearlong affair with his wife, Teresa Bagioli Sickles. Subsequent stories contained much additional detail, but these were the essential facts. The *Harper's* cover cleverly took advantage of its readers' knowledge

The Honorable Daniel E. Sickles in prison at Washington. (Courtesy of Library of Congress)

of the affair by setting the protagonists in the form of a triangle bisected by the fatal shot.

The press covered the story in breathless detail. The stories told how Sickles had received an anonymous letter on Thursday, February 24, informing him of his wife's relationship with Key. He had heard stories of a similar sort before but, assured by his wife and his friend that they were untrue, had dismissed them as malicious gossip. This letter was different. It had the address where the guilty pair met, in addition to other damning details. On Friday, Sickles commissioned a friend to investigate. His report was conclusive. Neighbors informed him that a young woman whose general description fit that of Teresa Sickles had regularly met Key at this house. Key normally went in through the front door, his lover through the rear. They had, as the letter charged, used a ribbon or string as a signal, something a number of the neighbors commented upon. On Saturday evening, Sickles confronted his wife. At first she denied everything but ultimately admitted the affair. Sickles demanded a written confession. His wife, her hand betraying her emotions, complied. Two women in the house witnessed her signature. *Harper's* used a facsimile as its front page on March 12, 1859. It began:

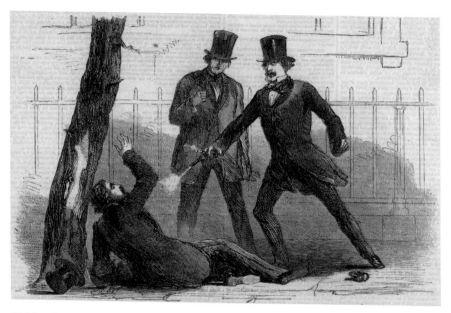

Sickles shoots Philip Barton Key over Key's affair with Sickles's wife, February 27, 1859, in Washington, DC. Samuel Butterworth looks on. (The Granger Collection, New York)

I have been in a house in Fifteenth Street, with Mr. Key. How many times I don't know. I believe the house belongs to a colored man. The house is unoccupied. Commenced going there the latter part of January. Have been in alone and with Mr. Key. Usually stayed an hour or more. There was a bed in the second story. I did what is usual for a wicked woman to do.

CAPITAL INTRIGUE: THE CONGRESSMAN AND THE U.S. ATTORNEY

On Sunday, February 27, in the middle of a conversation with his friend Butterworth, an agitated Sickles saw Key emerge from a clubhouse directly opposite his house. The congressman lived on Lafayette Square. At this point, accounts diverge. According to Butterworth's sworn statement at the trial, he left Sickles's house of his own volition, ran into Key without planning to, stopped merely to discuss the health of a mutual friend who happened to be a club member, and so witnessed the homicide as an innocent bystander. Early newspaper accounts had suggested Butterworth went out, at Sickles's behest, expressly for the purpose of detaining Key so that Sickles would have time to arm himself.

There were numerous other witnesses to the shooting. It was a mild day and the Square, situated directly across from the White House, was a favored area for walks. The testimony was of a piece. Two men, Butterworth and Key, were talking. A third man, Congressman Sickles, rushed toward them and shouted something on the order of (in Butterworth's words): "Key, you scoundrel, you have dishonored my house—you must die!" Sickles then drew a revolver and fired. He either missed or the gun misfired. Key rushed toward Sickles and attempted to wrestle him to the ground. Sickles pulled away, took out a second pistol, and raised it. Key backed away, drew something out of his pocket, and threw it at Sickles. Sickles advanced upon Key and fired again. Key staggered and fell, crying out (again in Butterworth's version), "Don't shoot me!" Sickles took out a third weapon, stood over Key and shouted, "You villain! You have dishonored my house, and you must die!" Then he fired a third time. There is some dispute over whether Sickles attempted a fourth shot. Butterworth said not. He swore that, after the third, he took Sickles by the arm and advised him to either walk up 16th Street to the attorney general's home and turn himself in or go to his own house and await the police. Some other witnesses claimed to have seen Sickles press yet another gun to Key's head. They did not hear it fire, however. All testified that they saw Sickles and Butterworth walk off together. After they had gone only a short space, Butterworth returned to where Key lay and picked up an object. It was a pair of opera glasses, the object that Key had thrown at Sickles. Butterworth then walked after his companion. He swore in court to retrieving the opera glasses and to giving them to Sickles rather than to the authorities. No one seemed to have thought this strange. What captured attention, first in the newspaper and magazine reports and then in court, was the irony of Key throwing his opera glasses at Sickles. Teresa Sickles had been in the practice of signaling to him when she would be free to join him by waving a scarf from a second story window. To see it from his clubhouse window, Key used the glasses.

The March 5, 1859, *Harper's* published a map of the area so that readers could see where the Sickles house and the clubhouse were in relation to each other—and to the White House. *Leslie's* did so as well on the same day. *Harper's* also provided detailed drawings of both the house and clubhouse. *Leslie's* offered its readers a similarly detailed illustration of the house Mrs. Sickles and Key had used for their assignations.

Once at the attorney general's, Sickles admitted to shooting Key. A constable arrived to arrest him. Sickles asked if he could return to his own house before going off to jail. The constable agreed. As with Butterworth giving the opera glasses to Sickles, no one appears to have thought this odd. The constable did obtain a promise from the congressman, before he allowed him to go up the stairs to where his wife was, that he would not harm her. The March 5 *Leslie's* offered its readers a wonderfully melodramatic version of the private conversation Sickles had with his wife, which included Sickles saying, "I've killed him!" What Sickles actually said is unknown. When he came downstairs again, however, he had his wife's wedding ring and a pair of diamond earrings he had given her as a wedding present. He also had, it turned out, a loaded revolver. The constable did not search the congressman; his possessions were not confiscated at the jail. This was not the only unusual feature of Sickle's confinement while awaiting trial.

He was able to receive visitors, and so many came that he was granted the use of the head jailer's apartment to receive them. The jailor's quarters, as portrayed in *Leslie's* of March 12, 1859, was scarcely sumptuous but was far more roomy and comfortable than Sickles's cell. The visitors came in a constant stream, each identified by the press. They included members of House and the Senate, members of Washington society, but not, the papers noted, President James Buchanan. The president did, however, send Sickles a personal note. Most painful for Sickles, according to the *Harper's* March 12 edition, were the visits of his wife's mother and her clergyman. Both told him that Teresa was distracted with grief, shame, and sorrow. The loss of her wedding ring, both told him, was more than she could bear. "Think of your daughter," they urged him. What would happen to her if her mother should suffer some sort of break down? Sickles relented. He returned the ring. But nothing could repair her marriage vows, the press quoted him as saying (*Harper's*, 1859, March 12, p. 168).

On March 12, 1859, both *Harper's* and *Leslie's* ran images of Sickles in prison. That of *Harper's* was the more bathetic. It showed a haggard sufferer, hands clasped as if in prayer, staring upward. Light illumined his face and the wall immediately behind, but the rest of the cell was in shadows. Its title was "Hon. Daniel E. Sickles in prison at Washington," but it might well have been captioned "More sinned against than sinning." In a later issue the magazine would editorialize against what it described as a publicity campaign to create sympathy for the Congressman. As the drawing shows, it did much to elicit that sympathy itself. *Leslie's* added a plaintive touch, Sickles's dog, who accompanied his master to jail.

Harper's itself editorialized on March 12, 1859, that Sickles did not need anyone's sympathies as far as his upcoming trial was concerned. If, as appeared certain, there had been a "guilty intrigue" between Key and his wife, "the public of the United States will justify him in killing the man who had dishonored his bed." As soon as Sickles learned of the affair, "he held the life" of his wife's seducer "in his hand." Of all the ways in which husbands might seek redress, the magazine continued, murder was best. It was the American way. The cuckold in France might challenge his wife's lover to a duel; in England the outraged husband might sue. Here he committed homicide and, terrible as that might be, it was "the most effectual, the wisest, and the most natural revenge." And, since this was the American way, and was becoming customary in much of Europe as well, there was not a jury in the country that would find Sickles guilty even of manslaughter, much less of murder.

Harper's view that no jury would convict Sickles was universally shared. Even the *New York Herald*, whose redoubtable editor James Gordon Bennett had been sued for libel two years earlier by the Congressman, offered the prediction that the jury would find him innocent. The trial might mean the end of Sickles's public career, Bennett's editorial continued, but only in New York. He could go west. He was a man of genuine ability. Perhaps in a decade or two a new constituency would return him to Congress. The *New York Times*, the city's other major Democratic daily, editorialized that the homicide in no way unfitted the congressman for office. Needless to say, it also expressed confidence he would be found innocent. Even those, such as editor and staunch Republican Horace Greeley of the *New York Daily-Tribune*, who disputed vehemently the notion that Sickles had a right to kill Key, agreed that he would not be convicted.

THE WAGES OF SIN: WHY THE CASE FASCINATED THE MEDIA AND PUBLIC

Given the universal expectation that Congressman Sickles would be acquitted, how can we explain the enormous interest the trial generated? Newspapers around the country printed extended excerpts of the testimony. The New York and Washington papers printed the entire transcript verbatim. Shortly after the trial was over, several books recounting the trial appeared, including one from Harper Brothers that included illustrations from their *Weekly* that covered the trial from gavel to gavel. *Leslie's* dropped its coverage right in the middle of the proceedings when the full details of Teresa Sickles's liaisons with Key were discussed in open court. The weekly editorialized that this was unfit for a family publication. The rest of the press, however, continued to print everything, right up to and beyond the jury's verdict. Why, in view of the foregone conclusion that Sickles would not be convicted, did the American public hang upon every word uttered in the courtroom? Why did *Harper's* and *Leslie's* publish illustrations, not just of Sickles and Key—*Leslie's* published a sketch of the inquest on March 5, 1859, showing

Key's body propped up against a chair—but of everyone and everything connected, however peripherally, with the case?

Surely the prominence of the murderer and his victim had something to do with this national fascination. Sickles was not just any congressman. He had served as President Buchanan's personal secretary when Buchanan was ambassador to Great Britain. He had then returned to the United States in 1856 to help secure the presidential nomination for Buchanan. When he went to Washington in 1857, he was not just a first-term congressman. He was the protégé of the president, a fact symbolized by his residence just across Pennsylvania Avenue from the White House. Similarly, Philip Barton Key was not just another U.S. attorney. His father, Francis Scott Key, is now best known as the author of "The Star-Spangled Banner." In 1857, he was also remembered as one of the pillars of the Washington bar. Philip's uncle was Roger B. Taney, chief justice of the U.S. Supreme Court.

Another source of fascination was Teresa Bagioli Sickles. She was very young, only in her early twenties. Although born and raised in New York City, she was usually described in the press as though she were a foreigner. Her parents were Italian. She had lived, prior to her marriage, in the household of Signor Lorenzo Da Ponti, the noted music teacher who had worked as Mozart's librettist on such masterpieces as "The Marriage of Figaro." Raised in this musical, Italian, Catholic household, she was as much an exotic to the readers of *Harper's* and *Leslie's* as if she were a Gypsy princess.

Da Ponti's son had befriended the teenaged Dan Sickles and had gotten him a scholarship to New York University, where he was a professor. Young Sickles moved into the Da Ponti home. He left after about a year when his mentor suddenly died, but he maintained close ties with the family. He had known Teresa since her infancy. After he left college, Sickles apprenticed himself to a lawyer and was admitted to the bar. He quickly made a reputation as a brilliant attorney. He also established strong connections to the city's Democratic Party organization, Tammany Hall. In fact, he was so successful that his father abandoned his own career in real estate to study law with his son and became the junior partner in the firm of Sickles and Sickles.

Despite his prominence and his long connection to the family, the Bagiolis refused to consent to Sickles's proposal of marriage to Teresa. She was only sixteen; he was in his early thirties. The couple married in a civil ceremony without her parents' blessing. Her family then relented. The couple married again, this time with John Hughes, Catholic archbishop of New York City, presiding. Some months later their only child, a daughter, was born. Almost immediately thereafter came Buchanan's invitation to accompany him to London. At first Sickles turned the post down. He had just become collector of the port of New York, perhaps the most lucrative patronage job in the entire U.S. government. He eventually changed his mind, however, and went off to England with Buchanan in 1853. A few months later Teresa and their daughter joined him. She found herself immersed in a world of social engagements, balls, and receptions.

Teresa Sickles found Washington to involve as much social activity as London. The Sickles gave a formal dinner every Thursday. Teresa was "at home" to other society ladies every Tuesday morning. With her husband she attended most of the major social events. After all, Congressman Sickles had the ear of the president; Mrs. Sickles was beautiful and charming. Teresa Sickles, *Harper's* reported, quickly became a fixture in Washington society. She was especially celebrated as a hostess who was capable of charming the most sophisticated while simultaneously making the most socially inexperienced feel at home.

What made the Sickles case so compelling to antebellum Americans was that it was a real-life morality play. The tragedy was all the more satisfying to contemplate because it carried its meaning on its surface. The moral was, "the wages of sin is death." The sin was seduction of a married woman. This was, as *Harper's* editorialized on March 12, a threefold crime—against the woman the adulterer misled, against the husband he dishonored, and against the society he threatened to disorganize.

Further, all of the protagonists agreed upon the meaning of their actions. *Harper's Weekly* of March 12, 1859, quoted an unnamed friend of Key who remembered him saying he was for "French intrigue. A fig for common license! French intrigue and romance, with a good spice of danger in it!" (p. 170). "Common license" would have involved mere flirtation; the use of "French" to modify "intrigue" meant adultery. Like the British, Americans tended to think of Paris as the capital of sin. At the time, the friend claimed not to know of Key's affair with Mrs. Sickles, but the same story commented that Key and Mrs. Sickles had not been very discreet and that all of Washington was abuzz with gossip.

If Key knew the risk he ran—indeed, relished it—then Teresa Sickles knew equally well the gravity of her offense. In her confession, written the night before the homicide, she described how she would meet Key. She could not recall the exact number of their assignations; they were too many. But she recounted in detail how she would look for the signal, enter the rented house through the rear, go to the bedroom, undress—this was the material *Leslie's* thought unfit for its readership—and do "what wicked women did."

Sickles also understood his role. "Key," he shouted that Sunday morning, "you have dishonored my house and you must die." He did not shoot his wife or harm her physically in any way. He took away her wedding ring and went off to await trial. He had acted in the "American" fashion (*Harper's Weekly*, 1859, March 12).

Philip Barton Key made an excellent villain. While in his twenties he earned a reputation as a ladies' man. Then he married, apparently very happily, in 1843. He and his wife had four children. When she died, Key returned to the social world of Washington as an eligible bachelor. "His ancient prestige" as a gallant returned, according to *Harper's*. "No man in Washington was more popular with the ladies."

Naturally, *Harper's* continued, there was "talk" when Key "abandoned the company of the heiresses and belles of the capitol" to spend all of his time with Mrs. Sickles. He was, according to most press reports, a talented lawyer, but one who did not work very hard on his cases. Instead he devoted himself to horses, cards, and the ladies. Key was tall and handsome; there was a hint of melancholy in his manner, of sorrow over the death of his wife, which made him a romantic figure. So did his eccentric taste in clothes. He often wore riding boots to social events and carried a crop (*Harper's*, 1859, March 12, p. 170).

He first met Congressman Sickles in early 1857. Key's tenure as U.S. attorney for the District of Columbia was very much in doubt. President-elect Buchanan was determined to turn out most officeholders and replace them with his own people. Sickles took a liking to Key and, as a close associate of Buchanan's, succeeded in keeping his new friend in his post. This made the affair all the more reprehensible. As *Harper's* editorialized on March 12, Sickles was not blameless in killing Key, but it was Key who was guilty.

If Key was all one could ask in a villain, Teresa Sickles made a perfect fallen woman. First and foremost, she shared the popular perception of her actions. Her "confession" that she had done what "wicked women do" made that plain. So did the letters of remorse she sent to her husband in jail. He had given her no cause for complaint, she wrote. He had always been everything a husband should be. The sin, and that is how she viewed her romance with Key, was entirely hers. Her grief, her mother told the Congressman, was so overwhelming that she feared Teresa might take her own life. Teresa Sickles did not plead her youth, but others did, as in the poem, "Judge not," published in *Harper's* on March 12, 1859. She had been still a child herself when she plunged into "society" at the Court of St. James. Shouldn't her husband have shielded her from the snares that awaited one with so little experience of the world? The greatest danger, some moralizing commentators noted, was a premature sophistication. Ought a young bride have been exposed to the cynicism of courtiers? Sickles, however, had been ambitious. To further his diplomatic and then political career, he had expected his wife to preside over dinner parties and to make conversation with ambassadors and their wives. He had expected her to attend balls and to dazzle onlookers with her beauty and charm. She had done this for six years and was still only twenty-two; and, those who began to sympathize with her would add, there was the child.

Daniel Sickles initially played the role of outraged husband to the hilt. He had trusted his wife and his friend. He had dismissed the early stories of their affair as mere gossip. It was only when confronted with the details in the anonymous letter that he acted. Even then, he had investigated first. Only after the evidence was compelling did he confront his wife. From her he exacted the "confession," signed in the presence of witnesses—proof he had used no force to obtain it. At the first opportunity thereafter, he did what a true American male was supposed to do.

Sickles, however, was something more, and something less, than a man bent upon avenging an insult to his honor. Key was the product of a "good" family. Sickles was a parvenu. He maintained a large house in an exclusive section of the capital, entertained lavishly, and spent freely on every hand. Yet he had no fortune to draw upon. Surely he could not have paid his bills on his congressional salary or on his earnings as an attorney. Yet he never lacked for money. James Gordon Bennett had an explanation. He editorialized in the *New York Herald* in 1857 that Sickles used his political connections to influence the outcomes of cases. There had been rumors to this effect in New York for years. How else had a young lawyer with no family connections risen so rapidly? Sickles's close connections to the New York Democratic Party, already nicknamed Tammany Hall, did nothing to dispel the rumors. Neither did his unsuccessful libel suit against Bennett. Most troubling were the rumors about his marriage to Teresa. Had she been *enciente*, the term the press used for "pregnant"? In February 1859, just two weeks before the shooting, they had marked their sixth anniversary. Their daughter was, as *Harper's* carefully put it, between five and six. If Teresa had been pregnant, it would explain why her parents so quickly changed their minds about consenting to the marriage. No one aside from the Congressman, his wife, and the family knew for sure. But, if Sickles had himself once played the part of the seducer, and that was when Teresa was just sixteen—it was a troubling thought, especially since the morality play required that everyone stay in character. Would they? Or, under the pressure of the trial, would some additional scandal surface? This was the answer, perhaps, to *Harper's* question: Since the outcome is a foregone conclusion, why is there such interest in this trial?

SICKLES'S DEFENSE: PASSION AND HONOR

The defense strategy promised to generate a good deal of controversy and drama in court. Chief Counsel James T. Brady, like Sickles a product of

Tammany Hall, and his colleagues needed to provide the jury with a theory of the case on which they could base an acquittal. After all, Sickles had killed Key quite deliberately in broad daylight in front of numerous witnesses and only a stone's throw from the White House. He had taken the law into his own hands. That act was first-degree murder, however much public opinion might sanction what the congressman did. Brady's task was to enable the jury to follow public opinion without openly disregarding the law. The theory he offered the jury was temporary insanity. News of his wife's infidelity had left Sickles crazed by grief, sorrow, and horror. He was not responsible for his actions. If the temporary insanity defense succeeded, it would be the first time in an American trial.

Under French law, as innumerable commentators in the press pointed out, a husband could shoot the guilty parties and not even be charged. It would be a "crime of passion." Such a defense, however, had no standing in English or American jurisprudence. Even if it had, the prosecution would argue at trial, it would not apply to the Sickles case. In order to commit a "crime of passion," the husband must catch his wife and her lover in the act. Sickles had not. Nor did he rush out and shoot Key as soon as he read the anonymous letter or even as soon as its allegations were confirmed. Instead he confronted his wife, observed the legal nicety of having her write out a "confession" that two witnesses attested she had done of her own free will, and engaged in a heart-to-heart conversation with his friend Samuel F. Butterworth the next morning. According to Butterworth's testimony, Samuel urged Sickles not to take any action, on the grounds that doing so would just spread the scandal. Sickles replied that it was already the talk of the town. In that case, Butterworth swore he told Sickles, "There is but one course open to you, as a man of honor" (*Harper's*, 1859, March 12, p. 169).

None of this, District Attorney Robert Ould would point out to the jury, was the behavior of a man driven to distraction and unable to control his actions. "The prisoner," he intoned in his opening address,

[H]ad come to that carnival of blood fully prepared. He was a walking magazine [of arms]. He was not only fully provided in the number of his firearms, but had also taken care to supply himself with their different varieties, each one of which, doubtless, possessed its peculiar excellence for the murderous work. To a nice and close calculator the contingency of an anticipated collision might call into requisition both Derringer and revolver. If before the time of the meeting any such idea passed through the mind of the prisoner at the bar, as would seem to be indicated not only from the number and variety of his firearms, but from the temporary armory with which he was provided, to wit, a convenient overcoat on an inconveniently warm day, it would seem that he did not reason carelessly.

Central to the defense's case was the testimony of Robert J. Walker, a former secretary of the treasury during the Polk Administration and briefly governor of the Kansas Territory in 1857 during the height of bloody strife there. Walker had not seen Sickles for a number of months when he called upon him at his home on Sunday, February 27, the day of the murder. It was around 3 p.m., Walker testified, saying,

As he came in his manner appeared excited. There was something strange and unusual about it. His voice was somewhat different from the manner in which I had usually heard him speak. He advanced and took me by the hand. I think he then said, "A thousand thanks for coming to see me under these circumstances." He had scarcely repeated these words, when I saw a great change in his appearance. He became very much convulsed indeed. He threw himself on the sofa, covering his face with his hands. He then broke into an agony of unnatural and unearthly sounds, the most remarkable I have ever heard—something like a scream, interrupted by violent sobbing. From his convulsed appearance he was in the act of writhing. His condition appeared to me very frightful, appalling me so much that I thought if it lasted much longer he must become insane. He was indulging in exclamations about dishonor having been brought on his house, his wife and child. He seemed particularly to dwell on the disgrace brought upon his child. Should think this continued ten minutes. Endeavored to pacify him. I turned from him to go for a physician myself, but he seemed to stop a little these violent exclamations, and finally they broke down. The spasms became more violent till they ceased. I think I must have been there something over half an hour. I accompanied him from there to the jail.

Then came an interruption. *Harper's* readers learned from its April 16 edition:

Mr. Sickles, during the statement of the witness was violently affected—breaking out into sobs and profusely shedding tears. E. B. Hart and Isaac Bell, one on each side, and Mr. Sickles, senior, together with others, accompanied him from the court room. The witness particularly, and many of the spectators, were moved to tears. The scene was one of deep interest. In some few minutes Mr. Sickles was brought back into court, his countenance still indicating extreme mental suffering, and the desolateness of his whole appearance awakening strong sympathy in the breasts of all who saw him. His father was much affected by his condition.

Walker's testimony and Sickles's reaction to it were the case for the defense. There were numerous other witnesses. Some testified to Teresa Sickles's frequent meetings with Key, necessary after Judge Thomas H. Crawford ruled that her "confession" was inadmissible because it would require her to testify against herself; that is, her admission of her affair could be used against her in a divorce proceeding. Other witnesses described the congressman's highly emotional state on the Friday and Saturday before the murder. But it was Walker, a distinguished public figure, an acquaintance but not an intimate personal friend of Sickles, who described his state of mind immediately after the shooting. Sickles's reaction in court provided a sort of corroboration, as lead defense attorney James Brady realized. Near the close of his summation to the jury he proclaimed:

Nature, Heaven, God Himself, in his heart-broken image, here became, here in this very court became, the witness of the torture by which, on that terrible day, the 27th of February, the prisoner was inflamed. You beheld the scene of the 12th of April. It was the same as that to which Robert J. Walker testified. Recall this scene. Think of how the proceedings of this court were suddenly arrested by the sobs of the prisoner, when the beautiful image of his poor child was revived by the words of Robert J. Walker, how he was bowed to earth, and how he writhed as though an arrow were buried in his heart; how, supported by his friends, he was led from this Court, his vision quenched in scalding tears, his limbs paralyzed, his forehead throbbing as though it had been bludgeoned by some ruffian, and his whole frame convulsed. Recall this scene. Think of this—think of the tears you shed yourselves as this stricken victim was borne by—think, think of it—and then may we well say to the jury, if your love of home will suffer it—if your genuine sense of justice will consent to it—if your pride of manhood will stoop to it—if your instinctive per-ception of right and wrong will sanction it, stamp "murder" upon the bursting forehead that has been transpierced with the thorns of an affliction which transcends all other visitations, and for the scandal, the dishonor, the profanation, and, in the end, the devastation which provoked this terrible outburst, this tempest of grief, this agony of despair. . . . Do this, do it if you can, and then, having consigned the prisoner to the scaffold, return to your homes, and there, within those endangered sanctuaries, following your ignoble verdict, set to and teach your imperiled wives a lesson in the vulgar arithmetic of a compromising morality, and let them be inspired with a sense of womanly dignity by a knowledge of the value you attach to the sanctity of the household, to the inviolability of the wife, to the security of the hospitable roof, and last of all, but above all, to the inherited traditions of an innocent but ruined offspring.

The jurors themselves had sobbed with Sickles. Could they doubt the depth of his suffering after sharing in it? It was not only God Himself who was a witness. Brady had made the members of the jury witnesses for the defense. What was the prosecution to do? The law and the evidence were on its side. But that counted for nothing if the jury identified with the defendant. There was one way, perhaps, to break that identification. If Sickles were a hardened profligate, if the congressman were so sunk in debauchery that the very idea of his being driven to distraction by his wife's infidelity became laughable, then the jury might decide their duty was to find the defendant guilty of murder. As assistant District Attorney Carlisle described the case,

There is [a] class—safe, quite safe from insanity, from such a blow as that—the confirmed adulterer, the open, shameless profligate—the man nurtured in brothels, the man breathing all his life the atmosphere of adultery and seduction; if there be such a man, he is certainly safe from the visitation of insanity because his familiar plaything has turned and wounded him.

If the court admitted Teresa Sickles's "confession," it "necessarily opens inquiry of the sort I have indicated," Carlisle continued. The judge did not admit the confession. Nonetheless the defense, in arguing for its admission, managed to convey its contents to the jury. Judge Crawford did admit testimony concerning Mrs. Sickles's trysts with Key. Sickles, he ruled, had shouted out that Key had "dishonored his bed." Therefore, testimony that went to show what he meant was relevant. By the time the defense had finished, the prosecution offered to admit the confession itself.

The prosecution did not introduce evidence about Congressman Sickles's fidelity, or lack thereof, to his wife. This was what *Harper's* later, in a story on May 14, called "the excluded evidence." According to this story, which originally appeared in the *New York Daily-Tribune*, the prosecution was concerned lest it lead to "retaliatory vengeance on the part of Mr. Key's friends." This seems unlikely since, were Sickles convicted, Key's friends would have no motive to seek revenge. More plausible is the second reason given, that the judge deemed it inadmissible. The materials prepared by the prosecution, as quoted by the *Tribune*, make it plain that they were intended to rebut the "confession." When Judge Crawford ruled that out, the prosecution's argument became moot. Could the prosecution have done more? The May 7, 1859, *Harper's* claimed that District Attorney Ould could and should have resorted to the same "trickery" used by the defense. He had allowed the discussion of the "excluded evidence" to take place in the privacy of the judge's chambers. Brady and his associates, on the other side, had argued each point of Teresa Sickles's confession in the presence of the jury. They had thereby made sure that the jury knew much of the case that was, in the law, inadmissible.

Even *Harper's* conceded, however, that the verdict would have been the same no matter what the prosecution did. The jury took just over an hour to consider the case that had taken twenty days to try:

Clerk—Daniel E. Sickles, stand up and look to the Jury.
Mr. Sickles stood up.
Clerk—How say you, gentlemen, have you agreed to your verdict?
Mr. [Reason] Arnold—We have.

Clerk—How say you, do you find the prisoner at the bar guilty or not guilty?
Mr. Arnold—NOT GUILTY.

At the words "not guilty," pandemonium broke out in the court. The audience cheered, defense attorneys embraced, and bystanders dashed off to spread the word. A crowd gathered outside to hail Sickles as he descended the steps, and people vied with each other to unhitch the horses of his carriage so that they might pull it themselves. His attorneys persuaded the congressman's supporters to allow him to ride to his hotel in peace, but the crowd insisted on accompanying him and then serenading him and his legal team. Ten of the jurors joined in the celebration. The verdict had taken them so long to reach, one explained, because one member of the panel requested time to pray before voting not guilty. Reason Arnold, the foreman, proclaimed his gratitude that he had lived long enough to serve on the jury that acquitted Sickles. Still a third juror, described by *Harper's* (April 23) issue as a "wag," commented that, had he been in Sickles's shoes, he would have used a howitzer rather than a pistol! Even after the congressman's lawyers requested the crowd to disperse so that Sickles could get some rest, the serenade continued.

AFTERMATH: FROM CELEBRITY TO CONDEMNATION

Dan Sickles was not just a free man; he was the man of the hour. Then, suddenly, those who loyally stood by him during his trial turned against him. The damning item that caused this change appeared in *Harper's* on July 23, 1859. It was a reprint of a story from the *New York Herald*. The story stated that Congressman Daniel E. Sickles intended to reconcile with his wife. He had abandoned the idea of suing for divorce. Instead he and his wife had agreed to bury "the past in the grave of oblivion." More startling still, "it is said their love is greater than ever." Mr. Sickles's "political and personal friends . . . are much disappointed at this event." They had loyally stood by him after he murdered Philip Barton Key. They would not stand by if he determined to "live together again" with his wife "in peace and mutual affection."

Sickles understood their feelings, but was determined. On July 19, he wrote to the *Herald* a full explanation of his decision, which *Harper's* reprinted in its July 30 issue:

If I ever failed to comprehend the utterly desolate position of an offending though penitent woman—the hopeless future, with its dark possibilities of danger, to which she is doomed when proscribed as an outcast—I can now see plainly enough in the almost universal howl of denunciations with which she is followed to my threshold, the misery and perils from which I have rescued the mother of my child.

He admitted that "it is very sad for me to incur the blame of friends and the reproaches of many wise and good people." Further, there were "many who think" the reconciliation "is to be fatal to my professional, political, and social standing. If this be so, so be it." Why would the friends who stood by him when he committed murder abandon him when he committed forgiveness? The injury Key had inflicted upon him and his family was supposed to be irreparable. That was why he had the right to murder Key. Shooting Key vindicated not just his honor, but also the sanctity of the home, the purity of domestic relations, and, most importantly, the husband's claim on his wife's affections. Forgiving his wife, reestablishing domestic relations, and proclaiming that their love was now stronger than ever reduced the magnitude of Key's offense, on the one hand; and on the other, undercut the moral—as well as the morality—of the national drama in which he had played the central role.

In ordinary times, reconciling with his wife would have ended Sickles's public life. It did put an end to his career in the Congress although he did, while serving out his term in the winter of 1860, take an important part in the debates over secession by helping to gain Democratic support for strong measures against the South. In February 1861, he promised on the floor of the House of Representatives to raise a regiment himself. In the event, he raised a full brigade. Brigadier General, and later Major General Sickles, fought in a number of battles including Gettysburg, where he lost a leg and, according to General Meade, almost lost the entire engagement by ignoring orders on the second day.

Sickles and Meade staged their own personal war over Sickles's conduct at Gettysburg. After Appomattox, a physically and politically rehabilitated Sickles took up the military command of the occupied Carolinas. His insistence upon defending the interests of former slaves irritated President Andrew Johnson, who removed him from that office; but Ulysses S. Grant, the next president, appointed the newly widowed Sickles general ambassador to Spain in 1869. In Madrid, Sickles attempted to reinvigorate the scheme of his mentor James Buchanan to pry Cuba free from Spain. Failing in that, he allegedly became the lover of the Spanish queen. He also remarried, converted to Roman Catholicism, and fathered two more children.

Nor was this the end. He helped arrange the disputed election of 1876 for Rutherford B. Hayes, served on the first Civil Service Commission, and was a stalwart Republican for decades. In 1908, he wrote a pamphlet supporting William Taft for president. In 1913, he returned for the fiftieth anniversary of Gettysburg, an honored guest not only because he fought and was wounded there, but also because he played a leading role in having the battlefield preserved as a national shrine. He was then past ninety years old. He gave no public hint that he ever regretted killing Philip Barton Key.

REFERENCES

Frank Leslie's Illustrated Newspaper. (1859, March 5).

Harper's Weekly. (1859, March 12, April 16, April 23, May 7, May 14, July 23, July 30).

Keneally, T. (2002) *American scoundrel: The life of the notorious Civil War general Daniel Sickles.* New York: Random House.

The trial of Hon. Daniel E. Sickles. (1859). New York: Harper Brothers.

15

The Ordeal of Harpers Ferry and the Trial of John Brown: Madman or Martyr?

Russell L. Hanson

In a campaign speech on October 25, 1858, William H. Seward called the boiling controversy over slavery "an irrepressible conflict between opposing and enduring forces, and it means that the United States must and will, sooner or later, become either entirely a slaveholding nation, or entirely a free-labor nation." Largely because of John Brown, the irrepressible conflict erupted sooner rather than later. A year after Seward's remarks in Rochester, Brown and twenty-one men brought guerrilla war from the plains of Kansas to the mountains of Virginia. They raided the federal arsenal in Harpers Ferry with the intention of distributing captured weapons to allies who would join them in liberating slaves throughout the South.

The raid was a bloody failure and ended in death for civilians and soldiers alike. Only five raiders escaped with their lives. Ten of their comrades were killed, including two of Brown's sons. John Brown and six others were captured by federal marines under the command of Robert E. Lee. They were summarily tried, convicted, and executed in Charles Town. Virginia's legal proceedings against these men accomplished what the raid did not, however. Northerners questioned the fairness of the trials, and when the "freedom fighters" were hung, there was a burst of sympathy for abolition. That triggered an equally strong reaction in the South, where support for secession

The Tragic Prelude, a mural of John Brown, by John Steuart Curry. (Kansas State Historical Society)

surged. Public opinion was polarized on sectional lines, and the battle was joined on April 12, 1861.

Brown's role in hastening the war was highlighted in an 1881 address by the African American abolitionist Frederick Douglass at Storer College:

If John Brown did not end the war that ended slavery, he did at least begin the war that ended slavery . . . and made this a free Republic. Until this blow was struck, the prospect for freedom was dim, shadowy, and uncertain. The irrepressible conflict was one of words, votes, and compromises. When John Brown stretched forth his arm, the sky was cleared. The time for compromises was gone—the armed hosts of freedom stood face to face over the chasm of a broken Union—and the clash of arms was at hand. (Douglass, 1881b)

Northern abolitionists revered Brown's unyielding commitment to emancipation, although they did not endorse his methods of liberation. William Lloyd Garrison, founder of the American Anti-Slavery Society, wrote, "He periled all that was dear to him, not to achieve liberty for himself, but to break the fetters of a race 'not colored like his own,' most wickedly abhorred, universally proscribed, and subjected to a bondage full of unutterable woe and horror." The author of *Walden* and "Civil Disobedience," Henry David Thoreau, declared, "No man in America has ever stood up so persistently and effectively for the dignity of human nature, knowing himself for a man, and the equal of any and all governments. In that sense he was the most American of us all."[1]

To Southerners, these eulogies were grotesque. For them, Brown was a liar and a thief, a vicious murderer, and an enemy of the republic. George Fitzhugh, a leading defender of slavery, called him a "blood-thirsty beast," and an

Alabaman writing under the name "A. Clarkson" referred to Brown as a "butcher" and "fanatic." Clarkson actually traced the fanaticism to Brown's Calvinism, claiming that "Misanthropy, hypocrisy, diseased philanthropy, envy, hatred, fanaticism, and all the worst passions of the human heart, were the ruling characteristics of the English puritans; and they continue to be the ruling characteristics of New-England Yankees" who were their descendants.[2]

Out of these conflicting judgments grew the legend of John Brown, the great enigma of the Civil War (Peterson, 2002, p. 73). Abolitionists saw him as a saint and seer, but slaveholders thought him mad and evil. Once the immorality of slavery was universally recognized, though, the case of John Brown presented a more complex question: is violence a legitimate response to unjust laws or not? This is of course a perennial issue in American politics, and has been since Lexington and Concord; hence Thoreau's contention that John Brown "is the most American of us all." Whether we accept that comparison will surely color our own assessment of "Old Brown of Osawatomie."

THE RAID ON HARPERS FERRY

According to Franklin Sanborn, a friend and admirer of John Brown, "The story of John Brown will mean little to those who do not believe that God governs the world, and that He makes His will known in advance to certain chosen men and women who perform it, consciously or unconsciously. Of such prophetic, Heaven-appointed men John Brown was the most conspicuous of our time, and his life must be construed in light of that fact" (1885, p. 247).

Brown's religious convictions came naturally. He was born in Torrington, Connecticut on May 9, 1800, to parents who were strict Calvinists and staunch abolitionists. They raised their son in the northeastern corner of Ohio to "build up and be a help in the support of religion and civil Order" (Villard, 1910/1966, p. 13). The area became a hotbed of abolitionism, and the evils of slavery were impressed on John throughout his childhood and adolescence. By the time he reached maturity, Brown was implacably opposed to slavery, though he was not an active abolitionist. As a young man he was preoccupied with earning a living, establishing a family, and securing an honorable place in the community.[3]

Brown married in 1820 and had three sons by 1824. To support his burgeoning family, Brown moved to northwestern Pennsylvania in 1825. There he built a large tannery—and also a large barn with a secret chamber for hiding fugitive slaves. His business collapsed in 1835, and the Brown family returned to Ohio. Around this time he began to entertain schemes for the liberation of slaves, enlisting his wife and oldest sons in the cause. No one acted then, as Brown was embroiled in a series of business failures that led to bankruptcy and brief imprisonment in 1842.

Two years later Brown became a sheep farmer, and then a wool broker, in partnership with Simon Perkins, the son of Akron's founder. The wool business required him to move to Springfield, Massachusetts, in 1846, where Brown met many leading opponents of slavery. One was Gerrit Smith, a wealthy abolitionist who set aside 120,000 acres of land in upstate New York for use by freedmen and their families. When the wool business also collapsed, Brown settled his family among black farmers in North Elba, New York. According to Frederick Douglass, it was then that Brown revealed his intention of recruiting free men and ex-slaves to wage guerilla war on slavery from mountain strongholds in the South. The development of a concrete plan of action may have been triggered by Southern efforts to expand slavery into the western territories.[4]

Brown became increasingly active in the abolitionist movement as controversy flared over the recovery of fugitive slaves. In January 1851, he organized the first (and only) branch of The U.S. League of Gileadites for freemen near Springfield.[5] He advised the Gileadites to arm themselves and make "clean work" in disposing of anyone seeking to apprehend fugitive slaves in the North, and further noted that a lasso applied to a single slave catcher might deter others from following. Brown clearly felt God's calling to resist the evil Slave Power, by force if necessary.

His sons shared this view of faith in action. Five of them emigrated to "Bleeding Kansas," where abolitionists supported the admission of a free state to the Union. They faced an uphill battle against proslavery settlers and the Border Ruffians from Missouri, who sought admission of Kansas as a slave state. When John Brown Jr. wrote asking for arms to repel attacks by lawless ruffians, his father obliged in person, bringing a wagonload of guns to Brown's Station, near Osawatomie in October 1855.

On May 21, 1856, Border Ruffians from Missouri sacked and burned Lawrence, the center of abolitionism in Kansas. Frustrated by the timidity of fellow abolitionists in the face of this violent attack, Brown led a small group of armed men on a retaliatory mission. On May 24, they captured and butchered five proslavery sympathizers on Pottawatomie Creek. On June 2, in a pitched battle at Black Jack on the Sante Fe Trail, Brown's men and their allies defeated a large posse that was pursuing them. The Border Ruffians later retaliated by massacring five free-state men at Marais des Cygnes, Kansas.

A wanted man with a price on his head, Brown left Kansas. He returned to Massachusetts, raised money, and gathered weapons, which he then transported to Kansas in 1857. He repeated the journey in the following year, with a side trip to a meeting of abolitionists in Chatham, Canada. His preparations complete, Brown led a December 1858 raiding party into Missouri, where they attacked three homesteads, killing one man, confiscating property, and liberating twelve slaves. A posse chasing the group was scattered in a showdown, and Brown's group moved slowly northward with the help of abolitionists on the Underground Railroad. They finally reached Detroit in early March 1859, when Brown put the newly freed slaves on a ferry to Windsor, Canada and freedom. The operation drew national attention; abolitionists disavowed Brown's methods, but praised his results, while proslavery forces branded him a murderer and thief. The legend of John Brown grew.

Brown's foray into Missouri was intimately related to his plans for a "Subterranean Pass Way," his name for a Southern extension of the Underground Railroad. The Way passed through the mountains and included "stations" defended by armed men who were prepared to rescue slaves from their masters by force. In 1857, he began to assemble and train a paramilitary force that came to be known as the Provisional Army of the United States. The Secret Six, a group of prosperous New England abolitionists, financed the military preparations, which were interrupted by a disagreement between Brown and his chief military advisor, who left the army and threatened to expose the plot.[6] To divert suspicion, the Secret Six persuaded Brown to furlough the army and return to Kansas, whence he launched the raid into Missouri.

The raid's success emboldened Brown, who planned an attack on Harpers Ferry, a federal arsenal constructed on a high ridge overlooking the confluence of the Potomac and Shenandoah rivers. The idea of invading Virginia and arming slaves with captured weapons frightened some of Brown's backers, who tried to dissuade him from carrying out the plan. The old Calvinist would not be deterred, however. He rented the Kennedy farm in Maryland, four and a half miles from Harpers Ferry. Pretending to be a prospector, Brown scouted the area and stockpiled arms, munitions, and supplies diverted from Kansas.

In a last ditch effort to halt the raid, Frederick Douglass traveled to a quarry near Chambersburg, Pennsylvania. He told Brown the plan was certain to fail and that an attack on the federal government "would array the whole country against us" (Douglass, 1881a, p. 350). Brown, though, was determined to attack slavery in its cradle, hoping to provoke a confrontation, as he had in Kansas. Toward the end of the second week of October 1859, Brown moved a thousand pikes and hundreds of carbines and pistols to a small schoolhouse near Harpers Ferry for distribution to runaway slaves who might join the raid.

Around 11 p.m. on Sunday, October 16, John Brown led sixteen white men, including three of his sons, plus five free black men across the Potomac River and into Harpers Ferry. They took control of the Baltimore & Ohio

Railroad bridge, occupied the U.S. armory and arsenal, and seized the nearby Hall's Rifle Works. Brown then dispatched six men into the countryside to take hostages and free slaves; meanwhile he confined forty leading citizens in the fire-engine house of the armory. In the confusion of night, a baggage-master at the B & O Railroad station—a free black man—was killed by the raiders.

Panic ensued as reports began to circulate that an invasion was underway and that slaves were rising against their masters.[7] Not knowing the size of the raiding party, townspeople were slow to react, except for one man who was killed resisting. For twelve hours, Brown and his men controlled the village, during which time the raiders could have withdrawn and made their escape to Pennsylvania. Brown stayed put, waiting in vain for slaves to join his party, and expecting to trade hostages for safe passage out of Harpers Ferry. Or perhaps he believed the outcome was in God's hands and was therefore willing to risk martyrdom in the cause of freedom.

By noon on Monday, the residents of Harpers Ferry were regrouping. Militias from neighboring towns arrived, and the combined forces began to close the trap on Brown's "army." One of Brown's men, a free black named Dangerfield Newby, was killed when the railroad bridge was recaptured. Another was captured and later executed when he sought to retrieve Newby's body under a flag of truce. (Watson Brown was also fatally wounded under a flag of truce later that afternoon.) Three other members of the Provisional Army were killed trying to escape across the rivers, and one was captured.

Shots from the enginehouse killed two civilians and wounded eight others. One of the dead was the unarmed mayor of Harpers Ferry, who was shot by Edwin Coppoc. The militia returned fire, and Oliver Brown was mortally wounded along with another raider. When night fell on October 17, Brown and four others kept watch over nine key hostages while tending their wounded comrades and mourning the dead.

The enginehouse was surrounded by a detachment of U.S. Marines under the command of Lieutenant-Colonel Robert E. Lee, who arrived by train from Washington late that evening. Brown's rear guard at the schoolhouse realized that the situation was hopeless and fled during the night. Four of these five men, including Owen Brown, made their way to safety. So did another man, Osborn Anderson, from the rifle works.[8]

Early in the morning of October 18, Lieutenant J. E. B. Stuart, who knew Brown from Kansas, met the captain under a flag of truce. He conveyed Lee's demand for surrender, which Brown, still hoping to trade hostages in exchange for freedom, rejected. Lee then ordered the marines to storm the enginehouse, and in a brief but bloody exchange the marines regained control of the armory and freed the hostages. One marine was killed, two more raiders died, and Brown was wounded by saber blows to his head and thrusts to his abdomen.

Governor Henry Wise arrived on the scene early in the afternoon of October 18, too late to declare martial law and execute Brown on the spot. He and several other politicians interrogated Brown, who defended his actions in terms that impressed many Northerners who read newspaper accounts of the interview. After extensive questioning, Brown and his men were placed in the joint custody of a U.S. marshal and county sheriff and conveyed to the jail in Charlestown. The ordeal of Harpers Ferry was over, and the trial of John Brown was to commence.

THE TRIAL OF JOHN BROWN

John Brown was guilty of capital crimes, as he himself admitted to Governor Wise. Whether he was fairly convicted of the specific charges levied against him by the State of Virginia was disputed, however. Northern sympathizers likened the proceedings to a legal lynching, while Southerners cited Brown's own statement that he was "entirely satisfied with the treatment I received on my trial. Considering all the circumstances, it has been more generous than I expected." On the other hand, Brown also complained of unfairness during the trial and subsequently described his impending execution as a "public murder," so we must review the legal issues ourselves, beginning with the question of jurisdiction.[9]

To seize the arsenal, Brown crossed the Potomac River from Maryland. As Virginian George F. Caskie declared in 1909, "When John Brown reached Harper's Ferry, his first act was to take possession of United States' property and overpower U. S. guards found there. When finally captured, it was by U. S. troops on U. S. property after a fight in which one of the U. S. Marines was killed. Were these occurrences to take place today, it will hardly be doubted that the jurisdiction of the whole matter would be taken by U. S. Courts" (Caskie, 1909, as quoted in Draper, 1940).

Federal jurisdiction was precisely the issue in 1859, however, and Governor Wise sought jurisdiction for Virginia. As Draper (1940) explains, the *Baltimore Sun* reported on October 22, 1859, "It appears that the prisoners are amenable to the United States and State authorities—to the former for murder, to the latter for treason." The paper added that the federal court would be in session the following Monday, and elsewhere noted that the federal district attorney for the Western District of Virginia was in conference with President Buchanan. The paper concluded, "The sending of the prisoners to Charles Town is believed to be a concession to the views of Governor Wise who claims to try them by the laws of Virginia."

In the aftermath of the *Dred Scott* decision, Buchanan surely understood that a federal court could not satisfy public opinion in Brown's case. A conviction would further inflame abolitionists against the federal government, while an acquittal would enrage the South and might be difficult to enforce. Buchanan bowed to expediency and allowed Virginia to proceed on all fronts without challenge (Strother, 1868).[10]

Virginia's success in claiming jurisdiction had two important practical effects. First, it meant that Brown was tried in the Circuit Court of Jefferson County, located in Charles Town, eight and a half miles from the scene of his alleged crimes. A local jury decided his fate, even though "There were no men in Jefferson County who had not prejudged Brown, and if ever a motion for a change of venue to another county was in order, it was in this case" (Villard, 1910/1966, p. 489). The outcome would have been the same in any other court of Virginia, however; Brown's best chance of obtaining an impartial jury was in federal court (Moore, n.d.).

The venue affected the trial's pace, too. John Brown was captured on October 18, indicted on October 26, and sent to trial on Thursday, October 27. Testimony was heard that day and again on Friday and Saturday. Sunday was a day of rest, and after deliberating forty-five minutes, the jury convicted Brown on Monday, October 31. He was sentenced to death on November 2 and hanged on December 2, 1859. John Brown's body was "a-moulderin' in the grave" two months after he revealed details of his plan to Douglass.

The pace was dictated by a Virginia statute requiring a speedy trial "unless good cause be shown for a continuance." The prosecuting attorney Andrew Hunter saw no good cause for delaying the trial; to the contrary, Hunter felt swift justice was needed to reassure the badly shaken community.[11] The governor was inclined to move quickly, too, demonstrating Southern resolve and depriving Northern sympathizers of any chance to rescue Brown, as some threatened to do in letters to Wise.

The Northern press, which swiftly and uniformly condemned the raid itself, became increasingly critical of legal proceedings that were reported daily over the telegraphic wires by the Associated Press. In his first court appearance, Brown asked for a delay, saying his memory was impaired by head wounds. He further complained that it was difficult for him to follow the legal proceedings because of hearing damage caused by saber cuts. Sketches of the gray-haired man lying on a pallet, his head bandaged and body surrounded by heavily armed guards, appeared in the newspapers. The Lawrence, Kansas *Republican* opined that "Such a proceeding shames the name of justice, and only finds a congenial place amid the records of the bloody Inquisition" (Villard, 1910/1966, p. 480). Even the northern Democratic press objected to the authorities' unseemly haste.[12]

In addition to his physical health, Brown's mental competence was a concern, at least to his lawyers. On the first day of Brown's trial, one of his appointed attorneys suggested that Brown was incompetent to stand trial, and introduced a telegram from A. H. Lewis of Akron, Ohio, detailing a history of mental illness in the family of Dianthe Lusk, Brown's mother. The lawyer, Lawson Botts, further informed the court that Brown disdained the insanity defense, at which point the prisoner himself emphatically rejected "any attempt to interfere in my behalf on that score" (*Life, Trial and Execution*, 1859/1969, p. 65).[13]

Botts was appointed counsel to the defense by Judge Richard Parker, along with Thomas Green, a lawyer who was the mayor of Charles Town. Most accounts of the trial portrayed Judge Parker as a fair man, although he was criticized for not delaying the trial until Northern counsel appeared to represent Brown. Brown dismissed Botts and Green after George Hoyt arrived from Boston and was joined by Samuel Chilton of Washington and Hiram Griswold of Cleveland. This was very late in the trial, however, and Botts and Green had already raised the most important points in Brown's defense, though they were hampered by the unavailability of witnesses who could not travel to Charles Town in time to testify.

The jury in John Brown's trial weighed the facts, but also had to interpret several key points of law (that being the jury's prerogative in Virginia). For example, special prosecutor Andrew Hunter argued that Brown was guilty of treason against the Commonwealth of Virginia, insofar as he meant to establish a new form of government modeled on a constitution drawn up at the Chatham antislavery convention in 1858. A copy of the constitution was found among Brown's papers at the Kennedy farmhouse in Maryland and was the basis for Hunter's contention.

Botts and Green claimed that the constitution was not different from the charter of any other private organization and that Brown's actions, though illegal, did not rise to the level of treason. Griswold further argued that Brown, not being a resident of Virginia, could not be convicted of treason against the state. The challenge had merit, based on precedents in common law, but these were not definitive and may not have been known to the court at the time of Brown's trial (Draper, 1940). In any case, the Chatham constitution was meant to govern the Provisional Army during its activities on the Subterranean Pass Way. While that might not have been treason against Virginia, it was treason against the United States, as a federal court surely would have ruled.

Brown was also accused of conspiring to incite rebellion among slaves. White fear of "servile rebellion" was strong in Virginia, especially in the wake of Nat Turner's 1831 uprising. Wise's local political ally, Andrew

Hunter, stoked those fears by levying the maximum charge against Brown (Lubet, 2001). The politically ambitious governor then neatly reassured whites by mobilizing the militia to secure order. At the same time, Wise and Hunter attributed Brown's failure to slave loyalty and devotion to their Southern masters. This message was directed primarily at Northerners, although the contradiction was too obvious to ignore; there was little reason to fear attempts to incite rebellion if slaves were truly loyal to their masters (Abels, 1971).

Attorneys Botts and Green were loyal Virginians, and they did not directly challenge the charge against Brown. They did formulate a reasonable defense against it, however. They argued that any action to incite rebellion could only have occurred in Maryland, on the way to Harpers Ferry, or in the federal arsenal itself. In neither case did Virginia have jurisdiction. Hunter disputed the point, brazenly insisting that Virginia retained jurisdiction for criminal acts committed on federal lands.

Additional charges were levied against Brown for the murder of three civilians and one marine. The indictment listed Brown as a principal in the first degree, not merely an accessory before the fact, to the crimes of assault and murder. During the trial, no witness accused Brown of participating in the actual murder of any of the victims; to the contrary, his lawyers elicited testimony about Brown's humanitarian treatment of the hostages. Hunter parried, suggesting that Brown was principally responsible for the deaths by virtue of having planned and led the raid.

Finally, after arriving on the scene, Chilton and Griswold challenged the indictment itself, saying the state could not levy multiple charges for a single set of actions. Virginia, they insisted, must prosecute a single charge, for it was impossible to defend Brown if the jury was allowed to reach a global verdict. Judge Parker denied the motion, in a ruling that was subsequently upheld by the Virginia Supreme Court of Appeals.

From a technical point of view, these are interesting issues, but in reality the outcome of John Brown's trial was foreordained, and everyone knew it. The jury convicted him on all counts, and Judge Parker set November 2 as the day of sentencing.

THE EXECUTION OF JOHN BROWN

When John Brown was returned to the Jefferson County courthouse for sentencing, Judge Parker asked the prisoner if he had anything to say as to why sentence should not be pronounced on him. Brown rose, and in a calm manner and clear voice delivered a speech that utterly transformed the situation. What had been the trial of John Brown became a trial of the peculiar institution Virginia shared with other southern states. This trial, too, ended in a guilty verdict in the court of Northern opinion, and the sentence was concurrent with Brown's.

Brown opened his remarks by saying, "I have all along admitted of a design on my part to free slaves. I intended certainly to have made a clean thing of that matter, as I did last winter, when I went into Missouri and there took slaves without the snapping of a gun on either side, moving them through the country, and finally leaving them in Canada. I designed to have done the same thing again on a larger scale. That was all I intended. I never did intend murder, or treason, or the destruction of property, or to excite or incite slaves to rebellion, or to make insurrection" (*Life, Trial and Execution*, 1859/1969, p. 94).[14]

Brown expressed no remorse for the killings that occurred, despite his best intentions. To the contrary, he justified his actions by invoking the New Testament,

[W]hich teaches me that all things whatsoever I would that men should do to me, I should do even so to them. It teaches me, further, to remember them that are in bonds as bound with them. I endeavored to act up to the instruction. I say I am yet too young to understand that God is any respecter of persons. I believe that to have interfered as I have done, as I have always freely admitted I have done, in behalf of his despised poor, I did not wrong but right. Now, if it is deemed necessary that I should forfeit my life for the furtherance of the ends of justice, and mingle my blood further with the blood of my children and with the blood of millions in this slave country whose rights are disregarded by wicked, cruel, and unjust enactments, I say let it be done. (*Life, Trial and Execution*, 1859/1969, pp. 94–95)

Having placed his trust in divine justice, Brown accepted the verdict of man-made law and received Judge Parker's sentence: the convicted man was to be hung in a public space in a month's time, on December 2.[15] Prosecuting attorney Hunter chafed at the delay, and Governor Wise feared the worst: he was convinced that raiders from the North were preparing to descend on Harpers Ferry to rescue Brown from the hangman's noose. Wise wrote the governors of Pennsylvania and Ohio, asking them to prevent raiders from organizing in those states. When they discounted the risk, the governor of Virginia turned to President Buchanan for military assistance.

Buchanan, too, thought Wise was overreacting to threats and rumors, though he did send Robert E. Lee with 264 artillerymen to guard the arsenal at Harpers Ferry until Brown was executed. The president felt it was the states' responsibility to repel raiders from other states, which Wise declared "teaches even Virginia a lesson of state right" (as cited in Scheidenhelm, 1972, p. 153). It was up to the commonwealth to defend itself, so the governor mobilized the militia and effectively placed northern Virginia under martial law (Villard, 1910/1966, p. 525).[16]

Many Southerners, and some Northern Democrats, applauded the security measures. Alluding to captured correspondence between Brown and the Secret Six, an editorial in the *Baltimore Sun* on November 28 averred,

When the first intelligence of the Harper's Ferry outrage came upon the public, it was almost overwhelmingly regarded as the act of a mere crazy, old fool. People never dreamed that it was the fruit and matured result—rotten at maturity, it is true—of a long and deliberately prepared plan. As fact after fact came out, however, there seemed to be more in it than at first appeared. Day after day and week after week we have the cumulative evidence that John Brown is in fact the representative of a very large class of the people of the North. (as cited in Abels, 1971, p. 315)

Wise could not ignore the possibility of another attack, but his reaction was counterproductive. As the New York *Independent* pointed out,

The Virginians have done everything to concentrate public attention on the scene. The exaggerated dangers into which their own fears betrayed them, the movements of the Governor and their militia, the telegraphic rumors and alarms, the suspicion and vigilance manifested towards strangers, all keep up the excitement until every newspaper in the land is filled with it, and every reader made familiar with all of its details. The indecent haste of the court to obtain a verdict of Guilty, the rude treatment of counsel from abroad, the disregard for the forms and properties of law—all the infuriate zeal of the Slave-Power in contrast to the manly demeanor and conscientious integrity of the prisoner, has excited universal discussion as to the principles of the case. (November 24, 1859, as cited in Abels, 1971, pp. 313–314)

As a result of that discussion, "When John Brown is executed, it will be seen that he has done his work more effectively than if he had succeeded in running off a few hundred slaves" (November 24, 1859, as cited in Abels, 1971, pp. 313–314).

With Northern opinion turning against Wise and Virginia, abolitionists sensed an opportunity. Instead of justifying Brown's actions or rescuing him from the gallows, they applauded his willingness to die for the cause. Of course, the canonization of Brown required that he first be hung. In a sermon at Plymouth Church in Brooklyn on October 30, 1859, the Reverend Henry Ward Beecher warned, "Let no man pray that Brown be spared. Let Virginia make him a martyr. Now, he has only blundered. His soul was noble; his work was miserable. But a cord and a gibbet would redeem all that, and round up Brown's failure with a heroic success" (Redpath, 1860/1969, p. 262).

Beecher's sermon was reprinted in a newspaper shown to Brown, who wrote "Good" in the margin. Thus, Brown accepted his appointed role in the abolitionists' morality play. As he explained in a November 8, 1859, letter to his wife and children, "for me at this time to seal my testimony for God and humanity with my blood will do vastly more toward advancing the cause I have earnestly endeavored to promote, than all I have done in my life before" (Sanborn, 1885, p. 586).

Brown played his part extremely well. Speaking of Brown's answers to questions posed in the interview on October 18 and his statement to the court on November 2, Thoreau (1859/1973) commented, "He could afford to lose his Sharpe's rifles, while he retained his faculty of speech,—a Sharpe's rifle of infinitely surer and longer range" (pp. 111–138). While he was in jail awaiting execution, Brown continued to fire this weapon with great effect. He received visitors, who described their conversations with Brown to the press, which promptly broadcast the interviews across the land. Numerous letters from Brown to families, friends, and sympathetic strangers were also printed or summarized in the newspapers. Knowing little of Brown's deeds in Kansas or at Harpers Ferry, many Northerners formed an impression of Brown as a saintly figure, an impression that Brown carefully nurtured (Abels, 1971).

Moderates in the North understood the political consequences of Brown's impending "martyrdom." They advised Wise to spare Brown by declaring him insane, which the governor refused to do. In fact, Wise publicly declared his belief in Brown's sanity and expressed great admiration for his courage, to the chagrin of Southerners who thought Wise had unwittingly played into the hands of abolitionists. Trying another tack, many Northern newspapers urged Wise to commute Brown's sentence, depriving abolitionists and "Black Republicans" of their martyr. The suggestion won support from a few Southern editorialists as well. The Kentucky *Yeoman* warned, "If Old John Brown is executed, there will be thousands to dip their handkerchiefs in his blood, relics of the martyr will be paraded through the North, pilgrimages will be made to his grave and we shall not be surprised to hear of miracles wrought there as at the tomb of Thomas à Becket" (as cited in Abels, 1971, pp. 343–344).

Most of the Southern press demanded final justice, however, and they expected support from the North for the execution of Brown. As the Richmond *Whig* intoned, "We call on the Northern people to assemble in every town, village, country and neighborhood and unite before the country and the world in denunciation" of Brown and his men (Abels, 1971, p. 316). Southerners were sorely disappointed by the response; Democratic newspapers in the North backed Wise and Virginia, but moderate newspapers (e.g., the *New York Times*) criticized the legal proceedings and warned against execution, while radical Republican outlets and abolitionist broadsheets excoriated Virginia (Barmann, 1961). Some even questioned the valor of the state's men, noting that Brown's small party seized and controlled a town of several thousand people, with at least 700 men.

The lack of support from Northerners "roared like thunder across the South" and had a much bigger impact than the raid itself (Peterson, 2002, p. 27). Virginians, stung by criticism and feeling betrayed by their countrymen, resolved to carry out the execution. Contemptuously rejecting the idea of commuting Brown's sentence, the Richmond *Whig* declaimed,

Though it convert the whole Northern people, without an exception, into furious, armed abolition invaders, yet *Old Brown will be hung!* That is the stern and irreversible decree, not only of the authorities of Virginia but of the PEOPLE of Virginia without a dissenting voice. And, therefore, Virginia, and all the people of Virginia, will treat with the contempt they deserve, all the *craven appeals* of Northern men in behalf of old Brown's pardon. *The miserable old traitor and murderer belongs to the gallows*, and the gallows will have its own. (as cited in Villard, 1910/1966, p. 500)

The *Whig* was right. On December 2, 1859, John Brown swung at the end of a rope for almost forty minutes before expiring on gallows erected in a large field southeast of Charles Town. Fifteen hundred militiamen, backed by additional cavalry and artillery, were on hand to repel any attempted rescue. Access to the site was restricted; only officials and a small crowd of onlookers witnessed the execution. Among the latter were Brown's secessionist counterpart, Edmund Ruffin, and an actor from Richmond named John Wilkes Booth. Also in attendance were at least three dozen journalists (more were prevented from covering the execution by a ban on reporters from abolitionist and Republican newspapers).

Church bells tolled, memorial services were held, and minute guns were fired in Northern cities from Boston to Lawrence on the day Brown died. In Boston, Garrison proclaimed, "Today, Virginia has murdered John Brown; tonight we here witness his resurrection" (Peterson, 2002, p. 23). Brown's corpse reached Philadelphia by train the next day; it was then shipped to New York and conveyed to a grave on the family farm in North Elba. All along the way, crowds gathered, honoring Brown and expressing their sympathy to Mary Anne Day, his wife.

JOHN BROWN'S BODY

John Brown was dead, but his spirit was very much alive in the land, and so was the controversy over Harpers Ferry. On December 5, Governor

Wise addressed the General Assembly of the Commonwealth of Virginia. He insisted, at considerable length and with evident vehemence, that the raid on Harpers Ferry "was an extraordinary and actual invasion, by a sectional organization, specially upon slaveholders and upon their property in Negro slaves." Virginia must "organize and arm" herself against the continuing threat (as cited in Scheidenhelm, 1972, pp. 132–153, at 133).

Senator James Mason concurred: "John Brown's invasion was condemned [in the North] only because it failed. But in view of the sympathy for him in the North and the persistent efforts of the sectional party there to interfere with the rights of the South, it was not at all strange that the southern states should deem it proper to arm themselves and prepare for any contingency that might arise" (*New York Herald*, 1859, December 15, as cited in Villard, 1910/1966, p. 566).

The senior Democratic senator from Virginia was determined to expose the Secret Six and link their activities to Northern Republicans. At Mason's instigation the U.S. Senate formed a special committee to investigate the raid on Harpers Ferry. Mason was named chair of the committee and was joined by Jefferson Davis (D-MS), G. N. Fitch (D-IN), Jacob Collamer (R-VT), and J. R. Doolittle (R-WI). The committee spent six months investigating the raid on Harpers Ferry, trying to determine whether Brown and his men acted alone or with the assistance of other people and organizations. Witnesses were subpoenaed, but most declined to appear before the committee. In fact, three members of the Secret Six left the country immediately after the raid, and Gerrit Smith suddenly developed symptoms of insanity that required institutionalization.[17]

In the absence of testimony from key witnesses, the committee's partisan differences were freely aired. The Republican minority issued a report that expressed little sympathy for Brown or his objectives, but saw no evidence of a larger conspiracy. No one interviewed by the committee was aware of Brown's plan, or "had any suspicion of its existence or design" before the raid (Villard, 1910/1966, p. 581). Indeed, Brown's men were not fully aware of his intentions until the last moment, and they initially resisted the idea when it was revealed to them. Neither was there any indication of a conspiracy to rescue Brown or his men from jail, so further incidents were unlikely, concluded Collamer and Doolittle.

The Democratic majority saw things differently. The "invasion" of Harpers Ferry by the Provisional Army was distinguishable from ordinary felonies "by the ulterior ends in contemplation by them, and by the fact that the money to maintain the expedition, and the large armament they brought with them, had been contributed and furnished by the citizens of other States of the Union, under circumstances that must continue to jeopardy the safety and peace of the southern states, and against which Congress has no power to legislate" (S. Rep. No. 36-278, 1860, p. 18).

Northern states had failed to enact "proper legislation against machinations by their citizens or within their borders destructive of the peace of their confederate republics" (S. Rep. No. 36-278, 1860, p. 13). Members of the Secret Six had contributed money and guns to John Brown without ascertaining his purposes or reasserting control when warnings were issued. "With such elements at work, unchecked by law and not rebuked but encouraged by public opinion, with money freely contributed and placed in irresponsible hands, it may easily be seen how this expedition to excite servile war in one of the States of the Union was got up, and it may equally be seen how like expeditions may certainly be anticipated in future whenever desperados offer themselves to carry them into execution" (p. 13).

Events overtook the committee before its reports were issued. On January 11, 1860, the Democratic Party in Alabama adopted a platform asserting "the unqualified right of the people of the slaveholding States to the Protection of their property in the States, in the Territories, and in the wilderness in which Territorial Governments are as yet unorganized" (Dumond, 1931, p. 517). The platform insisted "that it is the duty of the General Government, by all proper legislation, to secure an entry into those Territories to all the citizens of the United States, together with their property of every description, and that the same should remain protected by the United States while the Territories are under its authority" (Dumond, p. 517).

Shortly thereafter, Democratic delegations from the Deep South withdrew from the April 1860 presidential nominating convention in Charleston, South Carolina, when delegations from Northern states refused to endorse a platform plank similar to the one adopted in Alabama. The party reconvened in Baltimore in late June, with the same result. Southerners then nominated John C. Breckinridge of Kentucky, while Northern, or "regular," Democrats backed Stephen Douglas, the Senator from Illinois. Republicans rejoiced at the widening split among Democrats and nominated Abraham Lincoln on May 18, passing over Seward, who was perceived to be more radical.

On November 6, Lincoln received only 40 percent of the popular vote but 59 percent of the electoral vote. A political moderate, Lincoln's moral repugnance to slavery made him unacceptable to most white Southerners. Even before he was inaugurated on March 4, 1861, seven states seceded from the Union and formed a provisional government called the Confederate States of America.[18] They chose their own president, Jefferson Davis, and were soon joined in formal confederacy by four other states. Missouri and Kentucky remained in the Union, but secessionist slates of officers from both states were admitted to the Confederate Congress and two more stars added to the Confederate flag. Meanwhile, thirty-nine counties in western Virginia broke away from the Confederacy, established the Restored Government of Virginia, and aligned themselves with the Union. A new state of West Virginia was in the making, and it included Jefferson County, the home of Harpers Ferry.

On April 12, 1861, Confederate troops fired on Fort Sumter in Charleston, South Carolina, and the Civil War was underway. Within a week, secessionists in Virginia captured the federal armory at Harpers Ferry, which was only partially destroyed by the Union garrison as it evacuated to safety. More than 5,000 rifles—and the machinery for manufacturing many more—fell into rebel hands. The rebels were directed by none other than Henry Wise, who as governor presided over the execution of John Brown for his "treasonous" raid on the armory in October 1859.

HIS SOUL IS MARCHING ON

Union soldiers marched to war with John Brown's name on their lips. In the spring of 1861, the Twelfth Massachusetts Regiment sang "John Brown's Body Lies A-Moulderin' in the Grave" to the tune of a popular revival hymn, adding that "his soul's marching on." Other soldiers in the Union army adopted the song, until it was replaced by the "Battle Hymn of the Republic." The stirring hymn was written by Julia Ward Howe, who was married to one of the Secret Six. Some say that a line of her fifth verse, "let us die to make men free," referred to the example of John Brown, and Howe herself said she wrote the lyrics after hearing Union soldiers singing "John Brown's Body."

The legend of John Brown grew with the passage of time. It was expressed in a surprisingly large number of ways, as Peterson (2002) demonstrates so well. In addition to the song, there were poems, John Greenleaf Whittier's "Brown of Osawatomie" and Stephen Vincent Benet's epic "John Brown's Body" among them. There were plays, dramatic readings, and performances based on the events of October and November, 1859. There were novels and, somewhat later, screenplays and films. There were portraits, busts, museums, and even parks in places made famous by John Brown and his men. Above all, there were the histories charting the movements of all the principal actors, and biographies trying to make sense of them.

Many of these works were hagiographic or sanctifying, and it is still true that African Americans hold John Brown in particularly high regard (Quarles, 1974).[19] Some revisionists go to the other extreme, but the most interesting interpretations of Brown try to balance the justice of his cause and its eventual success against the violence and bloodshed he brought to the land. John

Brown was not a saint, but neither was he the devil incarnate. He was a man whose convictions gave him the courage to make war on slavery, but Brown's chosen form of warfare was itself immoral. Terrorism claims the innocent as well as the guilty.

The enigmatic legacy of Brown is captured in John Steuart Curry's mural *The Tragic Prelude*, which was appropriately painted in the Kansas state-house. The mural shows Brown as a colossus, or larger-than-life figure, striding forward. His eyes burn with the zeal of a true believer, and his left hand displays the Holy Bible, open to pages showing the Greek letters alpha and omega. Brown's right hand clasps a Sharp's rifle or "Beecher's Bible," and his outstretched arms form a cross with his erect body. Beneath his feet are two dead soldiers, one in blue, the other in gray. Their armies are ranged on either side of Brown, while Kansas burns in the background. Also in the background is a cyclone, recalling the prophet Hosea's warning that a people who turn away from God shall "reap the whirlwind."

The mural and its uneasy judgment would not have troubled Brown. When Congressman Vallandigham (D-OH) asked him immediately after the raid whether he acted alone or in concert with others, Brown (*Life, Trial and Execution*, 1969, p. 45) replied, "No man sent me here; it was my own prompting and that of my Maker, or that of the devil, whichever you please to ascribe it to."

NOTES

1. The quotation from Garrison's editorial in *The Liberator* of October 28, 1859 is reprinted by Redpath (1860/1969, pp. 303–315, at 305). Also in Redpath (pp. 17–42, at 30) is the quotation from Henry David Thoreau's October 30, 1859 lecture, "A Plea for Captain John Brown."

2. The Fitzhugh and Clarkson essays are reprinted in Scheidenhelm (1972, pp. 189–206), with quotations at 190, 205, and 199, respectively.

3. Villard (1910/1966) provides the most detail on Brown's life, Oates (1970) accounts for Brown's historical significance, Du Bois (1968/2001) illustrates African Americans' particular regard for Brown, and Warren (1929/2002) offers the counterpoint. Peterson (2002) assesses the many biographies of John Brown.

4. The Wilmot Proviso, offered by Representative David Wilmot (D-PA) on August 8, 1846, would have prohibited slavery in any territory acquired from the war with Mexico. The Proviso was blocked by southerners in the Senate; instead John C. Calhoun proposed the "positive protection doctrine," authorizing Congress to protect slaveholders' human property throughout the territories.

5. In the Old Testament the book of Judges tells the story of Gideon and a small group of poorly armed men who delivered the Israelites from the Midianites in a great battle near Mount Gilead. Apparently Brown derived the name *Gileadites* from this story.

6. The six were Thomas W. Higginson, Samuel G. Howe, Theodore Parker, Franklin B. Sanborn, Gerrit Smith, and George L. Stearns.

7. Eyewitness accounts and recollections of the raid on Harpers Ferry abound and are cited extensively in Villard (1910/1966), Abels (1971), and Oates (1970).

8. Four of the escapees later enlisted in the Union army, including Charles Plummer Tidd, who died of fever during the battle of Roanoke Island, where Confederates fought under the command of former governor Henry Wise. Owen Brown did not join the army; Russell Banks' *Cloudsplitter* (1998) is the fictional story of Owen's recollection of his father, the raid, and its consequences.

9. Compare Brown (*Life, Trial and Execution*, 1859/1969, p. 95) with Brown in Sanborn (1885, p. 613). Brown's statement of "satisfaction" is qualified by circumstances, but it is also possible that his later reference to "public murder" was made in the performance of his martyr's role.

10. Wise's political opportunism became clear during the trial of Brown's fellow raiders. The governor instructed prosecutor Andrew Hunter to try John Cook under Virginia law and turn Aaron Stevens over to the federal authorities for prosecution. Hunter announced this decision in court on November 7, vowing to use the federal trial to "strike at higher and wickeder game," that is, Brown's Northern co-conspirators. However, an investigative committee appointed by the United States suited Virginia's purposes even better, and on December 18, Governor Wise declared that Stevens would be tried in state court after all.

11. The local prosecutor, Charles Harding, an intemperate man who was deemed unreliable, was relegated to a secondary role in this important case.

12. For contrasting views on the fairness of Brown's trial, see von Holst's attack (1889), Wright's (1890) rebuttal, Caskie's (1909) assessment, and Draper's (1940) illuminating discussion of the legal issues it raised. Lubet (2001) criticizes the lawyers' performance in the trial.

13. Was the raid an act of madness? Many thought so at the time, and from a military point of view it was sheer folly. In his official report, Lieutenant-Colonial Lee said the raid was the work of "a fanatic or madman, which could only end in failure." On the other hand, David Hunter Strother (1868, p. 42), who witnessed the events at Harpers Ferry and survived the war, asked in 1868, "Who is there now, that thinks John Brown was crazy?"

14. Many have questioned the veracity of these claims, given Brown's statements to Governor Wise on October 18. Lubet (2001) suggests that Brown spoke after, not before, his conviction, so that no rebuttal could be offered.

15. On December 16, four of Brown's men were hung: John Cook, Edwin Coppoc, John Copeland Jr., and Shields Green. Aaron Stevens and Albert Hazlett were hung on March 16, 1860.

16. Hunter (1887, September 5) later admitted that "It was not for the protection of the jail and the repelling of parties who are known to be organizing with the view of rescuing Brown and the prisoners, but it was for the purpose of preparing for coming events," that is, "a great conflict between the North and South on the subject of slavery."

17. Parker was in Rome at the time of the attack, Douglass left for England by way of Canada, and Sanborn and Stearns fled to Canada, though Stearns returned to testify. Higginson was never called before the committee because, he thought, Mason did not seek testimony from those who would defend Brown's actions (Villard, 1910/1966, p. 529). Douglass (1881a, p. 330) offered a more sinister explanation: "I have never been able to account satisfactorily for the sudden abandonment of this investigation on any other ground than that the men engaged in it expected soon to be in rebellion themselves, and that not a rebellion for liberty like that of John Brown, but a rebellion for slavery, and that they saw that by using their senatorial power in search of rebels they might be whetting a knife for their own throats."

18. The November 10, 1859, Raleigh North Carolina *Register* predicted as much: "The outbreak at Harper's Ferry and the disclosures consequent thereon, the dangerous character of public sentiment in the North as manifested by the tone of the press and pulpit, lead unerringly to the conclusion that the election of a Black Republican to the Presidency is probable, and we must infer that it would be the signal for immediate secession of the South from the Union" (as cited in Abels, 1971, p. 378).

19. Douglass (1881b, p. 9) anticipated this devotion: "His zeal in the cause of my race was far greater than mine—it was as the burning sun to my taper light—mine was bounded by time, his stretched away to the boundless shores of eternity. I could live for the slave, but he could die for him."

REFERENCES

Abels, J. (1971). *Man on fire: John Brown and the cause of liberty.* New York: The Macmillan Company.

Banks, R. (1998). *Cloudsplitter.* New York: HarperCollins.

Barmann, L. F., SJ. (1961). John Brown at Harpers Ferry: A contemporary analysis. *West Virginia History 22*(3), 141–158.

Caskie, G. (1909). *The trial of John Brown.* Richmond, VA: Richmond Press.

Douglass, F. (1881a). *The life and times of Frederick Douglass.* Hartford, CT: Park Publishing Co.

Douglass, F. (1881b). *John Brown.* An address by Frederick Douglass at Storer College on May 30, 1881.

Draper, D. C. (1940). Legal phases of the trial of John Brown. *West Virginia History, 1*(2), 87–103.

Du Bois, W. E. B. (2001). *John Brown,* D. Roediger (Ed.). New York: Modern Library. (Original work published 1968)

Dumond, D. L. (1931). *Southern editorials on secession.* New York: The Century Company.

Hunter, A. (1887, September 5). John Brown's raid. *New Orleans Times–Democrat.*

The life, trial and execution of John Brown. (1969). New York: Da Capo Press. (Original work published 1859)

Lubet, S. (2001). John Brown's trial. *Alabama Law Review, 52*(2), 425–466.

Moore, G. (n.d.). *The trial of John Brown* (draft). The John Brown/Boyd B. Stutler Collection Database, West Virginia Memory Project. Retrieved from http://wvmemory.wvculture.org/imlsintro.html

Oates, S. B. (1970). *To purge this land with blood: A biography of John Brown*. New York: Harper and Row.

Peterson, M. D. (2002). *John Brown: The legend revisited*. Charlottesville, VA: University of Virginia Press.

Quarles, B. (1974). *Allies for freedom: Blacks and John Brown*. New York: Oxford University Press.

Redpath, J. R. (Ed.). (1969). *Echoes of Harper's Ferry*. Boston: Thayer and Eldridge, Arno Press, and the *New York Times*. (Original work published 1860)

Report of the select committee of the Senate appointed to inquire into the late invasion and seizure of the public property at Harper's Ferry, S. Rep. No. 36-278 (1860).

Sanborn, F. B. (Ed.). (1885). *The life and letters of John Brown, liberator of Kansas and martyr of Virginia*. Boston: Roberts Brothers.

Scheidenhelm, R. (1972). *The response to John Brown*. Belmont, CA: Wadsworth Publishing Co.

Seward, W. H. (1858). The irrepressible conflict. Speech delivered October 25, 1858 at Rochester, New York.

Strother, D. H. (1868). Lecture on John Brown. Delivered in Cleveland. West Virginia and Regional History Collection, A&M, Box 8, FF16 at West Virginia University Libraries.

Thoreau, H. D. (1973). A plea for Captain John Brown. In W. Glick (Ed.), *Henry D. Thoreau: Reform papers* (pp. 111–138). Princeton: Princeton University Press. (Original work published 1858, October 30)

Villard, O. G. (1966). *John Brown, 1800–1859: A biography fifty years after*. Gloucester, MA: Peter Smith. (Original work published 1910)

von Holst, H. (1889). *John Brown*. Boston: Cupples and Hurd.

Warren, R. P. (2002). *John Brown: The making of a martyr*. Nashville, TN: J. S. Sanders and Co. (Original work published 1929)

Wright, M. J. (1890). The trial and execution of John Brown. *Papers of the American Historical Association, 4*, 439–454.

Index

About the Editors and
the Contributors

FRANKIE Y. BAILEY is Associate Professor at the State University of New York, Albany. With Steven Chermak, she is co-editor of *Media Representations of September 11* (Praeger, 2003) and *Popular Culture, Crime, and Justice* (1998). She is author of *Out of the Woodpile: Black Characters in Crime and Detective Fiction* (Greenwood, 1991), which was nominated for the Mystery Writers of America 1992 Edgar Award for Criticism and Biography, and *"Law Never Here": A Social History of African American Responses to Issues of Crime and Justice* (Praeger, 1999).

STEVEN CHERMAK is Associate Professor and Director of Graduate Affairs in the Department of Criminal Justice at Indiana University. He is the author of *Searching for a Demon: The Media Construction of the Militia Movement* (2002) and *Victims in the News: Crime and the American News Media* (1995).

JOANNE BARKER is an attorney and Ph.D. student in the History Department at the University at Albany (SUNY).

SALITA S. BRYANT is Professor at the University of Mississippi. Her publications include "A Dreadful Pleasure: Reading the Early American Murderess, 1735–1812" (Dissertation) and "Here She Hangs a Strangling/ By her Neck a Dangling: Reading the Murderess in the New Republic"

(*Literary Interpretation Theory*, Fall 2004). Bryant is associate editor of *Liberties Captives: Narratives of Confinement in the Print Culture of the Early Republic*.

KAREN ELIZABETH CHANEY is Teaching Fellow at the School of Continuing Education, Harvard University. She is currently working on *American Crimes & Trials, Lizzie Borden*.

JENNIFER H. CHILDRESS is Professor in the Department of Political Science, Northern Kentucky University.

TAMMY A. DENESHA is a practicing attorney.

EMILY GILLESPIE is a teaching assistant and student in the Applied Behavior Science–International Relations and Comparative Politics, Peace and Security Program, Wright State University.

RUSSELL L. HANSON is Professor in the Department of Political Science, Indiana University–Bloomington. He has published numerous books and scholarly articles including *The Democratic Imagination in America: Conversations With Our Past*; *Political Innovation and Conceptual Change* (edited by Terence Ball, James Farr, and Russell L. Hanson); *Politics in the American States* (edited by Virginia Gray and Russell L. Hanson); *Governing Partners: State-Local Relations in the United States* (edited by Russell L. Hanson); and *Reconsidering the Democratic Public* (edited by George E. Marcus and Russell L. Hanson).

ANDREA L. KORDZEK is a Ph.D. student at the School of Criminal Justice, University at Albany (SUNY).

CAROLYN LEVY is a Ph.D. student at the School of Criminal Justice, University at Albany (SUNY).

JOHN McCLYMER is Professor of History at Assumption College. His publications include *War and Welfare: Social Engineering in America, 1890–1925*; *Images of Women in American Popular Culture* (edited by Angela Dorenkamp, Mary Moynihan, and Arlene Vadum); *"Gå Till Amerika": Swedes in Worcester, 1868–1993* (coauthored by Charles Estus); *The Triangle Strike and Fire*; *"This High and Holy Moment": The First National Woman's Rights Convention, Worcester, 1850, and the Origins of Feminism*; and *Freedom Summer: Mississippi, 1964*.

KATHRYN MUDGETT has received her J.D. and Ph.D. She is the author of several publications including "'I Stand Alone Here upon an Open Sea': Starbuck and the Limits of Positive Law" in *Ungraspable Phantom: Essays on Moby-Dick* (edited by John Bryant et al.); and "'Cruelty to Seamen': Richard Henry Dana, Jr., Justice Story, and the Case of Nichols and Couch," (*The American Neptune*, Winter 2002).

MARCELLA BUSH TREVINO is Adjunct Professor of History, Barry University.

KATHY WARNES is a journalist/historian and a doctoral candidate, University of Toledo. Her publications include local history books, journal articles, and fiction.

BRANDON K. WEBSTER is a Ph.D. student, Division of Criminal Justice, University of Cincinnati.